25—

1st

SO-AHC-436

Russia Abroad

Russia Abroad

Prague and the Russian Diaspora, 1918–1938

Catherine Andreyev and Ivan Savický

Yale University Press
New Haven and London

Copyright © 2004 by Catherine Andreyev and Ivan Savický

All rights reserved. This book may not be reproduced in whole or in part, in any form
(beyond that copying permitted by Sections 107 and 108 of the U.S. Copyright Law and
except by reviewers for the public press) without written permission from the publishers.

For information about this and other Yale University Press publications, please contact:
U.S. Office: sales.press@yale.edu   www.yalebooks.com
Europe Office: sales@yaleup.co.uk   www.yalebooks.co.uk

Set in Bembo by MATS, Southend-on-Sea, Essex
Printed in Great Britain by St Edmundsbury Press Ltd, Bury St Edmunds

Library of Congress Cataloging-in-Publication Data

Andreyev, Catherine, 1955–
Russia abroad: Prague and the Russian diaspora,
1918–1938/Catherine Andreyev, Ivan Savický.—1st ed.
p.   cm.
Includes bibliographical references and index.
ISBN 0–300–10234–8 (alk. paper)
1.   Russians—Czechoslovakia—Prague—History—20th century.
2.   Prague (Czech Republic)—Ethnic relations.   3.   Czechoslovakia—
Foreign relations—Soviet Union.   4.   Soviet Union—Foreign relations—
Czechoslovakia.   5.   Russians—Foreign countries—History—20th century.
I. Savický, Ivan, 1937–   II. Title
DB2624.R87 A53 2004   303.48'247043712'09041—dc22   2003022082

A catalogue record for this book is available from the British Library.

2 4 6 8 10 9 7 5 3 1

Illustrations in text reproduced courtesy of A. Koprivova, E. Musatova and I. Savický.

Contents

Eastern Europe, 1918–38

Acknowledgements

Both authors had fathers who were active in Russian Prague, but the intellectual journey from first being told about Russian life in inter-war Prague to being able to study that period was a long one. It was finally made possible by the combination of the Velvet Revolution in Czechoslovakia in 1989 and the collapse of the Soviet Union in 1991 which meant that the study of the Russian emigration was no longer a politically contentious subject. This released an enormous amount of information and everyone who supported our research deserves our very warm thanks. There are too many to be able to thank everyone by name, but we wish to single out a few of them.

Our thanks are due to the British Academy for funding a visiting fellowship to Prague, to the late Světlana Tejchmanová for her hospitality on her first visit to Prague. Dr Vacek and later Dr Klimová at the Slovanská Knihovna were unstinting in their help and many in the Slovanský ústav were exceptionally generous with their help and expertise. Anastasia Kopřivova's knowledge of the details of life in Prague was very valuable. We are extremely grateful to her and to Elena Musatova for allowing us to use some of their photographs. The Governing Body of Christ Church, Oxford helped with research grants and provided a stimulating environment in which to work.

This project was originally discussed in Prague and we are particularly grateful to the late Professor Ernst Gellner for his enthusiastic support. Professor Marc Raeff, too, both supported the project in the early stages and encouraged it along its way. His kindness and good advice have been very much in evidence. Professor Gleb Zhekulin's advice and help was also greatly appreciated. In Oxford many people should be thanked for their support but especially those who were prepared to read and comment on the manuscript, particularly Philippa Logan, Bob Service, Gerry Smith and Barbara Heldt. Their advice was invaluable and much appreciated. In the closing stages the whole team from Yale University Press deserve our heartfelt thanks. They go to Robert Baldock, for not giving up on us, to

Candida Brazil and Ewan Thompson for editorial advice, to Beth Humphries for all the effort put into copy-editing and to Jane Horton for indexing.

On a personal note, the late Gill Andreyev put a great deal of effort into finding old family friends and bringing people together. Jervoise Andreyev has been a stimulating reader and critic. Eteri Savická and Olga Doskářová in different ways provided much needed support in Prague, and John and Laura have helped in ways which cannot be put into words. Our thanks are due to all of them and any errors are, of course, our own. On the subject of Slavonic transliteration, we hope that this work is consistently inconsistent.

Catherine Andreyev and Ivan Savický

Introduction

Russian Action

'The Czech lands linger in my memory as an azure day and a single misty night,' wrote Marina Tsvetaeva, one of the outstanding poets of the Russian émigré community.[1] She considered the three years she spent there from 1922 to 1925 to be one of the most stable periods of her life. Looking back over her troubled and difficult existence, she saw Czechoslovakia as a haven where happiness, creativity and even optimism about the future were not out of place. For many other Russian émigrés, the time they spent in Czechoslovakia had similar connotations and was associated with memories of youth and of promise for the future. Tsvetaeva had lived in Prague,[2] a city which played a unique role as a refuge for the post-revolutionary Russian diaspora. This was the city where the academic élite of the Russian empire congregated and where, from 1921 onwards, young Russians continued the studies which had been fractured by revolution and civil war.

The policy of Russkaya Aktsiya (Russian Action) provided financial support to Russian refugees in the early 1920s and focused particularly on education, with the aim of sending educated Russians back to Russia. Unique in the annals of inter-war Europe, it was an extraordinarily generous gesture by the First Republic of Czechoslovakia. By the mid-1920s, however, it was becoming clear that the assumptions on which the policy had been based were mistaken. The exiled Russians would be unlikely to return home in the near future since the Soviet Union was evolving in ways which had not been foreseen. For the émigrés, too, there were dramatic choices to be made: should they abandon their Russian identity and try to assimilate? This was not at all easy, as Czechoslovakia was able to employ very few of them. Should they attempt once again to find a new and welcoming place of residence? But the onset of the Great Depression meant that foreigners seeking employment were unwelcome almost everywhere. Moreover, how were they to preserve the Russian culture with which their identity was inextricably linked? To abandon it seemed a betrayal of their homeland as well as of themselves.

The evolution of Czech policy forced changes on Russian émigré society. The attempt by the Russian community to survive in the difficult economic conditions of the late 1920s and early 1930s was further complicated by the increasingly tense international situation. The rise of Hitler meant that Czechoslovakia felt vulnerable. It needed an ally, but the West seemed unable and unwilling to understand Czech problems. So in 1934 Edvard Beneš, the Minister for Foreign Affairs who was later to become President, entered into full diplomatic relations with the Kremlin and in 1935 negotiated a Soviet-Czechoslovak agreement. Subsequently, the USSR made it clear that it was not prepared for its new ally to give any recognition or support to the Russian émigré community. The Munich agreement in September, which was seen as signalling the weakness of the West, was a mortal blow for Czechoslovakia. Then on 15 March 1939, the Nazis invaded. During the Nazi occupation, the remaining Russian émigrés struggled to survive. The last vestiges of their community were destroyed after the so-called liberation of Czechoslovakia by the Red Army on 8 May 1945. If for Czechoslovakia this did indeed mean liberation, at least until 1948, it signalled the end of the émigré community: leading members of émigré society were arrested and archives and other 'incriminating' evidence were appropriated by the Soviet authorities.

The Russian Emigration

Emigration from Russia was not a new phenomenon. Ever since Prince Kurbsky fled from Ivan IV in the sixteenth century, Russian émigrés had considered it their duty to impart to the government of the day – more often than not, without success – a sense of its moral unworthiness to govern. This attitude had been widespread in the nineteenth century, which had seen a whole range of political opponents established abroad. One of them, Alexander Herzen, sometimes called the Father of Russian Socialism, published *Kolokol* (The Bell) in London, a journal that is supposed to have influenced Alexander II's decision in 1861 to promulgate the Emancipation Edict to free the serfs. Many later political exiles were representatives of the more radical and revolutionary trends, while in the period from the 1890s to the First World War people tended to leave Russia and Central Europe for economic or religious reasons, to create a new life for themselves in North America.

The post-1917 exiles were very different: this wave of émigrés represented the political, social and intellectual élite of Imperial Russia. In many respects, and at least initially, these post-revolutionary émigrés, saw themselves as repeating the previous patterns of political exile. They considered themselves to be the Russian version of the French Revolutionary exiles, who were able to return within a generation. But the scale of the Russian exodus was much larger. Exact figures do not exist, but the total number has been estimated at about one and a half million.[3] In addition to those who actually left Russia, a further eight million people were already living in areas which had been part of the Russian empire before 1917, such as the Baltic States, Poland, and those parts of Bessarabia which declared independence after the Revolution. A significant percentage of these people were Russian by culture and so provided a readership for émigré publications.[4] Contrary to the popular myth, it was not just the aristocracy who left. They numbered approximately 140,000 – less than 10 per cent of the total. A very large proportion of émigrés could be considered members of the intelligentsia, and they represented the entire spectrum of political opinion. Around a sixth of them were university graduates and two-thirds had completed secondary education. Men outnumbered women by more than two to one. A large number of those involved, however, especially the young and the old, might have been defined as refugees rather than political émigrés. As such, these émigrés were the first to become embroiled in many of the issues encountered by subsequent waves of refugees, first in Europe and, after the Second World War, world wide.

Claudena Skran has suggested that more recent attempts to help refugees have been hindered by 'a lack of institutional memory' and this disregard of the experience of legislators and politicians in the inter-war period 'has meant that refugee practitioners have had to reinvent the wheel'.[5] The problem created by the Russian refugees after the Revolution and Civil War resulted in the creation of many of the institutions which are the precursors of today's United Nations High Commission for Refugees (UNHCR). The upheaval of the First World War displaced large numbers of people and it was assumed by politicians and the peacemakers at Versailles, as well as by these outcasts themselves, that in due course they would be able to return home. When this hope proved unfounded, the League of Nations had to cope not simply with the question of humanitarian aid to the homeless and helpless, but with more complex legal problems concerning the status of the stateless in the post-war world. Self-determination ostensibly had become one of the guiding principles in the delineation of statehood and national boundaries. Before the First World War, few people had or needed passports, and travel had been more a question of finance than of identity or legal status.

LEGAL STATUS

On 1 September 1921 Dr Fridtjof Nansen, the Norwegian explorer, began work as 'High Commissioner on behalf of the League [of Nations] in connection with the problems of Russian refugees in Europe'. In 1918 he had helped to solve the problems involved in the repatriation of Russian, German and Austro-Hungarian prisoners and internees and had negotiated with Herbert Hoover on the question of famine relief to Russia. His personal profile was very high. When the Russian refugees in Constantinople appeared to present an insoluble problem, Nansen was asked to help, setting in motion much of the organisation which has been developed and refined to the present day.

In 1921–22, the League of Nations attempted to provide a certain amount of security and legal protection for Russian refugees and similar protection was later extended to other dispossessed groups, for example Armenians and Assyrians. An inter-governmental conference in May 1926 defined a Russian refugee as 'any person of Russian origin who does not enjoy or who no longer enjoys the protection of the government of the U.S.S.R. and who has not acquired another nationality'.[6]

In order to provide some kind of legal status for Russian refugees, in July 1922 an inter-governmental conference in Geneva supported Nansen's suggestion that a specific certificate of identity be issued by individual governments to Russian refugees on their territory.[7] Fifty-four governments eventually accepted this proposal and the so-called 'Nansen Passport' was brought into being. Although this was not really a passport, in the inter-war period, for many Russian émigrés it served almost as a symbol of loyalty to Russia and opposition to the Bolsheviks. Their Imperial identity papers were not recognised, but to take the nationality of the country in which they had settled was often regarded as treachery to the Russian cause.

EARLY ATTITUDES TOWARDS THE EMIGRATION

Until recently very little attention has been paid to developments within the Russian émigré world. Initially, the émigrés considered the emigration a short-lived phenomenon, the product of specific mistakes made during the Revolution and the Civil War by those opposed to Bolshevism. They therefore analysed these events, attempting to present an accurate picture of Bolshevism in the hope that this would encourage the West either to enter into open conflict with Soviet Russia or at least put pressure on the Bolsheviks to modify their policies. In the early years the émigrés had little opportunity or desire for scholarly analysis so the first studies of the emigration were written by others.[8] Statistics or reports concerning emigration were usually produced with the intention of helping refugees deal with the question of legal status or employment. The census of Russian refugees in Yugoslavia carried out along the same lines as a census of the entire population was unique in the history of the Russian emigration and took place as early as 1921.[9] In the same year the historian S.S. Oldenburg attempted to define the countries of the emigration according to the relationship of the state and society to the Russian émigrés.[10] Publications with a historical approach were a rarity. An exception is a history of the army in exile, written after the evacuation of the Crimea during the efforts made to keep Wrangel's army intact.[11]

Attempts to organise

As it became clear that their exile was likely to last longer than initially envisaged, émigrés began to feel the need for unity. From the earliest days of emigration there had been calls for greater unity in the face of common enemies but until the infrastructure of émigré life had been established these appeals had limited effect. For example, the Reichenhall Congress in 1921 attracted monarchists, and the 'national' congress in Paris in 1921 was attended by the more liberal and left-wing supporters of intervention in the Russian Civil War. The conference of members of the Constituent Assembly, which met in Paris in January 1921, contained few dissenting voices and at the Sobor (Assembly) held at Sremski Karlovci in Yugoslavia in late November 1921 by the Russian Orthodox Church abroad, it was clear that those opposed to the dominant line were not welcome. Despite the rhetoric of unity, the emigration continued to split and new political divisions and groupings emerged.

Many pre-revolutionary political parties were unable to survive in this new situation. The Kadets (Constitutional Democrats) were split by Miliukov's 'new tactics' of encouraging revolt from within in order to bring down the Soviet regime. The Kadet Party, which had come into prominence as a result of the upheavals of 1905, had a broadly liberal outlook and members of this party had been in the majority in the Provisional Government in 1917. Miliukov's turn to the left appeared to compromise many liberal policies. A new political party, Krest'yanskaya Rossiya (Peasant Russia) emerged from the ranks of the Socialist Revolutionaries (SRs), who had espoused the idea of a revolution based on land. They had considerable support in the country and received the largest share of the vote in the elections to the Constituent Assembly convened in January 1918. Krest'yanskaya Rossiya accepted the need to place the agrarian question at the centre of the political agenda but toned down the revolutionary aspects. All of the new political movements, which included such groups as the Smena Vekh (Change of Landmarks), the

Eurasians and the Mladorossy (Young Russians), were impatient with the political solutions proposed by their elders and attempted to find new approaches to Russian politics. These newer groupings were more prepared to analyse the revolutions of 1917 in terms of Russian development, with the aim of discovering some positive aspects. The older generation, by contrast, argued that Bolshevism was an alien imposition on Russia, and there was an unexpected revival of the extreme right-wing Black Hundreds, which had disappeared following the February Revolution in 1917. Now they were not only trying to restore the monarchy but to return to the situation prior to 1905 when the autocracy had been forced to grant concessions. Even a Russian Fascist movement was formed, although it found few supporters in Europe.

In these conditions the all-émigré congress of 1926 was very different from earlier ones. It produced vigorous debates about the exact nature of political forces within the emigration, both as a whole and within individual countries. There was also discussion about the views of the silent majority of émigrés.[12] As might have been expected, the congress did not result in any unity and new groups and divisions continued to emerge.

THE IMPACT OF INTERNATIONAL POLITICS

The end of the New Economic Policy (NEP) in the Soviet Union, along with the start of collectivisation in 1929 and the harsh measures associated with this policy, meant that the chances of the Soviet system evolving into something more acceptable to émigrés were sharply curtailed. This led émigrés to develop a policy of greater activism and to attempt to form a cadre of activists to carry out acts of sabotage and terrorism within the Soviet Union and set up anti-Soviet organisations there. Such enterprises were veiled in secrecy, and almost all ended in tragedy but they have appealed to the conspiracy-minded. An organisation called the Trust was set up by General Kutepov in the 1920s with a view to engaging in clandestine activity in the Soviet Union. This is the best-known example of such organisations and has given rise to a considerable body of literature.[13]

Hitler's accession to power and the likelihood of war between the Third Reich and the Soviet Union forced another very difficult question on to the émigré agenda: whom should the émigrés support? The Nazi regime was opposed to the Soviet system but the price to be paid by the Russian nation if they accepted Nazi support in destroying the system would be heavy. On the other hand, although the Bolsheviks had deprived the émigrés of their homeland, they were keeping the empire together and were promoting industrialisation, which was of great value to Russia. These issues led to a radical reassessment of political attitudes and the new divides this created ran right through existing political groups.

Issues surrounding the study of the emigration also changed abruptly. As a result of the economic crisis and the worsening of material conditions, many émigré publications were forced to close. Unemployment grew rapidly and many individuals had to forget their literary or academic ambitions and concentrate simply on surviving. Economic difficulties were followed by increased political pressure.[14] With the rise of Hitler and the disappearance of free speech in Germany, opinions about the Third Reich and the Soviet Union had to be expressed with great caution and attitudes towards these two states began to determine the politics of all émigré groups. It becomes almost impossible to assess the political inclinations of the émigrés from published sources. The international situation changed as more states moved to establish better relations with the USSR. Soviet representatives began to put pressure on their new allies to oppose émigré political activity, and to insist that émigrés should be seen as refugees, not as political exiles, and should only receive humanitarian aid. At the same time, some states reacted against those groups who voiced their criticism of Nazism, particularly the Russian-Jewish émigrés.

CULTURAL IMPACT

These political changes had the effect of making émigré scholars concentrate less on the history and politics of the emigration and more on cultural questions. Moreover, the emigration now had to defend itself from the criticism of their host societies which had intensified during the depression.[15] Younger Russians were becoming increasingly denationalised and were assimilating into their host societies. In order to fight this trend it was considered important to show that Russian culture and scholarship were of fundamental significance and that they could be maintained in émigré conditions.

Unlike the political groups and parties, who tried to present themselves as being completely independent and as having a clear solution to both Russia and the émigrés' problems and who therefore tried to hide their connections, those concerned with cultural questions needed to establish wide-ranging contacts. Professor A.S. Yashchenko in *Russkaya Kniga* (The Russian Book), first published in Berlin in 1921, intended to create a forum which would unite and inform all the various Russian publishers. In 1922 this was replaced by *Novaya Russkaya Kniga* (The New Russian Book), which had the same aims and the same editorial board. In 1923 this closed down for lack of finance. However, although the attempt to unify émigré publishing was not realisable, one of the largest exhibitions of émigré editions was held in Prague and its exhibition catalogue is still of value today.[16] As Czech support for the Russians waned, the Russian Institute in

Belgrade tried to keep track of scholarly publications.[17] At the same time, reviews of work by émigrés in various areas began to appear.

Despite all the difficulties and the lack of central organisations, institutions or national libraries, the Russian diaspora managed to keep in contact. Fiction was reviewed fairly systematically in newspapers and the 'thick' journals of the emigration. These provided the conditions for a general overview of cultural life although in the inter-war period few wished to embark on such a project. The need to maintain unity and emphasise the cultural life of émigrés was stated quite clearly by Pio-Ul'sky, one of the leaders of the emigration in Yugoslavia when in 1939 he gave a lecture in Belgrade on 'The Russian emigration and its significance in the cultural life of other nations'.

THE EFFECT OF THE SECOND WORLD WAR

By the end of the Second World War, both the international situation and the emigration had experienced profound changes. A whole host of leading figures had died, including Miliukov, often seen as a leader of the liberal left, the more conservative P.B. Struve, and Markov II, a representative of the extreme right. Others became, at least temporarily, Soviet patriots, among them Metropolitan Evlogiy, widely accepted as the leader of the Russian Orthodox Christians abroad, and the 'ambassador' of the Russian emigration in Paris, V.A. Maklakov. Yet others were detained by the Soviet authorities or, as happened in the case of some Cossack generals, were handed over to the USSR by the West. The old émigré élite had disappeared and been replaced. The new wave of Russian refugees was very different from those who had been forced into exile by the Revolution and Civil War. This so-called 'second wave' had an outlook which was based on their experience and understanding of the Soviet Union. Often they had difficulty finding a common language with the older generation of émigrés. As a result, the social, cultural and educational level and attitudes of the politically active members of the emigration changed fundamentally, even if some of the older émigrés were still in positions of leadership.

The attitudes of the host societies altered as well. Immediately after the war, the Allies handed over Russians who were seen as anti-Soviet to the Soviet authorities. These included both those who had been Soviet citizens and those who had never come under Soviet jurisdiction. This policy of crushing anti-Soviet activity, which was much harsher than anything that had operated in the 1920s, was reversed with the onset of the Cold War. Russian émigré ventures were then given financial support if this fitted in with the overall policies of their host society. The independence of the Russian émigré press of the 1920s disappeared completely and émigré politics was subsumed into the politics of the host societies. Politically, the emigration was quite different.

POST-WAR STUDIES OF THE EMIGRATION

Representatives of the 'first wave' began to assess the cultural achievements of the emigration in the post-war period. The first major account was that of G.P. Struve,[18] who linked the developments in Russian émigré fiction with various trends in the social and political thought of the emigration. This work was severely criticised by Struve's contemporaries for lacunae and inconsistencies, especially in its extensive coverage of minor figures while major writers received less thorough treatment.[19] In the late 1960s, P.E. Kovalevsky attempted to produce a much wider-ranging work.[20] However, this was limited by the author's own experience and the materials he had at his disposal. Studies of individual cultural and literary figures were produced but the first real survey and synthesis was Marc Raeff's masterly study, published in 1990.[21] This placed the subject of the Russian emigration firmly on the international scholarly agenda, although material relating to émigré life in the countries of Eastern Europe which had been part of the Soviet bloc was not available to him. Since 1989 much new material relating to the emigration in these areas has been published.

Berlin, Prague and Belgrade, in that order, were collection centres for information about the Russian émigré community. The Second World War put a stop to this activity and after the war these cities fell into the Soviet orbit and most of the material became unavailable to scholars. Even in Yugoslavia, study of the emigration was taboo. For, although Yugoslavia had broken with Moscow, it had not abandoned Communist ideology, so the emigration had to be seen as counter-revolutionary and unworthy of study. The Russian Historical Archive Abroad (RZIA), the largest of the émigré archival collections, was removed from Prague to Moscow, and most information about its was inaccurate and incomplete. Only with publication of the full catalogue in 1999 was T.F. Pavlova able to give a fuller account of what had happened in the post-war period.[22]

In addition to the removal of archives, many émigrés were arrested and those who remained were unable to publish their memoirs. Those accounts that appeared simply confirmed the political pressure imposed upon the remnants of the Russian emigration.[23] There were occasional moments of relative thaw: for example in Czechoslovakia, the 1960s was a time when Slavists attempted to begin the study of Russian literary life in Prague.[24]

Researchers, therefore, had to rely on pre-war publications. Some, like S.P. Postnikov's 1928 volume, *Russkie v Prage* (Russians in Prague), were based on accurate and reliable work. Postnikov attempted to show what had been achieved during ten years in exile and provided a survey of the Russian institutions in Prague.[25] Analogous publications appeared in other centres of the Russian diaspora,[26] but the quality of such publications was uneven and they covered only a small part of the community's activities. Moreover, many tended to over-praise the authorities and ascribe much of the welfare of the émigré community to them. A corrective to this approach were the memoirs of those who had managed to escape abroad; in respect of Czechoslovakia, the writings of Novikov, Andreyev,[27] and others were of considerable interest, but these were fragmentary and, again, illuminated only small areas of émigré life.

Western studies gradually attracted the attention of those who were not émigrés themselves. These works tended to be more academic and less involved in grievances and disputes, although the sympathies and antipathies of the early researchers are usually very clear and illustrate their personal links with émigré circles. Owing to the variety of problems associated with émigré material, these scholars used archival materials from the host societies. This is particularly noticeable in the case of Germany, which had been linked fairly closely in various ways to pre-revolutionary Russia. Hans von Rimscha[28] was the first in this area and was followed by Volkmann and later by Robert Williams, whose book is arguably still one of the best histories of Russian émigré society in a foreign country. In such works the émigré communities were examined as an organic part of their host societies, which meant that the differences between the various centres of emigration were highlighted. Last but not least, links between the post-revolutionary and pre-revolutionary émigrés began to be discussed. This connection was one which many political activists had tried to forget once they found themselves again in exile. However, pre-revolutionary connections determined certain aspects of émigré life and helped some refugees to adapt to new conditions. This association raised questions about the universality of émigré experience.

The result of this interest and the availability of material meant that in Western Europe and America the Russian contribution, particularly in the sphere of cultural achievements such as music, ballet and art, was well known. The final years of the Soviet Union saw a gradual change in attitudes to the study of the emigration. Shkarenkov's book was published in 1981 and despite its obvious political bias was based on material which had previously been unknown to the Soviet reading public.[29] By the late 1980s, the emigration was becoming less of a taboo and a much more fashionable subject. Kostikov's work incorporated material from meetings with the few remaining representatives of the first wave of the emigration,[30] while Pashuto's research on historians was an interesting synthesis of scholarly analysis and personal contacts.[31] A number of articles appeared, but those who had access to special archive collections or who were allowed to travel abroad and speak to elderly émigrés were a tiny minority of the Soviet élite. Their privileged position tended to prevent them from gaining a proper understanding of émigré life.

The early 1990s saw the organisation of congresses for émigrés and their descendants and the opening of rich archival collections. In Russia there was a complete change in attitude and there was great demand for the works of émigré authors. In some cases, this was the result of simple curiosity and the feeling that forbidden fruit is always sweeter. Others saw the émigrés as bridging Russia and the West and believed they could explain certain aspects of Western society. Some considered that the émigrés had benefited from the freedom in the West, where they had the opportunity to discuss questions which affected Soviet society, discussions that were forbidden or dangerous within the USSR. The policy of the Soviet authorities of expelling those writers and artists who challenged state dogmas seemed to confirm this analysis. Much émigré writing was accepted as the truth, ostensibly written by those who were totally honest and whose predictions of the collapse of the Soviet system had been proved right. This kind of hagiographic and simplistic approach began to be replaced by the work of those who were studying the newly opened archival material, but the basic problem was that the West and émigré society were poorly understood, so that these studies tended to lack a contextual basis. Access to archives could not compensate for a poor understanding of émigré attitudes and insufficient knowledge of the press.

Studies of Prague

The situation in Czechoslovakia was considerably better. Here, prohibition on the study of the emigration lasted for a much shorter time. Access to pre-war publications was much simpler and the end of the 1960s was a period when Russian émigré literature could be studied seriously. During the 1970s and 1980s, some archival collections were studied and catalogued.[32] Many scholars had personal contact with well-known émigrés. Moreover, material relating to the emigration was held in a variety of Czech government archives,[33] as well as in the collections of a range of organisations and the private collections of politicians. Slavonic studies in Czechoslovakia and the study of linguistics could not ignore the contribution of Russian émigré scholars. In particular the émigré legacy was very clear with reference to the Prague Linguistic Circle in which N.S. Trubetskoy and R.O. Jakobson had played so prominent a role. Even when study of the emigration was prohibited, it was evident that émigrés had contributed much to fields as diverse as the question of Russo–Czech relations, art history, folklore and international law. V.A. Frantsev, the Slavist and literary specialist, A.L. Bem, a literary scholar and Dostoevsky specialist, and L.V. Kopecky, the philologist, were discussed in connection with their disciplines even if their émigré background was not mentioned.

These more welcoming conditions formed the basis for the rapid development of the study of the emigration after the Velvet Revolution of 1989. A leading role was played by Professor Sládek, who not only published his own research[34] but also took the initiative in creating the first joint publication by Czech and Russian scholars in a special edition of the journal *Slovanský přehled*.[35] This work was taken further by V. Veber,[36] in three volumes of research connected with the Seminar for East European History, attached to the Institute for World History at Charles University in Prague. In 1995 the Slavonic Library, in conjunction with the Institute for Slav Studies and the Society for East and Central European Studies in the Czech Republic, organised an international conference on the emigration and published the conference papers.[37] Concurrently, the Slavonic Library was preparing to publish a bibliography of all émigré publications which appeared in Czechoslovakia between 1918 and 1945.[38] This included the work not only of Russian but also of Ukrainian and Belorussian émigrés, regardless of the language of publication. These undertakings provided valuable information for scholars.

Collaborative projects were continued under the auspices of the Institute for Slav Studies. In 1996 the journal *Rossica* began to be published and it devoted a fair amount of attention to émigré studies. A grant enabled the formation of a research group, which published a collection of documents, as well as articles and a chronology of the cultural and social life of the émigré community in Czechoslovakia.[39]

In addition, M. Dandová and M. Zahradníková continued to analyse material held in the archive of the Museum of Czech Literature.[40] S. Tejchmanová[41] attempted to analyse the political development of the emigration, an undertaking that was perhaps premature and that required more preliminary studies. Putna and Zadražilová's book *Ruska mimo Rusko* (Russia out of Russia)[42] was not limited to Czechoslovakia and consisted of short biographies of personalities within the émigré community. I. Savický's work discussed the Russian émigrés in Czechoslovakia in relation to Russian politics and the earlier Czech émigrés and the Czech legion during the First World War and the Russian Civil War.[43] Kopřivová[44] has collected information and photographs to provide a detailed picture of émigré society at local level,[44] while Chinyaeva has discussed the financial aspects of Russian Action.[45]

Recent Research in Russia

At the start of the 1990s, scholars in Russia began to study Prague as a centre of Russian emigration. Russian historians were able to use the valuable archival material to be found in RZIA. Regrettably, as in the more general studies of the emigration, their work suffered from a lack of understanding of the general position of the emigration. The idealisation of the émigrés, an understandable reaction to the decades of criticism, frequently resulted in an uncritical acceptance of émigré material, and particularly of archival documents. Some researchers have not given sufficient weight to the émigrés' very difficult circumstances, which often forced both individuals and organisations to exaggerate their importance not only in order to justify their existence but also to persuade organisations with funds that their activities were worth supporting.

The second weakness of the research, especially in the first half of the 1990s, was the paucity of published sources available to Russian scholars. Because they did not have access to émigré publications, their research frequently lacked the context necessary for them to assess the value of the archival collections. Moreover, the lack of knowledge of Czech or of publications appearing in the Czech Republic could cause problems. For example, although Tejchmanová published interesting information about S.N. Prokopovich's Economic Cabinet,[46] three years later a Russian scholar tried to analyse the cabinet using the material in RZIA but obviously unaware of the article in Czech.

E.P. Serapionova is the author of the only monograph devoted to the Russian emigration in Czechoslovakia to be published in Russia so far.[47] An excellent example of the strengths and weaknesses of current research, this book is based on a range of archival materials hitherto unavailable to scholars. At the same time, the work demonstrated that the author was not fully conversant with the émigré press and other contemporary publications.

However, the interest shown in Russia in the study of the emigration is gradually addressing these problems. Publications continually add to our knowledge of the archival material that is now available for study. The interest in ideas which arose and were discussed by the émigrés, especially Eurasianism, also impinges on the study of the emigration and is gradually elucidating the situation.

Émigré Attitudes

Despite differences in opinion or alterations brought about by their position in their host societies, the émigrés were united by a common interest in

Russia and in the shared difficulties of refugee life in a foreign country attempting to come to terms with the cataclysmic effects of the First World War. The desire to preserve their national and cultural identity meant that émigrés were particularly dependent on the printed word. This was the only medium available to them for self-expression and for the exchange of ideas. It was also the way through which links could be maintained. Many of the intelligentsia subscribed to newspapers and periodicals from all over the diaspora, thus keeping abreast of a whole range of ideas. Through the printed word, the scholarly community of Prague maintained academic contact with other scholars, both Russian and foreign. Those who could do so – and these were mainly political leaders – visited other émigré communities. Since the entire inter-war period was suffused with the belief that a return home was imminent, much émigré activity was dedicated to ideas relevant to Russia's needs. For many Russians, this belief was a product of their human predicament: for them, Russia was a place in which stability and happiness had been possible. It was very difficult to imagine that this had passed for ever. It was also very difficult for the erstwhile ruling élite of the Russian empire to come to terms with the idea that they had so mismanaged affairs that the Bolsheviks, who had been the riff-raff of society and had been jailed and exiled for terrorism, bank robbery and many other illegal activities, had seized power and maintained it without the support of the majority of the population.

In addition, the politics of the 1920s in the Soviet Union seemed to confirm the contention that political changes might bring about a relaxation of dogma and that it *would* become possible for the émigrés to return home. The abandonment of War Communism and the inauguration of the New Economic Policy appeared to herald a review of ideology. Although a large number of the leading writers and philosophers were expelled from the USSR in 1922,[48] many other contacts continued. In particular, various Russian publishing houses were still able to publish abroad, especially in Berlin. The cessation of contacts in the 1930s, when Stalin closed the borders and resettled the population of the frontier regions, made it far more difficult for the old underground channels of communication to remain open. As a result, the majority of émigrés knew little about Stalin's policies and so did not always understand the full implications of what was happening. Some tended to interpret Stalinism as a return to more nationalistic ideas, in contrast to the internationalism of early Bolshevism. This seemed to indicate that the demands of ideology were giving way to the more traditional role of Russia as a Great Power. The hope that Soviet policies would be reformed and that a return home would be possible continued right up to the beginning of the Cold War.

Although Russian émigrés drew parallels between themselves and other political exiles they saw the circumstances of their exile as unique. Their exodus from Russia had been produced by the specific situation in that country and by the attitudes of the Bolsheviks to those who were described as reactionaries, White Guards and members of the bourgeoisie. Their position in exile and the difficulties they encountered were determined by the conditions of the post-war world, which hampered both assimilation and return to the homeland. However, although the Russian communities in Europe and the Far East adapted to their situation and tried to evolve responses which would help them in both the short and the long term, arguably these attitudes and responses were not altogether new and had been exhibited by the refugees and migrants who had swept through Europe for centuries. For example, the idea that exile was temporary, even though it might last a lifetime, is an attitude shared by most exiles, beginning with the most long-lived of all diasporas, that of the Jews.[49] However, when this idea proved difficult to achieve immediately they learned to build a new home abroad.[50] This pattern has been repeated over and over again by successive waves of exiles and refugees, both secular and religious, in Europe and the New World who have striven to survive in new surroundings while preserving aspects of their former lives and identities that they associate with the homeland which, paradoxically, has forced them to leave.

The situation in Prague highlighted many of the problems associated with aid to refugees. Yet despite the material hardships, the émigrés were to demonstrate a great deal of energy and ingenuity both in dealing with the immediate problems of refugee life and in their attempt to preserve and perpetuate Russian culture. Some of the solutions they found were very similar to those in other centres of the Russian diaspora. Others were specific to Prague, where the Czech state and society determined many aspects of life for the Russian community. Comparison with other waves of refugees and émigrés shows that they all emphasised the special nature of their predicament. Their unwillingness to examine similarities with other such groups is a common response in an alien environment, and is furthermore intrinsic to the need to maintain a cultural and national identity. The sense of specialness is not unique to any emigration. Moreover, this characteristic of refugee communities in the first half of the twentieth century can be widely observed in modern societies where the need to maintain a distinct identity becomes of vital importance in the face of the pressures of mobility within a multicultural environment.

The Russian émigré community saw itself as seeking temporary asylum and only gradually began to appreciate the attitudes of immigrants who sought to create a new life in better conditions. Their view of Russia and experience of the Civil War were instrumental in determining their attitudes not only towards Russia but also towards their host societies. The evacuation of the White Armies resulted in the most determined and obvious opponents of the Bolsheviks being abroad, and this had a clear impact on political developments within Russia. It also resulted in a significant proportion of educated and administrative personnel leaving Soviet Russia, which had a far-reaching effect on the problems encountered by the authorities in their attempts to run the state. It was this perceived need for an educated élite which was part of the impulse for Russian Action in Czechoslovakia.

Interest in the emigration within Russia has been generated by the view that the history of the Soviet Union and Soviet society would certainly have been enriched and would have been very different had this élite remained in Russia. The difficulty for many Russian researchers and scholars has been to assess the Western context which had such a significant influence on the evolution of the emigration. The history of the Russian emigration has to incorporate the changes in the Soviet Union with the international situation. Events within the host societies influence the development of the Russian émigré communities and also illuminate the differences and similarities between the main places of settlement. Any assessment of the achievements of the Russian emigration must take this range of pressures into account. These influences explain many of the failings and misjudgements of the Russian émigré community. At the same time, the energy and self-sacrifice displayed by so many individuals in what they perceived to be the pursuit of truth in the interests of the Russian people makes their achievements even more remarkable.

This study does not discuss literary or political émigrés in detail. Instead, it seeks to explain the origins of Russian Action and to analyse its impact on the Russian emigration in Prague. The reasons for the extraordinary generosity of the First Czechoslovak Republic and the causes of the failure of its policies vividly illuminate the attitudes and situation of the mass of the Russian émigrés and help to elucidate the views and actions of the emigration's leading personalities. They also clarify the relationship between Russian refugees, their host societies and Russia.

Chapter 1

Relations between Czechs and Russians

It could not have been predicted that Czechoslovakia would develop a policy of aid to Russian refugees or that Prague would become a major refugee centre. Neither was the existence of an independent Czechoslovak state a foregone conclusion. Masaryk, the first President of the Republic, achieved his aim of Czech independence through astute political manoeuvring. His perceptive understanding of influential trends helped him to prepare the ground for some of the diplomatic initiatives which facilitated the movement towards independence. Many assumptions and preconceptions altered as a result of the Russian Revolutions of 1917 and the ensuing Civil War. These events in Russia were a vital component in the process of the creation of the new Republic and its place in the post-war world. Subsequently, the need to develop policies with respect to the USSR played a crucial role in determining attitudes towards Russian émigrés. In 1921 the Czechs also became involved in dealing with the pressing needs of the Russian refugees in Constantinople after the evacuation of the Crimea. Humanitarian considerations began to overrule the initial assumptions about the way in which the Russian émigré community in Prague would develop.

The relationship between the Czechs and Russians is illustrated by the history of the Bohemian lands.[1] The creation of an independent Czechoslovakia was seen as the culmination of a long struggle, during which Czech national feeling had been subjected to intense foreign pressure. This outcome was in many ways quite unexpected. Czechs' interpretation of their history has stressed two factors which were integral to their understanding of the place of the First Republic in Europe. First, the Czechs saw their lands as a constituent part of Western Europe and never wanted to be understood as part of Eastern European development. Second, the Czechs considered themselves largely as equal players in the game and masters of their own fate, not in constant subjection to various imperial overlords. These concepts ran parallel to and interconnected with Czechoslovakia's relations with Russia and formed an important part of Czech attitudes to the Russian émigrés.

Czech History

Questions of national identity and links with brother Slavs, particularly Russians, were to some extent incorporated into the national myth. Some commentators argued that although in religious terms Bohemia and Moravia were in the Roman sphere and the Byzantine influence now seemed very distant, certain Eastern affinities survived, if only on the level of 'a difference in mentality and psychological outlook'.[2] The Christianisation of Bohemia and Moravia took place between the ninth and the eleventh centuries. The Great Moravian Empire was the first political organisation to unify Czechs and Slovaks, to accept Christianity, and to create a literary and religious Slav language from the teachings of St Cyril and St Methodius. However, for political reasons and because of Germanic influence, the Slav liturgy was rapidly abandoned.

Nevertheless, this connection and sympathy for a Slav religious past were seen as significant towards the end of the nineteeth century when the Czech lands became the most economically developed part of the Austro-Hungarian Empire and Czechs occupied influential positions within the economic life of their own country. With the creation of the Dual Monarchy of Austro-Hungary in 1867, Czechs once more asserted their national identity and began to achieve political parity with Hungary and Austria.

However, although for the most part Bohemia seemed to fall into the Western European sphere of influence, the question of national identity meant that, after a very long break, relations with Russia began to play a central role in Czech politics. The intelligentsia in Bohemia was small, culturally German and strongly influenced by German philosophy,[3] but it began to look towards Russia as movements of nationalism and pan-Slavism took shape.

Russia was viewed as a friendly and brotherly Slav nation and, as the only Slav Great Power, a possible bulwark in the struggle against Germanisation. To begin with, this was theoretical as few Czechs knew much about Russia and Russian life. In the middle of the nineteenth century, a very small number did travel to Russia and most were disappointed by what they found there. Nevertheless, when the Habsburgs were defeated by Bismarck in 1866 and the Dual Monarchy was created in the following year, the Czechs, who would have preferred a triple monarchy, tried to play the Russian card. Czech political leaders made a 'pilgrimage' to Moscow, where they were greeted politely but not effusively. Their efforts to involve Napoleon III in the struggle for independence were no more successful, and it became obvious that the attempts to play a part on the international stage had failed. Czech politics returned to the idea that the country had to fight for change from within the structures of the Austro-Hungarian Empire and had to rely on its own resources rather than finding a champion elsewhere.

In cultural matters, the Czechs were far more successful in finding an international audience. Czech culture tried to free itself from German authority, which had been dominant for the last century and a half. To begin with, Czech culture found inspiration by turning to the Slav past and to the heritage of the sixteenth and seventeenth centuries. In the latter part of the nineteenth century, the Czechs tried to establish direct links with European and American culture. The irony was that they did so by means of the German language.[4] The outward expression of these changes was the division of the university in Prague, which had been completely Germanised, into a Czech and a German university as well as trips by Czech writers, musicians and artists to France, Russia and the USA. Entry of Czech culture on to the world stage coincided with the flowering of Russian literature, music and theatre. Thus, knowledge of Russian culture acquired a special meaning, giving Slav culture an international significance and providing traditional and rather diffuse Russophilism with a new dimension.

Arguably, restricting Czechs to a minor role in the politics of Austro-Hungary resulted in large numbers leaving the Dual Monarchy. Chicago became the second-largest Czech city in terms of the number of resident Czechs, while small colonies of Czechs in Russia played a key role in helping to establish economic links with the Russian empire. A new type of Czech Russophile came into being: the entrepreneur who understood the Russian business world and who made money. He was far more interested in the enormous range of economic and financial possibilities opening up in Russia than in the rather vague idea of 'brother Slavs'. Such entrepreneurs favoured the idea of closer links and even unity with Russia: Czechs, they believed, could use their expertise to play a leading economic role in Russia, owing to their experience of industrial development in Bohemia. As a result of living there for long periods, many such Czech entrepreneurs developed an affection for Russia and her people. This, in turn, had a positive impact on the fate of Russian émigrés to Czechoslovakia after the Russian Revolution, for these Czechs formed the backbone of the National Democratic Party, led by Karel Kramář. Kramář, the son of a wealthy industrialist and married to the daughter of a Moscow manufacturer, was well educated and believed in the idea of a wider Slav brotherhood. He was to play a crucial role in the support provided for Russian émigrés in Czechoslovakia.

Before the First World War, the political programme of these circles of financiers and entrepreneurs was expressed in Slavophile and even pan-Slav terms. However, this was aimed simply at increasing the political role of the Czechs within Austro-Hungary. No one was actually considering the question of independence for the Slav minorities within the Austro-Hungarian Empire which included Czechs, Slovaks, Croats, Slovenes and some Poles and Ukrainians. Still less were they discussing any kind of Slav federation or liberation of the Poles from Russian hegemony. In practical terms, they hoped to create a much closer alliance between Slavs in the Austro-Hungarian Empire and Imperial Russia, to act as a protector of Slav interest. As a result of this, as V.Černý notes: 'the neo-Slavophiles were constantly in a state of internal contradiction ... caught between their duties towards the interests of the Slavs, and their responsibilities towards the states in which they lived, Russia and Austro-Hungary, and to which they owed conservative allegiance.'[5] The long-awaited First World War, which had found everyone unprepared, suddenly reversed all such assumptions. Previous certainties were questioned, including the position of state frontiers. What had previously seemed wishful thinking became the subject of sober calculation. The policy of co-operating with political authorities of the Dual Monarchy in order to reform the system from within now appeared to be treachery towards the national cause.

This change in attitude was seen first among the ordinary population and it was easier for them to signal this change than for politicians, who had a more vested interest in the status quo. A significant proportion of the population supported the idea of an independent Czech state, which few had considered prior to 1914. There were no opinion polls: people simply voted with their feet as could be seen by the behaviour of the troops. The Austro-Hungarian army was fighting the Serb and Russian armies, who were not seen as obvious enemies. Czech soldiers on the Russian front crossed over to the enemy individually, in groups or in military formations; finally, a whole regiment, including its regimental band, deserted to the enemy. Probably not all of these soldiers were aware that when they did so, the road back to Austro-Hungary was now firmly closed, since they were no longer simply deserters but traitors. But nevertheless in the prisoner-of-war camps, and at home in the Czech lands, there was a growing group of people for whom survival in a free society meant that Austro-Hungary could no longer continue in its present form. In the first year of the war such popular trends were Russophile, conservative and monarchical. This pro-Slav attitude was enhanced by the fact that contact with Russia was far more intensive than contact with France, England or other Western powers, so that the idea of Slav interdependence gradually transformed and developed into clearer political forms.

Tomáš Masaryk

To begin with, the Russophile-monarchical trend was widespread and had no competitors, although Masaryk considered that there was no future in these views. As he observed in *The Making of a State*: 'After all, I was right, and I think that one of my soundest political judgements and decisions was in not staking our national cause on the Russian card alone and in seeking, on the contrary, to win sympathies of all the Allies instead of sharing the mood of uncritical and passive Russophilism then prevalent.'[6] This was not the first time that Masaryk had run counter to public opinion. Amongst his generation of Czech politicians he was an exceptional personality and his life reflected this. He had many international contacts, and was an intellectual as well as a politician. His wife was American and from 1878 onwards he visited the USA regularly, where he had a wide circle of acquaintance in American academic, political and business circles. He visited Britain more than once, where he also managed to find contacts that would be useful to the Czechs. Before the war he travelled to Russia three times and corresponded with Russian scholars. He also had contacts in Germany, had studied and taught at the University of Vienna, and was a deputy in the Viennese parliament.

No other Czech politician had such a wide range of interests or of international contacts. Masaryk saw problems in a broader context and did not discuss them in a clichéd or stereotypical way. Consequently, he was often misunderstood. He seemed insufficiently patriotic and on occasion did not appear to understand the wishes of the Czech nation. After the war, these exceptional qualities and Masaryk's otherness were seen as his strength. After he became an émigré in 1915, a group of close colleagues formed around him but they were much younger and for the most part had lived outside the borders of Austro-Hungary before the war. Masaryk was born in 1850. Edvard Beneš, who was to become Foreign Minister of the Republic and who succeeded Masaryk as President in 1935, was born in 1880. Milan Štefánik, who supported Masaryk's views in exile, was born in 1888. Klecanda, who was very close to Masaryk, was born in 1890. One of the leaders of Czech society in Russia, he was one of the few who had a liberal outlook. In 1917 he was appointed as Masaryk's representative to the Czech legion. He died unexpectedly of illness in 1918. Dr Štefan Osuský, a Slovak lawyer from Chicago – who acted as a liaison between the nationalists in Prague and the National Council in Paris from 1917 onwards, and later became Czech Minister in Paris – was born in 1889. Even amongst Masaryk's opponents there was only one of his generation: all the others were much younger. Kramář was born in 1860, and acted as liaison with the Russian emigration. Rašín, a National Democrat who was very close to Kramář, was born in 1867 and was assassinated by anarchists in 1921. After independence, when he was appointed Minister of Finance, he had introduced monetary reform. Antonín Hajn, one of the progressive grouping, was born in 1868.

To his close colleagues, Masaryk was an unquestionable authority. This usually allowed him, after his emigration in 1915, to rely on the unity of Czech émigrés, an extremely rare phenomenon amongst emigrations in general. This was particularly important during the First World War as it distinguished the Czechs in the eyes of the Western Allies from the mêlée of other Slav émigrés – Poles, Croats and Serbs – who split into countless warring factions and advanced contradictory suggestions and demands. However, this unity among the Czech emigration did complicate relations with opposition circles at home. Policies and issues were not clarified, and hidden enmity bedevilled internal political relationships for many years after the creation of the Czechoslovak Republic.

The First World War was crucial to the attainment of Czech independence even if this process was extremely tortuous and could not have been foreseen by those who played a leading role in events. The Russian Revolution of 1917 and the Armistice in 1918 drastically altered the position and attitudes of the Czechoslovak legion in Russia and involved it at an important stage of the Russian Civil War.

The First World War was not at all popular in Prague and 'war with Russia and Serbia was felt to be little better than civil war . . . repugnant as an outrage upon Slav solidarity'.[7] The successful Russian advance into Galicia in August 1914 gave the impression, towards the end of that year and in early 1915, that the Czechs would be liberated in the near future by advancing Russian armies. Russian propaganda emanating from these armies seemed to confirm this view. In August 1914, the Grand Duke Nicholas published his manifesto to the peoples of Austro-Hungary and many unofficial copies found their way into the Czech territories. On 20 August, and on 17 September, Nicholas II met a Czech delegation. The Russian Minister of Foreign Affairs, Sazonov, also met them, on 15 September. The Emperor and his minister expressed the hope that the desire of the Czechs to recreate a Czech kingdom would be realised. But whatever was said at these meetings was expressed so carefully and with so many caveats that the Imperial Russian government was not committed to any course of action. However, it was decided that a volunteer force would be formed from those Czechs who had Russian citizenship.

In their retrospective assessments of the course of the War of Liberation, both Masaryk and Beneš emphasised the dual nature of the policies of the Russian Imperial government. Although they seemed to be making overtures to independent Czech sentiment, the Russian government did not wish to allow such nationalism to get out of control. Principles of legitimacy and legality were considered more important than nationalist or revolutionary pan-Slav ideas which consisted of nationalist politics based on ideas of natural law. The Russian government did not wish to make any declarations which would be binding. Czech prisoners of war and deserters were not encouraged to join the volunteer formations, and all such units were subordinated to Russian command. Furthermore, these units were dispersed throughout the Russian forces in order to prevent the creation of a large Czech formation which might become the basis of a future independent Czech army. However, despite such hesitancy the Russians did more than other powers prior to 1917 to foster Czech national feeling and recognised the Czechs as an independent nation. The Western powers chose to ignore the problem altogether. If it was considered at all, the confusing intertwining of the nations of Central Europe was seen as a slow-burning fuse which threatened to ignite, 'Balkanising' Europe and spreading chaos to the borders of Switzerland and even into the heart of Germany.

Masaryk drew up a table which showed the steps towards the recognition of the movement of Czech resistance,[8] and the recognition of the Czech troops and the émigré government as legitimate representatives of a power on the side of the Allies. This process developed very slowly. Although the Russian authorities were prepared to speak to the Czech representatives in 1914, in the West the only success, in Masaryk's opinion, during this period was the decision by the French Ministry of the Interior that 'loyal' Czechs should not be interned but should be given the same status as citizens of friendly nations. Masaryk did not mention that in the same year, in the French Foreign Legion, *Compagnie Nazdar* was formed. The creation of this company seems to have played a role in the decision taken by the French on the subject of loyal Czechs. Almost the entire company was killed near Arras in May 1915.

An alternative Russian policy on the Czech issue seemed unimaginable in 1914 and Masaryk did not raise the issue in his talks with Vsevolod Svatkovsky, a Russian journalist and intelligence officer whom he met in Italy in 1914. When discussing the situation with Robert Seton-Watson, a British journalist, Masaryk admitted that complete Bohemian independence was the ultimate goal, which might be realised only if the war was prolonged. At this stage Masaryk assumed that if independence were to be granted, the nation would probably prefer a monarchy to a republic and one with a Western prince rather than a Russian Grand Duke, a solution which Kramář advocated.[9] This lack of discussion amongst the exiled Czech leaders maintained the unity of all radical anti-Austrian forces regardless of whether they were Russophile or Western in orientation, monarchist or republican in attitude. In 1915 the Czech question reached a critical point. The deciding event of that year was the advance by the Central Powers on the Russian front in May 1915 which forced the Russians to abandon not only all Austrian territory, but also all Polish territories under Russian jurisdiction. Pressure on Czech politicians in Austria also increased. In addition to the arrest of other Czech deputies, Kramář and Rašín were sentenced to death as representatives of the pan-Slav movement. The arrest of the most active anti-Austrian politicians led to the so-called policy of activism at home; the hope was that support for the Habsburgs might result in a policy of federalism. The entry of Italy into the war did not change this. In January 1915, Masaryk left Italy for Switzerland, and finally became an émigré, having learned that he would be arrested immediately were he to return home. He established that none of the Czech politicians had any contacts with the French or British governments except for those he had set up himself. His contacts were unique for a provincial politician in opposition in the Austro-Hungarian Empire but totally inadequate for the head of a national liberation movement. Masaryk used all his energies to establish further contacts but had very few successes in 1915.

In Britain, his supporters – notably the journalists Seton-Watson and Wickham Steed – did their best to introduce Masaryk to those with influence. In 1916 he was persuaded to accept a lectureship at King's College, London and inaugurated the newly founded School of Slavonic Studies.[10] Asquith, the British Prime Minister, agreed to chair the lecture on 'The Problem of the Small Nation in the European Crisis', but owing to illness his place was taken by Lord Robert Cecil at the last minute. Masaryk achieved his first noticeable triumph in France in 1916, when the Foreign Minster, Briand, met him on 2 February and supported the plan to divide Austro-Hungary into 'her historical and natural elements'.[11] This was an important general principle, but the French did not follow it up with any concrete policies or help for the National Council. In Russia practical measures were taken to help the Czech national cause and in January 1916 the Czech unit fighting with the Russians was renamed the Czech Rifle Regiment. In April permission was given to form a brigade and then, in October, divisions were formed. Regulations for the creation of Czech formations were drawn up. However, these policies were subject to the contradictions that existed within the Russian Imperial government and the decision to create divisions of liberated Slav prisoners of war was revoked following pressure from Stürmer, the reactionary Russian Prime Minister, and the Empress. The Czech deputy, Dürich, who had been sent in 1915 by Kramář to help Masaryk, and who had then become Masaryk's deputy on the National Council and representative on the council in Russia, organised his own special National Council in opposition to Masaryk's 'westernising' tendency. Dürich's programme was far more pro-Russian and reactionary and expressed a classical idea of autocracy: monarchy, orthodoxy, nationality. The fact that he promised to convert Czechs to Eastern Orthodoxy, and that the council was financed by Stürmer's administration, completely discredited him in the eyes of the majority of

Czech prisoners of war and alarmed the Western Allies. However, although Dürich's project was approved by the Imperial Government, after the February Revolution it was repudiated by the Provisional Government.

The Impact of the Russian Revolutions of 1917

Thus, 1917 began very unfavourably for the Czechs. Most of the internal opposition had been crushed; the opposition abroad, having achieved recognition with great difficulty, had split and was to a large extent discredited. The military situation was not optimistic: a drawn peace which preserved Austro-Hungary seemed likely. But suddenly, as in 1914, in the course of three weeks, everything changed radically and the Czech question entered on the world stage.

The Allies had never had a clear policy on the formation of an independent Czech state. Masaryk maintained high-level and influential contacts in order to publicise the views of the Czech nationalists and promote the idea of independence, but the French and British were primarily concerned with the defeat of Germany. Even if it appeared that detaching Austro-Hungary from the Central Powers was a possibility there was no desire to commit the Allies to the support of the dissident nationalities within Austro-Hungary.

On 21 December 1916, President Wilson asked the warring states about their conditions for peace. The Allies replied on 12 January 1917. At the insistence of France, one of these conditions was 'the freeing of Italians, Slavs, Rumanians, Czechoslovaks from foreign control'.[12] This statement put the 'Czechoslovaks' into an exceptional position among subjugated nations which did not have their own state. In large part, it was the result of Masaryk's policies and agitation although it also demonstrates the degree to which the Entente politicians did not understand the national problem in Central Europe.[13] However, if this singling out of the Czechoslovaks was a surprise to supporters of Austro-Hungary, it was also opposed by Czech deputies at home. On 31 January 1917 the Union of Czech Deputies, which included most parliamentary deputies who had escaped arrest, sent a letter to Czernin, the Foreign Minister of Austro-Hungary, in which the policy of independence for the Czechoslovaks was rejected and in which they 'resolutely declared that the Czech nation, as in the past, now and in the future sees and will see the conditions for its development only under the Habsburg sceptre'.[14] Some Allied politicians were convinced that Austro-Hungary 'might conclude a separate peace if it was given a guarantee against dismemberment'.[15] Between March 1917 and April 1918 secret negotiations were conducted intermittently between Vienna and the British, French and Americans. Attempts to detach Austria from Germany were ultimately unsuccessful but while this process continued there was little willingness to support Czechoslovak independence.

The National Council abroad, after the exclusion of Dürich, had only one elected representative on it: Masaryk. All the other members had been appointed by Czech communities abroad, under fairly doubtful circumstances, and their legal status was at best questionable. The rejection of the National Council's activities by a fully representative political body could have led to the repudiation of its avowed policy of independence, a policy, moreover, expressed in vague terms. However, the February Revolution broke out in Russia and events began to move rapidly and unexpectedly. From 24 April 1917, when the Provisional Government finally agreed to the formation of the Czechoslovak legion, the fate of the Czech lands and Czechoslovakia began to be decided in Russia.[16] Marxist-Leninist Czechoslovak historiography of the 1950s insisted that, without the October Revolution in Russia, Czechoslovakia would not have existed. This argument requires one important qualification. It was not the programme of national self-determination advanced by the Bolsheviks but the struggle of the Czechoslovak military formations *against* the Bolsheviks which guaranteed favourable conditions for Czechoslovakia during the peace negotiations.

In April 1917 this was still in the future, but Masaryk, despite his fears about the possible development of the Russian Revolution, fully realised the importance of Russia's role in the new conditions. On 18 March he sent a telegram to Rodzianko, the President of the Duma, and to Miliukov, the Foreign Minister in the Russian Provisional Government. Masaryk knew Miliukov personally and Miliukov played a key role in the creation of Czechoslovak formations in Russia. On 16 May Masaryk arrived in Petrograd by a circuitous route.

From April onwards, the creation of a Czechoslovak legion under the command of Jaroslav Červinka, a Czech serving as a Russian general, started to move ahead quickly. But France rather than Russia was interested in these troops. Despite tremendous losses, the highest circles of the Russian command still believed that victory was possible and also believed that at their disposal was an endless supply of well-trained troops. The Russian army, in their opinion lacked arms but not soldiers. On this basis, Nicholas II had promised the French that a significant number of troops would be sent to the western front. The Provisional Government did not continue this policy, either because it had enough sense to see that it was not in its interest to do so or perhaps, more plausibly, because it had insufficient power. When it became clear that the promised transfer of Russian troops was not going to happen, the French mission under M. Albert Thomas considered instead the transfer of up to 50,000 Czechoslovak troops and prisoners of war to France. Masaryk, for his part, wanted the Czech troops to be visible in an important theatre of war. Thus on 15 June 1917 the first agreement between an Allied Power (France) and the Czechoslovak National Council was signed.

That this occurred in Petrograd but without the participation of the Russians can be seen as symbolic. From this point, until the signing of the peace accords, the Czechs and Slovaks fought for their own independence and decided the external conditions of their future state in Russia. The Russians did not play an active part in this process as they were preoccupied with their own internal problems. But the progress of the Revolution and Civil War in Russia gave rise to constantly shifting alliances and enmities. Thus policy on what was happening in Russia and its likely impact on Czechs became central to the Czechoslovak National Council, to the government in exile and finally to the government in Prague. This policy determined Czechoslovakia's place at the Paris peace conference, where the map of Europe was being redrawn and where the interconnections were intended to strengthen the Versailles system.

In June 1917 Masaryk, to some extent, foresaw this situation. The attempt to transfer Czechoslovak troops and prisoners of war to the western front was still under discussion. This seemed the most rational policy, although in retrospect the cost in terms of men killed and wounded would have been very high.[17] The situation in Russia made everything extremely complicated. The distances in Russia, the appalling transport, the defeat of the Allies on the southern wing of the eastern front, all turned what might have been a politically clear and, diplomatically, the most rational decision into a very difficult task. In the course of solving it, one aspect of Masaryk's policy became especially important.

In the first instance, the Czechoslovak National Council was interested less in Russian victory than in the victory of the Allies and their support for the future Czechoslovakia. To achieve this, it had been necessary to create Czechoslovak military formations and send them into battle. The February Revolution in Russia had made this possible and the Czechoslovak troops had won their first important battle on 2 June near Zborov. However, the need to maintain unity in conditions of rapidly polarising politics in Russia would not be easy. This had become clear during the so-called Kornilov rising. Masaryk adhered to a policy of unconditional support for the legitimate Provisional Government. But the government was opposed by the Commander-in-Chief, General Kornilov, whom it had appointed. Various ministers resigned to demonstrate that they would not support a mutineer, and the dividing line between legitimate and illegitimate power dissolved. The Czechoslovak legion did not support Kornilov, although there is some evidence of a Czech 'Kornilov' company. Moreover, Bolshevik propaganda began to have its effect.[18]

The creation of military divisions and the redeployment of Czech prisoners of war became an urgent necessity. The success of the October Revolution and the beginning of the Brest-Litovsk peace negotiations, at which the Soviet delegation put forward the principle of self-determination as one of the cornerstones of the negotiations, gave added hope to the internal opposition in the Czech lands and Slovakia. But the Czechoslovak units in Russia were placed in a difficult position by the refusal of the Allies to play a part in these negotiations. The situation was rapidly complicated by the declaration of Ukrainian independence by the Ukrainian Rada. This was recognised by the Central Powers and peace was signed with the Ukrainian People's Republic on 8 February 1918. As Czechoslovak units were in the Ukraine, they had to clarify their attitude to the initially autonomous and then fully independent Ukrainian government. Increasingly, questions of self-determination and nationalism predominated and the need to support Russians in their internal conflict came to be questioned by the rank and file.

After the collapse of the Provisional Government, Masaryk assumed a strict policy of non-intervention in internal Russian affairs and did everything in his power to hasten the deployment of Czechoslovak units to France and to guarantee their legal status as part of the French army. Although these talks had been going on for some time, the October Revolution and the danger that Soviet Russia was about to leave the war unilaterally undoubtedly speeded them up. On 16 December 1917, a decree signed by Poincaré, Pichon and Clemenceau and published in the *Journal officiel* on 19 December declared that the Czechoslovak army in France was an autonomous formation and fought against the Central Powers under its own banners while subordinate to the French High Command. Politically, it was subordinate to the Czech National Council, based in Paris. This was further elaborated in the 'General instructions on the constitution of an autonomous Czechoslovak national army' approved by Clemenceau on 7 February 1918.[19] On the basis of this decree, the presidium of the Russian department of the Czechoslovak National Council under the chairmanship of Masaryk declared on 18 January 1918 that 'with the agreement of the Government of the French Republic, the Czechoslovak units in Russia (in the Ukraine and in former Russian territories) are part of the Czechoslovak troops under the High Command of the French'.[20]

This provided the opportunity for Masaryk to conduct negotiations with all the relevant authorities in both Russia and the Ukraine. He was able to present himself as totally independent and as the representative of a foreign military formation on the territory of an Allied power which, following the collapse of the Provisional Government, had not been linked with any of the warring parties. In the course of these negotiations, Masaryk could define his perceptions of all these various groupings more precisely, and work out his 'Russian policy' for the future, which later determined his policy on the Russian emigration.[21]

Tokyo Memorandum

The so-called 'Tokyo Memorandum' was composed on 10–11 April 1918 in answer to questions by the American ambassador in Japan during Masaryk's return journey from Russia. It delineated the main ideas which governed Masaryk's policy on Russia. Although it is infrequently cited in the secondary literature, Masaryk emphasised the importance of this document by publishing the Czech translation in his work *The Making of a State,* where it was the only appended document. In it, Masaryk advocated that the Bolshevik government had to be recognised *de facto*, and stressed that the Bolsheviks were stronger and likely to be more permanent than their opponents – both inside Russia and amongst foreign governments – believed. He rejected the idea of support for the monarchists, whom he considered very weak and he did not expect the Kadets or Socialist Revolutionaries (SRs), to be successful in their attempts to organise opposition to the Bolsheviks. He envisaged that eventually some kind of coalition government, which would include the Bolsheviks, would be formed. Any democratic government of this kind would exert strong pressure on the Germans and Austrians to bring about far-reaching reform. The smaller nations such as the Finns, Poles, Estonians, Latvians, Lithuanians, Czechs, Slovaks and Romanians needed a strong Russia as a counterweight to Germany and Austria. The Allies also had to support Russia for this reason and Masaryk considered that, once Germany had conquered the countries to the east, she was likely to turn towards the West. Masaryk also advocated the formation of an autonomous Ukrainian republic within the Russian sphere, as an independent Ukraine would be a German satellite.[22]

At this point, the First World War had not yet come to an end and Masaryk was trying to get the Czechoslovak legion transferred to France. He hoped this would be possible after reaching an agreement with Trotsky. It became clear that the Czechoslovak forces would have to leave Russia by journeying across Siberia, as the military situation meant that they could not cross Russia's western border. This journey was bedevilled by attempts to involve the Czech troops in the various conflicts of the Russian Civil War. In May the Czechoslovak legion revolted. The causes of this are unclear. Eyewitness accounts and scholars disagree on the extent to which it was a reaction of frightened and maltreated evacuees. It can also be seen as a result of machinations by the Allies to find a *casus belli* for intervention in Russia against Germany and her perceived Bolshevik allies. Moreover General Gajda, an anti-Communist, was attempting to mislead the Czecho troops, who were far more sympathetic to socialism and resented his policies.[23] By the end of May, local conflicts had developed into a full-scale war between the Czechoslovak legion and the Bolsheviks. Many attempts by a host of individuals and agencies to achieve a peaceful withdrawal were unsuccessful.[24]

Masaryk's policy as expressed in the Tokyo Memorandum began to be put into practice. Offers of alliances with General Alekseev (Supreme Commander in 1917), Kornilov and Semenov were rejected. In those territories over which they had some control the Czechoslovaks began to enter into agreements with, and in some cases assisted in the formation of, various democratic governments consisting of moderate left-wingers. Thus, they helped in the formation of the Committee of Members of the All-Russian Constituent Assembly (Komuch) led by the Socialist Revolutionary V.K. Vol'sky in Samara, which subsequently recognised 'the independence of the Czechoslovak state and its highest institution of power, the Czechoslovak National Council'.[25] They also signed an agreement with the Provisional Siberian Government in Omsk, led by the Trudovik P.V. Vologodsky and co-operated with the left Kadet and SR Ural *oblast'* (provincial) government in Ekaterinburg.

As a result, on 8 September 1918, in Ufa, the State Conference met with the aim of creating an all-Russian government. The complexity of the problem is emphasised by the fact that 23 different authorities were represented,[26] including *oblast'* governments, various independent Cossack *voisko* (armies), as well as a variety of national governments including those of Bashkir, Kirghiz, Turkestan, Turko-Tatar, Siberia and even Estonia. Also included were representatives of the Union of Zemstvos and Towns, and central committees of SRs, Mensheviks, Trudoviks, Kadets, and the Union of the Rebirth of Russia. Amongst all these representatives and within most of these organisations there was little agreement or unity. Despite this, the Temporary All-Russian Provisional Government was created and worked out a programme of general aims and policies, which was accepted unanimously on 23 September.

Members of the new government swore their allegiance and then the welcoming ceremony began. The Trudovik, S.F. Znamensky, on behalf of the members of the General Assembly welcomed the members of the new government, and after him B. Pavlů, deputy chairman of the Czechoslovak National Committee was invited to speak. His words were a reflection of Masaryk's policies: 'Throughout the unending struggle, we have long awaited that moment when we could once again welcome the creation of a new Russia – a united Russia, great, free and democratic, that Great and Powerful Russia, which once again will guarantee both your freedom and ours. . . . No one can feel the triumph and greatness of this moment more than we do.' It seemed that Pavlů was absolutely correct and that Masaryk's programme was now close to realisation. The Czechs had not only awaited this moment but had played a significant role in bringing it about. Pavlů was the only representative of any Allied power.[27] This was not simply because the Czechoslovak corps was the only realistic military force on the side of the Entente, which had opposed the Bolsheviks, but also because most of the Allies were not keen to see the resurrection of a great and powerful, albeit democratic, Russia.[28]

But the All-Russian government created with such difficulty was a fragile entity. Of ten members and their substitutes elected in Ufa, one, the Kadet Astrov, resigned as soon as he heard about the elections and the government programme. Another, General Alekseev, had little time to hear of his election, as he died in Ekaterinodar (Krasnodar) on 8 October 1918. However, according to General Denikin, Alekseev would not have accepted this nomination.[29]

But these were minor complications. Events in Siberia and Europe began to develop so fast that even Masaryk's ideas, which were based on an exceptional understanding of the situation and a realistic assessment of what could be achieved, were rapidly overtaken. Thus, his original idea had to be considered in radically altered circumstances. The creation of the All-Russian government in Ufa was followed less than a month later, on 28 October 1918, by the announcement in Prague of the creation of an independent Czechoslovak state. On 3 November, Austro-Hungary capitulated and on 11 November Germany signed the Armistice at Compiègne. This radically influenced the attitudes of the troops in the Czechoslovak legion.

At the end of September it had seemed that the aims of Czechoslovak politics had been achieved. A democratic Russian government had been created and it was thought that, with Czech help, it would be able to overthrow the Bolsheviks who had signed a treaty with the Central Powers. The Russian front could be formed once more, and after the Allied victory Czechoslovakia would have loyal and indebted allies. But when the war ended a month later, everything changed. Now that there was an independent Czechoslovakia, the main concern of the Czech troops was to return home; there was very little reason for them to continue to fight in a conflict that had never been particularly popular and which now was largely irrelevant to their main concerns. The Czechoslovak Republic existed and the main aim of the Czechoslovak legion had been achieved: it would not now be transferred to another theatre of war, but could return home, where it was awaited and needed. As a result, the fighting qualities of the legion deteriorated rapidly.

On 18 November 1918, Admiral Kolchak carried out a coup in Omsk, overthrowing the government and declaring himself the 'Supreme Ruler of the All-Russian state'. As Ullman writes, Kolchak's *coup d'état*

> met with the warm approval of the British military authorities in Siberia. There are some indications that British officers at Omsk actively connived at it, and there is no doubt that Ward's 25th Middlesex battalion covered the streets of Omsk with machine guns during the hours immediately following the coup, thus effectively discouraging possible interference by any other armed force, such as Czech units garrisoned nearby.[30]

Left-wing members of the All-Russian government, who would not agree to co-operate with the right-wing 'Supreme ruler', were arrested: some were killed, others exiled, and many left Russia on the ships that carried the Czech troops to the West. For the majority of officers and men in the Czechoslovak legion, the struggle in Russia lost any meaning. Monarchists were in the minority and it was difficult to believe in Kolchak's democratic credentials, especially when one experienced his regime at close quarters. Even inveterate Russophiles began to see that they were not helping 'the right kind of Russia'. There were many images of Russia during the years of the Civil War, but in this period the huge distances, torn by various fronts and ideological and national passions and even by the personal ambitions of a number of ruthless or charismatic personalities, meant that none of these images bore much relation to reality. The Czechs began to understand that they were not fighting for the democratic Russia which Masaryk would have liked to have seen but for British and French interests. The realisation that they were little more than mercenaries would hardly rally already disaffected troops. Furthermore, the financial demands of these mercenaries could not be met.

The Czechoslovak legion did what it could. Kolchak's opponents were evacuated, with the exception of a few who were killed in the first few days after the coup, and those who preferred to serve the Supreme Ruler for the sake of Russia's greater good. Once they returned home the Czechoslovak legionaries were treated as national heroes, but they had come back too late: much had already been decided in the new republic without their participation.

Throughout this period, Russo–Czech relations were a mixture of politics and questions of national identity. If Russia might in general be seen as the Great Power most likely to support its fellow Slavs, in practice its immediate political concerns tended to take precedence. Imperial Russia was anxious not to follow a radical nationalist agenda, although progress was made in the direction of Czech national aspirations. The Provisional Government, and particularly Miliukov, supported Masaryk's ideas but their brief tenure of office meant that they were an ephemeral ally. After the October Revolution, the attitude of the new Bolshevik government to the question of Czech independence was not altogether clear. In December 1917, a declaration advocated the right of self-determination for Bohemia.[31] Yet Masaryk was not uncritical of Bolshevism,[32] and he did not support the new regime. Moreover, the activities of the Czech legion meant that the Soviet authorities saw the Czechs as allies of the West. Once the legion had withdrawn to Czechoslovakia, overtures were made to establish diplomatic relations.[33] On 25 February 1920 the Soviet Commissar for Foreign Affairs G.V. Chicherin sent his first note expressing the hope that Czechoslovakia would not join in an anti-Bolshevik coalition.[34] (As yet there were no official Czech–Soviet diplomatic relations.) Beneš replied six weeks later in an evasive fashion, but in 1920 there were unofficial trade talks in London which Beneš attended. Moscow was concerned by Czechoslovak relations and the part the Czechs might play in the Polish war, and subsequently by her role in the Little Entente. The Soviet authorities tried to achieve an alliance with Czechoslovakia by all means available but *de jure* recognition of the USSR was granted only on 6 June 1934 and was forced on Czechoslovakia by the growing menace of Nazi Germany. The development of these policies was reflected in the emerging Russian émigré society.

Russians in Czechoslovakia, to the End of the Russian Civil War

On 28 October 1918, the independent Republic of Czechoslovakia was declared in Prague. Events had moved very fast and as a result of international diplomacy, the end of Austro-Hungary, the activities of Czechoslovak politicians and the attitudes of the general public, events coalesced to bring about the creation of the new state without bloodshed.

In the international arena, President Wilson in his 'Fourteen Points' address on 8 January 1918 advocated 'the freest opportunities for autonomous development' for the peoples of Austro-Hungary but did not advocate their independence. Only on 29 May did the American Secretary of State Robert Lansing announce that the 'nationalistic aspirations of the Czecho-Slovaks and Jugo-Slavs for freedom' had the 'earnest sympathy' of the United States government.[35] The French, British and Italian prime ministers associated themselves with this declaration five days later.[36] Wilson's policy was becoming increasingly anti-Austrian. At the same time, the revolt of the Czechoslovak legion meant that Allied politicians became more aware of Czechoslovak aspirations. On 30 June the French government recognised the Czechoslovak National Council in Paris as being representative of the Czechoslovak case and in August the British followed suit. On 3 September, the United States government recognised the Council as a *de facto* belligerent government, and hence began official recognition by the Allies of the fight for Czechoslovak independence.

The Allied offensive against the Central Powers in August 1918 alarmed the leaders of Austro-Hungary as it became clear that, even if a defeated Germany survived, Austro-Hungary might not. The Austro-Hungarian leadership in Vienna proposed that Berlin and Vienna should begin joint peace negotiations. When Berlin declined, hoping for a successful outcome, Vienna proposed the discussion of peace terms. This offer was rejected. On 4 October Berlin and Vienna sent similar notes to President Wilson suggesting a discussion of peace terms on the basis of the Fourteen Points, which had advocated national self-determination. In the case of Austro-Hungary, American policy had developed since the Fourteen Points as the USA had recognised the Czechoslovak National Council. Thus, while replying to the German government immediately, Wilson delayed his response to the Austro-Hungarian leaders. On 16 October, the Emperor Charles issued a manifesto authorising nationalities to form committees. Masaryk, in order to counter the renewal of negotiations between Vienna and Washington, declared Czechoslovak independence on 18 October. Wilson in his reply to Vienna on 19 October stated that, since the USA had recognised the aspirations of the Czechoslovaks and the Yugoslavs, they had to determine how the Austro-Hungarian government should act in order to grant that liberty. This reply caused panic in Vienna, where it was thought that the Czechs and southern Slavs would demand full independence and bring about the dismemberment of the entire empire. On 21 October the Austrian deputies withdrew from the Reichsrat and constituted themselves into a provisional assembly. The Austrian army was disintegrating and on 27 October the Austro-Hungarian government asked for an immediate armistice. When this news reached Prague on 28 October, it was taken to mean that the Austro-Hungarians had recognised Czechoslovak independence and it was declared that 'an independent Czechoslovak state had come into being'.[37]

Developments in the international arena were paralleled by the activities of Czechoslovak politicians both within the Czech lands and in exile. These were the creation of the 'Provisional Government of the Czechoslovak Lands in Paris', the National Czecho-Slovak Committee in Prague and the Czech Union of Deputies, all of whom discussed both how independence should be achieved and eventual forms of government. From the middle of

1917 it had become quite clear that sooner or later it would become imperative to co-ordinate the activities of the émigrés and the internal opposition, and that this could not be done at one remove but would have to involve face-to-face discussion. The agreement of the Viennese cabinet was essential but this appeared too much like capitulation, so was not gained until 1918, when delegates from Czechoslovakia on the way to Geneva stopped in Vienna and talks began in the Hotel Beau-Rivage on 28 October.

At this meeting the internal opposition to Austro-Hungary was represented by five leaders of the National Committee and the Czech Union and two economists. The Provisional Government Abroad was represented by the Foreign Minister Beneš, and three other politicians. Masaryk was in the USA and Štefánik in Siberia. This was the first meeting of representatives of all the leading political forces struggling for the liberation of Czechoslovakia. Talks on the shores of Lake Geneva went on for four days and most important questions were discussed. With the popular assumption that an independent Czechoslovakia had been recognised, the Czech opposition announced that it took upon itself all the responsibilities of executive power and that all Austro-Hungarian laws were recognised by the new power until they could be revoked by a constituent or a national assembly. These measures helped prevent chaos and disorder. The inauguration of the new state was not without its ironies. The National Committee which had taken power had not been aware that the Paris Committee had declared itself the Provisional Government. And as all the political leaders were absent at the moment of the declaration of independence, a third group of individuals came into being: 'muži 28 října' (the Men of 28 October), some of whom complicated the working of the new state. The delegation of the Prague National Committee returned from Geneva on 5 November, to a great welcome. It was only after the abdication of Emperor Charles six days later and the formation of an Austrian Republic that the creation of a confederation of the states of the Habsburg Empire was no longer a possibility. The first year of the existence of the independent Czechoslovak Republic was spent in establishing its authority, clarifying attitudes and trying to formulate policy. Most arguments, polemics, projects and ideas were connected in some way with the 'Russian question'.

To begin with, the situation was complicated by the fact that the German minority in Bohemia had attempted to define their own position the day before independence was declared, and they represented almost a quarter of the population of the Czech lands. Masaryk wrote that he was heartened by the fact that in the course of two to three weeks, the Germans had created half a dozen organisations. This bore witness to the fact that the Germans were really in complete disarray when faced with the defeat of the Central Powers, and would have meant that any German irredentism could easily have been crushed. Czech formations, most of which were rather amateur, and formed on the basis of the sporting organisation Sokol, established order. Crushing the Slovak Soviet proved a little more difficult. But it must have been clear to the politicians that the new government was in need of an army which had some combat experience, and that army could only be found in Russia.

More importantly, the action of the Czechoslovak legion in Russia was an ace in the hand of the new government at the Paris peace conference. In the words of Lloyd George: 'The story of the adventures and triumphs of this small army is indeed one of the greatest epics of history; it has filled us all with admiration for the courage, persistence, and self-control of your countrymen, and shows what can be done to triumph.'[38] The Western powers wanted the defeat of the Bolshevik government, but there was no consensus about how this should be achieved. In view of the opposition of the Russian population, the Allies could not intervene unilaterally, but the Czechoslovak legion was already involved in the Russian Civil War and was greatly admired. Some politicians hoped that they would be able to use the Czechs to further their aims.

For Czechoslovakia the Russian question fell into three parts: firstly there was the question of the fate of the Czechoslovak legion in Russia; secondly, what was the policy towards those Russians who were already in Czechoslovakia? and thirdly, what was the policy towards newly arrived Russian refugees? All of these subjects were interlinked, but were decided separately.

The Czechoslovak government had the freest hand when it came to dealing with Russians who were already on Czechoslovak territory in the first months of the Republic's existence. By the summer of 1920, there were 8,000–10,000 Russian prisoners of war. Since by that stage some had already been repatriated, it is likely that at the end of 1918 there had been approximately 15,000.[39]

By December 1918 the 'Union of Russian Officers in Prague' had been formed, and had applied to the Prime Minister Kramář, and to the Minister of Defence, Klofáč, with the request to create a military formation from these POWs. The request was granted and on 31 January 1919 the 'Training Company of Russian Officers and Volunteers' was formed. It consisted of 100 officers and 28 volunteers in Terezín, and 1,200 POWs concentrated in Choceň, as the basis for further units. Bolshevik propaganda, in the opinion of a representative of the Volunteer White Army, was unsuccessful, although it became necessary to return ten soldiers to the camp at Josefov because of their political unreliability. The training company had to prepare the POWs for a return to military service and the 'struggle against the Bolsheviks in the ranks of the Russian armed forces for the purpose of restoring order in Russia by means of calling a legislative assembly'. It was assumed that this formation would support Denikin's Volunteer Army.[40]

However, the situation changed radically after discussion of the Russian question at the Paris peace conference. In a letter to A.Rašín, the Foreign Minister, Beneš wrote that France had become convinced of the impossibility of further direct armed intervention in Russian affairs owing to the unwillingness of the French to fight any longer. But certain political circles in France did not accept this policy and were concocting various risky plans to intervene, based on Polish help. In Beneš's view this strengthening of Poland represented a risk for Czechoslovakia (and almost immediately border disputes and disagreements about the Polish minority broke out). 'In these circumstances in Russian political circles here [i.e. Paris] a new plan has been thought up: to create an army of POWs in Czechoslovakia, to concentrate the Russian formations as far as possible and give the control over the army to the Czechoslovak government, and thus to do on Czechoslovak territory the same as we did with our troops in Russia.'[41]

Russian politicians were even more afraid of turning the Poles into a crack anti-Bolshevik force than were the Czechs, as they considered that anti-Bolshevik action could easily turn into an anti-Russian struggle. Thus, it is not surprising that the 'Czech plan' was supported by exponents of various political tendencies: Prince L'vov (the first head of the Provisional Government) and Maklakov (a prominent Kadet), Sazonov (who had been foreign minister in Imperial Russia), Chaikovsky (revolutionary and Civil War figure) and Savinkov (a former terrorist). But Beneš's position was made more complicated by the fact that the head of the Czechoslovak delegation, Prime Minister Kramář, was an enthusiastic supporter of the 'Czech plan' to create units which could intervene in Russia. Bearing these facts in mind when reading this letter, it is surprising how far Beneš tried to push through a policy of non-intervention in an extremely unfavourable situation. He emphasised that he 'considered it tactless' from the point of view of Czech foreign relations to 'a priori reject all Russian proposals', but he suggested that the Russians must show what they were capable of organising before one began to think of Czech help. From Beneš's letter we can see that few seemed to adopt this approach. The Russians and Kramář were of the opinion that it would be possible to create a corps 100,000 strong from Russian POWs in Czechoslovakia and Germany, supported by the Allies, and also a 150,000-strong Czechoslovak volunteer corps which would advance into

Russia under the slogan: 'Liberate the Czechoslovak legion in Siberia'.
Beneš wrote:

> I do not believe in enterprises of that size. So I told Savinkov that we
> would agree to support the formation of Russian units on
> Czechoslovak territory but with very limited aims in view, i.e. the
> creation of units without enormous political plans or invasions of
> Russia . . . I would wish that we first had a realistic base to start with
> before I began to build various plans and to carry through a wide
> ranging policy towards Russia, i.e. intervention. I emphasise this point
> of view, which only in part agrees with the plans of Savinkov and
> Kramář.[42]

Given this point of view, the whole 'Czech plan' was doomed to failure.
Beneš stressed that he was not sufficiently *au fait* with the situation in
Czechoslovakia, but this statement must be seen as part of his diplomatic
language when writing to his coalition partners in the ranks of the
independence movement. In any case, whether this was extreme caution or
an attempt to force those who supported Kramář to back the Masaryk–
Beneš point of view, even this sceptical attitude to the possibility of forming
Russian, and particularly Czech 'White', units on Czechoslovak territory
was over-optimistic. Even in the camp at Choceň, where according to the
letter of the representative from Denikin's Volunteer Army everything was
going well, the recruitment drive for the Volunteer Army put into action
on 27 June was a complete fiasco.[43] This recruitment drive gave the odd
impression of some kind of raid on the POWs almost with the aim of
upsetting things. A six-man commission arrived in the camp, then Pavlov,
a Russian staff captain in the presence of the commission addressed the
troops and explained the reason for the call to service. The representative of
the Ministry of Defence, Captain Papoušek, of the Czech legion, assured
the Russian troops that this was entirely voluntary and that nobody would
be forced to join the Russian corps. After this there was a short period for
the men to consider the offer. As no one signed up, the period for
registration was closed.[44] Papoušek was Masaryk's private secretary, and a
close adherent of Masaryk's views during the First Republic.

So it appears that the Masaryk–Beneš grouping was subject to three
conflicting pressures. In the first place there was pressure from the French,
who wished to intervene in Russia and use the Czechoslovak forces to the
maximum extent. Secondly, the Bolsheviks were also pressurising the
Czechs. Their peace-loving declarations alternated with more hostile
actions and constant Communist agitation directed towards bringing down
the 'bourgeois' Czechoslovak government, Thirdly, from within the

government itself, the right wing led by Kramář attempted to put its policy into action. The Masaryk–Beneš group tried to manoeuvre between all these conflicting interests and at the same time to minimise intervention in Russian affairs, which was impossible to avoid totally in the circumstances, and to carry out the policy expressed in the Tokyo Memorandum. This policy could really only be implemented in relation to the Russians in Czechoslovakia. To begin with, the hope of transforming the prisoners of war into an active military force came to nothing. Even if the total fulfilment of this idea was over-optimistic, creating just one division as Beneš had suggested would have been possible. However, it seems that much more effort was directed to doing the opposite.

Thus, largely because the rank-and-file POWs did not wish to intervene in the Russian Civil War on any side, it was relatively easy to dismiss the 'Paris' ideas presented by Russians, Czechs and French supporters of intervention. The representatives of the Russian Volunteer Army, whose powers were in any case imprecise and unclear, were disbanded without any fuss.

A series of events in the summer of 1919 fundamentally altered the internal political situation in Czechoslovakia. This shifted the debate among various Russian political forces over the question of Czechoslovak policy on the Russian question from Paris to Prague.

On 15 June 1919, local government elections took place and Kramář's party lost heavily. On 8 July Kramář's cabinet resigned. Kramář never held government office again, although members of his party continued to occupy ministerial positions. But although many of them agreed with their leader on conservative policies with regard to internal affairs, they did not share his enthusiasm for the Whites, and to a large extent handed over decisions on the Russian question to the Ministry of Foreign Affairs under the direction of Beneš.

As the Civil War wore on, support for intervention grew less enthusiastic and the belief in the possibility of victory by the anti-Bolshevik forces declined catastrophically. In 1920 Great Britain officially refused General Peter Wrangel (who had become head of the White Army after the defeat of Denikin) any help in the Crimea. France actually recognised Wrangel *de facto* but had much greater hopes of the Polish forces. There were lots of ideas about how best to use the relatively small territory of the Crimea and the far Eastern Republic to establish some kind of 'home lands' of freedom on Russian territory, which would then act as an example and centripetal force for the rest of Russia. The 'White ideology' witnessed rapid changes, with acceptance of peasant and nationalist demands and those of the Cossack *voisko* but most of this had little effect and these changes, for the most part, came rather too late to influence the progress of the Russian Civil War. The peasants had a clear image of the White movement and Wrangel's decrees on land did not reach them. Even if they had, in all likelihood they would not have been believed. Furthermore, the anti–Bolshevik forces were becoming more right-wing in tone, as the Civil War polarised the issues and did not allow for shades of grey. All in all, for the majority of European politicians, the Russian Civil War was drawing to a close.

The number of Russian refugees was increasing rapidly. Many civilians who had retreated with General Yudenich's White Army in North Western Russia were arriving in the West, followed by the military personnel of the army. A few were evacuated from Murmansk. Many more refugees fled from Novorossiisk, and more significantly from Odessa to Constantinople and the Balkans. In Harbin, on Chinese territory but shielded by the special status of the Chinese Eastern Railway, arose a whole 'city on wheels' with a population of 20,000. It was during this period that the numbers of Russian refugees became statistically significant, growing from a few thousand to hundreds of thousands of people, making it necessary to deal with the problem on an international level and in the terms of international law.[45] Dr Nansen was appointed High Commissioner for Refugees by the League of Nations.

For Czechoslovakia, this was of exceptional importance. The last contingent of the Czechoslovak legion finally escaped Russia in March 1920 and the alliance with Kolchak's forces, which had tied the government's hands, could be abrogated. However, it was not quite the leave-taking from Russia for which Masaryk had hoped and worked. Partly as a result of French and British policies, the Czechs were unable to save the democratic government which they had helped to create, and they had had to hand over Kolchak to the Bolsheviks. At the same time, part of the Russian gold reserve had disappeared. After the brilliant beginning to the Siberian campaign, which even before independence had cast the Czechoslovak legion as an important player on the world stage, the end was rather dismal. The Czechs were accused of treachery on three counts: betraying the democratic government, betraying Admiral Kolchak and stealing the Russian gold. All of this affected relations between Czechoslovakia and the Russian emigration.

The flow of refugees into the Czechoslovak Republic was increasing daily, although it was much less than that experienced by the Baltic States, Germany, Turkey or Bulgaria. For the most part, refugees got through from the Ukraine and Belorussia, although many considered themselves either Ukrainians or Belorussians and did not describe themselves as Russians. To begin with, few of the political élite were to be found among them. The majority were members of the lower middle classes who were victims rather than actors in the Civil War. The politicians among them were not well known or influential. Yet they formed the 'political layer' of Russian émigrés who had to react to events in Russia, and to the changes and expression of Czech politics towards Russia.[46]

The collapse of the White fronts led to an intensification of Czech–Soviet relations over the question of an armistice in Siberia; over the repatriation of prisoners of war; and finally on the question of some kind of official representation even without full diplomatic status. The first official Soviet mission was formed in Prague on 20 July 1920 and consisted merely of representatives of the Soviet Red Cross, but discussion about such representation forced a regrouping of the political spectrum in Prague, particularly amongst the émigrés.

Czechoslovakia's Russian policy had to be viewed in the broader context of the international situation. The exceptional generosity of the Czechs towards the dispossessed should not be seen purely in humanitarian terms. From the time of the Tokyo Memorandum onwards, all Czech policy was based first, on the idea of bringing non-military pressure to bear on the Soviet Union, and secondly on the need to support anti-Bolshevik democratic forces, in order to create a democratic socialist bloc that might be able to withstand dictatorship from both the right and the left. Masaryk held very firmly to the conviction that a 'White' victory would lead to a counter-revolutionary terror and the rebirth of autocratic rule or some other form of dictatorship. For that reason, he supported internal opposition forces: those who did not wish to leave the country and who tried to place all possible legal forms of pressure on the authorities and on that part of the emigration, the SRs and Kadets, who supported Miliukov's 'new tactics', and who were prepared neither to reject the Revolution completely nor to become apologists for the Bolsheviks, such as those belonging to the Change of Landmarks movement. The link between providing aid to the starving in Russia – originally through the Obshchestvenny Komitet Pomoshchi Golodayushchim (Public Committee for Aid to the Starving) headed by S.N. Prokopovich and his wife E.D. Kuskova, who were subsequently exiled and became leading members of the emigration in Prague – and help to the émigrés can only be understood in this light. In both cases, it was an attempt to strengthen a particular political grouping which would have led to a democratic Russia.

The changing international situation after the evacuation of the Crimea was also of fundamental importance. General Wrangel had taken over as Commander-in-Chief after Denikin's resignation. The French government had recognised Wrangel's government *de facto* and consequently was in a very tricky situation after Wrangel's defeat by the Bolsheviks and the evacuation of his army from the Crimea. The French rapidly announced that with the end of hostilities on Russian territory, they did not consider

themselves responsible for Wrangel's government and assisted in the evacuation purely from humanitarian motives.

This meant the end of the army and the transformation of all evacuees
into refugees. This had already occurred without much difficulty in the
cases of Yudenich's and Kolchak's armies, and those serving with Denikin
who had not ended up in the Crimea. However, Wrangel's commanders
turned out to be more capable, and his troops more stable than Denikin's.
In both the command and the rank and file were people who had already
been tested by defeat and had experienced the collapse of morale. In the first
few months various not unexpected events occurred: several thousand
Cossacks returned to Russia, where they had been promised an amnesty;
others left for Brazil or enlisted in the French Foreign Legion or elected to
work in agriculture or in industry in France, whose workforce had been
shattered by the war. Nevertheless, the kernel of the army, in difficult
circumstances in the camps at Gallipoli, Lemnos and Chataladzhe, did not
wish to disband and dissolve into the refugee masses. France, therefore,
faced the problem of forceful liquidation of an Allied army. This was fairly
simple legally but the political position was affected by the fact that a
significant part of the electorate had invested in Russia before the war and
was demanding the overthrow of the Soviet order, a repayment of debts and
continuation of the struggle. Morally, the French situation was complicated
by the fact that she was the only victorious Allied power that had supported
Wrangel's enterprise.

France's attitude was decisive for Czechoslovakia as she was the most
important guarantor of the independence and sovereignty of the new state.
Russian officers in the higher ranks of the Czech army were replaced, for
the most part, by French officers. In particular, the French General Pelle was
Chief of Staff of the Czechoslovak army and during the period of
heightened activity by Hungarian Communists and the creation of the
Slovak Soviet Republic for a short time was even appointed Commander-
in-Chief of the army. In 1921 he held the position of French General
Commissioner in Turkey, and the problem of the evacuated army and
accompanying refugees came under his jurisdiction.

Thus when General Wrangel sent a memo to General Pelle demanding
the preservation of the army and suggesting that this could be done by
settling various units in different countries, including Czechoslovakia, it is
not particularly surprising that Pelle read this to the Czech representative in
Constantinople, Dr Světlík. The latter instantly informed Prague that:

> I indicated the difficulties associated with supporting and billeting the
> troops and also that the internal political situation in the Czechoslovak
> Republic would not allow the Czechoslovak government to meet

General Wrangel's wishes. General Pelle replied that he was well aware of these difficulties . . . and greatly regretted that the French government had been drawn into Wrangel business, which was now costing France so much in both trouble and expenses.[47]

Both men expressed, diplomatically but accurately, the position of their respective governments: the Czech refusal to accept Wrangel's units and the French desire to get rid of this problem as well as the accompanying trouble and expense. The solution, in line with the Russian policy of the Czech government, was not to take the military formations but to accept some of Wrangel's former soldiers in their personal capacity, to include them in a different category, not as soldiers, but as agricultural workers or students. This regrouping of the evacuees from the Crimea solved a number of problems for the Czechoslovak government: it helped France and it was a response to the demands of the numerous Russophile circles in Czecho-slovakia to help Russian refugees.[48]

Yet it was extremely unlikely that such a policy statement could be implemented in a clear-cut way in the complex post-war world. The Russian Civil War produced a host of new problems and the new Czechoslovak Republic had to deal with a highly complex situation both internationally and within its own frontiers. In its policy towards Russian refugees it had to maintain a judicious balance between humanitarian needs and political realities. In the event, the Czechoslovak Republic was extra-ordinarily generous towards Russian exiles. Its support for Russian scholars and academic endeavour was exceptional. Although such a programme could not reverse the fundamental reasons for the existence of the exiles, it provided the opportunity for many of them to deal more constructively with the vicissitudes of émigré life.

Chapter 2

Politics and the Emigration

The experience of revolution and civil war permeated all the activities of the Russian émigrés. While Masaryk and the Czech legion were struggling with the rapidly changing situation within Russia, the émigrés debated the questions of intervention and support for the White forces in Russia and, by implication, their attitudes towards Czechoslovakia. These arguments were further complicated by disagreement over the form that future government in Russia might take. The 'Russian ambassador', V.T. Rafal'sky,[1] behaved modestly and diplomatically and did not interfere in Czech internal politics. This enabled him to preserve his position and influence throughout the existence of the First Republic, and to some extent to represent the right-wing counterbalance to the attempts by the Socialist Revolutionaries, with government backing, to monopolise the distribution of aid to the refugees. Others were less diplomatic or circumspect.

Émigrés in Czechoslovakia

Initially, the main objective of the émigré press and of the dominant group of Socialist Revolutionaries was to influence Czech policy on Russia. They had experienced the situation at first hand and were closely affected by the outcome. They paid scant attention to the émigrés, as their sojourn abroad was presumed to be very short. But there was little consensus among the exiles on what government policy should be. The first edition of *Russkoe Delo* (Russian Affairs), a newspaper for Russians in Prague, appeared in April 1919 but did not take a clear line on Czechoslovak policy. Indeed, this would have been difficult as the divisions over the Russian question had not yet crystallised. In the first issue, following a dryish leader, there was a welcoming message from Boris Savinkov, the revolutionary activist, who was on good terms with both Masaryk and Kramář. Savinkov's slogans: 'Republic, Federal State, Land to the Workers' and repeated calls to reconvene the Constituent Assembly were similar to Masaryk's views but had little in common with those of Kramář. However, the message addressed to the emigration was far more likely to please Kramář and upset Masaryk. It echoed Burtsev's famous slogan: 'Either Lenin or Kolchak–Denikin. There is no third way. He who does not support Kolchak–Denikin must support Lenin.' Burtsev, a long-standing member of the SRs, had become famous in 1909 when he unmasked Azef, one of the most notorious of the agents of the tsarist police, as being the head of the terrorist branch of the SRs. He advanced the slogan in support of Kolchak and Denikin during the Civil War and split with his erstwhile colleagues.

Thus, the émigrés were being exhorted to 'Hurry home, armed, in serried ranks, with beautiful songs of Liberty! . . . Home for a future free, democratic and united Russia!' as I. Tupikov, the heart and soul of the editorial office, wrote in his article 'Examples of Life (Prague Impressions)' under the revealing pseudonym, Ivan the Czech. His editorial line was that the White struggle should continue and intervention should be supported. Tupikov also advocated the use of SR slogans and expressed respect for the experience of the Czech legion in Russia.

During the period of the elections and Kramář's subsequent resignation a 'delegation of Russian public activists to the Slav states' led by E.A. Efimovsky arrived in Prague. Efimovsky, considered to be Denikin's un-official representative, immediately embarked on a political struggle with the intention of influencing the internal political situation of Czecho-slovakia. Using his contacts, he determined the editorial outlook of the first Russo–Czech newspaper in Prague: *Slavyanskaya Zarya* – *Slovanská zora* (Slav dawn). From the second edition, Efimovsky became the editor and attempted to adopt a similar tone to Tupikov in *Russkoe Delo*, but did not keep it up for long. By 5 October 1919 Efimovsky had produced an unattractive picture of government policy: 'The reality of Czechoslovak politics demonstrates that Czech political circles (albeit not all) are not content with passively watching events and go much further and at the same time are moving away from the idea of Russia Reborn.[2] . . . Kramář and his supporters are Russia's faithful knights. But it is no coincidence that Kramář is no longer in office.' The author concludes that if Czechoslovak policy is to continue in this direction then when Russia becomes strong again she will have to repudiate those 'friends'.

Efimovsky did not confine himself to journalism. On 29 October 1919 he gave a public lecture on 'Reborn Russia and her Enemies' in one of the grandest and most prestigious venues in Prague, the City Hall. The hall was full; the majority of those present were Czech and included the right-wing élite. According to the report in *Slavyanskaya Zarya* the lecturer was warmly applauded. Any scepticism one might have over a report in a newspaper edited by the speaker is unjustified, as the account was substantiated by the hostile Czech press. The fact that this was so widely reported in newspapers of very differing views proves that Efimovsky's opinions struck a raw nerve. Furthermore, his provocative lecture, supported by various Czech political circles, was delivered on the day after the first anniversary of Czech independence and the day after the first address of the President to the nation, and the lecture was a criticism of the politics of that nation. Czechoslovakia was sharply contrasted with the Kingdom of the Serbs, Croats and Slovenes which was presented as a true friend of 'Russia Reborn' while Czechoslovakia, if she did not alter her policies, was seen as Russia's enemy. Given the military situation, and particularly the unclear and contradictory information about the Russian Civil War, this still sounded threatening.

Shocked by the pro-monarchist and anti-government tone *Russkoe Delo* found it necessary to distance itself from Efimovsky's lecture and by implication to excuse Kolchak's and Denikin's governments, stating publicly that 'The Executive Committee of the Union of United Slav Organisations' of which Efimovsky was the official representative, was 'a fiction'.[3]

At the same time, representatives of a 'third way' – the SRs – were arriving in Prague. For the sake of a 'Future Russia', they rejected both Lenin and Kolchak–Denikin and the whole idea of intervention. This group held views which were closest to those expressed by the Czechoslovak government and for the most part its representatives had left Russia with the Czech troops escaping from the Bolsheviks and from Kolchak. These SRs were welcomed triumphantly, particularly Ekaterina Breshko-Breshkovskaya, the 70-year-old 'Grandmother of the Revolution'.

However, it would appear from the Czech press that, despite official audiences and positive comments from the left-wing papers, the weakness of Czech support for the SRs could not be hidden. Traditionally, Russophile groups were, for the most part, very conservative. The new-Russophile circles which were pro-Communist and which, in the words of the poet Mayakovsky, learned Russian 'because Lenin spoke it' were not interested in émigrés. The left looked towards the West, notably France. A large part of the Czech legion which had co-operated with the SRs during the Civil War and understood their potential importance was still in Siberia. Government circles, the leadership of the right-wing Social Democrats, the National Socialist and Agrarian parties and their press supported the SRs, but their meetings did not attract as large a Czech audience as meetings of the right-wing Russophile groups.

Efimovsky put the question bluntly: 'Why were only those Russians who assisted in Russia's decline or hindered her regeneration granted official audiences in Prague? Why do ordinary Russian patriots or those who had always worked for pan-Slav links between Russia and the Czech lands have to be silent or guiltily hide their patriotism, or have accusations made against them and have to suffer all kinds of public criticism?'[4] If the vocabulary of the Civil War and journalistic extremism was ignored, the question was valid. It might have been phrased in the following way: 'Are the Czech authorities going to support only the opponents of the Whites and intervention? Although they spoke of a democratic Russia, they did nothing to bring it about.' This was the question which faced the Czech government. In the light of the reply, relations to the Russian emigration would have to be decided.

But before anyone could answer this question clearly, the situation in Russia on the various fronts in the Civil War changed radically and between December 1919 and the end of March 1920 the majority of the White forces were defeated or disarmed. The Northwestern Army which had advanced on Petrograd in the summer of 1919, and was later under the command of General Yudenich, was disarmed in Estonia in December. This was a prelude to a whole series of defeats of White forces. In January 1920, Admiral Kolchak in Siberia transferred power to Ataman Semenov, and on 7 February Kolchak was shot after the Czechslovak legion had signed an armistice with the Bolsheviks. Red Army troops entered Odessa on 30 January. On 13 March, Allied intervention in the north came to an end and the Whites left Murmansk. On 26 March, Novorossiisk was surrendered by the White forces. Thus most of Russian territory was controlled by Red forces and by April 1920 only the Perekop isthmus in the Crimea remained a battlefront. As a result, although the Civil War was not over, belief in the possibility of victory by the Whites had all but disappeared. Support for the anti-Bolshevik forces from the European powers also dwindled. The number of Russian refugees increased dramatically and became an international problem as well as a national tragedy.

Czecho–Soviet relations had to address not only the armistice in Siberia but also the vexed question of repatriation of prisoners-of-war and the need to deal with official representatives of the Soviet Union even if those did not yet have full diplomatic status. Such discussions were bound to have an effect on the émigré political circles in Prague. Even Tupikov, hitherto polite, began to use a different kind of language when commenting on a restrained reply by the Czechoslovak government to a note from Chicherin:

> There can be no middle way on this question. We already have bitter experience of the result of an attempt to find a middle way when it came to the question of intervention. Instead of direct and open, strong and decisive military action, there has only been feeble support for Russian anti-Bolshevik forces. [This has led to] the treacherous

'neutrality' of Allied forces at a moment when a decisive attack would have been able to deliver Bolshevism a mortal blow. As a result [we see] the ruin of Russian armies and the shameful flight of the Allies.[5]

This reverse in war should have had a profound effect on the diverse opinions within the emigration. The growing number of refugees required some response from Russian émigré political circles and it seemed as if the two Russian newspapers in Prague, finally, would be able to find a common language. The Civil War in Russia was coming to an end, a whole variety of governments had also come to an end, and the Soviet authorities, by means of their representatives abroad, were beginning to turn their attention to the émigrés. Logically, this common enemy should have united the émigrés. However, émigré logic was of a different order. The partial end of the Civil War brought many calls for unity abroad yet the process of fragmentation was only speeded up. Russian émigrés, whether in Paris, Berlin or Harbin, deplored the 'cursed Russian inability' to organise and unite. However, while recognising this self-criticism, calls for unity accompanied by rapid fragmentation are characteristic of most emigrations in the modern era. The Russian émigrés were no exception.

On 22 April 1920 Ivan Tupikov, in *Russkoe Delo,* developed the reasons why the emigration needed to unite:

> The Russian emigration may shortly be faced with the appearance of Soviet representatives in Czechoslovakia. . . . At the present moment the émigré colony is completely fragmented and devoid of any legal representation of its interests. It is scattered through various separate circles and organisations . . . divided by political disagreement . . . the Russian emigration, on the whole is a formless mass which any free and easy Bolshevik commissar or representative of the Czech authorities can easily deal with. . . . Unity is essential. If we miss this opportunity, we will bear witness once more to the cursed Russian inability to organise.

These ideas could hardly have been more clearly expressed and followed on the heels of an article two weeks previously which dealt with the pressing questions of the hour and which in both style and content was very similar to Efimovsky's approach. In the next issue of *Russkoe Delo,* on 24 April, the leading article by Tupikov, entitled: 'Belittlers of the Russian Peasantry', was an attack on Efimovsky and the views expressed in *Slavyanskaya Zarya.* In it, Tupikov stated that there had been an attempt to avoid polemics in order not to split the forces of the emigration. This was not in fact correct, as Efimovsky's lecture had provoked criticism, but now, to quote Leo

Tolstoy, Tupikov felt that 'I can no longer be silent.' He considered Efimovsky's ideas monarchist and feudal and criticised him sharply. Efimovsky challenged Tupikov to a 'literary court of honour' and Tupikov accepted, in order 'to prove the complete wretchedness of the behaviour of those heroes of literary and political decadence whom I described as "belittlers of the Russian peasantry."'

The importance of this incident was the conclusion drawn from it by the Czech authorities. There was nothing new in the fact that rival publications, although calling for unity among the émigrés, immediately disagreed sharply. But the decision to clarify their positions in court was unusual. The vitriolic attacks in the press on the motives of their opponents could have been expected, even if it was ironic that the cause of the disagreement should be the call for unity. It is hardly surprising that nothing came of all the many similar projects for unification. The Czech authorities, who were well briefed about the activities of the Russian colony in general and in particular the views of those who were politically active, decided that the question of organising the Russian emigration must not be left to the émigrés but must be undertaken by the Czech authorities themselves.

Czech Policy

The Czech government decided that it needed to find an agency which could implement its policy: it did not wish to do so openly, as this would expose it to every cross-current in Russian émigré politics. Moreover, the Czech government was not really interested in the emigration as such, but rather considered that its priority should be to influence events in Russia in the support of democratic tendencies there. The SRs, they felt, could help them to achieve this aim. It was only later that the SRs began to turn their attention to the emigration rather than to events in Russia. The first documentary evidence of this change in policy came in May 1920. When discussing the activity of a Russian aid committee, the Czech government stated that: 'We are interested in creating a centre of progressive Russians in Prague.'[6]

Throughout his period of office, Masaryk's influence was of paramount importance and he played a key role in Russian Action. In addition to the National Assembly, two unofficial centres of power emerged: Pětka (the Five) and Hrad (the Castle group) both of which consisted of people close to Masaryk.[7] The Five was made up of Antonín Švehla (Agrarian), Alois Rašin (National Democrat), Rudolf Bechyně (Social Democrat), Jiří Stříbrný (National Socialist) and Jan Šrámek (Populist). They met informally and helped to achieve a consensus in the National Assembly. The Castle

(*Hrad*) group consisted of Masaryk, Beneš, Josef Scheiner, a banker and head of Sokol, the sporting organisation, Alois Rašin, the Minister of Finance, Jaroslav Preiss chairman of the Trade Bank, and Přemysl Šámal, head of the President's chancery. The composition of the Hrad group varied but it remained very influential. For the émigrés the existence of such a group which was not dependent on elected representatives provided some kind of stability in a system that was changing constantly.

The SRs were able to use government policy and personal contacts to strengthen their position in Czechoslovakia. As Mark Vishniak, a well-known SR journalist noted:

> Thanks to his personal contacts and authority Alexander Kerensky was able to obtain promises of material help for the cause of Russian freedom and culture from Tomáš Masaryk and Edward Beneš. This friendly action was all the more magnanimous because, in contrast to future Czech 'action' towards Russian and Ukrainian émigrés, it was not tied to the compulsory sojourn in Czechoslovakia of particular individuals or institutions. After the end of the Prague talks, at the beginning of June 1920 Kerensky called a meeting of his closest adherents in Paris.[8]

Czech money enabled the SRs first to acquire the Russian newspaper in Berlin, *Golos Rossii* (Russia's Voice), which then became *Dni* (Days), to found the 'thick journal' *Sovremennye Zapiski* (Contemporary Notes) in Paris and to start publishing the political paper *Volya Rossii* (Russia's Freedom/Will) in Prague. It is important to note that although they were acquired by SRs, none of these publications was the official voice of the SR Party. This was initially because the party disintegrated fairly rapidly, and new 'right' and 'left' groupings were formed or were excluded for collaborating with Kolchak or Denikin and the like. Furthermore, the émigrés did not wish to act independently, and remained in contact with the party centre in Russia. Thus, the Prague group was not formed until 29 November 1922 although the mutual aid budget was created on 14 April of that year.[9]

However, although there was no official SR organisation in Prague, there was a great deal of activity around *Volya Rossii*. The leading article of the first edition on 12 September 1920 spelt out its political line. The editorial board was clearly opposed to the two existing Russian newspapers in Prague. The article declared that *Volya Rossii* was fighting for democracy as the basic prerequisite for socialism. Since the idea of socialism was fairly fluid, that could be accepted by *Russkoe Delo*. But, the editorial continued, in order to achieve this aim, it would struggle against dictatorships both right and left wing. 'Both of these dictatorships – the Bolsheviks and the reactionary generals – betrayed Russia.' The Bolsheviks betrayed Russia to the Germans while 'Reaction as personified by Denikin, Wrangel, Yudenich, Kolchak, Semenov, Miller and all the groups and parties supporting them including the Kadets in their struggle for power have betrayed Russia into the hands of the Japanese, the Poles, the Romanians, the Allies and concur in the dismemberment of Russia. . . . The psychology and politics of dictators of both camps is identical.' Because of this, neither the Whites nor intervention could be supported. This view was completely unacceptable to Efimovsky, who shortly afterwards left Prague to lead 'a small but noisy' party of constitutional monarchists in Berlin.[10] It was also unacceptable to the democrat Tupikov and to the majority of émigrés, who had become refugees by accident and for whom General Wrangel represented their best hope of returning home. They were less worried by the prospect that he might 'sell Russia down the river' to the Japanese or the Allies. However, these political declarations were not really directed at Russian émigrés in Prague. They were addressed to the Russian people, and only in passing to the emigration. To begin with, *Volya Rossii* paid little attention to the Russian colony in Prague or to Czechoslovak policies on the Russian question.

The defeat of General Wrangel in November 1920 and the end of the White movement had raised the question of the creation of a Russian émigré community in Czechoslovakia and of who should be considered as acceptable members of such a community. After the evacuation of the Crimea the number of refugees had increased substantially and it became clear that the emigration would be fairly long lasting. The Czechoslovak Republic with its active policy towards Russia could not escape making a decision on this matter. It is not clear whether Czech politicians persuaded the SR politicians to address the problems of the Russian colony in Prague, or whether the SRs themselves decided to turn their attention to 'local' matters. It is likely that the wishes of both groups coincided. However, SR success in this area was significantly helped by the Czech authorities.

In contrast to what occurred in Yugoslavia, the democratic Czechoslovak government could not openly create a single-party Russian political authority to deal with the refugees. They were not working with the monarchists who were used to directing affairs from above but with the SRs who were more used to underground activity. So the SRs – unable to count on the support of the general mass of émigrés, who were still hoping for the victory of the White Army – started to work gradually from a position of considerable strength, given their allies within the government. On 24 November 1920, *Volya Rossii* published an announcement of the 'initiatory group', which was trying to form the Russian Society for Mutual Aid. This was not an original idea: it had been considered before. However, now the group was up and running. It had not only acquired legal status, but had opened a club, which was run every evening in the restaurant U Jungrů, a labour exchange, legal help, a cake shop, a carpenter's workshop and, a little later, a bookbinder's. These beginnings could only be welcomed and no one in the Prague emigration opposed them. Moreover, there was no longer any Russian publication which could oppose *Volya Rossii*.

The activity of the Society for Mutual Aid was not criticised in the Russian-language press although everyone in the colony knew that the SRs were behind its activities. The life of the community centred on the dining room, the cafés and restaurants: anywhere where one could eat, as a significant proportion of the émigrés lived in night shelters, if not under bridges, or rented corners of rooms where they were forbidden to light a kerosene stove. Those who were able to rent separate rooms, with the right to use a stove, or even with a bathroom and kitchen, were very fortunate.[11] However, the eating places had to be cheap, not those intended for tourists, and it was preferable to be able to order in Russian and to meet one's own kind, to be able to chat, and to read Russian language newspapers. The newspapers on offer, however, were usually determined by the political orientation of the café.

To begin with, this kind of centre could be created only by the Czechs, as there had not been a sufficiently large and wealthy Russian colony in Prague before the war. The Russophile sympathies of the owner of one of the largest of the Prague hotels, Beránek, created this kind of meeting place in his hotel, also called Beránek. The majority of Russians did not know of the link with the surname of the owner. Berberova recalls: 'Beránek means sheep in Czech. Little sheep are drawn on the walls, on the doors, are embroidered on the pillowcases, decorate the menu and smile at you on the bill. Khodasevich says that we live in a herd of little blue and pink sheep. Some have ribbons, others gilded horns and still others little bells round their necks. A [model of a] sheep stands at the entrance of the hotel, shakes its head and says "Baa".'[12] Perhaps Mayakovsky scholars have established the link between this Czech hotel and the lines the poet allegedly wrote: 'The Czech is gentler than a sheep, there is no little man gentler than him.'[13] In any case, the views of Khodasevich and Mayakovsky seem to have been similar, but the comfort which both young poets found amusing was probably greatly to the taste of most Russians in Prague.

Beránek, both the man and his hotel, to paraphrase Mayakovsky,[14] played an exceptional role in the creation of 'Russian Prague'. The hotel was a haven for hundreds of Russians during their first days and weeks in the city, and for those *en route* to other places. More importantly, it became the cultural centre of Russian Prague, allowing the Česko-Ruská Jednota (The

Czech–Russian Union) to meet regularly and without payment in the Japanese dining room. 'Russian scholars, writers, journalists, musicians, singers and artists . . . [met regularly] and shared the fruits of their scientific and artistic collaboration with Czech society, which in its turn got Russians acquainted with the products of Czech genius.'[15] There were also regular evening meetings on Fridays organised by the cultural-educational committee of the Union of Russian Students. This was now reported in *Volya Rossii*, which had become much more interested in the activities of the emigration.

As well as the activities in Beránek, the Czech–Russian Union developed a programme of events elsewhere which included dancing, acting and opera. It is more than likely that Khodasevich and Mayakovsky, Berberova and Tsvetaeva would not have approved of these programmes, but they pleased most of the émigrés of that time, and more importantly most of the activities were developing under the Russo–Czech standard. Czech settlers of the late nineteenth and early twentieth centuries who had become assimilated into Russian life but who had been expelled by the Civil War in the same way as Russian refugees, as well as the old Russophile Czechs who had struggled against German influence were all involved. The majority had no pretensions to belong to the intellectual élite or to the artistic avant-garde and were broadly middle class. These people generously welcomed the émigrés and bore the lion's share of the costs of organising the joint cultural events. They aided gradual assimilation in Czechoslovakia. However, the Russians were still homesick, and did not have enough of their own, purely Russian things.

V.L. Burtsev began to take part in the game. In 1921, in the Paris newspaper, *Obshchee Delo* (Common Cause)[16] based on material sent to him by L.F. Magerovsky, he revealed that the Prague SRs had organised the Russian eating house with a view to advancing their political views, which to Burtsev's mind were unacceptably pro-Soviet. Events unfolded rapidly. The eating house had opened without a name, and then was declared as belonging to the Russian Society for Mutual Aid, which apparently had nothing in common with *Volya Rossii* and was gaining the reputation of being a useful enterprise. However, this did not calm things down. One thing became clear: the SR system of trying to work behind anonymous organisations was not effective. It was too easy to ascertain the political basis of their activities. They had too few figureheads and their political links and sources of finance could easily be discovered. If the SRs were to occupy a leading position in the Russian colony in Prague, they had to find some other way of doing so. This was quite obvious both to the SRs and to their Czech sponsors.

In the spring of 1921, therefore, there were 'private meetings' whose aim, yet again, was to create a united non-party émigré organisation which would keep a tally of the number of Russian citizens in Czechoslovakia, would find shelter for those who lacked it, would provide free food and petty cash for those who were unemployed and penniless and could give help and advice on employment, medical care, the legal right to reside in Czechoslovakia, education, and the setting up of independent schools, courses and libraries.[17]

Hitherto, the literature on this question has stated that this was a purely private initiative. It was simply that 'those who had worked in the Union of Zemstvos and Towns in Russia decided to create an organisation to help refugees from Russia, which would derive its authority not from official credentials but from the trust of the refugees themselves'.[18] Although the humanitarian motives of those involved should not be belittled, political considerations played a decisive role.

This programme differed little from earlier proposals except that it was implemented rapidly and effectively. This was the result of the Czech decision 'to create a centre of progressive Russians'. This time no lip service was paid to 'non-party unity'. On 7 March 1921, nine SRs declared themselves the founders of the Union of Russian Zemstvos and Towns in the Czechoslovak Republic (Zemgor). Three of them had participated in the state conference in Ufa and four had worked in the administrations of Barnaul, Samara and Ufa, areas which had had links with the Czechoslovak legion in Siberia. All of these people had at one time or another been elected on to various bodies and administrations in Russia. Members of the Zemgor had played key roles in the organisation of the war effort during the First World War and on occasion during the Civil War. It was, perhaps, simply coincidence that only SRs met in Prague. But this coincidence meant that the organisation worked far more smoothly, as there was no inter-party bickering, and made relations with the Czechoslovak authorities much easier, as some of the founders already had links with members of the Czechoslovak Ministry of Foreign Affairs. In these conditions, from an émigré point of view, miracles began to happen.

In an article in March 1921 in the only official SR publication, *Revolyutsionnaya* (Revolutionary Russia), Alexander Kerensky wrote: 'A miracle has occurred! A third force, which only yesterday was being denied, is now not only recognised by all, but has become the only agency in which all hope and trust are placed.' In a broader context – that of Russia or the world – this was a great exaggeration, even if there had been a substantial shift away from the Whites and towards revolutionary democracy as represented by the SRs. In the smaller world of Czechoslovakia, which had already issued warnings about the inadvisability of depending on the White generals, Kerensky's assessment had some measure of truth as the

Czechoslovak government no longer had its hands tied either by its main ally, France, or by the need to oppose its right wing.

Thus, the last of the series of private meetings, which took place on 17 March 1921, was declared the first of the organisational meetings and a three-man provisional committee was elected to draw up the constitution. This was all accepted in an opening meeting, presumably of the original nine members, and rapidly received legal recognition from Zemská Politická Správa. The speed was remarkable, particularly from government institutions which disliked haste, but even this did not please the organisers. On 19 April, even before legal recognition was official, talks had begun with the Legiobanka about a long-term large loan to be paid back on advantageous terms. This agreement, which was signed on 27 May, was unusual even in the annals of banking. The bank advanced one million crowns' credit. (For purposes of comparison, the Czechoslovak state budget in 1921 was 20,000 million crowns and the capital of the bank was 70 million crowns.) The rate of interest was 6 per cent per annum and the loan would be paid off 'when the normal business of the Union of Russian Zemstvos and Towns was renewed on Russian territory and the business of the union would be merged with it'. At the time when this document was signed there were nine members of the Union in the Czechoslovak Republic, when representatives of the Zemgor in Russia could be numbered in thousands. Given the very generous terms, payment of the interest seems a minor detail, and moreover 'prior to 1925 the Legiobank would not demand the payment of interest and there was ground for hope that the Legiobank would agree to the proposals of the Zemgor that all extra interest payments would be excluded from the agreement'.[19]

The Legiobank was the largest and most powerful of the banks founded after independence in Czechoslovakia. According to official records, the original capital consisted of funds that had accumulated or had not been paid on time to the Czechoslovak legion in Russia. Some of the money was derived from trade with the legion and was subsequently used to form trading companies. A court case was brought in Soviet Russia against one such firm, and right-wing émigré circles averred that the Legiobank had been built up on the proceeds of Russia's stolen gold reserve. An enormous literature exists on these issues. In outline the situation was as follows: at the beginning of 1920, a large part of the Russian gold reserve was in Kolchak's hands. Eventually this was handed over to the Soviet authorities but a certain amount was lost.[20] Recent research shows that there has been much erroneous speculation on this subject and that most of the gold reserve was spent on legitimate projects. Legiobank was, however, linked with the new government. The government, like the SRs, needed some form of neutral cover. It could not openly support the SRs and subsidise the Zemgor as its political complexion was abundantly clear not only to members of the emigration in Prague, but also to right-wing Czech circles and émigré representatives from Paris to Belgrade and Sofia. Therefore the government started to finance the Zemgor indirectly through the Legiobank. Later that year the government provided the Zemgor with a further subsidy of 560,000 crowns when it was already up and running.

When one considers the fact that the Czechoslovak government spent 10 million crowns on the Russian refugees in 1921, the sum of one and a half million crowns as an initial loan to a new and small organisation seems very large. In addition the Zemgor received a further loan of 90,000 crowns from the Legiobank, and it is likely that subsidies for specific purposes were also paid to the Zemgor, although officially allocation of funds for specific purposes and to specific institutions only occurred in 1922. Considerable sums were spent on bringing the Russian school, as well as more than 2,000 Cossacks and 1,000 students from various institutions of higher education, from Constantinople to Czechoslovakia. In addition, a large amount was spent on the care of war invalids who were being brought to Czechoslovakia by the Czechoslovak Red Cross.

By the end of April 1921, it might have seemed that the nature of the Russian emigration in Czechoslovakia had been decided. By creating a representative body, the Czechoslovak government was able to shed much of the responsibility for distribution of aid to the émigrés, and for shaping the Russian colony. The Zemgor was to select those who would be granted refuge in Czechoslovakia. As the Zemgor report stated:

> The attraction of Czechoslovakia for the refugees was met by restraint on the part of the government, not because they lacked sympathy and understanding but because of their general plan to regulate the flow of refugees. Relations with the refugees were not simply regulated by humanitarian concerns but were dictated by long-term state and political objectives. Czechoslovakia preferred to concentrate certain categories of refugees within her borders, particularly students, scholars, writers and farmers. The Czechoslovak government did not simply filter those refugees who were independently trying to get to Czechoslovakia according to its preferred criteria but actively assisted the migration of appropriately qualified refugees from other states.[21]

Those supporters of the White movement and of intervention in Russia who were in Prague realised the danger which the creation of the Zemgor represented. The main divisions among the émigrés at that time were not along the left–right divide but over the question of the best way in which to fight the Bolsheviks. Some considered that the only way of overthrowing the Bolshevik regime was through military defeat. The right tended to dominate this group but it also included a large number of former SRs and those Kadets who did not accept Miliukov's 'new tactic'. A second group, whose kernel was formed by the SRs, considered that the struggle had to occur within Russia and that the Bolsheviks could be overthrown using the tactics which had been used to oppose tsarism. Politically this group was the most monolithic. A third grouping placed its hopes in the internal evolution of Soviet power. This was expressed in the Smenovekh movement (Change of Landmarks). The political composition of this group was very varied, but all of them believed that the Bolsheviks had achieved the national objective of the recreation of the state, which had been faced by total collapse, and had thereby unified national forces. The idea of a Great Power attracted many on the right wing, whereas the idea of reconciliation with the Bolshevik reality attracted those on the left.

Within all these groups and trends, right- and left-wing factions could be found. This was often useful for establishing links with different political groups in countries of exile. After Kramář's departure, it became impossible for the monarchists to influence government circles in Czechoslovakia. Thus, instead of monarchist opposition to the Zemgor, it was opposed by the Russian Society of the Working Intelligentsia (Russkoe obshchestvo trudovoy intelligentsii) an organisation which, even in title, was democratic to the core. Its most active member was L.F. Magerovsky, who had already acquired a reputation by opposing the SR dining room. The society managed to get an audience with the Minister of Foreign Affairs, Beneš, and gave him a document which expounded the idea that the government should hand out aid to refugees and give the émigrés themselves a subsidiary role. This would have meant that the Czechoslovak executive would have to transfer émigré political arguments into the arena of Czechoslovak internal policy, a situation which would have been exploited by both right and left wing alike. However, the government was trying to avoid this situation by giving the responsibility for administering aid to a Russian representative body. The need to isolate émigré life and help for refugees from the internal politics of the newly created government was considered essential. The opposition of the German national parties, the growth of the radical left, which in 1921 formed the Communist Party, and the increasingly strained relations between the parties of the right and the centre all put pressure on the government. Since the Russian question was seen as having a particular importance, the attitude towards the emigration could become a key element in the political intrigues of any grouping if the government allowed itself to be drawn into this game.

It seems that some of the 52 members of the Society of the Working Intelligentsia understood this, for at the same time as making representations to Beneš, they began to try to find an émigré organisation which could co-operate with the government and which was not the Zemgor. They invited 12 Russian organisations to a meeting on 21 April 1921 to create a central organisation to protect the interests of Russian refugees. A year earlier, on 26 April 1920, a meeting of this type had been called and that had created a Russian Committee in the Republic of Czechoslovakia to unite all émigrés 'regardless of political beliefs, gender or religious affiliation', in order to facilitate relations with the authorities, protect the interests of the émigrés, keep a record of the numbers and so on: in other words, to carry out the programme which was later carried out by the Zemgor.[22] A year later there was no trace of this Russian Committee, even in the memory of the organisers of the new, analogous enterprise.

What had changed was the Czech authorities' policy. There is no other explanation for the boldness of members of the Zemgor. In reply to the suggestion that an executive rather than a Russian Committee should be formed consisting of representatives of various organisations, the Zemgor representatives replied that this was unnecessary as the Zemgor was already carrying out this function. This was said ten days before the official registration of its constitution by the Czech legal authorities – in other words, before its legal existence. The meeting collapsed in disarray. Representatives of six organisations left in protest; the remaining six, realising that the majority was behind the Zemgor, passed a motion criticising the organisers and their supporters for involving 'the refugee masses in political discord, behind the scenes intrigue and antagonisms'.[23]

The Zemgor emerged victorious from this but the bickering did not stop. A new Russian newspaper *Ogni* (Lights) was published on 2 August 1921 in Prague, and in the second issue an article on 'The Russian colony in Prague' stated: 'Politically, up to the present time the Russian colony in Prague has been represented by a circle of SRs grouped around the notorious *Volya Rossii* and the Zemgor.' In the following issue, on a different topic, this theme was continued: '*Volya Rossii* wants to square accounts quickly with those who are no less democratic than themselves and must protest about this tiresome "Kerenshchina" in all its guises.' In this case Kerenshchina – a pejorative term in the émigré lexicon associated with Kerensky and signifying vacillation, hypocrisy and lack of principle – was represented by the Zemgor, whose actions, apparently, aroused the indignation of the entire colony. 'The abnormal monopolistic position of the SRs' "Zemgor" will inevitably lead to miserable unpleasantness,' warned the author.[24]

The 'indignant' Russian colony, however, was powerless in its struggle with the Zemgor, which was beginning to receive the money from the bank loan. In June, the Zemgor opened an employment office, in August a hall of residence, a dispensary and a dentist's surgery and in November a library and reading room. All émigrés needed these facilities, and to oppose the Zemgor in Prague was becoming, to say the least, increasingly problematic. Nevertheless, there was one more attempt to get the control of aid to the Russian émigrés out of the hands of the Zemgor. At the end of November, Masaryk met an émigré delegation consisting of Prince V.M. Volkonsky, A.V. Novikov and the tireless Magerovsky. They thanked the President for his help and asked him to transfer the question of aid to the Czechoslovak Red Cross.[25] This did not happen.

The centre of the struggle for the character of the Russian colony in Czechoslovakia was being moved on a different plane. The Zemgor had to try to influence the composition and behaviour of the 'refugee masses' which were reaching Czechoslovakia. Although by November 1921 there were still only 6,000 refugees in Czechslovakia, the word 'masses' linked the SRs with the Bolsheviks, who used the same word. From the end of 1920, however, Czechoslovakia was faced with a new problem: the need to help groups of refugees evacuated from the Crimea. The question of influence took on a new aspect: which groups would be welcomed and who would decide? The question referred to individuals, not masses, but in much greater quantities than the number of refugees already in Prague.

Criticism of the Zemgor continued in the Russian press outside Czechoslovakia. Even the most democratic states in the 1920s were fairly tightly restricted by laws on publication, and by the unspoken limits of public opinion as well as by financial considerations. The Russian press outside Russia was subject to various unwritten laws, but publications were also closely linked to the diaspora community and the press was, at the time the freest press in the world. This meant, however, that a critical assessment of the situation in one country frequently had to be found in the press of another. For example, to study the situation in the Russian colony in Yugoslavia the Russian press in Czechoslovakia or France was useful. To understand developments in Czechoslovakia, the Yugoslav or Russian press in France was essential. The only people in Czechoslovakia to declare that the Zemgor was an organisation that belonged to a political party were Soviet representatives or Czech Communists. Thus, although Czechoslovakia was one of the most democratic countries in Europe at the time, the mechanisms of influence seemed to be operating. The demands made on émigré publications were complex. They had to be sensitive to the needs of the refugees, and also a means of communication between the émigrés and the government. Analogous processes were unfolding in all countries where there was any significant number of refugees.

Russian Action differentiated Czechoslovakia from all the other states which accepted refugees. It encompassed help to children and invalids, and peasant resettlement in Czech enterprises, but most of all it was noted for the welcome it afforded to Russian students to continue and complete their education. Russian scholars, academics and writers were paid in order to guarantee worthwhile education for Russian students and younger scholars and conditions were created in which they could continue their activities.[26] This academic facet of Russian Action was unique and from 1924 enabled Prague to be seen as a major academic centre in the Russian émigré community. However, this policy cannot be understood without reference to Czechoslovakia's Russian policy in the broader context of the international situation.

Cossack Agricultural Workers

The first documentary evidence referring to the organisation of selected groups of refugees is dated 3 August 1921; that is, at the beginning of the action to help the starving in Russia. However, it is evident that this policy was being prepared somewhat earlier. Gorky's appeal to which Masaryk responded was published on 13 July and the question was discussed by the Czechoslovak government on 28 July. On that day Masaryk wrote, in a frequently quoted letter to Beneš, that 'one must not forget about the myriad of Russian citizens, living between us and Europe, whom we now support'.[27] This referred to aid to the starving and also implied that help being prepared for the émigrés should not be curtailed as a result of the aid that was being sent to Russia.

A dispatch of the Czechoslovak Ministry of Foreign Affairs to their representative in Constantinople demonstrated that the Czech authorities had put in a good deal of effort into grasping the situation in which Russian refugees in the Bosporus found themselves and had a reasonable understanding of the disposition of political forces:

> The government of Czechoslovakia invites up to 800 students to the Republic with a view to providing them with the opportunity to complete their education. Apply to Mrs Alexandra [this should be Adelaide] Vladimirovna Zhekulina and the Russian professorial board and with them begin to prepare to leave. Go to the French institutions and particularly to General Pelle, and request support for our action. The selection of students must be carried out jointly with Mrs Zhekulina and the Russian professorial board. . . . If possible, check that we are not sent undesirable elements in the guise of students.

Telegrams from the Deputy Foreign Minister Girsa defined what was meant by 'undesirable elements'. In one sent on 7 September, these elements were said to be organised military units and those who were too left-wing or too right-wing. In the next telegram, two days later, there is a request not to allow Wrangel's people to influence the selection and a demand that members of Wrangel's staff should not be let in, in the guise of students, is repeated at the end of September.[28] This was unrealistic and it became impossible to avoid the influence of the 'Wrangelites'.

It appears that the Czech government had hoped in the first instance to invite peasants, which illustrates its thinking on the question of Russian refugees in general. These peasants played little part in the life of Russian Prague as they were thinly spread and there were no leading cultural personalities amongst their number, whereas academic circles and Russian life in general contained many such figures. But at the outset of the Russian Action, 800, later increased to 1,000 students, as well as 4,000 peasants, were invited to Czechoslovakia. Thus, to begin with, it was assumed that these types of émigré would dominate, at least quantitatively. It has been put forward that such emigration was encouraged in the interests of the large landowners who needed labour after the war.[29] Once again, there was not always the required interaction between the government of the country accepting the émigrés and the multifaceted and divided émigré society. The Czechoslovak government sometimes refused to grant visas or even deported émigrés, but more frequently gave financial help to certain groups, so that they would favour particular types of refugees. However, since resources were limited, it was necessary to find new political solutions to émigré problems.

After the instruction of 7 September 1921 to accept 1,000 students and 4,000 agricultural workers a telegram followed on 12 October stating that: 'Only agricultural workers may be brought into Czechoslovakia and not less than 50 per cent must be Cossacks. In order to pick the Cossacks, negotiations must take place solely with the "Agrarian Cossack Union." Financial support will be organised by Zemědělská Jednota (the Agarian Union – a Czech organisation) and Russian organisations will be excluded. The Ministry of Foreign Affairs will deal with cultural needs. Girsa.'[30]

This did not mean that students would not be allowed to enter. It seems most likely that this telegram was the result of the fact that dealings with the students were not turning out as the Ministry wished. The minister was trying to prevent the same thing occurring with the peasants and hoping to stop the policy getting out of his control. This is clear evidence of the Ministry's constantly improving understanding of the real nature of the emigration from the Crimea, and the relentless search for an acceptable political ally. It would seem that soundings had been taken before the political directive, as the first group – consisting of 80 people sent by the All-Cossack Agrarian Union – arrived in Czechoslovakia in June 1921.[31] A second group of 42 Cossacks arrived in August. There is little doubt that they were picked by the same union. Political soundings were carried out quietly.

At the start of plans for Russian Action it was assumed that it would not be a problem to find peasants among the Russian émigrés, but to find those who were 'acceptable', as opposed to those who might be of use to large landowners, was acknowledged to be more difficult. Unexpectedly, there turned out to be another problem. Although representatives of all social groups could be found within the emigration, its composition, as a German diplomat remarked, was that of 'a social pyramid standing on its head'.[32] There were simply very few peasants or agricultural workers. Moreover, they had left Russia not as peasants but as soldiers and they were submerged in an unwelcoming environment. According to the figures provided by the Russian Command, among the 30,000 refugees of the Crimean evacuation could be found 5,220 agricultural workers, landowners and gardeners, or 17 per cent of the total.[33] Figures for refugees in Yugoslavia are very similar.[34] Furthermore, some of these 'agricultural labourers' were purely amateurs before the Revolution, those who might come to help with the scything on the first day of the harvest, while others became agricultural workers during the Civil War and the years of famine which had made them leave the cities. So that even the 'agricultural workers' were in fact an amorphous mass, not united in any way and including the rich and poor, those who had worked on the land for generations and those who had come to it simply by chance. The group included those who came from the fertile black earth areas as well as those from the poorer northern areas. Some had been caught up by events, others had left in uniform as part of military units. They had no leaders and were not used to organising themselves except on local, communal, village principles which were completely unsuitable to the conditions of landlessness abroad.

It turned out that the only apparently united group amongst these so-called peasants were the Cossacks. And they were united less by profession than by the idea of estate. Arguments about the origins of the Cossacks are age old and they flowered in emigration but the most important point was that the Cossacks represented a state within a state. On their own territories they had privileges which singled them out from non-Cossack inhabitants. They created their own order, which was democratic for themselves and repressive for the rest. The Russian Imperial Government guaranteed their privileged position but limited their internal democracy by appointing *atamans* (Cossack leaders) and rejecting those who were democratically elected. Nevertheless, the Cossacks remained loyal to the Tsar and were a bastion of Imperial power at least until the Revolution of 1905. After that, the position changed. Almost all Cossacks, regardless of wealth, were involved in agriculture but they developed a consciousness of themselves as a privileged estate with divisions along party lines. This was vividly illustrated during the Civil War when both 'Red' and 'White' Cossacks made their appearance on the political scene, as well as Cossacks fighting for 'a whole and undivided Russia', those who sought autonomy and did not wish to get involved in 'Russian' affairs, and those who supported an independent Ukraine. Similar trends were to be found throughout peasant society in Russia, but they acquired a much clearer organisation amongst the various Cossack *voisko* and in various joint-*voisko* organisations.

It is impossible to know whether Deputy Minister Girsa had considered all these aspects when he sent his telegram. However, it gave the whole subject a political meaning which the accepting Czech organisations had not wanted. As a result, the outcome was not liked by anyone. The All-Cossack Agrarian Union had been created in 1921 in Constantinople as a way of uniting Cossacks, for the most part those who had served in Wrangel's army but no longer wished to obey the leadership which had failed. The Czech authorities had, meanwhile, begun to look for support from groups such as the SR who did not want Russian military units favoured. This brought new problems in its train, since the SRs, who represented revolutionary democracy, had acquired the pejorative name of 'Ni-nisty' amongst the right wing for their slogan: '*Ni Lenin, ni Kolchak*' (neither Lenin nor Kolchak).

The agricultural emigration distanced itself from the influence of Russian organisations, including the Zemgor, even in cultural questions. This demonstrated a lack of trust in émigré organisations. The Zemstvo organisations in Russia had not exercised authority in the Cossack areas, which had their own independent structures. Even for democratic Cossacks, subordination to the alien structure of the Zemstvo would simply have been insulting. Thus the Czech authorities sought to create the equivalent of a 'Cossack Zemgor' and the All-Cossack Agrarian Union was intended to provide this kind of structure.

The aim of the Czechoslovak government – to accept 4,000 agricultural workers, of which at least half would be Cossacks – never became a reality. The figures of the administrative commission of Russian agricultural workers at the Agrarian Union of Czechoslovakia, which organised everything connected with this, show that by January 1922, 2,098 agricultural workers had arrived in Czechoslovakia. Since the All-Cossack Union stated that they had sent more than 2,000 Cossacks, it would appear that the number of non-Cossack agricultural workers was very low indeed.[35] Including those who arrived later, the usual figure for the Cossacks quoted in the Czechoslovak press was 2,500–3,000. The numbers begin to decline after 1924, but the Cossacks remained the only politically active force among Russian agricultural workers in Czechoslovakia.

The government hoped that they would be able to control this Russian agricultural emigration through the All-Cossack Agrarian Union and the Czech Agrarian Union. However, the former could not bring about unity. In the Soviet Union an amnesty had been granted to those who had been in the White Army but who were of peasant or worker origin. This affected agricultural workers so that in the second half of 1922 'the leadership of the union, almost without exception, reset their sails, recognised the Soviet government and called the Cossacks to return home',[36] according to the main publication of the reconstituted union, albeit on the Czech-language page, which was intended more for the employers of the Cossacks than for the Cossacks themselves. Consequently, by the beginning of 1923, 'The All-Cossack Agrarian Union has very few members and does nothing,' stated *Khutor* (the Farm), detailing nine other Cossack organisations. 'However, the political sympathies of those at the head of most of the organisations are those of left-wing intelligentsia, with a tendency towards socialism. These views prevent them from being sufficiently impartial towards their work and they become involved in agitational propaganda of a political kind,' noted one anonymous observer.[37]

These comments show that there had been some success in assessing the political nature of the Cossack émigrés despite the confusion with the All-Cossack Agrarian Union, but that the Czech Agrarian Union did not completely share the pro-socialist sympathies of the government towards the Russian emigration. During the period of rapid growth of Communist influence in the country, there existed a 'red–green coalition' in Czechoslovakia of Social Democrats and the agrarian interest, but this was a forced alliance as opinions on various political questions differed widely. These differences were all the more marked when it came to the Russian emigration. The Foreign Ministry, bearing in mind the needs of their Russian policy and their aim of preparing those forces who might be able to oppose the Bolsheviks, supported the socialist line. The Agrarian Union, on the other hand, which was trying to get Czechs to employ Russians on their farms and wished to keep possible conflict to a minimum, supported agrarian policies.

Moreover, the attitudes of the Cossacks were greatly affected by the difference between their former life in Russia and their position in Czechoslovakia. From the point of view of the employers, it was desirable that clashes of interest between landowners and their employees should be minimal. The main slogan of the Czech Agrarian Party and Agrarian Union was: 'The village is a family.' When the Cossacks arrived in Czechoslovakia and were distributed through the large estates, they were exploited more than local workers. While this might have been tolerable for prisoners of war, who were mostly of peasant origin and from the central Russian provinces where their land holdings had been small and not particularly productive, it was unacceptable for the Cossacks. They were used not only to owning their own land but also to running their *stanitsas* (villages) in their territories. So conflicts arose from the early days after the Cossacks' arrival in Czechoslovakia. From the fragmentary information in the press and in archival material the development of events can be reconstructed to some extent. Being in the position of farm-hands on large estates in a worse position than the local labourers, the Cossacks began to look for employment on small land holdings, expecting to find the patriarchal conditions with which they had been familiar at home. But in Czechoslovakia the position was very different and it became necessary to intervene to improve the position of the Cossacks on large estates. A wide-ranging programme was inaugurated to enrol the Cossacks into agricultural training schemes, from some of the most basic courses to higher education institutions.

For the Czech Agrarian Union, arguments within the agricultural sector of the Russian emigration meant that they had to intervene in disputes between capital and labour. The government was not really interested in arguments between the left and the right wings of the Cossack community; it was more concerned with its policy towards Russia.

At the first conference of representatives of the All-Cossack Agrarian Union on 23 May 1924, V.T. Vasiliev announced that the agricultural workers had been the first to arrive and the first to feel that as skilled labour they were unnecessary. As a consequence, the union, which was in constant contact with the government from 1923 (two years after the arrival of the Cossacks), began to organise 'Unions in other countries in order to find work for members of the union who had received preliminary training in the Czechoslovak Republic'.[38]

If this idea had worked out, then the 'Czechoslovak Cossacks', who had received both professional training and some experience of democracy in Czechoslovakia, might have had an important influence on the Cossack mass, as with the exception of those few who had been enrolled into the border guards in Yugoslavia, most Cossacks in other places lived in very difficult conditions and had no hope of any training, or even of higher education. The Cossacks from Czechoslovakia would have been a practical illustration of the advantages of a democratic system with a strong social policy, which could help an individual in the struggle for survival even in the extremely arduous conditions of refugee existence. Furthermore, the graduates of Czechoslovak institutions were bound to publicise the success of Czechoslovakia as a cultured and developed country, and indeed did so. The young state was in great need of such publicity. Finally, once these people returned to Russia, they would help the Czechs to trade in the Russian market by establishing a special relationship between the future Russia and Czechoslovakia.

For this to happen, however, it was essential that this future Russia should be politically SR-Left Kadet, as the actions of the Czechoslovak legion in Siberia, the policy of non-intervention by the Czechoslovak government on the international stage, not to mention the betrayal of Admiral Kolchak, finally spoilt relations with all interventionist and 'White' circles. Thus from the point of view of Czechoslovakia's Russian policy, it was essential to support the left, even radically left forces, even if this led to complications over the way in which the émigrés adapted to local conditions.

The organisers of the All-Cossack Agrarian Union wrote openly in the Czech press that their basic policy consisted of 'organising the Cossack emigration, that is tearing it away from reactionary circles and dealing with the questions of labour and legal rights'. This signalled a rift between the policy of the Ministry of Foreign Affairs and the policies of the Agrarian Union, which allowed émigré groups to exploit the contradictions between the organisations.

This discord meant that, at the moment when the All-Cossack Union was reformed, a right-wing opponent arose from another apparently apolitical organisation to which the government could not object. At the end of the conference in 1923 a 70-strong 'agricultural group' presented a declaration which was not made public. It stated that

> In view of the fact that the agricultural conference in Prague . . . turned out to be political . . . and not [the] agricultural [one] to which we had been invited, and that the union would not accept a number of Cossacks as members, . . . that we were not allowed the freedom of expression . . . that the presidium did not reply to certain questions, we the undersigned Cossack agricultural workers, who enjoy the hospitality of the Czechoslovak government and people and do not wish to be involved in political intrigues, consider that the conference was undemocratic, did not respond to old Cossack traditions and did not express the feelings of the Cossacks who are employed in agricultural labour, nor does it represent Cossack-agricultural workers to the Czechoslovak authorities and we are leaving the union.[39]

Those who left formed the Union of Cossack Agricultural Workers and, although there were calls at the meetings of the All-Cossack Union 'to settle the dispute amongst the Cossacks in the Czechoslovak Republic', the split continued until the time when Russian Action began to be wound up, and at that point splits and schisms started to multiply. Obstacles to unity in 1924 were not only the personal disagreements between the leaders of the two unions, neither of whom wished to be subordinate to the other, and the fact that two different Czech organisations – the Foreign Ministry and the

Agrarian Union – were involved. Cossacks were divided over political issues and their allegiance to their own regions and over the basic question which divided the emigration: should they be preparing a military campaign against Moscow, or would Bolshevik power be overthrown by other means, from the inside?

This fundamental divide was manifest in the attitude towards the émigré Conference of Russia Abroad in April 1926. Despite the fact that the Cossack newspaper *Kazachiy Put'* opposed this 'monarchical' conference in a very similar manner to the main SR publications, *Revolyutsionnaya Rossiya, Volya Rossii* and *Dni*, the 'Russian agrarians in the Republic of Czechoslovakia' sent eight delegates to the conference, and two of them were members of the organising committee.[40]

So the Foreign Ministry's attempt to create an 'SR' agricultural emigration which would be directed by an organisation like the Zemgor failed. This might have worked had they been dealing with Russian peasants. But there were very few representatives of such peasantry in the emigration as a whole, and those that existed were lost in a socially alien milieu and could not create any organisations of their own with which the Foreign Ministry could have had dealings. The Cossacks were the only group of the rural population with whom it was possible to deal and they had a special position. This complicated matters from the outset. Furthermore, the Czechoslovak organisation, the Agrarian Union, which was responsible for carrying out this policy, soon adopted a different point of view from that of the Foreign Ministry. In order to implement its Russian policy, the Foreign Ministry had to overcome hostile attitudes within the Agrarian Union and found that it was unable to put its original ideas into action.

Students

In the case of Russian students coming to Prague the situation was even more complex. Russian students who found themselves abroad had been deeply affected by revolution and civil war, experiences that coloured the views of everyone. Those who needed help and wished to come to Prague turned out to be very different from the kinds of students whom the Czech authorities had originally wanted to invite. Moreover, the institutions and agencies which the Czech government had hoped would implement their policies were unable to do so and the government had to delegate the responsibility for getting these students to Prague. Professor Lomshakov and A.V. Zhekulina had a crucial role in this and their initiatives profoundly affected both how Russian students reached Prague and the openings which were available to them.

By the end of the First World War there were a few Russian students in Prague and this number increased during the course of 1919. On 30 November 1919, in a room belonging to the Czech–Russian Union (Česko-Ruská Jednota: CRJ) there was a meeting of the Constituent Assembly of the Union of Russian Students. The constitution was accepted and the executive elected. To begin with there were 40 members of the union.[41] Professor B. Morkovin welcomed the students on behalf of CRJ, saying, as reported by the newspaper *Slavyanskaya Zarya*, that he hoped 'Russian students would work for the creation of a Russian federal but not bourgeois republic. . . . The new Russian republic must be based on socialist principles.' A student representative replied to the welcome with the assurance that 'Russian students were always progressive'.[42]

Morkovin took care to distance himself from an attitude which appeared to be synonymous with socialism, but the declarations of intent certainly sounded socialist, beginning with the word: 'Comrades!' Subsequent announcements were quite unsophisticated and make one think that the students must have been schoolboy SRs, who had been evacuated from Siberia with the Czechoslovak legion. If not, it is difficult to see how 40 Russian students could suddenly have arrived in Prague.

The original declaration states that 'Russian students may with pride turn the pages of the history of the liberation of the Russian nation. Leading the march of eternal progress, and being the most active fighters for freedom and a better future for their people, Russian students were far from being national chauvinists, and called all nationalities inhabiting Russia comrades, under the glorious banner of struggle.'[43] The various political divisions in the emigration had not yet made themselves clear. The right-wing paper *Slavyanskaya Zarya* announced the calling of the student assembly, whereas the declaration was published by the relatively left-wing *Russkoe Delo*. Apart from publishing this announcement, neither paper commented on this student activity.

News of this new organisation disappeared for almost a year from the pages both of the Czechoslovak and the Russian press in Czechoslovakia. The SR, O.S. Minor returned to the question in September 1920 in *Volya Rossii*. According to him, the Union of Russian Students had 122 members in Prague. They were 'young people who had fled both the violence and terrorism of the Bolsheviks and the Volunteer Army'. These young people, in the opinion of the author, would be very valuable for Russia, but apparently, even in Prague, 'Russian students are not accepted on various courses for ridiculous reasons such as, there was insufficient food and lodging for 122 students in a city with a population of half a million . . . Unwillingly one is forced to seek another reason for the hounding of Russian students in Prague – the need to prevent the spread of Bolshevism.'[44]

The students under Minor's wing were not Bolsheviks, but it was difficult for the majority of Czechs to be sure about this. Communists had not declared themselves in Czech party politics, or amongst Slovak, German, Carpathian and of course émigré political parties. Masaryk and the employees of the Ministry of Foreign Affairs understood this much better. Refugees from both right and left were comprehensible and they were not upset by the word 'comrades'. However, while they were trying to create the new state they had not got the time to deal with 122 students: they would have to be considered at a later date. The question of who should be invited to Czechoslovakia had been clearly formulated by the middle of March 1921. Nevertheless, the decision not to admit those who had served with Wrangel did not help them to deal with those whose views appeared to be extreme. It simply produced another dimension of the problem for the Czechoslovak government, which wished to have a far-seeing Russian policy. The question of which Russian students to accept took on a new importance.

It seems it is a mistake to date the beginning of Russian Action from the telegram of 3 August 1921. This telegram, written in Czech, stated that the Czechoslovak government invited 800 students. However, in Czech, the word 'students' could apply to schoolchildren as well as to those studying in further education, but it did not carry the same connotations in Russian. The fact that the selection of these 'students' was carried out with the help of A.V. Zhekulina, a pioneer and activist in school education, suggests that it was the Czech meaning of the word student that was intended.

Adelaide Vladimirovna Zhekulina (1866–1950) was one of the prime movers and personalities of the emigration, and yet she is mentioned only in passing in the literature. She devoted herself to the unseen practical work of creating and preserving Russian schools, organising Russian cultural life and providing financial help to thousands of people. She did not write about her activities and writers on this subject sometimes forgot to mention the names of those who undertook basic and unglamorous work. Zhekulina was busy with the day-to-day problems of these enterprises and did not write sparkling articles in the press or publish learned works about the 'emigration's children', or address those problems which would now be subsumed under the heading of 'identity'. There was no real tradition or desire amongst women in particular to write in this kind of way. Yet in Prague there were at least three such women: A.V. Zhekulina, Countess S.V. Panina (1871–1956) and Princess N.G. Yashvil' (1861–1939). All undertook important work and were regarded by contemporaries as leading lights of the émigré world. They were, more or less, members of the same generation and came from wealthy aristocratic families. They were already known in Russia, where they had become involved in socially useful activities once they were widowed. All of them spoke several languages well and had many useful contacts both in and outside Russia.

Before the Revolution, A.V. Zhekulina founded a girls' school (gymnasium) in Kiev, which became famous throughout Russia. By all accounts she was a talented teacher with a vocation but she did not just depend on her own talents: she made a serious study of the findings of education specialists both at home and abroad, including American theories, which at that time was exceptional in Russian pedagogical circles. In politics, as in her approach to education, she was a liberal and supported the Kadets, although it seems that she did not engage in political activity. After the outbreak of war, she began to work in the Sogor–Soyuz gorodov (All-Russian Union of Towns), which tried to organise help for the army, in the first instance medical aid. This kind of work suited both the personality and the political convictions of Zhekulina. Her former pupils testify that she was, first and foremost, a good person who was loving without being sentimental. It was natural for her to help people in need but she was a sensible person with a practical approach who did not simply do good works in order to salve her conscience. She wanted to help people to get on their own feet, and to prepare them for life. Her liberal convictions led her to do this through social activity. It is no coincidence that later on she became one of the organisers of a society to study the self-government of towns in Czechoslovakia. From the moment that Russians found themselves abroad, she worked tirelessly to help Russian children and young people whose education had been cut short by the whirlwind of civil war, trying first of all to get them into educational institutions in Constantinople and then to evacuate these institutions to other more welcoming countries. She was successful to a large extent, and many children received a secondary and often higher education as a result of her efforts in the extremely difficult circumstances of emigration. She evacuated the school which she had organised, from Constantinople to Moravská Třebová in Czechoslovakia. Here she became chair of governors of the school. She was also made chair of the Sogor and was head of the Society for Care of Russian Children, where she worked to raise funds and to open kindergartens for those born during emigration.[45]

Zhekulina was given responsibility for choosing the students and schoolchildren to be sent to Czechoslovakia, along the lines indicated by the Czechoslovak government. However, things did not work out quite as intended. To begin with, the schoolchildren had experienced four years of a world war and three years of civil war, and were no longer the children in school uniform of the pre-war years. As Rudnev explains:

> The classes of the younger age groups were relatively small, whereas the final years were very full . . . in 1922 there were four parallel forms

for the eighth (final) year, and for those who had completed their schooling in Constantinople and were waiting to be accepted into higher educational institutions in Czechoslovakia, it became necessary to create an additional ninth class. Among these pupils there was a significant number of participants in the Civil War; not infrequently they had been injured and maimed, and had been officers who had been decorated.[46]

Even children of normal school age bore little resemblance to their contemporaries of 1913. More than 30 per cent were orphaned, while more than 40 per cent thought that their parents were still alive but had remained in Russia and had no contact with their children. Only 20 per cent of children had both parents living in Czechoslovakia. Most had gone through dreadful experiences and their understanding of life was not childlike, their habits were not those of children and they found it difficult to study. Given the nature of their life so far, schools had to resemble institutions for delinquents more than pre-war gymnasiums, even if in social origin the pupils were not so different from those in gymnasiums.[47]

It would have been perfectly possible to have selected these children on political grounds. It is to Zhekulina's great credit that she did not do so. It is also to the credit of the Czechoslovak authorities that they did not try to expel those seen as 'unsuitable', as had happened, for example, in Belgium. Quite the reverse: the authorities did their utmost, in collaboration with the teachers, to provide opportunities for the children to re-enter normal life, although to begin with the results were not particularly encouraging.[48] Nevertheless, the children remained at school and the rates of success began to improve as the children, once again, became accustomed to the rhythm of school life.

This liberal approach was less appropriate for the teachers. Muffled criticism of the political ethos at Moravská Třebová can be found in the sources and in the end the authorities appointed a new headmaster. It would also appear that the gymnasium was very pro-White in sympathy, which was hardly surprising since a third of the pupils had lost their parents during the Civil War directly at the hands of the Red Army or as a result of Bolshevik policies.

However, the representatives of the government had no intention of using education to instil ideas of class hatred. It must be stressed that the unique feature of the Czechoslovak policy towards the émigrés was that when they realised that their aims were not being put into practice, the authorities did not begin to apply restraints, but placed their hopes in the power of democratic ideas and experience of life in a democratic state, and simply prevented the inculcation of ideas which were diametrically opposed

to their own. The subsequent fate of those who were educated at Moravská
Třebová was very varied politically, professionally and geographically, as a
substantial number left Czechoslovakia, and the school provided a free
choice of careers. The Cadet corps in Yugoslavia, by contrast, pointed its
pupils in one direction so that during the Second World War many found
themselves in the ranks of pro-Nazi formations in Yugoslavia. Thus, as far
as children were concerned, even if the authorities did not manage to put
their original ideas into practice, they were able to ensure that extreme
views within the emigration did not predominate and to provide a broad
education within a broadly democratic framework.

Higher Education

The issue of older students in higher education was more complicated. Like
the pupils of the gymnasiums, they bore little resemblance to their pre-war
predecessors. On average they were between three and five years older and
their experience of three years of civil war made them more mature. Some
kind of political selection of these students was necessary. The Czechoslovak
authorities hoped that the Russian Academic Group in Constantinople
would do that, taking into account the tension between Wrangel's
leadership and various Russian social and public institutions. However, even
here the government was unsuccessful.

A re-examination of the origins of the academic side of Russian Action
shows that the initiative did not simply come from President Masaryk, as the
literature frequently asserts. Masaryk knew Russia well, but his attitude
towards her was quite critical. Furthermore, he had direct experience of
emigration and knew what a corrupting effect émigré life had on the
personality. At the very least, until the crushing of the Kronstadt rising in
March 1921, he had more faith in left-wing anti-Bolshevik forces within
Russia and aided the creation of left-wing émigré centres which would
maintain links with the internal opposition. Such groups had resources to
publish propaganda and channel it back into Russia. He does not seem to
have been interested in any kind of general welcome for the émigrés, and
may have considered this harmful, being well aware that there was no
employment for them. Masaryk's attitude was in stark contrast to the
situation in Yugoslavia and Bulgaria, where there was a strong awareness of
the lack of qualified people. Serbia had also suffered immense casualties
during the war and needed both officers and lower ranks in the armed
forces. So it is quite likely that the initiative to create a Russian academic
community in Prague did not originally come from Masaryk but was
ascribed to him at a later date by grateful left-wing circles who were aware

that in the 1920s Masaryk had actively taken part in the development of Russian Action and, as it wound down, used his private means for charitable enterprises.

Masaryk's name is absent from contemporary sources. *Studencheskie Gody* (Student Years) describes the early days in the creation of a Russian academic centre financed by the Czech authorities:

> During the first months of its existence, the Union of Russian Students was getting nowhere and only when K.K. Fiksel' became chairman and V.V. Shrut deputy chairman, both of whom were well acquainted with Czech society, did it become possible to win the sympathies of the government, Czech students, professors and the public. This prompted the leadership of the Student Union to place the student question in a much wider context and prepared the ground for calling the first all-student émigré conference . . . from that point on the activities of the Union increased at a feverish pace. The government provided the necessary resources to publish a journal and to organise a conference.[49]

Another source states that 'by the beginning of 1921, following the initiative taken by the deputy Foreign Minister Dr V. Girsa, a state cultural and educational plan for aid to Russians was formed'.[50]

Placing this in a wider context, it is striking that nothing really worked without government aid. This also applied to the Zemgor, which began to expand its activities once it had received financial help from the government. It appears that the above document refers to March–April 1921, when the Kronstadt rising was defeated in Russia and discussions with General Pelle over the resettlement of Wrangel's troops abroad were taking place. The individuals involved are also of interest. Before the war, Dr Girsa practised medicine in Kiev and was one of the steadily growing number of Czechs in Russia. Nothing is really known about Fiksel' and Shrut, apart from their surnames and the fact that they had graduated from institutions of higher education in Czechoslovakia by 1922; the fact that they had contacts within Czech society makes it probable that they were Russian Czechs. Even if they had not known Girsa in Russia, they would still have had a common language with him since they all belonged to the minority left wing of the Czech colony.

The Czech government had intended to create a student movement throughout the emigration, not to form a Russian colony in Czechoslovakia. There are analogies with the support given to the SRs. Their publications and activities in Berlin and Paris were supported, and some sources state that this also applied in Poland and Finland. The Czech government did not wish to have all this concentrated in Czechoslovakia and forbade political activity on its territory. They would not accept the revolutionary activist Savinkov and his colleagues, and demanded that émigré conferences should be apolitical and that there should be no interference in internal affairs in an attempt to influence policy on émigrés. In other words, the government was quite prepared at this juncture to support the left wing of the emigration throughout Europe but was not yet considering the possibility of creating a major academic centre in Czechoslovakia.

Such a centre was something quite different, as the commentator from the Union of Russian Students understood very well. He continued: 'At this time, it was hoped that academic questions would be settled advantageously (and material problems too) as the Russian professor and the Union of Russian Engineers come to the aid of the students. Professor A.S. Lomshakov is the leader of this enterprise.' This commentator chose his words very carefully. Both academic and financial questions were due to be discussed and decided at the student conference. The author understood that the problems of students in Czechoslovakia had been partially solved but that in addition to the activities of Professor Lomshakov other factors were involved.

From this it appears that there had been a fundamental change in the thinking of the Czechoslovak government over the question of the emigration. Instead of supporting progressively minded Russians on a Europe-wide basis, they now concentre on creating a Russian academic centre in Prague. Our source states that Professor A.S. Lomshakov led this enterprise. Like Zhekulina, he has disappeared from the literature.[51] Yet Lomshakov was a key personality within the Russian emigration in Prague. Arguably the creation of a viable academic community in Prague was to a large extent the result of his efforts, his contacts within Czech society and his sensible and practical approach to the problems he encountered.

In contrast to Zhekulina we do at least have a short outline of his biography in an article by E.A. Vechorin,[52] and his official papers are in the Czech archives. Many of these are official service records and refer to his academic career and his work in industry and only in passing do they mention his efforts on behalf of the emigration which became the main part of his life from 1921 to 1939. The full extent of his activity – his role not only in Prague but in the entire émigré community – still awaits assessment; however, it is not possible to understand the emigration as a social and cultural phenomenon without analysing the role of personalities such as Lomshakov. It was people like him who transformed the refugee mass into a structured community which was then able to survive for a relatively long time. Some of the characteristics of these personalities pre-ordained them both for this role and for future oblivion. They seem to have been a distinct type and radically different from the political leaders who were the pride of the emigration, well known in other countries, and whose names have been preserved for posterity.

Zhekulina came to be known affectionately as 'Grandmother Zhekulina', in the 1920s, when she was not yet 60. Professor Lomshakov was an eminent engineer who became a member of the Prague Polytechnic Institute: he could never have been nicknamed 'Grandfather' even a month before his death at the age of 89. Yet a comparison of these two active individuals demonstrates many similar traits of character.

Lomshakov was born in 1870, the sixteenth and last child of a priest in the remote Siberian town of Barnaul. From childhood he was deeply religious, but in his own words he grew up among the children of the street, in an unsentimental atmosphere as severe as the Siberian climate: the frosts reach −55°C, yet society was fair and ordered by unwritten rules. He was educated in the cadet corps, to which, according to his memoirs, he owed a great deal: 'it provided an unshakeable feeling of comradely duty, a sense of discipline, taught one to carry out one's duties accurately, and fixed an understanding of Russia's greatness, the duty of loyalty towards her, of patriotic and national pride'. Lomshakov then went to the St Petersburg Technological Institute and, after graduation, worked at the Okhtensky gunpowder works, which had achieved notoriety after a series of explosions. Here he began his work as an inventor, for which he later received recognition when working in one of the best known of Russian industrial enterprises, the Putilov works. His design for a furnace was awarded a medal at the World Exhibition in Paris in 1900 and at that time he began to teach in various Russian institutions of higher education. At the age of 33 he became a professor, and in 1905 he was actively involved in politics and was elected as a Kadet deputy to the Duma in 1906. During the war, he was involved in the development of the armaments industry, and during the Civil War he found himself in the south with General Denikin.

Professor Lomshakov arrived in Prague on 6 April 1920. Originally, he had been appointed to Czechoslovakia as a representative of the Department of Trade and Industry and the Department of Finance of the Commander of Armed Forces in Southern Russia. This was an important position, as at the time of his appointment the Czech legion appeared the only force that realistically might support the Allies in Siberia and still seemed a possible ally in the struggle in the south, given Kramář's policies. But by the time Lomshakov arrived in Prague, the government which had given him a particular task no longer existed and Czechoslovakia had already strongly declared its opposition to intervention. His original tasks were clearly impossible to fulfil.

This did not mean, however, that he did not act. We do not know whether he tried to contact General Wrangel's government or whether he attempted to carry out any of their directives, but we do know that from May 1921, he organised the Society of Russian Engineers and Technical Specialists. By then he was employed by Škoda, one of the largest industrial firms in Czechoslovakia, and had contacts with influential industrialists and in academic circles.

The Society of Russian Engineers and Technical Specialists did not simply try to find work for its members. In Postnikov's *Russkie v Prage*, the description of the society's activity states that

> From the beginning of the society's existence, the management became involved in aid to Russian students; on the suggestion of the Cultural and Educational department of Sogor in Constantinople, the management requested permission from the Czechoslovak government to allow 250 students with technical training and 700 university students to enrol in educational institutions and to provide financial help for the journey.[53]

But Lomshakov who worked very hard to make this plan a reality was not mentioned. In addition, it appeared as if the initiative had come from Sogor, but we do not know whether Sogor would have acted if they had not received optimistic reports from Prague. Sogor was largely Kadet in outlook, whereas the Zemgor was more influenced by the SRs, who had nothing in common politically with Lomshakov. However, in October 1921, according to the *Zemgor Bulletin* in Paris: 'the answers from Czechoslovakia, received via Professor Lomshakov, exceeded all expectations'.[54] This refers to the invitation to Russian students. It would be logical to assume that Professor Lomshakov told his party friends about this earlier and more systematically. Why was Lomshakov not mentioned in Postnikov's work?

Nor was Lomshakov mentioned in the chapters dealing with the Committee for the Provision of Education for Ukrainian and Russian Students in the Czechoslovak Republic or in the section describing the Union of Russian Professors, although a number of other publications mention him in this context. Vechorin, an engineer, directly states that he 'formed the Committee'. The Prague Russian paper, *Nedelya* (The Week) noted on 3 October 1930 that 'Nine years ago, on the initiative of the President of the Škoda works I. Šimonek, the Managing Director Dr F. Hanuš and Professor A.S. Lomshakov, with the participation of prominent political, social and academic figures, help for Russian students was organised.' In addition, an invitation to deputy Hajn, dated 6 August 1921,[55] exists, signed by Professor Lomshakov on behalf of the preparatory committee. He became the first and permanent chairman, the one who determined the destiny of Russian students, and enemy No. 1 of the SR newspaper, *Volya Rossii*. The angry attacks on Lomshakov, no less than the many tributes and expressions of thanks from student and academic organisations in the period 1922–23, demonstrate the exceptional part he played. Nevertheless his role is not mentioned by Postnikov, and since this work has become the main source for information on the Russian emigration in Prague, Lomshakov has 'disappeared' from history. The reason that he did not appear in Postnikov's work was that he was the head of the various organisations described and he edited the sections about the work of these bodies. He was a modest man and self-advertisement was not fashionable at that time. The general account of Russian Action was written from the point of view of the Prague Zemgor, which although not at odds with the committee in 1928 had no interest in praising Lomshakov. Thus, his very important contribution was not emphasised.

Altogether, the beginning of a Russian academic centre and help to the student body shows the different influences at work. In March–April 1921 representatives of the new management of the Union of Russian Students, who were probably Russian Czechs, contacted Deputy Minister Girsa and proposed the creation of a pan-European if not a world émigré student movement with generally left-wing but anti-Bolshevik views.[56] This was in line with the politics of the Czech government and was not expensive to promote: only three issues of the journal *Student* ever appeared, plus the organisational costs of a conference that met in October. On the whole, it followed official policy. It created the United Russian Émigré Student Organisation (Ob'edinenie Russkikh Emigrantskikh Studencheskikh Organisatsii: ORESO) with its main office in Prague. This was useful for the young republic, which needed international channels of communication. For the time being, it was also cheap.

The question of bringing students to Czechoslovakia and supporting them was only indirectly linked to the student union. The smooth operation of the international student movement might have encouraged the supporters of Russian Action in Prague, but did not do more than that. Lomshakov had hopes of influencing very different circles. He had little concern with the left-wing groupings around the Ministry of Foreign Affairs. His contacts were with the old-style Russophiles, largely conservative, who belonged to the National Democratic and Agrarian political parties, as well as with his colleagues, engineers who were largely apolitical. These were the circles in which he found himself as a result of his profession and of the authority originally conferred by Denikin. In any case, right-wing circles, prompted by Lomshakov (and not by Masaryk) began to agitate on behalf of the students. Documents in the archives attribute the plan for Russian Action to Kramář and A. Švehla.[57] But it is more than likely that these various forces were united by Lomshakov over the idea of creating a Russian academic centre. He was the only prominent émigré who was welcomed equally by the President and by the former premier, which later almost proved fatal for him.[58]

The main enemy of all charitable undertakings in any period are financial institutions, and Czechoslovakia was no exception. Already by 1921 the guardians of the budget were indicating that expenses were rising above the intended expenditure, even though Russian Action had hardly started. The original estimate of 10 million crowns had been multiplied by ten but in 1924 the expenditure of the Foreign Ministry alone on Russian refugees was 100 million crowns. In these conditions it became more difficult to argue the case for bringing in further groups of Russian students. Things happened on an *ad hoc* basis and it was often a case of first come, first served. Russian Action became much larger than had originally been planned, but this was the result of a strategic change by the Czech government in their Russian policy.

In a confidential memo addressed to Monnet,[59] which for some in-explicable reason has not received the attention of researchers, the principles of this policy are stated. M. Monnet was the French representative on the Nansen Commission for help to the starving in Russia. The Czechoslovak side stressed that the famine was not fortuitous and that there were insufficient funds to overcome its effects. Feeding the starving was not the most serious problem. It was necessary to produce enough specialists from the local population to organise agriculture so that the famine could not recur. Masaryk did not advocate the use of foreign experts in this situation as he was well aware that such people frequently did not understand the language or local culture sufficiently well to be of much use.

The Czech authorities knew that Russia had its own well-qualified intelligentsia, but since they 'had suffered enormous casualties as a result of civil wars, famine, etc., in the first instance one must help the refugee Russians abroad and make them work to help their own country. For this to happen it is essential to provide the opportunity for them to complete their education abroad, and to provide them with the opportunity of returning to their native country and worthwhile employment.' Up to this point, this memo repeats the ideas of the Tokyo Memorandum, which had also expressed the hope that Russia would be recreated by the efforts of its intelligentsia, in a different context. Then follow points which were purely of relevance to the emigration.

The text stated that Czechoslovakia was providing education for 5,000 Russian and Ukrainian students. (This was an obvious exaggeration, even if 'students' included pupils at secondary school.) It went on to say that 10,000 Russian students in Europe had no opportunity to continue their education. France had spent vast sums of money on the Russian emigration but there was a danger that other countries, probably Germany, would reap the benefits. The Czech author emphasised that 'It is quite clear that the conditions and the place where these people receive their education will be of great importance for future political and economic life.' He continued: 'The German representative at the conference said to me, after listening to the Czech speech, that he was sure that Germany would accept the rest of the Russian students on the same conditions that were announced by the Czechs. The danger is immediate.'

The author of the memo went on to consider how best to avoid this danger. He thought that the ideal solution would be for the Russian students to complete their education in France but then adduced arguments against this: education in France would be four times as expensive as in Czechoslovakia and the majority did not know French so would need an extra year to learn the language. There was a clear assumption that a related language could easily be learned by Russians and Ukrainians without any special preparation.

At that time Czechoslovakia was able to take a further 5,000 students 'into its schools and universities' if the French government would pay for them. Since Czechoslovakia was linked to France both politically and culturally, the effect would be the same as if these people had studied in France. In conclusion it was stated that this matter must not be delayed in view of the measures which might be undertaken by the German government. Czechoslovakia was prepared to place at France's disposal not only her schools and universities but all the influence she had amongst Russian professors and students in the emigration. The last sentence of the memo read: 'For your information I enclose Professor Lomshakov's report of January 1922.'

This document, amongst others, clearly demonstrates that Russian Action was not simply charitable and that Lomshakov played a central role in both analysing the situation and putting forward solutions. Moreover, Czechoslovakia was pressurising her patron. She was demanding cash in the interests of economics, culture and influence in the future Russia – threatening that otherwise Germany would provide those influences. Three years after the end of 'the war to end all wars', this was a powerful argument. Nevertheless, like the Tokyo Memorandum, this Czech document had no consequences. France, entirely taken up with internal and European problems, considered that Russia was out of the game for a long time and that Germany should be kept on its knees for many years, if not for ever. The spirit of the tiger, Clemenceau, still influenced French politics.

Between August 1921, when the Czech representatives in Constantinople received their instructions to prepare the first groups of students for evacuation to Czechoslovakia, and January 1922 there was great change. Originally the intention was to accept 800 selected students; by the end of this period they would be accepting 10,000 if not all Russian émigré students. The main factor in this radical reappraisal seems to have been that Masaryk became disillusioned with the idea of creating an SR centre in Prague and in particular with the idea that the Zemgor could select a sufficient quantity of politically acceptable students. At the same time, he became convinced that Lomshakov could organise and run the operation apolitically, which in effect meant that right-wing students would be accepted, provided they did not engage in any politics. Masaryk's great merit was not that he initiated Russian Action but that he correctly assessed the rapidly changing situation, the realistic opportunities available to Czechoslovakia and her various allies amongst the Russian emigration, and put his ideas into practice. He thus achieved the optimum result from the point of view both of the government's Russian policy and of the effectiveness of help to the émigrés, given that finances were limited.

The mistaken assumptions of the Ministry of Foreign Affairs about the need to bring SRs to Prague were clearly delineated by Lomshakov. The 'official' historians, Davats and L'vov, of Wrangel's army in exile stated: 'The question of sending one hundred students from Gallipoli to Prague might not have been raised, if it were not for the Commander-in-Chief, who asked what was happening.'[60] Considering the reasons for this, L'vov and Davats in the first place thought that since the army was struggling to maintain unity, officers would not be allowed to leave, and secondly that the army at least had rations, whereas refugees were in an even more difficult situation and help to them had to be a priority. 'Third, we do not rule out this possibility, it seemed undesirable to bring a close knit group "of reactionary minded people" to Prague as the men of the 1st corps seemed to many.' In the event, 'one hundred men from Gallipoli' did get to Prague, and in the period when the book was written there was still a possibility of sending more people to Prague which probably explains the authors' careful phraseology and diplomatic wording.

Finally, it was owing to Professor Lomshakov that men from Gallipoli could get to Prague. The conditions made it imperative to move the troops out of Turkey for humanitarian reasons. But to left-wing Russians and Czechs, these remnants of the White Army symbolised the worst aspects of the White struggle. The possibility of evacuating these men to Prague was mentioned 'in a private letter ... and General Kutepov was told immediately. Informing them of the steps which had been taken, Professor Lomshakov was concerned about the troops at Gallipoli, expressing the conviction that it was they, disciplined and stoical, who would provide some of the best students.' According to S. Shevlyakov, 'when General Kutepov was shown Professor Lomshakov's private letter, in which the possibility of taking 300 students to Prague is mentioned [once again this makes one think that the remaining 500 must be schoolchildren, and that this letter was sent at the same time as Girsa's August telegram], he immediately telegraphed back: "I can send 500".'[61]

It is not known whether Kutepov actually sent this to Lomshakov, but undoubtedly he reported it to the Commander-in-Chief, and General Wrangel then became involved in Constantinople. This occurred by the end of September 1921, and radical changes were happening in Prague where the Committee for the Provision of Education for Russian Students and the Union of Russian Professors were formed. Lomshakov was the head of the Russian side in both cases.

This was the first major defeat for the Zemgor. A parallel organisation to administer aid to the émigrés had been formed and had been given jurisdiction of the section of the emigration with the greatest potential. Furthermore it was under the leadership of a man who had arrived in Prague as Denikin's representative. Denikin was hated by the SRs and his representative had links with conservative Czech circles.

The difference in attitude between the SRs and Masaryk is striking. Masaryk very quickly came to value Lomshakov's qualities and businesslike approach, although he had no sympathy for Denikin and his relations with Kramář were steadily worsening. Thus without hesitation he agreed to work with Lomshakov and referred the whole thing to the Ministry of Foreign Affairs, even though the initial impetus for this had come from those with whom he had little in common. The President wrote a personal testimonial, which he gave to Lomshakov when he went to the USA on a fund-raising trip: 'I strongly support Professor Lomshakov as irreproachably honest and energetic; he has every right to discuss this matter on behalf of all Russian academic organisations abroad.'[62] By contrast it seems that the SRs could not repress their ideological and personal dislike of Lomshakov as a more successful competitor in organising Russian Action, although the earlier harsh criticism ceased.

As a result of Lomshakov's work, in the first instance in opposition to the politics of the Foreign Ministry and subsequently in collaboration with it, a Russian student community was formed which bore little resemblance to the one originally planned by the SRs and the Foreign Ministry. The first students arrived from Constantinople in December 1921, and the 'Gallipoli hundred' with them.

The number of students in Prague rose rapidly until there were 1,474 by the beginning of 1922.[63] These 'Constantinople students', as they were known, although some of them had arrived from Gallipoli, Salonica and Tunis, were displeased with the activities of the poorly supported left-wing student union. On 18 December 1921 a general meeting was called, which continued for three days and at which a new management was elected and a new constitution drawn up. In essence the union experienced a take-over by conservatives, although this was covered up by the demand that the union should be apolitical.

The question of what was understood as 'political' and 'apolitical' by the emigration at the time was central to the argument. At the very beginning the SRs presented themselves not as a political force but as the frequently anonymous organisers of various socially useful projects, for example help to prisoners of war, the mutual aid societies, and finally the Zemgor. The Czechoslovak authorities provided patronage for non-political activity of left-wing circles. This helped them to achieve their aims without conflict, or more often disarmed the criticism of right-wing circles in Czecho-slovakia. But in émigré circles this was an open secret, and the emigration itself began to unmask crypto-SR and left SR activity, as by now the SRs had lost their unity and were not a political organisation in its original meaning. Starting with the 'SR eating place' and ending with the Zemgor, these organisations found themselves subject to criticism by émigrés who had links either with influential Czech circles or with the Czech press. It became increasingly clear that this kind of crypto-political influence was not producing the right results.

Using the excuse of being apolitical, the right wing, more than once, was able to exclude the left, or was able to create right-wing organisations in opposition to the left, as happened with the organisation of the Cossack agrarians in opposition to the All-Cossack Agrarian Union. These examples refer to the period 1922–24, but the first organisation to make use of the requirement to be apolitical was the Union of Russian Students in collaboration with the Committee for the Provision of Education for Russian Students. They did so with the express intention of reversing existing political attitudes.

On 11 February 1922, *Volya Rossii* announced that students who were being supported by the government of Czechoslovakia were 'being subjected to a sustained assault from reactionary circles in the Russian emigration. These circles have successfully seized the direction of student life through the medium of the Committee for the Provision of Education for Russian Students'.[64] In some other articles these 'reactionary circles' were explicitly identified with Professor Lomshakov. However, this attack was not expressed in terms of monarchical or White Guardist propaganda but based on the demand to be apolitical. The most reactionary document of the committee, which was published by the newspaper was 'Regulations for Russian Students supported by the Committee for Aid to Russian Students', the first point of which stated:

> Recalling the conditions which they had accepted, students promise to refrain from participating in political activity. The following can be considered political activity:
> a) active participation in the activities of one of the local or Russian political parties;
> b) making party political propaganda speeches;
> c) writing and distributing political pamphlets;
> d) carrying out the orders of political parties;
> e) taking part in political demonstrations.

These regulations simply spelt out the conditions to be accepted by students who were financially supported by the Czech government. There was nothing which overtly linked these conditions with reactionary groups in the emigration. Government aid for the émigrés was supposed to be apolitical and purely humanitarian, and the Foreign Minister Beneš constantly emphasised this in both parliament and the press. In reality, of course, this was pretty unusual. Until mid–1921, the government financed not only left-wing newspapers such as *Revolutionnaya Rossiya* and Miliukov's *Poslednie Novosti* and also supported a variety of general émigré organisations on the left whose true nature was concealed by titles such as the All-Cossack Agrarian Union or the Union of Towns and Zemstvas. The creation of the Committee for the Provision of Education for Russian Students marked a change from the previous policy. The question of being apolitical began to be taken seriously and not simply seen as a way of limiting the activities of the more conservative.

The SRs, however, were correct in thinking that implementing these demands meant that the right wing was becoming stronger because of the changing attitudes within the emigration. The majority of Russian refugees particularly loathed Alexander Kerensky, who had to conceal his presence in various émigré centres. He was accused, along with the rest of the Provisional Government after Miliukov's resignation on 4 May 1917, of the collapse of the army and the destruction of the state. Many of the Socialist Revolutionaries were accused of aiding the Bolshevik victory by their attacks on the Whites.

The actual situation was far more complex, and SR agitation had not weakened the Whites, as many conservative theoreticians knew full well. The SRs had led many anti-Bolshevik rebellions from the rear, and thus aided the White movement. The Whites had behaved no better than the Reds, and in some cases worse, and were hated just as much by the peasantry. Thus erstwhile opponents of the 'Red Terror' fought against the 'White Terror' and there were also the so-called 'Green' or peasant risings. However, a million refugees were not analytical sociologists who could discuss the causes of events dispassionately and calmly. They were a mass of deprived people who found themselves in difficult circumstances. The natural reaction was to find someone to blame.

The Russian émigrés, like all other émigrés, considered that the main cause of evil lay in those who had expelled them from their homeland. They saw these victors as representing the forces of evil, as the product of hell and the devil. Every emigration has sought to show that their tragedy is not merely local but the result of the march of Antichrist on the world. In the 1920s, most of Europe and the so-called civilised world was permeated with ideas about the differences between races, and the characteristics of the Jews. For the Russian émigrés, the number of those of Jewish origin in the Central Committee of the Bolshevik Party seemed to add force to the accusation that the Bolshevik coup had been the work of a 'Jewish conspiracy', and anti-semitism spread rapidly.

But this explanation could not properly satisfy the emigration. A handful of bandits could hardly have overthrown a healthy nation, so the hunt continued for the devil's assistants. For the Russian émigrés this focused on the left, where one might find Jews and Freemasons, who since the time of the French Revolution had been considered the instigators of upheaval. However, Jews and Freemasons were a nebulous target so, until the objects of hatred could be identified, tangible objects of criticism were needed. The SRs served as such a target.

An SR author gave a characteristic and accurate analysis of the state of mind of Russian students in Prague.[65] He argued that the bulk of the refugees from Constantinople were remnants of the White armies. Politically, they were completely unsophisticated, but given their memories and experience of the Civil War had a tendency to sympathise with the right wing. The author argued that in addition to this mass of right-wing sympathisers there was a second type of person: whereas the majority of front-line combatants found themselves in Gallipoli, 'the rear with all its dregs, counterintelligence, special units and so on, were disembarked in Constantinople'. He claimed that it was many of these who became students and began to play an influential part in subverting SR intentions for the student body.

This article is characteristic of a number of attitudes; in particular the author hid his identity by using the initials 'A.K.' This was very rare for long articles in *Volya Rossii*. It seems likely that the author was a student who feared ostracism; subsequently, an author of vivid articles about student life signed himself 'Student'. No less telling was that this anonymous author did not dare to criticise the Gallipoli veterans, the backbone of the White fighting forces, but only attacked the dregs of the White armies. Although the majority of the emigration had not served in the armed forces, those who had were respected and attacks on them by those who had left the country a couple of years before the conflict ended were seen as unacceptable.

A.K. correctly observed that people were influenced not by clear political attitudes but by their memories and experiences. This was expressed more precisely by N.V. Bystrov, who represented the left wing of ORESO. He thought that the majority of students did not wish to join either the monarchists or the democratic groups 'preferring to be "untamed"'. These categories are made up of the so-called middle ground of the students, who in actual fact must be added to the number of conservatives.'[66] This was an accurate assessment of the situation and was the reason why he was extremely irritated by all forms of the 'apolitical'. Later Bystrov worked for the Foreign Ministry but even in 1923 he strongly opposed the apolitical line insisted on by the Czechoslovak authorities. The old Union of Russian Students, which was financed by the Czechs, had convened a congress of students with the slogan: 'All strength, all attention must be directed towards one goal – a sensible use of time for study. All political passions and discussions must be put aside.' This attitude seemed to him like a betrayal. However, this was a misrepresentation of the situation and at the time the Czechoslovak government did all in its power to neutralise political extremism.

The Czech authorities could not organise a political congress of students because both the right and the left wing would have opposed financial support for their opponents and this would have cut across purely humanitarian aims. In addition, in the circumstances described above, allowing complete freedom of political action would have led to a right-wing victory. The SRs never advocated such complete political freedom, simply political freedom for the left, with limitations on the activities open to right-wing groups, which in fact was the case in Czechoslovakia, where for instance, pro-Habsburgs propaganda was forbidden.

The Czech authorities realised the complications that would arise from support for the left wing and restrictions on the right wing, both from the point of view of influencing the emigration and, in this particular case, in relation to the academic world. They refused to support SR circles, and tried to obtain guarantees of self-limitation from those moderate conservatives and right-wing Kadets who were represented on the committee of the Student Union and on Sogor.

The SRs had no intention of backing down and, when the reformed Union of Russian Students in Czechoslovakia seemed too right-wing to them, they created an 'independent group', which on 22 March 1922 became the Russian Student Union. According to Magerovsky, by 1923 the union had very few supporters. The main union had 1,700 members and the new Russian Student Union just 120.[67] 'Student' wrote in *Volya Rossii* that the Union of Russian Students announced: 'The majority of officers have a particular psychology with particular traditions. We are a corporation.'[68] 'Student' cites one attack on the Jews and Freemasons as an example of the rampant reactionary attitude; this case reached a disciplinary tribunal. One student shouted at another: 'I murdered 15 Jews in Russia, and I can always murder another. We should have killed more of you in Russia – we ought to organise a pogrom here too.' It appeared that his friends supported this sentiment.

An example which is just as surprising occurred at the opening of the student club, Russkaya beseda which had been made possible by Rafalsky, the Russian ambassador.[69] In the presence of Kramář, Chirikov and Amfiteatrov, only eight out of 60 to 70 students were prepared to sign a message of sympathy that was to be sent to the Nabokov family after the assassination of Nabokov in Berlin. This is despite the fact that the message was to be sent to the Nabokov family not to his political colleagues, and thus was not a political gesture but one of human sympathy. During an attempt on the life of Miliukov, Nabokov had thrown himself between Miliukov and the assailant. V.D. Nabokov was a well known lawyer and politician, a member of the Kadets and father of the writer, Vladimir. He did not accept Miliukov's new tactics and in 1921 had spoken in favour of support for the army. His death shook those of all political persuasions and his murder was condemned by delegates to the monarchist congress and General Wrangel as well as by the more left-wing groups.

Such episodes created a very damning picture of student life in the Russian community in Prague, and *Volya Rossii* chose these examples only in order to protect its own reputation. The Czech press also described such incidents and even the Soviet representatives officially protested against the hounding of students with Soviet citizenship who supported the Smenovekh (Change of Landmarks) movement and who had formed their own union.

Yet despite such efforts to paint the Russian students as reactionaries, it must be emphasised that almost all these incidents occurred in the first few months after the arrival of the students in Prague. Not everyone found it easy to free themselves from the psychological strains of civil war, exacerbated by defeat, during the materially and morally difficult conditions of the first year of exile. As a result, changes in attitude occurred slowly.

But an understanding of the development of émigré views does not seem to have been widespread and French officials, at least, were ill informed.

Exactly five years after the arrival of the first students in Prague, on 26 October 1926, the French Foreign Ministry asked its ambassador in Czechoslovakia whether it was true that 'the International Association of Russian Students, which was created to maintain monarchist attitudes among Russian youth . . . was gradually accepting the ideas expressed by the leaders of the Soviet regime?'[70] France was interested in this, as 'at a moment when Soviet Russia lacked intellectual elements, it would be interesting to know whether new ideas could not be brought in by young people who had acquired a high level of political training in Europe and whose presence in the ranks of the administration and government could have a useful influence'. According to the French, ORESO was hostile not only to the monarchists, but also to the moderate left-wing attitudes represented by Miliukov and Kerensky.

A copy of this letter exists in the Czechoslovak Foreign Ministry archives, the original having been lent by the French ambassador for a day. The answer includes no reference to the letter, and simply mentions a meeting held on 22 November. It is not clear who signed it. However, a comparison of the letter and its answer, following a meeting between the ambassador and a high-ranking official of the Foreign Ministry, is of interest. In the first instance, the lack of understanding by the French of the evolving attitudes within Russian émigré society and the policy of Czechoslovakia towards them is striking. Czechoslovakia, having provided the funds to set up the student organisation ORESO, made an effort to ensure that it would be anti-Soviet, but also apolitical, and not an organisation set up to propagate the monarchist ideal. Gradually this was being put into effect. It is not at all clear why the letter refers to the monarchical parties of 'the Grand Dukes Nikolai and Aleksei' when in addition to the Grand Duke Nikolai Nikolaevich the pretender was the Grand Duke Kirill Vladimirovich. But perhaps most intriguing is the fact that the French authorities were considering whether the émigrés might be used to facilitate the evolution of Soviet power – the idea which formed the basis of the whole Russian Action. However, at the time when this might have been possible, during the famine and the formation of the NEP, no one would even consider, let alone accept, Czech policy.

In reply, the Czechs explained that the Democrats were gradually gaining support even if they were not yet in the majority. At the same time, more of the student body were interested in understanding the Soviet Union although the idea of returning (*vozvrashchenchestvo*) had very little support. The author of the document indicated that difficulties were created for returnees by the Soviet side as well, although not in equal measure for Russians and Ukrainians. 'Interested parties welcome those intellectual émigrés who wish to return to the Ukraine. This is the result of the rise of

Ukrainian nationalism and the reduction, which is clearly felt, of the number of intellectuals in that country.' In other words, the Czechs emphasised the success in reorienting students towards democratic ideas but expressed scepticism about the possibility that they would return to Russia and exercise any influence on the Soviet authorities.

This letter can be viewed as an early assessment of what had been achieved in the development of aid aimed at Russian students. The initial idea of choosing and inviting only the progressive section of the Russian emigration, those who were Democrats or SRs, turned out to be impracticable unless only an extremely small number of people were to be invited. This was in its turn undesirable, from the point of view of the government's Russian policy, the pressure being exerted by Russophile circles in Czechoslovakia and because of the French requirements to break up the army and dissolve the concentration of refugees in Constantinople. When it became clear that the initial ideas had to be modified, Lomshakov advanced the idea of accepting large numbers of students into higher educational institutions in Czechoslovakia. His proposal was supported by the National Democrats, some representatives of the agrarian parties, and also by industrialists, in particular the directors of the Škoda works, and by the professors of the Prague Polytechnic. The belief that the central figure in all this was Professor Lomshakov is supported by the fact that the first concrete proposals emanated from the Union of Russian Engineers in May 1921, which he had formed and of which he was president for many years, and also by the fact that these plans were supported by circles to which Lomshakov was linked.

Masaryk and Beneš, who were the authors of Czech foreign policy, saw the possibilities presented by this policy oriented towards students. They also appreciated Lomshakov's abilities and allowed him in effect to direct operations. Having decided against selection, the Czechoslovak authorities decided to accept the majority of Russian student émigrés. However, this policy required financial support from the French and the Allies. When this was not forthcoming, the whole enterprise was left half finished. The other condition for putting this policy into action was that it must be kept apolitical. Given that right-wing monarchical views predominated amongst the students, it was necessary to ensure that these views did not receive any further encouragement and that they should develop into an integrated system of political beliefs. Contrary to the views of the French Foreign Ministry, it became possible to prevent ORESO from becoming a hotbed of monarchism, which would undoubtedly have occurred if ORESO had been allowed to develop without interference. At the first conference of ORESO not held in Prague, there was an attempt to place the union under the patronage of the Grand Duke Nikolai Nikolaevich or at least make the union monarchist. But by this time democratic ideas were so popular that this pro-monarchist action was not successful. It is noticeable that after 1926, when Czech government aid began to decline, many student organisations moved to the right. From this one may conclude that the Czech authorities to some extent were mistaken in their idea that the White Guard students would democratise, influenced by life, study and employment in a democratic environment.

Although the general direction of development had been correctly predicted, the speed of this development was much slower than expected. This was the result not simply of the psychological effects of the Civil War, but also of new aspects, including disillusionment with democracy, which turned out to be incapable of guaranteeing employment and a reasonable standard of living for its citizens. This was not a Russian or an émigré phenomenon but a feature of the inter-war period. Émigrés suffered even more than the citizens of the countries in which they found themselves. As foreigners they were often the first to become unemployed and the instability of political systems did little to help them.

The nature of an emigration means that its development does not coincide with that of the host societies. The fundamental mistake of Russian Action in general, and in relation to the students in particular, was that both the government of Czechoslovakia and the émigrés assumed that they would be returning home after a few years. The two sides imagined this return rather differently. Most student émigrés thought that they would be returning home with unfurled military banners following a leader on a white stallion, whereas Beneš in his discussions with Soviet representatives in 1927 tried to ensure the return of the émigrés to Soviet Russia on honourable terms.

But those who had completed their education in Czechoslovakia were not able to return to Russia, nor was there any work for them in Czechoslovakia. As the country became stronger and more confident, Russian émigrés found themselves in a very difficult position. There were two realistic options to be followed: either to emigrate once again further west, or to the more reactionary society in Yugoslavia, the other border areas of the Soviet Union, Poland or the Baltic States; or to become involved and assimilated into Czech life and to remain there in the long term, a turn of events which Russian Action had tried to prevent.

One fact is very striking: in Czechoslovakia when Russian academic life was expanding, no daily Russian newspaper was being published in Prague. During 1919–21, when there were only a few hundred Russians in Prague, there were four newspapers. In the mid-1920s when there were more than 20,000 Russians in Prague, there was not a single newspaper published for the Russian colony there. *Volya Rossii* aimed at a wider audience than Prague. When the number of émigrés declined, newspapers appeared once again. This was not true of other centres of emigration. Newspapers

appeared as soon as a group of Russians settled anywhere, even if there were
no trained journalists among them. Many of these publishing ventures met
an untimely demise owing to lack of funds; nevertheless, they were always
followed by new attempts to form a Russian press. There was always a
demand for a Russian paper, even if it was not enough to keep the
publication going for long. This was one of the basic ways in which émigrés
tried to keep in touch and maintain their identity as Russians in
unfavourable and alien surroundings. Why then was there no newspaper in
Prague? The most obvious answer is that there was no sense of an immigrant
community. Prague had created a working atmosphere in which people
were preparing themselves for a return home to Russia. Thus the
eventual failure of these aspirations was felt more acutely.

This disillusionment led to a reaction against those ideas which had
formed the basis of Russian Action, and also against the system which had
tried to put them into practice. That the White struggle had been delayed,
if not totally rejected, began to seem like a mistake. It began to seem that
the years of study had been wasted. Their knowledge was not needed. New
polarisations emerged within the emigration, and democratic ideas were
increasingly rejected. This brought about the rise of right-wing totalitarian
elements and, to a much lesser degree, left-wing pro-Soviet sympathies.
Against this background, one can see that the success of the democratic
section, which had been the aim of Russian Action, was still significant.

One must conclude that Russian Action had been the result of a range of
ideas and policies that had been brought into a more orderly system by
Czech statesmen. It was not founded on dogmatism, but assessed social,
psychological and even personal factors. Its humanitarian programme was
planned to last for several years, at the end of which the Russians would be
able to return home. No contingency plans were made in the event that this
should prove impossible. Consequently, the aims of this policy were never
achieved. For many of the scholars involved in the expansion and
development of Russian life in Prague, these five years were wasted in the
sense that their colleagues who had been trying to become accepted into the
academic world of other societies were well ahead in the game, even if
initially it had been even more difficult for them. For others, it was a very
valuable experience which allowed them to escape the horrors of evacuation
and refugee existence and to reassess and reorient their efforts.

The SRs Do Not Give Up

With a certain amount of excitement and anxiety the Russian colony in
Prague awaited the inauguration of the Russian Law Faculty in Prague, on

18 May 1922. The names of the staff were known; students had registered. Many hoped that this was the first step towards founding a full-scale Russian university abroad.

The SRs did not join in the general celebrations. The attitudes of the staff and students did not allow them to hope that the Law Faculty would be an exponent of the ideas of democratic socialism which were being developed in SR circles, especially by the party leader V.M. Chernov. The SRs feared that monarchist ideas or, worse, those of the 'Black Hundreds' would be expressed in the faculty. They also realised that they had lost the battle for influence over the Russian academic community in Prague.

Two weeks before the opening of the faculty, V. Vasiliev published an article in *Volya Rossii* entitled 'The Professional and Technical Education of Russian Refugees in Czechoslovakia'. In it he asserted: 'There is evidence to support the view that many of those refugees now trying to acquire higher education would prefer professional and technical training if the possibility arose. And this, perhaps, would not only be better for the refugees themselves, but would also suit the states concerned – Russia and Czechoslovakia.'[71] However, in 1922 most Russians still saw themselves as exiles due to return home in the near future and those institutions which offered technical training of this nature, such as the Russian School of Automobiles and Tractors,[72] were not particularly popular. For the most part such employment meant moving still further away, with individuals becoming isolated from Russian communities. Vasiliev's comments would apply when they assimilated into their host societies and became immigrants rather than political exiles.

The other hindrance from the point of view of the SRs, who aimed to educate not only specialists but also those active in social spheres, was the practical nature of such training, which limited the possibility of political influence. However, the fact that these schools were founded by the Zemgor and financed by the government meant that some opportunities for such influence did exist. In trying to exert influence they inevitably came into conflict with the right. The SRs did not have enough members to provide all the teaching and training staff and had to co-operate with those of other views and opinions. This was not easy, as the SRs' political interests took precedence over everything else. When the SRs were faced by opposition, in order to keep their influential position they began to argue that the émigrés were bored with politics, and that they were largely occupied with survival and the need for stability so that the future would be less uncertain. While this became true eventually, the SRs began to express such ideas several years before they were commonly accepted. The combination of their political attitudes and their refusal to countenance a campaign to restore Russia, contrasted strongly with the so-called apolitical attitudes of the more conservative émigrés who tried to preserve existing views and who resolved to return and work to help Russia. Up to the mid–1920s, such views predominated amongst the Russians in Prague.

Conflict was therefore inevitable and was not favourable to the SRs. They set up the Railway Training School, after the founding of the Russian Law Faculty, as the first part of a practical programme of training. It was established in December 1922 by the Zemgor, with the agreement of the Union of Engineers, led by Lomshakov. The following year it became the School of Transport. Members of the engineering union quickly became involved in the practical side. A unique body was formed: the inspection committee, which with the director, the academic council and the inspection council, made sure that resources were used properly. This Inspection Committee, created with parity of members between the Zemgor and the union, had one aim: 'to make sure that the interests of the union and the Zemgor coincide, while dealing with the day to day running of the School and removing any friction between the various bodies running the Training School'.[73] SR political influence was undoubtedly limited by such a policy.

The conflict between the SR organisers of the Russian refugees in Czechoslovakia and those academics and scholars who were determined to build on the foundations provided by Czech aid, can be seen clearly in the history of the Russian People's University (Narodny Universitet) in Prague. This was also organised by the Zemgor. In 1952 M.M. Novikov, the Principal of the university throughout its existence, published his memoirs. Like all such recollections, these are subjective and sometimes make mistakes in the detail, but they give a vivid impression of the atmosphere and of the arguments between the SRs and the academic side. The SRs who had arrived in Czechoslovakia with the Czech legions from Siberia, after Kolchak's coup in Omsk, were those who had 'struggled against right and left'. The academics were the liberal professors who had been invited by Lomshakov and Van-der-Flit, who were active in the Union of Russian Professors. These were P.B. Struve and P.I. Novgorodtsev, principal of the Russian Law Faculty, who had both been honorary members of the Gallipoli Veterans, and left wing in Imperial Russia although they now supported the Whites. Novgorodtsev was able to involve specialists who would not have agreed to work for an SR clique. However some, such as Academician N.P. Kondakov, never forgave Novgorodtsev for making this compromise. The arguments were probably not so much caused by fundamental disagreement over political ideas as by socio-psychological differences, which determined how they aimed to reach their goals. Psychological incompatibility, frequently a result of difference in experience, then became ideological conflict. M.M. Novikov recalls, 'our right wing colleagues, of course, could not collaborate with a socialist organisation, even on matters of an educational character'.[74] This was quite unlike Shanyavsky's People's University where, according to Kizevetter, 'Octobrists, Kadets, SRs and SDs [Social Democrats] all worked closely together'.[75]

It is not clear where the idea of creating the Russian People's University originated. Its name and development in the last years of its existence are sufficiently muddled to confuse most scholars. Modelled on Shanyavsky's People's University, it was intended to provide adult education of a type similar to that offered by British university extension courses or German *Volkshochschule*. In Imperial Russia, Shanyavsky's People's University was slightly more professional than its Western counterparts, but did not become a real university producing a complete higher education. Its staff were more highly qualified than the norm, as they included a number who left Moscow University in 1911 in protest against the limiting of academic freedom.[76]

The SRs saw the value of this kind of institution for the émigrés in that it would allow some sort of systematic education of deprived groups in a society, and the Zemgor organised it but did not have enough properly qualified staff. There were great difficulties emanating from the left in the Zemgor. 'Members of the Zemgor wished to run everything themselves so that the academic side were simply the executive of their wishes. We were well acquainted with such a tactic. It was tried repeatedly by the Tsarist government, and then was brought to completely grotesque levels by the Communist government,' wrote Novikov bitterly. After lengthy discussions an agreement was reached according to which the academic side would be run by the academic staff with representatives of the Zemgor, and the practical aspects would remain within the purview of the Zemgor, and this included the financial side. The university was opened on 16 October 1923 with Novikov as chairman of the Council. Novgorodtsev and Kizevetter were his deputies. Of the staff, somewhere between 70 and 80 were also employed by other institutions which provided them with their main source of income.

Difficulties continued. P.D. Klimushkin, who was appointed 'Director' by the Zemgor, tried to interfere in the academic side, using his financial powers to do so, and told Academician Struve, the philosopher, economist and politician, and Professor Lossky, a philosopher of international standing, to lecture on a more popular level. Once, when it was suggested that he was taking his powers too far, he replied that he understood his 'autonomy more widely'. Novikov commented that this was typical both of Klimushkin's educational level and of Zemgor policy.

Finally, the Society of the People's University was given legal standing in

1925 and government subsidies went to it directly, despite opposition from the Zemgor. The Ministry of Foreign Affairs, which had good relations with the Zemgor, nevertheless allowed businesslike people, organisers and specialists to get on with their work, rather than giving preference to politicians. The Russians were also helped by their Czech colleagues, particularly Professor Zdeněk Bažant, who rather like some other key individuals has fallen out of the history of the emigration even though he tried to help the families of colleagues who were arrested and taken to the Soviet Union in 1945.

Once the Zemgor was sidelined in its attempts to influence the People's University, it increasingly became simply a refugee organisation and had fewer links with the Russian academic community in Prague. But it would be unjust not to recognise the valuable role played by the Zemgor in alleviating some of the problems exprienced by Russian refugees. They may have lost the battle for ultimate control and did not manage to turn Russian Prague into their base but they still played a leading role in the very active cultural and academic life of Prague in the 1920s.

In Russian academic life in Prague, criticism and intrigue surrounded Novgorodtsev. In his recollections of Lomshakov, P.N. Savitsky wrote:

> One of the most major intrigues unfolded in 1923 and was directed against one of the founders and creators of the Russian Action in Prague, P.I. Novgorodtsev. Several members of the Russian Academic Group in Prague considered P.I. Novgorodtsev, who had done so many good things, too 'left-wing' and decided it was necessary to remove him from posts which he held with A.S. Lomshakov at the head of most academic organisations in Prague. Since Novgorodtsev died in 1924, Lomshakov did not have time to neutralise all these attacks, but he played no part in them, just as he was not involved in all such activities.[77]

Other sources, such as the diaries of Academician N.P. Kondakov, the elder of academic society in Prague, who would not agree to sit at the same table as Novgorodtsev, seem to indicate that all of this happened because Novgorodtsev did a deal with the Zemgor.

The politics of the Russian Civil War permeated every aspect of Russian émigré life and explained many of the allegiances as well as enmities within the academic world. It is, therefore, an interesting paradox that as the policy of creating a Russian academic centre in Prague was developed, existing preconceptions altered. Both the Czech government and individuals like Lomshakov appear to have been motivated more by practical considerations than by ideology. As a result the Socialist Revolutionaries, through the agency of the Zemgor, were far less powerful than has frequently been supposed and were unable either to select like-minded refugees to come to Prague or to influence the mass of the student body once they had arrived.

Chapter 3

The Russian Academic World in Prague

I could not genuinely appreciate Prague: it seemed to
me to be nobler than Berlin and more out of the way.
Berberova, *The Italics Are Mine. An Autobiography*

A Russian academic centre in Prague was initially envisaged as a place where
Russian refugees could complete their studies and refresh their skills and
knowledge. After a short interlude of study abroad these students would
return to Russia to work in the new Soviet state which was so short of the
educated élite it required to run the country. As this vision receded, so the
Russian community needed to adapt to changed circumstances. The wish to
acquire skills for Russia had to give way to the need to earn a living in Europe.
At the same time Russians needed to preserve their own culture not only for
their children and a future Russia but also for themselves, so that their identity
did not become totally lost in an alien environment. The story of the Russian
Law Faculty in Prague is highly symbolic of the problem faced by the Russian
academic world and by the wider émigré community. It was created with a
very specific aim in view and when this turned out to be impracticable, it had
to close. In many ways this signalled the end of the heyday of the Russian
Action in Prague. But other institutions continued their work and the Russian
archive abroad (RZIA) which has been rediscovered has achieved renewed
scholarly importance. Some institutions such as the Kondakov Institute were
founded after the high point of academic activity in Prague, but still managed
to acquire an international scholarly reputation. Lastly, Prague was closely
associated with the ideas of Eurasianism which have attracted renewed interest
in Russia since the late 1990s.

Formation of the Russian Academic Centre

Despite all the aid for Russian refugees, the attitude of many émigrés to
Czechoslovakia was ambivalent. N.N. Alekseev, an expert in constitutional

law, was invited to form and develop the Russian academic centre in Prague. His comments illustrate the complexity of the situation in which academics found themselves.

At last I have moved from Asiatic to European countries. I have moved to Prague, where I have been invited to fill one of the so-called 'free vacancies' for Russian professors, and as one humorist puts it, I have got a place in an almshouse with a pension attached. (It is an almshouse in the full sense of the word, as hitherto we have been living there and it is the Czech word for almshouse.) I can't say that the impressions of Czechoslovakia have been totally comforting. I am not referring to the fact that all the undertakings here do not seem at all durable – one could come to terms with that as nothing in life is durable now. I am alarmed by the dreadful boredom and poverty of life here, its unbelievable parochialism and patriarchy. I do not feel at home in the society in which I find myself, and which I am no longer used to – the velvety baritone of Pavel Ivanovich [Novgorodtsev], the academic gossip and intrigues, the charming wives, in other words all the nonsense which I used to avoid in Moscow, but cannot avoid here. Given my first impressions, one would like to be able to view Prague simply as a temporary stage . . . I find Berlin very attractive and given the opportunity I would willingly exchange Prague for it.[1]

Alekseev saw things very differently from those who had no other options and simply ended up in Czechoslovakia. His succinct letter is an accurate reflection of the doubts which assailed academics in Prague, which they saw as a temporary location for émigré activity. Unlike those working on the land, for instance, for whom it quickly became clear that Czech agriculture was more advanced, Russian scholars were justified in thinking that the old Russian cultural centres, although too few for a large empire, were nevertheless more productive and fruitful than provincial Prague had been in recent times. Berlin, Paris, Vienna and even Oxford, not to speak of the wealthier cities in the United States of America, were all worthy competitors to Prague

Prisoners of war had only one question to decide: should they return to the motherland, to their families and the places they knew and cared for, where everyone spoke an understandable language, or should they stay abroad, where they would be foreigners but where it was more cultured, in general the economic conditions were much better and where indisputably it was much safer. For those who were invited or who arrived in an organised way, the reactions were different: they were concerned much less with making comparisons with conditions at home, or with conditions when they left Russia, than with their expectations of Czechoslovakia. These expectations were complex. If there was a shared experience of exile and desire to return home, this was modified not only by the changing policies of the Czech government towards the emigration, but also by the evolution of the Soviet Union, which seemed stronger and more stable than many émigrés had assumed. As the likelihood of a speedy return home gradually disappeared, the émigrés were forced to adapt to the possibility of a protracted stay abroad, and began to see themselves and to behave more as immigrants than as exiles. This too was not a straightforward evolution and was influenced not only by economic necessity but also by the political divisions both within the emigration and by the politics of their host societies. Humanitarian needs and educational aspirations often cut across political divides and these currents can be traced in the attempts to create a Russian academic centre in Prague.

Alekseev's remarks help to clarify the thought processes of many Russian intellectuals in their decision to accept or reject the proposals of the Czechoslovak government which, given the conditions of émigré existence, were most attractive. In order to evaluate Prague as an émigré centre and to understand the dynamics of the Russian emigration, one must not only consider those who lived and worked in Prague, but also examine the question of who was invited but never arrived. S.L. Frank, the philosopher, did not respond to Struve's invitation to come to Prague, partly because of increasing tension between them.[2] Struve had moved to Prague in 1922 in order to teach at the Law Faculty. I.A. Il'in, another philosopher, 'refused the attractive invitation to come to Prague' and started to give lectures in Berlin. Although in material terms conditions were not as good, Berlin was a world centre for academic philosophy. P.A. Sorokin, a sociologist, left Prague after a year although his conditions of work were extremely favourable. Amongst other leading academic figures P.B. Struve and G.D. Gurvich, a philosopher, jurist and sociologist, left Prague as early as 1925, when Russian academic life was flourishing. Alekseev's letter demonstrates the kinds of question asked by the Russian intellectual élite as they tried to decide where they should go.

The first requirement was stability. After three or four years of constant travel – from Petrograd to Moscow, from Moscow to the Don or Samara, from there to Odessa or Tomsk, and then on to the Crimea or Harbin and after that Gallipoli, Constantinople or even Yokohama – even a few years of peaceful work was valuable. For, as the émigrés said, misquoting one of Lermontov's poems: 'Flight for a time is not worth the effort, and flight for eternity is impossible.'

However, whether Prague was a stable environment was questioned by many from the outset, and others felt the sands shifting even before the first signals to wind up Russian Action were given. Those who were well informed knew that this would be the case as early as a year after the opening of the Law Faculty, which many had hoped would be the heart of a proper Russian university.

V.A. Frantsev was a Russian scholar who was a Czech specialist and a corresponding member of the Royal Czech Academy of Sciences from 1901. He became a full member of the academy in 1904 and was invited to become a professor in Charles University in 1919. He was thus in a strong position in Prague. He wrote to his friend Ikonnikov in Kiev in July 1923: 'It is sad that Vera Ivanovna [his wife] is finding life hard. Her hope is to find a better position for us, but I am convinced that this has no foundation. I am well aware of how things stand here, and that my judgement is correct.'[3]

On the other hand, Prague had many attractions. It was seen as a cultural and academic centre. To those coming from Constantinople, Sofia or Belgrade, Prague seemed to be a European city and Asia was left behind. This feeling was expressed by N.S. Trubetskoy, the linguist and leading member of the Eurasian movement, in a letter to Petrovsky of 3 August 1922. Describing his travels in Bulgaria and Yugoslavia where he sought some kind of fairly durable haven, and writing of his journeys 'through Central Europe, sniffing the air and looking for somewhere to shelter', he states that he had considered Vienna. 'It seemed very attractive to live in a proper cultural centre, with a wonderful library and with a scholarly environment.'[4]

The first and most important condition for the creation of a cultural centre was the existence of sufficiently large libraries. There were many émigré complaints from Sofia and Belgrade about the lack of one or other fundamental work in various areas of knowledge. In respect of libraries, Prague represented an almost ideal city which fell just a little short of the really large centres such as Berlin, Paris or London. Furthermore, it was possible to get access to literature which had been published in Soviet Russia. Some of this literature could be obtained in Yugoslavia with difficulty whereas in Paris it was almost impossible to find these publications. Many Russians, however, were put off by the seemingly provincial nature of Czechoslovakia. One can illustrate this with the chance remark of S. L. Frank, who in his memoirs wrote that in the autumn of 1924 he arrived for a conference of Russian–Christian youth in the suburbs close to Prague. The conference in fact was taking place in Přerov in Moravia, about 200 kilometres from Prague as the crow flies, which was considered a very distant province. For people who were used to Russian distances and to travelling to their dachas or visiting their estates, which could be 1,000 kilometres away, this was incomprehensible.

Provincialism was not simply a question of geographical distance but was reflected in intellectual life as well. Despite the gradual de-provincialisation of Czech national life, the desire for national independence and for national self-determination led to a kind of introversion, a tendency strengthened by the creation of an independent state. Czech scholars who had had to make their careers in Vienna, when Bohemia had been part of the Austro-Hungarian empire, returned to an independent Czechoslovakia and were regarded with suspicion. Czech–German relations got much worse. In Prague where there was a German university which depended on the support not only of German national groups but also of the German-speaking Jewish intelligentsia, conflicts were rarer and as a rule not as dramatic as those in the German areas along the frontiers of Czechoslovakia. Nevertheless, co-operation between the Czech and German universities in the early years of the First Republic was unthinkable.

All of this made it more difficult for members of the Russian intelligentsia to enter Prague cultural life. Professor M.M. Novikov, who had been Vice-Chancellor of the Russian People's University for 15 years and who had been energetic in promoting Russo–Czech co-operation, wrote much later that 'the most difficult part of the Czech character was its extreme national-ism, which developed markedly amongst the middle classes and sometimes amongst the intelligentsia'.[5] Arguably, this was a mistaken assessment. Czech nationalism was not unusual or particularly virulent. National feeling rather than any organised ideology of nationalism by and large dictated the Czechs' actions and reactions in a given situation. For example in 1913 almost no one was thinking about the creation of an independent Czech state. In 1938 no one thought about the post-war deportation of the German minority in Czechoslovakia. In both cases the Czechs reacted to events which they had not brought about and were anxious to protect their interests. This did not mean that xenophobia did not exist but Czech nationalism did not get in the way of attempts by the Russian emigration to co-operate with Czech society.

In the academic world there were other factors which created difficulties. Rather than too few members of the intelligentsia in Czechoslovakia there were too many. During the existence of the Austro-Hungarian empire many Czechs as well as those of German origin had careers in the Austrian part of the Habsburg monarchy. Now this option was closed to them. The creation of new universities in Brno and Bratislava did not mean that foreigners had to be invited, as the pool of indigenous specialists was quite sufficient. This was in stark contrast to the situation in Yugoslavia or Bulgaria where there were far more academic jobs for Russian émigrés. The arrival in Czechoslovakia of more than 100 lecturers from Russian institutions of higher education represented dangerous competition. Amongst the newly arrived Russians were a number who had an international academic reputation. In many documents and memoirs of the time there is a stress on the need for self-restraint by these Russians. Even in the creation of Russo–Czech institutions, for example the Russian People's University, or in various joint publications there was a constantly repeated request not to upset the Czechs.

As Professor Novikov intimated, the attempts at joint action between the eastern and western Slavs created serious difficulties; not simply because the Czechs did not want competition but also because of the different outlooks of the two nations. Furthermore, the attitudes of the Russians were not straightforward. As Trubetskoy noted:

> the attitudes of the Russian émigrés to those amongst whom they live is on the outside not only very respectful but often extremely enthusiastic. However, when they discuss these same foreigners amongst themselves then it turns out that they are lower species worthy of contempt. Whereas for the older generation this is fairly clear . . . among the younger Russian émigrés you can already see the growing complexity of these psychological processes; complexities which remind one of the psychology of Jewish members of the intelligentsia. On the one hand they are almost ashamed of being Russian, on the other hand they almost are proud of it. On the one hand they happily want to be the same as everyone else and to assimilate themselves into the surrounding society. On the other hand they are repelled by this society and despise it.[6]

When reading Trubetskoy's article it must be remembered that this characterisation of the Russian emigration appeared in a piece about racism which was directed against the Nazi anti-Semitism that had been used to attract Russian and Ukrainian émigrés to the National Socialist standard in Germany. In addition, definitions of the older and younger generations must be combined with an understanding of their different levels of education. Nevertheless Trubetskoy catches the essence of the situation: i.e. one would be naïve to think that the Czechs did not realise the lack of sincerity of some of the compliments paid to them and that they disliked the superiority shown by many of the Russians in their midst.

Further to this basic nationalistic feeling, intellectual approaches and values differed. Since the beginning of the twentieth century in Russia there had been a gradual evolution in intellectual fashion amongst the leading members of the intelligentsia from Marxism towards idealism, as can be seen in the change of outlook of such people as Father Sergei Bulgakov or the philosopher Nicholas Berdiaev. This idealism developed into a more general religious outlook and then, under the influence of war, revolution and exile, to an affirmation of the positive aspects of the Eastern Orthodox faith. This meant that many members of the intelligentsia abandoned not only Marxism but also positivism, economism, liberalism, and many of the other dominant intellectual ideas of the second half of the nineteenth century.

In Czechoslovakia on the other hand, the complete opposite could be observed. The collapse of the Austro-Hungarian empire led to a massive departure from the Catholic Church which had been closely associated with the 300-year-old Habsburg yoke. Some Slavophiles hoped that this would end in a return to the Orthodox Church, which in their opinion had retained the purity of the traditions of the early Apostolic Church. This did not occur, and there was no religious revival or return to religious consciousness. An important part of those who left the Catholic Church declared themselves to be atheists and others formed a Czechoslovak Church, which was concerned less with matters of dogma than with national problems.

Sergei Levitsky, a philosopher, recalled an episode which illustrated this mutual incomprehension:

> My university teacher, the Czech professor Kozak [a positivist], during a lecture recommended various new books and mentioned Lossky, adding that we should not read him since he used intuition and was a mystic, which had no part in serious academic philosophy. When I tried to defend Lossky, Kozak rebuked me and advised me to keep my Russian, reactionary, befuddled, philosophical musings to myself.[7]

Such disagreements were not the result of national differences but simply of the varying trends in intellectual fashion.

To begin with, the Russian lecturers and professors in Czech institutions attracted huge audiences but these left fairly quickly when they found they did not understand academic terms. Attempts to deliver lectures in French were equally unsuccessful, as few Czechs knew French well. As a result it became necessary to lecture in Czech but the similarities between Czech and Russian made the question of learning the language accurately very difficult, particularly for people who were no longer young. The average age of most university lecturers was about 50. Some of the grammatical errors in the lectures delivered in Czech by Russian scholars were widely repeated as jokes. Such difficulties were much less acute in technical areas. There were thousands of Czech soldiers who had fought in the Czech legion in Russia and tens of thousands of prisoners of war who had spent several years in Russia. Thousands of Russian-Czechs had decided to return to Czechoslovakia after the Revolution as well as hundreds of people occupied in business and specialists in various areas who had worked with Russians before the war. Here people used both languages freely.

In the academic area in general and particularly amongst Slavists and historians, various Slav disputes were taken much more to heart. In the nineteenth century the growth of Russophile feelings among the Czechs had been followed by periods of disillusionment, especially after the crushing of the Polish rising in 1863. By the 1920s it had become very difficult to be pan-Slav owing to the number of inter-Slav conflicts; in addition to the Russo–Polish conflict, there was the question of Russian–Ukrainian as well as Ukrainian–Polish relations and Serb–Bulgarian relations. At certain points the Ukrainian émigré community in Czechoslovakia was as large as the Russian one and this tended to make relations between them more stressful. The government made efforts to lessen the conflict between these groups and to make them agree on federal lines but these successes were short-lived. Such types of national feelings meant that both Russian and Ukrainian academic life were fairly isolated in Czechoslovakia. This in turn led to the creation of a more or less autonomous structure of schools, cultural and academic institutions.

The attitudes of the Czech authorities contrasted with the activities of those SRs who were active in the Zemgor and who wished to influence the émigrés for their own ends. The SRs were much more likely to indulge in tactical changes. After the arrival of the mass of students, the SRs began to put more stress on refugee attitudes whereas at the outset they had completely ignored émigré life. Gradually the SRs realised that they had to deal with ideas completely different from the committed revolutionary attitudes they had previously experienced. It was no longer a question of a small, ideologically committed élite but rather of a mass emigration where the majority had been forced to leave their country in order to save their own lives. Unexpectedly for the SRs, moreover, the emigration was for the most part 'counter-revolutionary', in that those who left had fought in the ranks of the White Armies and had left with those armies.

The SRs quickly began to understand that this was not so much a committed intellectual position as the result of what the people had lived through: for them the only conceivable return home was by military force with their leader on a white horse. These people had to be given a rest and could not be drawn into politics too quickly. The émigrés had to be allowed to become involved in the day-to-day processes of refugee life, as this would help to calm the emotional impact of the Civil War. Living in a democratic Czechoslovakia would persuade them of the positive aspects of a democratic order. It was essential to convince them that their dream of a new military intervention in alliance with one or other of the Great Powers was extremely unlikely to materialise. Therefore the SRs tried not to discuss a return to Russia but preferred to address the possibilities of employment abroad. It fell to the Czech government to remind the émigrés that study and training in Czechoslovakia were just a preparation for their work in Russia, that they had a patriotic duty to their own country, and that the Czechs did not wish to and could not accept the émigrés permanently.

Russian academic life was built on altogether different assumptions. Both the Czech authorities and the Russian organisers agreed from the beginning that this academic world should not simply be Russian academics in exile. Members of the academic community had to refrain from political activity and, therefore, from any attempts to overthrow the Soviet authorities. But neither could it be an immigrant organisation, because the graduates of the Russian academic institutions in Czechoslovakia must not consider that they were bound to get work there. Russian students had to see themselves as students of a foreign country or of an institution abroad and realise that once they had finished their education they would return home. Initially the newly arrived students enrolled in Czech institutions but the number of these Russians increased rapidly. On 1 October 1921 the Committee for the Provision of Education to Russian Students had 61 students on its books, who were already living in Prague, while by January 1922 there were 1,319 students.[8]

Russian Academic Institutions in Prague

As we have mentioned, one of the most useful sources on the history of Russian Prague is Postnikov's volume *Russkie v Prage*.[9] This not only provides a description of a whole range of institutions and activities but is also an indication of the way in which these émigré enterprises were changing. Postnikov's collection of reports on various institutions was published in 1928 to commemorate the tenth anniversary of the founding of the Czech Republic. During these ten years the Russian émigrés had moved no nearer to their desired goal of a return home and the nature of the emigration had changed. Regardless of their wishes, the émigrés had to settle down, earn a living and assimilate: increasingly they were becoming part of the labour market and less of a political factor in the foreign policies of their host societies.

The Russian emigration was no exception to the general rule in the histories of various emigrations, that wars help to maintain the original identity of the emigration. Other examples are the Czech Protestant refugees during the Thirty Years' War or the German anti-Fascists during the Second World War. Postnikov's publication has to be understood in this context. After ten years in Prague, although the émigrés still considered themselves political exiles it was becoming increasingly necessary to emphasise their achievements there. Postnikov tried to stress that he was concerned with the first ten years of the Czech Republic rather than in producing a conclusion to ten years of the Russian emigration. To make his volume seem more scholarly and objective, he invited the non-political Russian institutions in Prague to submit reports on their activities. Reading the rather dry prose, it is nonetheless clear that two very different attitudes were represented. Some authors of the reports thought of their activities as a continuing living entity, although they would conclude with the statement that the institute had been forced to close. Others saw their task as the production of an obituary on a project or institution which, although still in existence, was clearly doomed to closure. Postnikov's work is a unique and valuable source. Despite the attempts to produce a scholarly and unbiased document, it was written on the basis of raw emotions.

The recent work of the academic bibliographers of the Slavonic Library in Prague is an equally interesting publication although it is written in a completely different way.[10] The authors examine more than 5,000 known books, series and periodicals of the Russian and Ukrainian emigrations, which were published in Czechoslovakia between 1918 and 1945. In addition to the material provided by organisations and publishers, the authors have added both secondary and archival information. This reveals in great detail the complicated net of frequently unexpected interconnections within the emigration.

Russian Universities

A very modest beginning to the Russian academic centre in Prague was the creation of the 'higher supplementary Russian educational courses', which added Russian law and history to the programme of the Czech universities in Russian subjects. These courses tended to be very general.[11] This attempt to use existing resources was never fully developed,[12] as the Union of Russian Professors quite rapidly received permission to invite Russian scholars to Prague to continue their research and to teach. The creation of a Russian university seemed to be a real possibility.

THE RUSSIAN LAW FACULTY

On 18 May 1922 the idea of creating a Russian university began to be put into practice. The management of the Union of Russian Academic Organisations Abroad created a constitution for the Russian Law Faculty based on the general constitution of Russian universities in the form that had operated until the October Revolution. It was headed by the tireless Professor Lomshakov and the administration of the Law Faculty was organised by Professor Novgorodtsev. It was characteristic of both that neither paid any attention to the political disagreements amongst staff and students and concentrated on the academic questions. As a result, both were vigorously attacked and criticised but, as this opposition was not united and the staff and students represented a wide variety of opinion, Lomshakov and Novgorodtsev's efforts met with success. They managed to bring together people of very divergent outlooks in the one aim of educating future Russian administrators and lawyers. Unfortunately, Novgorodtsev died before he could be sure that people were prepared to co-operate in this project.

This concept of higher idealism, of devoting oneself to the cause of creating the educated élite which Russia would need in future, was an aim that united both the organisers of the Russian academic community and the Czech government. But in many ways, to work for and achieve this aim, those involved had to be prepared to be rather isolated from Czech society. Nowhere was this more evident than in the study of law.

At the opening of the Russian Law Faculty, Lomshakov observed that in the areas of technical education, science and philology Russian students could be educated either in Soviet Russia or in the West. For Russian student lawyers this was not the case, as the law was only partly inter-national: the larger and more important section of the subject was national. Education in foreign law faculties could widen horizons, but could not replace the teaching of the Russian Law Faculty. But this was a two-edged sword. Because the education available in the Russian Law Faculty in Prague had to be based on national needs and concepts, it could not be seen as equal to the education provided by the legal faculties of the Czech and German universities in Prague; its qualifications were not recognised anywhere else. The organisers understood this. Speaking after Lomshakov at the opening ceremony, Novgorodtsev said:

> We are starting this venture in very confused circumstances and in the face of an unknown future and it demands first of all definite, calm and sure leadership, making great efforts and having great faith in Russia. One of the students enrolling here answered my question as to why he had chosen the law with the comment: 'I believe in Russia.' That is correct. The creation of the Russian Law Faculty is based on belief in Russia, on the belief in her future and on the belief in the rule of law.[13]

This was the basic distinction between the Russian Law Faculty and earlier academic institutions. Despite avowals from both the Russian and the

Czech side that they were creating these institutions for the strengthening of Slav unity, the assumption was that this would not occur immediately but after a return to Russia. This ushered in a period of about four years which saw considerable isolation of the émigrés from Czech society.

The Law Faculty began its work with 13 professors and academic teachers and 255 students. The spring of 1924 saw the high point of the Law Faculty, with 488 students. There were a number of well known scholars on the staff, including the Academician P.B. Struve, Professor M.M. Katkov, and Professor E.V. Spektorsky, a specialist on the seventeenth century and the history and philosophy of law. G.V. Vernadsky, a young historian, taught in the faculty and among the more junior lecturers were G.D. Gurvich,who achieved an international reputation a little later as a French sociologist, Father G.V. Florovsky who later wrote *The Paths of Russian Theology*, and P.N. Savitsky, one of the founders of Eurasianism.

But the death of Novgorodtsev in 1924 meant that a notable figure in Russian law and university life was lost. He was succeeded by D.D. Grimm, a specialist in Roman law and one-time Rector (i.e. Vice-Chancellor) of Petrograd University. In 1924 Gurvich was given a year's leave to prepare his dissertation and left for Berlin. After that the list of those leaving reads like a roll-call. During the academic year 1925–26, Academician Struve, Father Sergei Bulgakov, Florovosky and the lecturer Zaitsev left for Paris. A.A. Chuprov died aged 52 and Ya.D. Sadovsky, destined for a professorship, died aged 33 from tuberculosis. Then Grimm left for the University of Tartu, A.V. Makletsov was invited to Lublin, and Vernadsky left for Yale. In 1925 the number of students accepted dropped to 54, and in 1926 ceased altogether.

The teachers at the Law Faculty were not only lecturers but were also involved in the publication of lectures and textbooks. Prague had few Russian textbooks in its libraries. The position was gradually being rectified, but even so there were not the quantities of books that students required. In the course of five years the Russian Law Faculty produced law text books of which well over half were new texts by the academic staff. Further publications were published by the YMCA press. These publications were not easy to produce but in the conditions in Prague formed an important part of academic life.

During this period there was a marked change in outlook of the students who, through bitter experience, began to realise that they would not be returning home immediately and had to see themselves as immigrants rather than as political exiles. This was vividly illustrated by the self-imposed levy to pay the publication costs of texts needed for their courses. In 1923–24, the students raised 45 per cent of the costs, in 1925–26 this fell to less than 5 per cent and in the following year it ceased altogether. The tiny amounts of money that the students had at their disposal went into a new fund which was intended to support the graduates during the almost inevitable unemployment after they graduated. The fifth anniversary of the founding of the Law Faculty was more like a kind of wake and the Vice-Chancellor, who had already packed his bags, as he was leaving in June, finished his speech with the words: 'We have done everything that we could. Let Russia judge us.'[14]

The feeling of decline did not simply apply to the Russian Law Faculty but could be sensed in relation to all the attempts to create a Russian academic centre in Prague. The decline was clear to many although the process of deterioration was not uniform.

The Russian People's University

The Russian People's University played an important role in émigré life but its position in the history of the Russian emigration is still unclear. There were no émigré universities in the accepted sense of the word – that is, educational institutions accepting students. No proper Russian university ever existed. People dreamed of creating such an institution but they were only able to create the law faculty. Moreover, the People's University did not have any students and there was no pool of people from which students could be taken. In Russian Prague and also to some extent in Brno and Bratislava, émigrés were given the chance of a complete education in local schools and therefore the idea of an extension course lost some of its immediacy. By the second year of its existence, the director, Novikov, admitted that the Russian People's University needed to be organised differently: 'If one goes on with courses for too long the very quickly changing audience . . . drops in numbers and alters in character.' [15]

The university had to adapt to circumstances and it did this in radical ways. The original idea of having something similar to extension courses did not work out because, although Prague was almost the only place where courses could be organised, owing to the concentration of teachers and possible students, these courses did not live up to expectations. Trying to turn the courses into individual lectures or mini-courses in Prague did not produce the hoped-for results either. However, the concerts and, from the second year of the university's existence, the literary historical evenings were most successful. The concerts and evenings were devoted to individual Russian and later Czech composers, or to individual writers. They began with a talk from a specialist, then the composer's music was played or there were readings of the author to whom the evening was devoted. Frequently these kinds of evening attracted an audience of between 200 and 450, and they were the only part of the university which was financially self-supporting. Their popularity was helped by the presence of very gifted musicians in Prague, often Czech as well as Russian. Such evenings showed that the émigrés required an emotional expression of their feelings for their motherland rather than a practical link.

Prague was almost too full of Russian links and reminders. These sentimental symbols were often more important than membership of Russian educational institutions. Russian halls of residence were open to Russian and Czech students. There was a wide range of cultural, professional, political and crypto-political organisations in addition to all the domestic crafts and trades typical of most émigré and immigrant societies and of national minorities. These organisations created such a dense network of links that the problem was often not that there was insufficient national support, but that students failed to become involved in the wider activities of society and were marooned in an inward-looking series of organisations. There were not enough Russians in Prague to create a Russian version of Chinatown; but there were enough of them to produce Russian islands. In addition to the Russians themselves, these islands included members of the non-Russian national minorities of the Russian empire as well as individuals from Russo–Czech society who supported the émigré community. All this enabled some people to live in Prague for 20 years without using the Czech language very much and with few links beyond people of their own kind. However, in the provinces there was much less contact with Russian culture and this could be seen very clearly in the number of people who attended the lectures organised by the Russian People's University outside Prague. Although Professor Novikov attempted to maintain ties with the élite of the Russian academic world – specific ties both with Russia, and with international academic life – the work of the university increasingly tended towards discussion of Russian culture for an immigrant society.

There was a distinct change in the work and attitudes of the Russian People's University as the whole impetus for the creation of a Russian academic community in Prague began to wind down. The year 1928 saw the end of annual reports and the publication of the first volume of academic work by those teaching at the university. This indicated that there had been a complete change in direction. At the outset, lecturers had been seeking an audience and very often had idealistic notions about helping Russia. By 1928, it was clear that this was not going to happen and so scholars were trying both to maintain links with other academics and to publish their own work, which might help to provide an income. As in all émigré institutions, politics played a crucial role throughout. And even when in the end Novikov had managed to free the university from the clutches of the

Zemgor activists and gather the whole of the academic and cultural élite of Russian Prague around the university, certain names, such as Lomshakov, Mrs Zhekulina or Prince Dolgorukou, never did become associated with this particular enterprise. For the SRs in the Zemgor, such people were unacceptable and this illustrates the furious passions which raged round all émigré undertakings.

Practical Training

THE AGRICULTURAL CO-OPERATIVE INSTITUTE

One of the earliest academic institutions to be set up was the Russian Agricultural Co-operative Institute, on 20 May 1921.[16] The first term began on 2 October and took the form of courses run by the co-operative movement. Sixty-three students enrolled and 57 graduated in May 1922. In émigré conditions these were extremely good results. The programme of courses was widened and the course of study was extended: first to 14 months, and later to three years. At the same time four-month courses were brought in for those who had been unable to finish their secondary education. The teaching focused on three areas: the co-operative movement, business and agriculture. By 1928 the institute had accepted 585 students, of whom 259 had graduated, 48 with the title of engineer, and 154 were still enrolled on courses of study. In 1930 the institute closed. This institute was unique in many ways: it was formed before the whole idea of creating an academic centre in Prague had been discussed. It was founded at the same time but was independent of the Zemgor and thus had features not found in other academic institutions in Prague, illustrating the difference between the idea of creating a Russian academic community as originally conceived and the way in which it turned out.

The impetus for the creation of the institute originated in the Congress of Russian Co-operatives in Prague and the Slav Co-operative Conference in May 1921. The Czech government approved of the idea and provided some financial help. However, almost 45 per cent of the money came from Russian co-operative organisations; 40 per cent was obtained from other organisations and individuals, and only 15 per cent was state aid. Even during the second year of the institute's existence, the Moscow People's Bank covered a third of the expenses of the institute and the government only guaranteed the payment of grants to students. In its third year, the institute came to depend totally on financial support from the Czech government but until the very end of all the various émigré academic and scientific institutes, it remained a relatively inexpensive establishment to support, as a fairly high proportion of those enrolled in it did not need a grant. The fact that this institute was relatively inexpensive for the government probably explains why it closed fairly late on. The political attitudes of the staff were also interesting. The director, Marakuev was a Don Cossack by origin. He had wide interests and was well regarded by staff and students. He was one of those who was arrested by the Soviet authorities in 1945 and was never heard of again. Although the institute was engaged in the discussion of co-operative agriculture, which was said to be a subject close to the interests of the Socialist Revolutionaries, in many ways it was more capitalist. Here the issues which had arisen in the disagreements between landowners and Russian agricultural workers were repeated and discussed. The institute had much closer ties with the Union of Czech Agricultural Co-operatives and the Ministry of Agriculture, which was linked to the Agrarian Party, than with the Ministry of Foreign Affairs, the National Socialists or the Social Democratic Parties which were the particular supporters of the President. The emphasis the institute placed on research as well as teaching linked it closely with the other institutions of Russian academic Prague. The institute published six volumes of its work which appeared first as *The Co-operative Movement and Agriculture* and later as *Notes of the Russian Institute of Agriculture and the Russian Co-operative Movement in Prague*.

THE RUSSIAN SCHOOL OF AUTOMOBILES AND TRACTORS

By contrast the Russian School of Automobiles and Tractors had nothing in common with the idea of creating an academic centre. The Czech Ministry of Foreign Affairs was convinced that cars and tractors would play an important role in the future economic life of Russia and planned to prepare as many émigrés as possible for practical activity. The Foreign Ministry suggested to the Zemgor that this kind of training would be useful and gave permission to open this so-called school.[17] So it was opened in August 1921 as a driving school that would provide an official qualification. The Zemgor saw this as a way of providing refugees with the opportunity to obtain a qualification and find employment fairly rapidly. Industrialists became interested in the school, as it was seen as a way of extending and developing Czech and Russian contacts in industry.[18] As a result, several large industrial enterprises, beginning with Škoda, financed the undertaking. Workshops were set up, the Ministry of Defence provided three vehicles and the Ministry of Foreign Affairs provided grants. In 1926–27 very short courses were organised, presumably for those graduates of other institutions who were unemployed. In 1928 three-quarters of the 712 enrolled found work.

The nature and development of this training illustrates that the Czechs were engaged in putting through their own policies with regard to the Russian émigrés and the USSR; they were not developing an émigré policy.

THE RUSSIAN BUSINESS SCHOOL

The history of the Russian Business School is a clear illustration of the difficulties inherent in émigré life and serves to show how idealistic and unrealistic was the whole idea of trying to create a Russian academic centre. The Committee for the Provision of Education for Russian Students set up the school in 1923 to provide an opportunity for former students in Russian business schools to complete their education. The Ministry of Foreign Affairs, however, required the school to help those Russian students who were not making progress in the Czech Business School and to prepare people to work in Russo–Czech trade. Therefore emphasis was placed on learning the Czech language, which was an obstacle for Russian students.

At first, ten-month courses were organised: these accepted 50 students with bursaries and ten who paid for themselves. In the autumn of 1923, the courses were changed into two-year courses and 40 students with bursaries and four privately funded students transferred to these courses. By February 1925, 40 people had successfully completed the course. However, in March 1925 the financial support of the school was withdrawn, and in April it closed. The hopes of the Union of Russian Academic Organisations Abroad to make this into an all-Slav business school were not realised. The link between the Business School and the development of Czech–Russian trade helped it to obtain initial funding but this direct business link meant that the Business School became one of the least effective of the Russian academic institutions in Prague. Under the New Economic Policy (NEP) the Soviet economy was accelerating surprisingly quickly and those who wanted a rapid return on their investment had to work with the Soviet authorities, rather than with the emigration. This was already clear by 1924 and one must assume that the Ministry of Foreign Affairs was just waiting for the first set of graduates to finish their studies before closing the school. The syllabus was too specialised for any of the graduates to be able to affect social consciousness in the Soviet Union even though, as was typical of so many émigré educational institutions, the teaching staff were far more highly qualified than was usual in a business school. The director was a university lecturer, U.D. Zhilaev, A. V. Zen'kovsky who later became the head of the Pedagogical Bureau, was on the staff, as were P. A. Ostroukhov and P. N. Savitsky, lecturers in the Russian Law Faculty. But the very narrow programme did not allow these lecturers to use the full range of their abilities and so, in terms of publications, the Business School was one of the least successful of all the Russian institutions.

Pedagogy and Schools

THE RUSSIAN PEDAGOGICAL INSTITUTE

All this is particularly obvious when the Business School is compared with the Russian Pedagogical Institute of J. A. Komensky which began its activities six months later, on 1 August 1923. Those with secondary education had been accepted into the Business School, whereas only those who had finished higher education and had a teaching qualification were accepted by the Pedagogical Institute. Exceptions were made for those who had many years' teaching experience and for those who simply wanted to listen to lectures. This, of course, limited the potential number of students but, even so, on the first course there were 88 students, far more than in the Business School: 50 had grants, 14 paid for themselves and 24 came just for the lectures. When the Pedagogical Institute was closed in 1926, 100 students had graduated from the two-year course, two and a half times more than those who finished the Business School. The institute produced ten times as many publications as the business school, and the level of teaching was excellent. The staff included Academician V.A. Frantsev, Professor A.A. Kizevetter the historian, V.V. Zen'kovsky a philosopher and historian, S.N. Bulgakov the theologian, I. I. Lapshin, and A. L. Bem, a specialist on Dostoevsky who has been termed the *spiritus movens* of the Russian colony in Prague.

The reasons for these differences can be seen both in government policies on the Russian emigration and in the expectations of the émigrés themselves. The Business School had the practical task of preparing managers for Russo–Czech trade, whereas the Pedagogical Institute was preparing organisers of educational work in Russia. In the opinion of many Russians and Czechs such educational work was not only of Russian interest but had repercussions for the rest of the world. Educational issues were at the core of debates within the Russian émigré community in Czecho-slovakia. Many considered that the lack of education among the Russian people and most of the other nations of the Russian empire was one of the main reasons – if not the key reason – for the catastrophe of the Revolution and the horrors which followed it.

There were at least two main approaches to this problem and these arguments were not just specific to émigrés but can be found in many societies. Some Russians considered that education needed to be improved. Others argued that poor education in pre-revolutionary Russia produced a half-educated populace that undermined society and religious faith, which together maintained the existing order. At the same time, any form of education raised expectations and it was the gap between reality and such expectations which led to revolutionary situations.

Russian émigrés of a democratic turn of mind had observed that a whole range of Russian authors, some of whom were fairly obscure, had produced examples between the sixteenth and nineteenth centuries of the low levels of Russian culture and resistance to education. These émigrés tried to promote the idea of a new school which would defeat these tendencies. This new school would be based on the examples produced by Jan Amos Komenský, an important seventeenth-century figure in education. He was a bishop of the Protestant Church of the Czech Brotherhood and a controversial philosopher who created his own holistic system of knowledge combined with mystical elements. He was forgotten during the Enlightenment but was rediscovered by the positivists and attracted increasing attention at the end of the nineteenth century during the debate over the meaning of progress. In Russia, education became one of the central intellectual questions in the run-up to the Russian Revolution, and in this connection interest in Komenský grew faster in Russia than elsewhere. As early as 1892 at the Military School there was a Komenský Department. Serious analyses of Komenský's works appeared in Russian and the works themselves were published in new translations. For the emigration it was equally important that he was an émigré invited to Britain by the British Parliament. He had influenced the fate of Sweden at the point of her greatest importance and had known both kings and princes in Poland and Hungary. He was a teacher, who at the height of the Religious Wars had acquired significant acceptance; his book *Orbis pictus* was used by some of his worst enemies, the Jesuits. Yet he never ceased thinking about his own country.

For the Russians in Prague he was an excellent example of an émigré. Language would have been no barrier for him since educated society everywhere would have been familiar with Latin, and he had every opportunity to make a successful career in the various societies and courts to which he was invited. Nevertheless, he sacrificed this success in order to save his contemporaries and co-nationals in exile – from the baleful influence of the surrounding society following de-nationalisation, and from betraying their faith. Komenský taught in the school at Leshno in Poland and wrote a short course for the reform of schools in the Bohemian monarchy. He used his authority to influence European politicians in the interests of the liberty of the Czech-Bohemian crown, although his highly placed patrons were often displeased with this use of his powers on matters that were of no concern to them. They wanted textbooks and a programme of reform for their own schools.

For the Russian émigrés it was also important that he was a Czech and the pride of the Czech nation, and that he was admired by President Masaryk, who shared his concern with the importance of education. The education course at the Pedagogical Institute included a section on Komenský himself. In contrast to much of the rather formulaic praise heaped on Masaryk as a thinker, this interest in Komenský among the Russians was genuine. It was an example of the link between the democratic Russian emigration and Masaryk's educational goals. As a result, education became one of the most successful areas of collaboration between the émigrés and representatives of the government's Russian policy. They shared the aim of the re-education of Russians so that they would be ready for life in a democratic society. The means to achieve this was to be the restructuring of schools and all non-school educational institutions. Since this was a long-term project it was not affected in the same way as the Business School by short-term considerations and short-term changes in the political situation.

The Pedagogical Institute existed from August 1923 to 1926, and was directed towards reorganising education in Russia. Its graduates could not wait: they had to return to Russia at the height of their powers in order to carry out their aims. Many students had had their education cut short by the Revolution and Civil War. They had been accepted by the institute on the assumption that they would then be able to find employment in Russia, not abroad. It became clear that this was not going to be possible and a crisis soon developed as there was no employment for them in Czechoslovakia either. By the mid–1920s the number of Russian pupils in secondary schools was decreasing and so there were fewer positions for teachers. Even if the funding had continued, the institute would have had to close through lack of students.

The Pedagogical Institute was not the only tool to be used in this educational restructuring. The Czech authorities wanted much wider educational action that would influence the émigrés as a whole, and that would link up with their initial aim of supporting democratic forces throughout the emigration. This matched the desires of the liberal-democratic part of émigré society. Educational work in the emigration, given the circumstances, was extremely complicated and had to be carried out on many different levels. The help afforded by the Czech government reflected the difficulties of the situation. In the first instance the government provided funds to organise a conference of those who worked in Russian schools abroad.

THE PEDAGOGICAL BUREAU

By the end of 1922 the Organisational Committee for the Conference of Teachers in Secondary and Junior Russian Schools Abroad was formed and this body published two issues of its journal in 1923. In April 1923 the first conference took place, financed by the Czech government, and the Union of Russian Academic Organisations Abroad and the Pedagogical Bureau dealing with the affairs of primary and secondary schools abroad were formed. The Pedagogical Bureau was financed by the government and was a very active body. Between 1923 and 1931 it published the *Bulletin of the Pedagogical Bureau*, which became *Vestnik* [Herald] *of the Pedagogical Bureau* and the *Vestnik of the Pedagogical Bureau & the Union of Russian Teachers Organisations Abroad*. These publications contain evidence of the Second Congress of Russian Teachers Abroad which took place in Prague in July 1925, but there are also reports of other congresses in 1924 and 1925, as well as local meetings of representatives of Russian schools in Yugoslavia and Bulgaria. The All-Émigré Conference for the Struggle against Denationalisation took place in October 1924 and there were further meetings. The unknown author in Postnikov's volume produced a laconic entry on the Bureau's work, but was undoubtedly correct in his assessment that by 1928 the Bureau was at the 'centre of émigré cultural and educational work'. The Bureau was closely involved in the organisation of the 'Day of Russian Culture' which became a general émigré festival and annual event.

Gradually, the priority for those in education became the need to maintain and preserve Russian culture abroad; this was always in tension with the need to survive, which often required more assimilation into foreign environments. The journal *The Russian School Abroad* was published in Prague in 1923, initially by S. I. Kartsevskiy but by the end of the year by the Zemgor using Czech government funds. A collection of articles *The Russian Teacher in the Emigration*, was published in Prague at the end of 1926. All this meant that much less was written about Soviet schools. The Bureau was involved in organising two other important events: the conference on pre-school education abroad in July 1927 and the conference on extra-curricular education in July 1928. Like the conference on the problem of denationalisation among schoolchildren, these conferences demonstrate that émigré's were becoming increasingly concerned with problems encountered in the emigration rather than problems in Russia.

The focus of activity changed and the idea that Russian émigrés would return to teach in the Soviet Union receded. The Pedagogical Bureau began to carry out a different programme and to direct its interest to both pre-school and extra-curricular education for Russian children abroad. The main aim was the retention of the language and the feeling of being part of

Russian culture so that the children could use their talents after they returned to their motherland in the distant future. In some respects, this was a harsh experiment which entailed a certain kind of schizophrenia, and taught the second generation what might be termed typical émigré attitudes, which meant that although they lived abroad the focus of all their activites continued to be Russia. Émigré children received an excellent education in Czechoslovakia. But this was followed only too rapidly by exceptionally complex political problems. The Second World War saw the Czechs under Nazi control and raised the question for second-generation émigrés of how best to oppose Bolshevism. Was it better to be allied with the devil against Stalin? However, any support for Nazi Germany would have been a betrayal of their Czech contemporaries. Most émigrés did not do this: instead they waited for the Red Army to liberate them and many attempted to work towards Allied victory.

SCHOOLS

There were two Russian schools in Czechoslovakia, one at Moravská Třebová and the other in Prague itself. A.V. Zhekulina had evacuated a Russian school from Constantinople to Moravská Třebová, where a camp of huts was made available for the school by the Ministry of Foreign Affairs. This became an institution with over 40 buildings in which Russian children of both sexes were housed and educated. Many of the pupils were deeply traumatised by their experience of revolution, civil war and evacuation.[19] Initially the school had to deal with these psychological scars and with the fact that some of those who needed to complete their secondary education were far older than was normal. Most of the teaching was in Russian. In 1928, the school came under the auspices of the Ministry of Education and was included as part of the Czechoslovak educational system. In the 1930s, when the number of pupils began to fall, the school was amalgamated with the Russian gymnasium in Prague.[20]

As a result of the Zemgor opening a Russian primary school in Prague in 1921–22, and setting up a summer camp in 1922, the gymnasium opened in September 1922 with five classes and two preparatory classes.[21] Numbers grew rapidly. In the first there were 60 pupils; by mid-1926 there were 320. The educational programme was broadly similar to that in Czech schools with additional teaching of Russian history and geography, religious education, Russian language and literature. Teaching was in Russian but the Czech language was a compulsory subject.

Educational questions had implications far beyond the restricted world of pre-war Russian academic life in Prague. The interest in education and the theoretical and practical character of the work in this area indicate that the émigrés still expected to return home. The fact that most teaching was carried out in Russian is further proof of this. The kind of education provided was on the whole of a very high quality and gave children a relatively happy childhood in difficult conditions; however, it produced many difficulties in adulthood – the cruel paradox of emigration.

Research and Cultural Bodies

THE RUSSIAN INSTITUTE

The changes in Russo–Czech policies, the changing relations between the Czechs and the Russian émigrés and between Czechoslovakia and the Soviet Union, as well as the complexities of Russian émigré politics itself, are all reflected in the history of the Russian Institute. It was established at the last meeting of the Second Congress of Representatives of Russian Academic Organisations Abroad on 16 October 1922.

To start with, this was seen as an academic institute which would be involved in a study of all aspects of Russia. However, by this time most of the aid to the Russian emigration was being directed through the Zemgor, which had no interest in supporting an academic institution which it saw as the product of Professor Lomshakov's ideas. The SRs, who had not been able to maintain their influence over the shape and nature of the academic emigration as a whole, had sufficiently good relations with the Ministry of Foreign Affairs to take a leading role in the study of Russia. They had created their own institute but managed it in such a way that the Czech government began to be rather less generous.

Both Lomshakov and Novgorodtsev continued to push their ideas through. Novgorodtsev produced a new constitution which was accepted in November 1923 and which extended the functions of the institute, adding an educational role to the research. Lomshakov gained funds from non-governmental sources, which were essential if they were to begin their work. Lecture rooms for the humanities, which were largely intended for an émigré audience, were found in the Prague Polytechnic where Lomshakov taught, but far more important was the special industrial department which prepared lectures intended for Czech trade and industrial circles that were interested in the Russian market. These lectures took place in the Czech Chamber of Commerce.

This is the first example of a systematic attempt to create business relations of a non-partisan type between the emigration and Czech society. But it could only last for a limited time. The longer the émigrés stayed abroad, the more out of date their contacts became. The businesslike discussion between two equal business partners turned into an experimental attempt to discover what was happening, or might even be seen as a form of sovietology. Thus, as the position of the émigrés altered, so the interest in collaborative trade projects with the Russian Institute diminished.

In 1929–31 the Russian Institute published three volumes of articles on the humanities in Russian, designed for a Russian émigré audience. In this the institute could not compete with the Russian People's University, and in the area of sovietology it was no match for Prokopovich's Economic Bureau. Nevertheless, its modest aims and governmental financial support enabled the Russian Institute to survive until the end of the First Czech Republic in 1938. The institute had no regular members of staff, but its directors were first Academician Kondakov, followed by Academician Struve and finally Academician Frantsev. Amongst the lecturers were some who also taught at the Russian Law Faculty: Professors Bulgakov, Kizevetter and Lossky.

RUSSIAN HISTORICAL ARCHIVE ABROAD

There was, however, in Prague an institution of a completely different kind – the Russian Historical Archive Abroad (RZIA). In the last ten years a great deal has been written about it,[22] both specialist and general, and archival material has been published. Most of the archive is to be found in GARF, the State Archive of the Russian Federation in Moscow, although certain sections have been handed over to other archive collections in the former Soviet Union. Some of the more sensational studies have confused rather than clarified the history of the archive, and have made it out to be the NKVD's main source on the emigration.

The idea of creating an archive originated with the Zemgor although the attempt was fairly amateur. In February 1923 it was decided that in addition to the Zemgor library there should be two archives, one relating to the Russian emigration and the other relating to Czechoslovakia. The fact that the second archive was even considered shows how little the founders understood about the processes of creating an archive. When after a few months very little material had been collected, and it had not been catalogued, it was decided in September 1923 to concentrate on the creation of an archive for the Russian emigration as an independent academic institution. Specialists were asked to collaborate, in particular Professors Kizevetter, Shmurlo and Myakotin. In April 1924 the Ministry of Foreign Affairs began to finance this archive; from 1928 it was run by the Ministry, although the committee and directorship created in 1924 continued their work. Despite the fact that funds for the archive were fairly limited, the extensive links of its directors with émigrés throughout the world meant that a wide range of documents could be obtained. This was greatly helped by the fact that because of the difficult financial position of many émigrés and the lack of interest in Russian archival material in their host societies, they certainly could not sell the archives, or even donate them elsewhere. As a result, the Russian Historical Archive Abroad grew very rapidly and became one of the most important archive collections of the Russian emigration, containing material dating back to the pre-revolutionary emigration of Herzen and Ogarev.

To begin with, political differences prevented the co-operation of the Zemgor with the directorate of the Russian academic organisations, and national and regional conflicts made it difficult to collect all the material from participants in the Civil War. But the attempt to recall and understand the turbulent years of the Revolution and Civil War predominated and material from the entire Russian ethnic and political range was accepted. Much is due to the first director of the archive, V. Ya. Gurevich, who was nominated by the Zemgor, and, subsequently, to the Czech director of the archive, Jan Slavík. Both these men, despite their strong political views, did not interfere in academic research: indeed Jan Slavík played an active role in this research. However, since many donors stipulated that their archives should only be opened at a given point after they had deposited them, much material could not be properly catalogued or worked on, and some was not opened until the 1990s, in Moscow. In the intervening period, the most important part of the archive consisted of published materials: leaflets, posters, newspapers, magazines, brochures and books – that is, the material which made up the library of the archive. Postnikov, in the bibliography which he published in 1938,[23] showed how important this collection was for the history of the Revolution and the Civil War. The value of the library of the archive for the history of the emigration itself is only now becoming apparent, because the library, as opposed to the archive itself, remained in Prague and has become part of the Slavonic Library. In contrast to almost all the other institutions of Russian academic Prague, the archive and its library, which began on a very restricted basis and did not have a large role to play in inter-war society in Russian Prague, will gain greatly in value and importance in the future.

COMMITTEE OF THE RUSSIAN BOOK

Once it became clear that the émigrés would not be going back home in the foreseeable future, the question of whether all their efforts had been in vain began to be debated. How should all their ideas and efforts be preserved, or were they doomed to oblivion? These kinds of thoughts united everyone and the emigration began to consider its legacy.

1. The staff of the Russian Law Faculty.

2. The Russian Historical Archive Abroad (RZIA), 1934. Standing from the left: P.A. Skachkov, P.S. Bobrovsky, M.M. Zaitsev, D.I. Meisner, I.D. Golub, M.A. Kovalev, F.T. Aspidov, E.F. Maksimovich, N.P. Tsvetkov, V.M. Krasnov, M.S. Stakhevich. Sitting from the left: L.F. Magerovsky, A.F. Izyumov, Jan Slavik (Director), S.P. Postnikov, G.P. Antipova.

3. (*top*) The Automobile-Tractor School, late 1920s. The director N.E. Sergeev is seated in the middle.

4. (*above*) A school dining room, late 1920s.

5. (*left*) Father Michael Vasnetsov, Bishop Sergii and Father Isaakiy, Easter 1944.

6. On the steps of the Church of St Nicholas after Princess Yashvill's funeral, 15 June 1939.

7. The Pedagogical Bureau. A.V. Zhekulina is seated on the left.

above, left to right:
8. Professor Lomshakov.
9. Professor Kizivetter.
10. Professor Novgorodtsev.

11. P.B. Struve and K. Kramář

12. A.V. Zhekulina.

Sergei Varshavsky summed it up: 'The idea that it was necessary to collect and systematise all the spiritual riches created by the Russian emigration in the form of books, in all areas of knowledge, had to come from Prague, the haven for so many Russian cultural and educational institutions.'[24] Varshavsky was a member of the directorate of the Committee of the Russian Book. It was not surprising that these ideas should first have been expressed in the period 1922–24 when it became clear that emigration was going to be a long period with cultural achievements of its own. It would be easier to create some kind of lasting record while the Czech government was still interested in using the emigration as a possible way of influencing the development of the USSR.

In addition, for both Russians and Czechs there was one further reason: the need to defend the émigrés from attacks by the Czech left and by the public at large. There were almost too many Russians and, in particular, too many students. By 1 January 1922 there were 1,390 students on grants; two years later there were 3,245, or more than 10 per cent of all students in Czechoslovakia. The Czech public objected to the fact that these students were not paying fees and even received government maintenance grants. Furthermore, people complained that the students met in each other's rooms or flats and had noisy gatherings in the evenings. This kind of criticism simply illustrated that Czech and Russian habits differed. Czechs tended to get up much earlier and met in cafés and beer cellars rather than entertaining at home. And the overall number of students included Ukrainians, but no one was inclined to sort out the differences between the two. Such misunderstandings were reflected in complaints to the government that government spending was supporting the feckless life of counter-revolutionaries when their own people were in poverty. It had to be proved that the students and other émigrés were not simply spongers but were engaged in culturally valuable enterprises. The Committee of the Russian Book wished to prove this by mounting an exhibition of Russian books – that is, books published both in emigration and in the USSR. It was to be limited to textbooks and academic research.

A meeting was called for 25 May 1923 to which representatives of 39 Russian and Czech institutions in which Russian students were enrolled were invited. A number of these groups did not see eye to eye. The Committee to Guarantee the Education of Russian Students, the Union of Russian Academic Organisations and the Union of Russian Engineers were all profoundly disliked by the Zemgor and the newspaper *Volya Rossii*. The editors of *Krest'yanskaya Rossiya,* the right-wing SR paper, and Struve's *Russkaya Mysl*, which was becoming increasingly conservative, were also present. Despite this range of views, no one walked out of the meeting, as happened so frequently in other attempts to unite members of the emigration. Finally, the committee was created and its initial aims were achieved. It proved very difficult to obtain Soviet publications, partly because of the demands of Soviet bureaucracy, and so this part of its role, which could so easily have become a serious bone of contention, was dropped. As the effort to organise an exhibition developed it became evident that the aim of the committee had become the attempt to show what had been published abroad. This also involved keeping track of the book trade and acquiring all the relevant information about émigré publications. On 8 June 1924 an exhibition was opened of 3,000 Russian books published abroad and 600 periodical publications.

A number of specialists were asked to contribute, regardless of their political attitudes. These included such diverse figures as E.A. Lyatskiy and M.L. Slonim, who had radically opposing views on both politics and literature and who frequently disagreed at meetings of the Union of Russian Writers and Journalists. The élite of the Russian Law Faculty was included, as well as the Countess V.N. Bobrinskaya, and S.A. Ostrogorsky, the personal doctor to the Emperor Nicholas II's children, who later became director of the Russian Pedagogical Institute in Prague. The bibliography was compiled by the indefatigable bibliographer and SR, S. P. Postnikov.

Arguably, at that moment only the question of publishing could have united such a diverse body of people. Some of the surveys were obviously written in a hurry and the authors approached their subject in various ways, so that different degrees of bias emerge. Nevertheless, it was the first survey of this nature and of this quality. The article on periodicals by V. A. Rosenberg and S. P. Postnikov laid the basis for subsequent statistical and socio-statistical research on Russian periodicals. Despite the rather elementary methods of analysis and collection of information, their knowledge and understanding of the emigration make their work often rather better than more recently produced surveys based on new archival materials and methods of statistical analysis.

Since most of the émigré world considered publishing to be part of their mission and the best way to justify their activities while in exile, full runs of publications were sent to the committee in Prague. The creation of a permanent way of monitoring all these publishing ventures turned out to be impossible: it was easier to ask people to do something once rather than ask them to keep on doing it and many émigré publications and publishers did not last long. Thus in order to maintain continuity and achieve completeness the committee needed to be able to buy some of these publications. In addition, an extensive correspondence was required, to maintain the flow of information. In other words, this kind of enterprise would have needed a building in which to store books, staff to buy and catalogue them and compile bibliographies for publication, all of which called for financial resources which were not available to the committee. By 1924 the government of Czechoslovakia was unlikely to provide the support necessary for this kind of work. The Soviet Union was achieving international recognition and the émigré community seemed increasingly unimportant. Nor did this kind of idea really fit in with Masaryk's foreign policy.

The Russian Historical Archive Abroad (RZIA) collected unique materials on various key questions of the development of Russia in the years of revolution and civil war. The importance of this both historically and politically was quite clear to Masaryk and the archive continued to receive financial support. By contrast, the Committee on the Russian Book chronicled the achievements of the émigrés. After the exhibition and the publication of *Russkaya zarubezhnaya kniga* (The Russian Book Abroad), further financial support was not forthcoming and the committee was forced to close.

INSTITUTE FOR THE STUDY OF RUSSIA

Russian Action was coming to an end. It was no longer possible to consider opening new educational institutions, but there was a growing interest in studying information from the Soviet Union which was arriving in ever greater quantities. By 1923 the Soviet government had brought order to the gathering of statistical information. Material from the Central Statistical Directorate and Gosplan was published regularly, and material was also published in economic journals and newspapers, and in various official publications. There were also the stenographic reports of organisations such as the Conference of the Soviets, as well as party conferences.

It was sensible to use the academic and intellectual powers of the Russian emigration to study these materials and here again the interests of the émigrés and the Czech authorities coincided. But, unlike the gathering of all kinds of publications, in the appraisal of this information from the USSR, politics still dominated. It is difficult to assess whether the Russian Institute could have become an academic centre for the study of Russia but one can say with some assurance that, for the competing Institut Izucheniya Rossii (Institute for the Study of Russia) founded in April 1924, the chances of becoming so were extremely small.[25]

This institute was an SR organisation led by talented ideologues, theoreticians and revolutionaries who, however, had none of the right habits of mind for scrupulous, analytical academic work. V.M. Chernov, who had been the last SR leader and the chairman of the Constituent Assembly, was more interested in attempts to resurrect the Party and to develop constructive forms of socialism. S.S. Maslov, head of the Department of Agriculture and Co-operatives, spent most of his time and effort on the new party of Krest'yanskaya Rossiya (Peasant Russia) which was largely created from right-wing SR elements and rejected many socialist tenets. A.V. Peshekhonov, who was head of the Economic Department and for a short time had been a minister for supply in the Provisional Government in 1917, appeared to have had some experience as a statistician in his youth, but since 1901 had devoted his life to politics. Peshekhonov began to move to the right politically but, after the defeat of the Volunteer Army which he had supported, he again moved towards the left wing. During the existence of the institute he became a Soviet employee and worked as an economic consultant, although the Soviet authorities never allowed him to go back to Russia. None of these individuals could have been expected to provide impartial, systematic and analytical work for the institute even though it had been constructed for that purpose.

There were 23 departments which were supposed to cover all aspects of life in Russia. These departments were further divided into 214 areas and still more subsections and all current information was collected under these headings and collated on cards. This card index was supposed to be the fundamental work of the institute, and on the basis of it the institute was to prepare reports for the Czech government. Yet despite these intentions, the institute did not become an important source of information for the government, so there was no impetus to maintain it. Neither did non-governmental organisations, that might have been able to support it, require its work.

Notes of the Institute for the Study of Russia illustrates why there was no enthusiasm for its work. The largest proportion of the publication, in terms of both size and quality, consisted of historical essays, for example the work of A.N. Chelintsev dealing with land-owning before the Revolution. Quite a lot of ink was expended on dealing with questions which interested Socialist Revolutionaries. For instance, Chernov wrote about the black re-partition of land in 1918 and V. Lutokhin discussed the Provisional Government's agrarian policy of 1917. Given the aims of the institute, it is puzzling that so many articles should be devoted to agrarian politics in post-war Europe. However, if the institute is viewed as an academic and theoretical centre which was developing agrarian policy for Russia, its activities fall into place. For an analysis of agrarian policies the long-term perspective and foreign experience were important aspects. Those directing the institute appear to have understood that this was in fact its real purpose, but by 1924 it was not expedient to say so openly.

The argument between Kramář and Beneš in 1926 in which Beneš as a spokesman of the government declared that it was not possible for émigrés to return home as political leaders – a statement which was in complete contradiction to the experience of the Czech political emigration – was a sign that this was not the moment to create a centre whose task was political and conceptual. However, the members of the institute were either unwilling or unable to adapt to such changed circumstances. The appearance of the third volume of the institute's work in Czech did not save the situation: even though this volume was an attempt at a systematic analysis of the contemporary situation in Russia, it was too static and too ideological.

PROKOPOVICH'S ECONOMIC BUREAU

S.N. Prokopovich's Economic Bureau had a completely different approach.[26] Although he was active in politics, Prokopovich's approach was based on academic interest rather than political or conceptual theorising. Perhaps this was due to the fact that he had been expelled in 1922 rather than emigrating during the Civil War. Those who had lived for those five years under Soviet rule did not simply refer to the Soviet Union in clichéd ideological terms. Like the philosophers N.A. Berdiaev and S.L. Frank among many others, Prokopovich saw that elements of the Soviet regime coincided with the wishes of the masses and that the evolution of the regime to some extent depended on pressure from those masses.

Prokopovich aimed to produce an analysis of the USSR which could distinguish between the different elements of dogma and ideology, utopianism, pragmatic development of policies, and the natural processes of the evolution of the regime. He realised that both émigrés and foreign specialists required accurate information in order to assess the situation and to make realistic predictions. For Prokopovich, producing the material for a clear analysis was of paramount importance, whereas the Institute for the Study of Russia considered that ideological schemata should take pride of place.

Prokopovich's office had begun its work in Berlin but its financial position was very weak and much of the work was really a product of the enthusiasm of the members of the office, so the invitation from the Zemgor to come to Prague was a life-saver. It is not known how the Zemgor envisaged co-operation between Prokopovich's office and the newly founded institute. Both organisations tried to work together – an unusual state of affairs within the emigration – but differences rapidly became apparent. Prokopovich did not reject all theoretical work. The first issue of the *Economicheskiy Vestnik,* published in Berlin, opened with an article by Struve dealing with the economic situation and a consideration of what was meant by 'equilibrium'. Discussion of this question continued on the pages of *Vestnik,* and other articles of a similar theoretical and methodological nature were published in the 12 volumes of the *Russkiy Economicheskiy*

Sbornik, which were published in Prague from February 1925. But the majority of articles analysed the Soviet economy on the basis of current information.

However, the most important part of *Sbornik*, from the second issue onwards, was a section entitled: 'A Review of Russian Life', in which this emotive subject was tackled in a most scholarly way. When the subsidy for *Sbornik* ceased in 1928 it was not difficult to turn this into the core of the subsequent publication, *Bulletin*. The quality of the research was so high that it is still of value for scholars today. This excellence determined its later fate, and the financing of *Bulletin* continued throughout the years of economic crisis. The Ministry of Foreign Affairs continued to support the Economic Bureau even when the USSR was recognised by the Czechoslovak government and an alliance was signed with the USSR. Prokopovich's work was as necessary to the government as to academic institutions, and the Bureau's publications were valued in other countries as well. In 1940, Prokopovich left occupied Czechoslovakia for Geneva. The *Bulletin* began to be published in English and was subsidised by the Carnegie Foundation, demonstrating even more clearly the evolution of its attitudes and position.

The development and fate of these two institutes in Prague, both designated for the study of Russia, logically and symbolically bring to an end a heroic experiment: the creation of a Russian academic centre in Prague. Such institutions survived if they turned away from working for a future Russia and towards the demand for their skills abroad. Nor was it simply a linguistic question, although language barriers created more problems for the Russian emigration than for other European emigrations because almost no one in Western Europe knew Russian and the Russian intelligentsia itself had no second language in common. Knowledge of German had been fairly universal before the First World War but German was unacceptable to part of the emigration and some accepting host societies after the war; French had not yet had time to replace German. There was growing interest in English but this was not universal even in educated circles. But even the change in the use of language and structure did not help the Institute for the Study of Russia, whereas the Economic Bureau survived using Russian. Survival of such institutions depended on the kinds of questions addressed and the way in which such questions were approached.

THE KONDAKOV SEMINAR

One group of historians and archaeologists who gained international scholarly recognition despite all the financial difficulties and political changes facing the émigré academic community were those associated with the Kondakov Seminar and Institute.[27] Founded on 22 April 1925, shortly after the death of N.P. Kondakov, the seminar was intended to continue Kondakov's work in Byzantine studies, archaeology and the history of art. In 1926 a volume in Kondakov's honour was published.[28] Financed by Charles Crane, an American businessman, diplomat, philanthropist and a close friend of Masaryk, it was followed by 11 similar volumes published over the next 15 years. These volumes contained articles from scholars all over the world, and as the members of the seminar emphasised that they were strictly non-political, early volumes even contained articles by Soviet scholars. Articles in various languages served to publicise the activities of the seminar very effectively. The first directors of the seminar were Professor A.A. Kalitinsky and G.V. Vernadsky. Vernadsky's departure for Yale in 1927 was a serious blow which, followed by the onset of world economic depression, made the position of the seminar difficult. However, it did have a wide range of influential contacts and also managed to make money from its publications. Princess Yashvill, another of the leading lights of émigré society, was closely linked with the activities of the seminar. Her knowledge of languages, her wide circle of contacts and the high esteem in which she was held all helped to support the work of the Kondakov Seminar. In 1928, the seminar was given additional help by President Masaryk, who provided the funds for two students: N.E. Andreyev and E.I. Mel'nikov. In 1931 after a move to new premises, the seminar was reorganised as an institute, which served to tighten up its structure. However, the international economic situation meant that the possibilities envisaged by members of the institute for the development of their work never came to full fruition. N.E. Andreyev later became librarian, secretary and during the war was acting director until his arrest by the Soviet authorities in 1945.

Although most of its leading members had left Prague during the Second World War, Andreyev managed to keep the Kondakov Institute independent of both the Czech and German authorities. It continued to exist in formal terms until its closure in 1948. The history of the Kondakov Institute is an interesting example of the evolution of the Russian academic émigré world. Founded after the heyday of Russian Action and developed at a time when many other institutions could no longer function, the Kondakov Institute never saw itself as playing a role in Russia in the future. Instead, it tried to bring together the scholarly world in a common endeavour. At the same time it experienced the difficulties inherent in the émigré condition.

Achievements of Academic Institutions

By 1928, around 2,000 Russian students had graduated from educational institutions and a further 1,500 graduated in the period 1928 to 1931.[29] Of those, 784 graduated from Russian institutions.[30] However, given the infrastructure of the Russian academic community, students who were studying in the Czech system still had close ties both with Russian academic interests and with their own culture and could attend additional courses, for example through the Russian People's University.

The societies of engineers and technical specialists, and of doctors and agricultural workers, all took the place of cultural organisations: they established links with Russian student organisations in the various faculties and provided welfare both directly and indirectly. Large numbers of people could become involved. In July 1923 a six-day trip was organised to visit a variety of agricultural projects, and 65 students took part. In the conditions of the emigration, this was a significant figure: a little later, organisers of courses in the Russian People's University could only dream of lecture audiences of this size. Only the historian A.A. Kizevetter, well known as a first-class speaker, was able to attract an audience of between 90 and 300 listeners for his fairly long series of lectures about problems in Russian history. In 1925, Professor S.A. Ostrogorsky gave a course of lectures on aspects of marriage to about 80 listeners, and although in both cases the majority of the audience were students, neither course of lectures had any direct link to any specialist course of study.

The results of teaching can rarely be seen immediately. Had the graduates of the Russian Law Faculty been able to return to Russia, they would have had an important role to play. There had been a shortage of good lawyers in pre-revolutionary Russia, and after the beginning of the First World War the number training was cut in both number and quality. By the beginning of NEP, no lawyers were being trained. In such circumstances, 500 qualified lawyers who were familiar with Soviet law and had experience of Western legal systems would have been useful even in a country the size of Russia.

But all this is counterfactual history. These people were never allowed to return home and there never was any possibility of assessing their education. The majority of these graduates had to leave Czechoslovakia and a very large part of them had to change professions or to add to their legal training in those countries in which they settled. Furthermore, lawyers needed to know languages well and had to be able to express themselves clearly. To learn a language sufficiently well to be able to do this after about the age of 30 is not easy. Moreover, in all legal systems there are certain assumptions and culture, and cases have to be presented in particular ways. Even for those graduates of the Russian Law Faculty who became lawyers, it is very difficult to know and to assess what they learned from the Law Faculty and what they acquired through later experience. Lawyers are an extreme case. A comprehensive knowledge of national law and of foreign languages, the interpretation of unwritten codes and practices and an understanding of the psychology of the accused and of juries – all these factors made it more difficult for them to assimilate into their host societies. The Russian Law Faculty had been founded for that very reason: so that Russian lawyers with a foreign education would be able to return to Russia.

However, it was not much easier for teachers, who could lose authority in the eyes of their pupils because of an accent. Doctors might lose the trust of a patient if they did not seem able to communicate properly. In general, it was easier for émigrés to assimilate in professions where non-verbal communication was more important, and it was even easier when the results of that profession could be seen in practice. Engineers, for example, had a better chance of assimilation. Their role in Czechoslovakia has not really been assessed, although it is undoubtedly important. Russian émigrés played a key role in the American aviation industry and in engineering generally, but it seems that in the USA many had lost their close ties with their Russian background and had become more assimilated into American society. Moreover, the unequal legal status of the émigrés which meant that, as foreigners, they often could not have their own firms or acquire property, played a significant role. In Czechoslovakia this also applied to architects who worked as unnamed partners in firms.

It is no less difficult to assess the academic activities of Russian scholars who found themselves in Prague between 1922 and 1927. They often worked in areas which were distinct from one another. Only a very large body of scholars well versed in the history of their own disciplines could assess all the research and publications in Russian Prague, and this is not a realistic prospect. A historian of the emigration as a cultural or academic phenomenon must work with the assessments of others, but this is still insufficient for the study of an emigration in which priorities changed and the normal context of academic work no longer applied.

A larger group of people gave most of their energy to the business of teaching. Teaching in institutions of higher education usually combines well with research, which complements and strengthens it. Students were far more varied than in normal conditions and, as a rule, had fallen out of the usual academic pattern for at least three years. It was almost impossible to repeat a year, as many of the teachers taught various courses in a range of institutions. An example would be Kizevetter, who taught in the Law Faculty, in the Pedagogical Institute, in the Philosophical Faculty of the Czech Charles University, gave lectures at the Russian Institute and at the Russian People's University.

Among the Russian émigrés teaching had its own peculiarities. Frequently, neither the students nor the teachers had the usual resources of textbooks or other sources. Vernadsky's comments are fairly typical and form the preface to his *Outline of the History of Law of the Russian State*:

I hesitate to publish this outline which is the result of lectures which I gave at the Russian Law Faculty in Prague during the academic year 1922–23. The outline was put together in fairly difficult circumstances. On the one hand many sources and publications were made available to me. (It is sufficient to note that one cannot find a complete edition of the Russian Imperial Law Codes in Prague.) On the other hand I am a historian who had to grapple with the question of the history of law. I might not have published the *Outline* had there not been an obvious need for it in view of the poverty of the Russian book trade abroad.[31]

With minor alterations, almost anyone involved in Russian studies would have subscribed to this statement. Moreover, almost all the general developments after the First World War meant that pre-war assumptions had been overturned. International law had radically altered, democracy was in crisis, as was religion. Economic theory had developed very rapidly and war, as ever, had stimulated technical advances. The use of aviation, the use of gas, and communications all called for new approaches. In other words, there were almost no areas in which the pre-war assumptions still held and many questions in the humanities and sociology had to be rethought, particularly in the light of Russian and émigré experience. As a result almost all textbooks had to be rewritten.

In a course on the history of international law which he gave in the Russian Law Faculty, M.A. Tsimmermann emphasised a number of approaches which bear the clear imprint of the Russian émigré experience. He stated that

it is essential that from the outset we must distance ourselves from attempts by contemporary legal positivists to discuss the question of the development of international law purely in terms of the moment when that international law came into existence . . . based on the assumption that it is the product of either Romano–Greek civilisation or Christian in origin . . . these assumptions form the basis of conclusions about the limits of the development of international law in the future. As a result, the rejection of the past formulations is tied to the teaching about the impossibility of international law emerging from various constraints. . . . The possibility of maintaining theoretical approaches to the subject while the form of international law is transformed, is rejected.[32]

In the first place, he rejected the stress on Eurocentrism and the assumption that the influence of Romano–Greek civilisation should be the norm. This is in part a product of disillusionment with the Western Allies, and in part the influence of the Eurasian movement. Furthermore, in this statement one can see a reflection of the general discussion about new forms of law. The idea of 'Soviets without Bolsheviks' was advanced by Savinkov as a political slogan but was also seen as an idea which was possible theoretically and which might be a desirable form of government once dictatorship had been done away with.

Similarly, Professor M.I. Rostovtseff's idea of the history of the ancient world quite obviously carried the assumptions of post-Russian-Revolution thinking. He seems to have defended the idea of analogy between antiquity and contemporary developments.[33] P.A. Sorokin's sociological theories are determined to no small extent by his Russian background. Sorokin spent less than a year in Prague but acknowledged that his time there was very fruitful. He published a whole series of articles in Czechoslovakia, which formed 'the theoretical basis of work which I later produced in several volumes while teaching at Minnesota University and at Harvard'.[34] He had brought out with him from Russia the draft of *Sociology of Revolution*, a book that brought him international acclaim. Although he was far from the centres of émigré community, Sorokin kept in touch with his Russian colleagues in the Law Faculty, who helped him assemble the material for another book, *Social and Cultural Dynamics*. Both Rostovtseff and Sorokin became known internationally. Neither was in Prague for long but both recognised that the academic world there had been valuable to them and believed that it would be influential in educating the next generation of scholars. Both used their experience of Russia in developing their ideas.

During the first years of the émigré community the scholarly questions asked in philosophy,[35] social studies[36] and economics,[37] were of a very general kind, on Christianity, culture and civilisation.[38] These were followed by more concrete questions. For example, was the idea of natural law an equitable one? This provoked fierce arguments. The post-war years also gave rise to widespread debates embracing the crisis in religion, in democracy, in socialism – even the crisis of the co-operative movement.[39] Among Russian émigrés arguments about the crisis of the West, of Europe and of the Romano–Greek civilisation predominated. These kinds of question have always been debated within scholarship but in the émigré community the proportion of published works on such issues was surprisingly high.

It was essential for Russian émigré scholars to publish in Russian: it was seen as their moral duty to do so. But the Czech government financed émigré publications in order to help Russian academic life, not to make Russian scholarship known internationally. Finally, the majority of those who settled in Prague hoped that they would be able to return home and wanted to do so with a number of published works. Examining Russian publications in the period 1922–26, it seems that only one article in them appeared in a foreign language, Professor E.V. Anichkov's article in French, 'What is Art in the View of the Great Scholastic Teachers?'[40] (This was on such a specialised subject that there could hardly have been a large readership in Russia and furthermore it was the sequel to a work which had been published in a specialist French publication in 1917–18.) Between 1926 and 1928 several publications appeared in Czech but this was not an attempt to appeal to a world audience, just a rather late attempt to interest local society in Russian problems when the government was winding down the whole Russian Action.

Chapter 4

Identity and Attitudes

Preserving a Russian identity in emigration was not easy, as the politics of inter-war Europe meant that it was often disadvantageous to be a Russian émigré. Economic necessity made the problem even worse. Particularly after the onset of the Great Depression, many countries gave priority to finding employment for their own nationals. Many Russian émigrés felt that abandoning their Nansen passports and acquiring foreign nationality was a betrayal of their loyalty to Russia. Yet this was the only course of action open to them. The Russian academic émigrés in Prague had been inspired by the idea that they would be able to return home to Russia and work for the ideal of a just and free democratic society and this aspiration had underpinned the support afforded to the Russian refugees by the Czechoslovak government. But in the event Russia was unable to take them back and many had to emigrate elsewhere; others found that assimilation into their host society was the only way to survive.

The Russian Orthodox Church

Russian Orthodoxy seemed one way of maintaining links both with fellow compatriots and with the Russian homeland. The idea that after the Revolution the Russian Orthodox Church abroad became an important centre of émigré life is a frequently repeated assertion, but is poorly documented. Interestingly enough, Postnikov's overview of Russian life in Prague[1] contains almost no mention of church life, and in particular no reference to the parish of St Nicholas, although many recall that believers as well as some of the atheists in the émigré community went to church as a way of maintaining contact with other members of the Russian community. In Prague, Bishop Sergii is still remembered as a warm and spiritual man, an outstanding pastor greatly loved by his parishioners who stabilised and enhanced the life of the Church.[2] However, church archives have either disappeared or been destroyed and the picture remains fragmentary.

The need to support and reaffirm the identity of exiles was not straightforward. Religion could not be divorced from politics and what was happening in the USSR. The main cause of schism and dissension amongst the émigrés was the issue of authority and the role of the Patriarch. This had a direct bearing on organisation and politics in the Church and was a result of the problems facing the Russian Orthodox Church in 1917. As the recollections of Archbishop Evlogii show,[3] while not directly involved in the upheavals of 1917, the Church could not fail to be affected by the revolutionary atmosphere and the Synod was rapidly inundated with demands for the election of bishops and the discussion of church affairs. In the spring of 1917 there were renewed demands for the convocation of an All-Russian Church Assembly or Sobor to discuss pressing questions of church life and organisation. Such a Sobor had been mooted in 1905–6, but Pobedonostsev, Ober (Chief)-Procurator of the Synod, had put a stop to further discussion. A Sobor was convened in Moscow and opened on 15 August 1917 in the Uspensky Cathedral (Cathedral of the Assumption), the largest of the cathedrals in the Kremlin. Twenty subsections discussed matters relating to all aspects of church life, but the problem, which was to affect all subsequent church relations, was whether the Church should continue to be governed by the Synod, or should elect a Patriarch and return to the tradition which had been destroyed by Peter the Great. Peter had abolished the Patriarchate and by so doing had limited church autonomy, making the Church part of the state apparatus. However, in 1917, the more left-wing members of the Sobor, in particular members of the intelligentsia who were professors of theology from the theological academies and universities, tended to support the idea of the Synod as a way of producing communal leadership and avoiding the possibility of dictatorship. Those members of the higher clergy concerned with the spiritual life of the Church had felt that they could not deal with these matters if the needs of the Church were constantly subordinated to the state. Furthermore, it was apparent that in the revolutionary atmosphere strong leadership was desirable. When Tikhon, the Metropolitan of Moscow, was elected Patriarch on 5 November 1917, there seems to have been some feeling that at last there was a father-figure who would stand up for the Church.

This decision to concentrate power in the hands of one individual – the Patriarch, who would remain in Moscow and therefore be subject to Bolshevik pressure and control, and with whom Russian exiles and the Russian clergy abroad could have less and less contact – became one of the main causes of splits in the emigration. Should the Patriarch be seen as the servant of God who had to be obeyed as the purveyor of God's will, or was that will being corrupted by the machinations of the Bolshevik regime? The question of the position of the Patriarch was ineluctably linked with the question of power and influence in the Church. Beyond the boundaries of the Soviet Union, the question of the autonomous churches complicated the situation still further.

On 15 April 1921, the Provisional Administration of the Russian Orthodox Church authorised Metropolitan Evlogii to run the Orthodox churches of Western Europe with the proviso that this would continue only until relations with the Patriarch were re-established.[4] This was confirmed by the Patriarch by an order which Evlogii received in the summer of 1921. The order was not universally welcomed by the Orthodox world abroad, and at the Karlovci conference in Serbia, Evlogii's authority was challenged. Evlogii's arrival had been delayed, allegedly by visa complications in Berlin, and he arrived after the Presidium of the conference had been elected. It rapidly became clear that the monarchists were the moving power at the conference. They renamed the conference the Sobor of the Russian Orthodox Church abroad, and a resolution was passed affirming that the Church stood for the restoration of the Romanov dynasty. It was suggested that a declaration to this effect should be sent to the League of Nations and to the major powers. Evlogii opposed this on the grounds that it would make things very difficult for the Patriarch and for the Church. News of the debate and resolution reached the Patriarch through the press reports in *Obshchee Delo* and, as Evlogii had feared, it worsened the situation for the Patriarch and led to the trial of the Metropolitan of Petrograd, Veniamin. Bishop Sergii of Prague supported Evlogii's opposition to the resolution of the Sobor.

Tension between opposing factions in the Russian Orthodox Church continued. In 1926 there was a split between those who accepted the authority of the Patriarch in Moscow, and those who sanctioned the authority of the Sobor. This schism did not resolve the problems, and friction concerning who had authority over the Orthodox churches in Europe continued.[5] Then in 1930 Metropolitan Sergius announced to foreign journalists in Moscow that there was no persecution of Christians or of the Church in the USSR. This produced a storm of indignation in the émigré community and Evlogii was placed in an invidious position. He did not wish to encourage further divisions but could not sanction such blatant disregard for the truth. In the face of mounting criticism, Evlogii tried to argue that Sergius had not committed a heresy and that this was a political act. Despite this, schism was unavoidable. At the beginning of Lent in 1930, the Archbishop of Canterbury, Cosmo Gordon Lang, invited Metropolitan Evlogii to Britain to pray for the suffering Church in the Soviet Union.[6] Evlogii accepted. Shortly afterwards, he was ordered by Metropolitan Sergius to explain his actions and to condemn his political criticism of the USSR. Evlogii replied that his actions were religious, not political. His answers were obviously not considered satisfactory and an order was received removing Evlogii from his position in charge of the Russian Orthodox Church in Western Europe and transferring the position to Bishop Vladimir of Nice. Vladimir, however, refused to accept it. Finally, Evlogii appealed to the Patriarchate of Constantinople, which accepted jurisdiction over the Russian Orthodox Church in Western Europe. Although this clarified matters, tensions continued.[7]

In Czechoslovakia, the situation was confused by the position of the Czech Orthodox Church and the problem of the scarcity of priests in the émigré community. Most records suggest that the number of clergy leaving Russia was very low, and this did not make the organisation of church life any easier. In Prague, the Archpriest Stelmashenko had been running the parish but there had been difficulties in his relations both with some of his parishioners and with the Czechoslovak authorities.[8] He was subsequently appointed to a church in Nice. Further, when Bishop Sergii arrived from Poland in 1922 there was a power struggle with Father Savatii, a Czech who had studied at the Kazan Theological Academy and who returned to Prague after the Revolution with a view to becoming the incumbent there, but the Russian colony did not get on with him. However, Savatii appealed to the Patriarch in Constantinople and was made Bishop of all of the Czech lands. He returned to Prague and renewed hostilities with Bishop Sergii, with whom he had to share the church of St Nicholas on the old town square. Shortly after this Savatii was removed from power and Bishop Gorazd was appointed head of the Czech Orthodox Church. Relations with Bishop Gorazd were much better, but the legal and administrative position of the Russian Orthodox Church remained unclear with the Czech Orthodox Church retaining official control over church affairs.

The church of St Nicholas had been the church of the Russian consulate before the First World War. The permanent iconostasis was removed and was replaced with a movable one which could be installed when the church was not being used by others. Bishop Sergii was found a room with a Czech landlady, and eventually her flat became a centre for Russian life, with regular Thursday teas which were attended by émigrés from all walks of life. Bishop Sergii was much loved and admired for his pastoral qualities by Russians and non-Russians alike. A parishioner recalled that he never seemed to have any gloves or pairs of socks even in cold weather, because he had always given them away to those in greater need.[9] Another remembered how on a visit to Estonia Bishop Sergii had discussed church matters with his parents,[10] but had also impressed the local fishermen with his interest and understanding of fish! At the end of the Second World War, Bishop Sergii was moved first to Vienna and then to Kazan, where he died in 1952. Bishop Sergii was assisted by Archimandrite Issakiy, formerly a

White Army officer, who allegedly suffered a great deal as a result when he was arrested in 1945 by the Soviet authorities, and by Father Michael, son of the painter Vasnetsov.

Because the use of the church of St Nicholas was dependent on the agreement of the Czech authorities, the Russian community, with the support of Kramař, built a chapel at the cemetery at Olshany,[11] which contained the graves of many leading émigrés.

The Russian Student Christian Movement was also active in Czechoslovakia. Despite having a considerable following in the Kingdom of the Serbs, Croats and Slovenes and although the headquarters was established in Paris, a journal appeared in Prague in 1922–23, *Dukhovnyi Mir Studenchestva* (The Spiritual World of Students) which found a following in Prague. The movement also organised a successful conference in Přerov, in October 1922. However, its journal seems to have folded once various professors of theology moved from Prague to Paris.

The Russian Émigré Press

The gradual change in attitudes is very evident in the Russian émigré press. At first the Russian press in Prague had focused on Russia or the emigration as a whole and had addressed the issue of intervention in the Civil War. However, by the end of the 1920s and early 1930s, it had become the press of the Russian colony in Czechoslovakia.

Slavyanskaya Zarya (Slav Dawn) was published during the Civil War in 1919 and 1920 and its main objective was to persuade the Czechoslovak government to become involved in a new intervention in Russia. But despite its confident, even belligerent, tone, this newspaper did not last long and its editor, Efimovsky, moved to Berlin. It was succeeded by *Volya Rossii*, which was first published on 12 September 1920. To begin with, the editors concentrated on events in Russia; their entire commentary dealt with Russian political issues and they had almost no interest in the emigration. The editorial of the first issue was signed by O.S. Minor a prominent member of the SRs. It illustrated the weakness of the SRs who in 1920 were stating: 'we will endeavour to turn the Russian people's conscience to the correct understanding of the main ideas and principles of the state and social building of the February Revolution of 1917'. It was extraordinary, when the Civil War was in full swing and the weaknesses of the White Armies were becoming more evident, to suggest that the Russian people would be interested in a re-evaluation of the February Revolution of 1917, when the achievements of that revolution had so obviously been overtaken by events. The editorial went on:

The dictatorships of Bolsheviks and reactionary generals were both betraying Russia. . . . The psychology and policy of both of them was exactly the same. . . . We strongly believe that it is only sincere and honest but at same time merciless criticism of both forms of violence upon the free will of the Russian people, criticism guided by the principles of democracy and socialism, that can help the Russian people to recover, to gain strength and with one powerful movement to shake off the whole army of dictators–parasites from the left and from the right.

This was an expression of Socialist Revolutionary views but could scarcely be deemed realistic or practical advice. At this period the newspaper was full of slogans which for the most part referred to events of 1917. For example: 'Defence, development and consolidation of the principles of the March revolution! Freedom and civil rights! A democratic federal republic! Power to the Constituent Assembly!' The slogan 'Land to the Workers' was more ambiguous, but nevertheless the general tenor of the newspaper was clear. It was addressed to a readership in Russia.

These views were challenged by G.A. Aleksinsky, the editor of *Ogni* (Lights), which was supposedly a non-political publication. In the first edition, of 8 August 1921, he accused the Socialist Revolutionaries of idolising the Revolution and ignoring the real history of their countrymen. He continued: 'We bend down before the sufferings of our people. We would sacrifice everything and give our lives and strength to save and free our own people. And these are the lights following which we will find the lost way to our motherland.' Should anyone have been misled as to the real direction of these high-blown sentiments, the next issue, on 15 August, revealed that Aleksinsky was looking forward to the unity of all brother Slavs to fight for 'freedom of Russia, against cholera, Bolshevism, plague, Lenin, Trotsky, starvation and the Council of People's Commissars'. He argued that instead of 'organising hospital trains equipped with anti-cholera vaccination drugs and quinine' they should have called for support for a force to join General Wrangel's troops, which apparently would have liberated Moscow and finished off 'the stinking corpse of the Bolshevik power'. This would allow the 'best people', regardless of party affiliation, to speak for Russia.

The arguments conducted in these publications were a prolongation of the Civil War. For one side, Wrangel was as much of a dictator as were Lenin and Trotsky. For others, Wrangel was the obvious commander of a force to liberate Russia. Although some considered the policy of non-intervention pursued by Czechoslovakia the only sensible approach, others saw it as disastrous and even a betrayal of the Russian cause by their brother

Slavs. But, despite these obvious disagreements, both newspapers had one element in common: they were not interested in the Russian colony in Prague or in Czechoslovakia in general. They addressed their remarks to the population of Russia. Any appeal to the émigrés was simply to direct their attention towards the best way of reviving Russia. *Volya Rossii* continued to be published until 1932. Gradually, it began to turn its attention towards the émigré community, but this was never its main focus of interest.

During the 1920s there were a variety of periodical publications addressed to specific groups within the emigration but it was only at the very end of 1928 that a new newspaper *Nedelia* (the Week) appeared. The editorial of the first issue, on 22 December 1928, was titled 'Nasha Zadacha' (Our Task) and explained that the aim was not to produce a political broadsheet or to engage with the eternal questions, but to meet the demand of thousands of Russians in Czechoslovakia, who wanted to know what was happening in Russian circles, where best to use their abilities and experience, where they could buy or sell and where they could go to relax. The editorial was emphasised as it was clear to the editors that this was their strong point. The majority of émigrés were tired of thinking about insoluble political issues, and wanted to live in the present without losing contact with their community.

Nedelia was replaced by the newspaper *Edinstvo* (Unity). This had a Czech title as well, which was a sign of further assimilation of the Russian community. During the second year of the paper's life, it published a revealing piece by Professor A.A. Kizevetter, the historian, one of the most popular lecturers of the émigré community. Entitled 'Na Novyi God' (For the New Year) and published on 7 January 1932, this editorial praised the Russian émigrés because, as Kizevetter said, they were worthy of it and were frequently subjected to attacks from all sides. He continued: 'I feel sure that the Russian community as a whole can expect a fair judgement from history.' Kizevetter suggested that a record should be kept of the creative achievements of the émigrés.

The tone of this article is more like that of an obituary, or perhaps birthday greetings to a very elderly and respected individual: their achievements are praised, it is still possible to hope for good health, but nothing concrete is proposed. To some extent the tone could be attributed to the author's age. He was 65 and his obituary was published in the newspaper a year later. More credibly, the newspaper simply reflected the views of its readership. The older generation of émigrés had little to hope for except that their efforts during their exile should be understood and appreciated.

A slightly younger generation reacted to the ruin of their hope of returning home in a different way. Their views were represented by a new newspaper, *Novosti* (News). According to the editorial of the first issue on 19 December 1934, 'The life of the Russian colony in Czechoslovakia is taking on a definite shape. There are Russian inhabitants of Czechoslovakia and not simply guests staying temporarily.' The paper intended to address the needs and interests of these Russians which were different from members of the Russian diaspora in other countries. There had been a gradual transformation of the Russian community into an ethnic minority which had put down its roots into a foreign country.

A comparison of the editors' lives is also interesting. E.A. Efimovsky (1885–1964), a former Social Democrat, went on to found a monarchist party, even if compared with other monarchist groupings it was relatively moderate, even left-wing. O.S. Minor (1861–1934) came from a rabbi's family. As a law student he joined the extremist terrorist organisation Narodnaya Volya. He was arrested in 1883. From then until 1902, when he emigrated for the first time, his life consisted of imprisonment, penal servitude or exile, with only short periods of freedom. He returned to Russia after the 1905 Revolution and shortly afterwards was imprisoned once again. He was in exile during the February Revolution. He returned to Moscow and immediately became involved in politics. As head of the Moscow Duma, he played an important role in making the Duma a centre of resistance to the Bolsheviks during the first months after the October Revolution. At the beginning of January 1918 he was arrested by Bolsheviks but was soon set free and in January 1919 he emigrated. During the first months of his emigration he believed that democratic forces would lead the armed struggle with Bolsheviks and therefore he approved of the policy of intervention. However, he rapidly became disillusioned and lost faith in both the White movement and the Allies.

Although G.A. Aleksinsky (1879–1967) was born into an aristocratic Russian family and was almost 20 years younger than Minor, there were many similarities. He was expelled twice from university, in 1899 and then again in 1902, for taking part in student disturbances. Owing to some liberalisation of the regime he was allowed to take his final examinations in 1904. The following year he joined the Bolsheviks in Moscow, and then in emigration he switched from one group of Social Democrats to another. However, at the beginning of the war he espoused 'defencism', the policy of defending Russia against external threat, a policy which was at odds with the ideas of the Bolsheviks. Aleksinsky worked with like-minded Social Democrats and Socialist Revolutionaries to unmask Bolsheviks as agents of German imperialism. From the war until the beginning of 1920, the views of Minor and Aleksinsky on most major questions were very similar. But Minor lost faith in the White movement, whereas Aleksinsky saw the Whites and intervention as the only way of defeating the Bolsheviks. All these arguments and disagreements were typical of the period of the Revolution, Civil War and early years of the emigration. It is particularly striking that, despite political differences, the political leaders among the émigrés at this period were indifferent to the emigration. Their main concern was the fate of Russia and this united them all, whether they were 'professional revolutionaries' or right-wing extremists, supporters of the White movement or those opposed to intervention.

This generation of political activists was followed by very different editors of the Russian press abroad. First of all they were much younger: *Nedelia* was edited by V.I. Ilinsky (b. 1895) and S.Ya. Savinov (b. 1897) and *Novosti* by K.K. Tsegoev (b. 1894). Thus they were all members of a younger or 'second' generation. This was not a definition which was simply chronological, as the older generation included such people as Gurvich (b. 1894), Savitsky (b. 1895), and Jakobson (b. 1896) who had graduated and worked in Russia. So when they arrived in Prague their attitudes had to some extent been formed by their experience of the old regime and, moreover, they arrived as teachers rather than as students of the 'second generation'.

Differences in age and social position resulted in a different level of involvement in the local community. Although Russian students lived relatively secluded lives, Russian professors often found themselves in a very small and close-knit community. Furthermore, economic questions such as employment or housing were usually less acute for those who represented the older generation of teachers. At the same time, the so-called younger generation still had very strong connections with Russian culture. They had vivid memories not only of the tragic years of the Revolution and the Civil War but also of the peaceful years before the war. All of them tried to contribute to literature and journalism exclusively in the Russian language. This strong connection with their own culture while abroad was vital for them; returning to Russia was no longer their primary aim.

Those trends which can be illustrated by reference to the editorials in Russian newspapers can be further substantiated by developments within the Russian press in Czechoslovakia in general. A new style of publication was emerging which focused on a very particular audience. It was not dependent on any form of government support but either raised money from sales or was supported by its publishers.

A good example is the journal *Russkii Vrach* (Russian Doctor) regularly published in Czechoslovakia from 1934 to 1940. From the second issue it was subtitled 'Publication of the Union of Doctors – Citizens of the Republic of Czechoslovakia'. Here all connections with the emigration, even of legal status, were cut. While most émigrés were still stateless and carried Nansen passports, doctors who had managed to find employment or considered that it would be easier to do so if they were Czech nationals, adopted Czech citizenship.

Another long-lived publication was *Morskoi Zhurnal* (Journal of the Sea) which paradoxically appeared regularly (from 1928 to 1941) in a country which was totally land-locked. The driving force behind this venture was Lieutenant M.S. Stakhevich, a 1913 pre-war graduate of the Petersburg Marine Corps. He was also the chairman of the Prague Wardroom, an organisation of marine officers and naval cadets. Nevertheless, no matter how active he was he could not possibly have started his activities had it not been for the 76 students from Bizerta who arrived in Prague in March 1922. The remnants of the Russian navy based in the Black Sea had been transferred to Bizerta in Tunisia. Although all these students were supposed to have graduated by 1928, a number must have found employment in Czechoslovakia and thus guaranteed a readership for the journal.

Czech Language

The academic Russian world was invited to Czechoslovakia with the idea that this would be a temporary haven before its return to Russia. The need to dedicate itself to Russia is part of the explanation why this group of highly intelligent people, with well-honed skills in communication did not find their relations with Czech society easy. The experience of those who were less academic could be quite different. In May 1929 a Congress of Russian Agricultural Workers was held in Prague. The correspondent of *Nedelia* noted that, despite many difficulties, the Cossacks had settled down fairly well and that an interesting process of Russo–Czech assimilation could be observed.[12] Of all the groups within the emigration, he wrote, it was the peasants and Cossacks who had adjusted best to the social life and customs of the local population and had learned the language. After the congress, a dinner rounded off proceedings and Cossack and Slovak songs alternated with Czech and Russian conversation. In fact the newspaper correspondent was not totally accurate, in that the majority of the Russian and Cossack peasant farmers never formally learned Czech: they just acquired a working knowledge through everyday contact. Even 30 years later it was still possible to come across people in Czech villages who had become completely assimilated but who spoke an extraordinary mixture of Russian and Czech which was clearly understood in the locality. They used a mixture of quite complex structures, as well as Czech folk expressions, which no one would have learned at school. This mixture of Russian and Czech had a clear utilitarian function but it would have horrified any grammatical purist.

The question of language was central to most academic concerns.

Similarities between Slav languages had led in the first instance to the feeling that translation was unnecessary. In actual fact this could lead to many errors in understanding and mistakes because the main ideas and vocabulary seemed so similar. The Czech and the Russian intelligentsia could communicate in German although in the immediate post-war years this was largely taboo. Once the hope of a rapid return to Russia evaporated and it became clear that any Russian academic community in Prague was likely to be a transitory phenomenon, the question of which language should be used by the Russian scholars abroad became increasingly important.

The changing nature of the Russian academic world can be seen in N.M. Mogiliansky's article, 'The People's University'.[13] Mogiliansky, the founder of the Department of Ethnology at the Russian Museum in St Petersburg, had been a lecturer at the Sorbonne and then at the Russian Pedagogical Institute in Prague. In 1927 he became head of the Department of Natural and Applied Sciences of the People's University. Commenting on a brilliant lecture on Chekhov given by S.V. Zavadsky, at which there were only 20 or so young people and a few grey-haired men present, he asked: 'Where is our Russian audience? Where is the audience that three or five years ago filled the lecture halls?' Mentioning that many graduates had left the country and that others had to provide for themselves by hard physical labour, he stressed that was not the whole story, as 'the halls at the dances during the holiday season were packed and Russians of all ages hung round the dusty rooms full of cigarette smoke'. He did not find it surprising that, in Paris, the People's University had turned into a kind of polytechnic for industrial skills in its struggle for survival. But he saw Prague as a unique place, where there was still the luxury of engrossing oneself in pure science. He complained that the émigrés did not appreciate the opportunities open to them and were more interested in material questions.

Mogiliansky was obviously correct in one aspect of his commentary: Russian student life had disappeared. The academic atmosphere which had filled the lecture halls of the People's University during its early years no longer existed. But he was not fair to the so-called young Russian intellectuals in Prague. Even in Russian Prague's heyday, Russian students were older than average. By 1930 there were far fewer students in the 20–25 age group as they would all have had to have left Russia as children. The majority of recent graduates were aged around 40. That is the age when, even in normal circumstances and with a solid financial background, people start to lose interest in acquiring masses of new cultural information. But arguably it does not mean that they also lose interest in 'pure science'. On the contrary, people concentrate on their own profession and seek connections in the international academic world. This was also happening in the émigré world.

N.S. Trubetskoy, one of the leaders of Eurasianism, argued in December

1930 that it was quite normal for young people to disperse their energies over a wide area. He went on to assert that maturity brought concentration. This referred to both choice of subjects and the means by which they were propagated. Thus, for émigrés, the question of language became very pressing. Who should be addressed and in which language?

> To write in Russian for Russian scholars who attend 'congresses of Russian scholars abroad', is even more pointless than to write in Slovenian or Latvian: our Russian works hardly ever appear in Russia, but even if they do they are forbidden and cannot be quoted, whereas foreign writings of the same authors published in foreign scientific journals have a good circulation in Russia. Moreover, they are immediately famous in the whole Europeanised world.[14]

Trubetskoy did not mention the third factor which, for many, was the most important. Writing in another language and becoming part of the local or preferably the European academic community was far more profitable. By that time Trubetskoy was a professor at the University of Vienna and so perhaps the economics of the question was of less immediate importance to him. Trubetskoy's succinct exposition of the language question provides a good definition of the form in which a 'mid-career crisis' affected Russian émigré scholars. Both Mogiliansky and Zavadsky were born in 1871 and had been invited to Prague in the period 1921–23 as scholars with an international reputation. Czech government provision, however modest, cushioned the difficulties of emigration and, at 50 years old, both men preferred to work in Russian for the future of Russia. A decade later, it was not really possible for them to work in any other way, but this meant that they no longer had a real audience within the emigration and could not reach a Russian audience in the USSR. Thus they could not train their own successors in their disciplines in Russian. The professors' house – in fact a block of flats occupied by many leading members of the Russian academic community – in Prague acquired the nickname 'the common grave', which only served to emphasise their isolation.

This isolation was exacerbated by attempts to preserve Russian identity. In 1924 Zavadsky, a specialist in Russian civil law, created 'The Circle of Champions of the Russian Word' attached to the People's University. This had great difficulty in developing its activities. In 1929 a publishing venture 'Edinstvo' was launched. Its main aim was to unite the Russian, Ukrainian and Belorussian émigré communities based on scientific proof of the real unity of these three 'branches' of the same nation. A few brochures were published. Zavadsky lost touch with his own profession. Both men died in Prague: Mogiliansky in 1933, and Zavadsky in 1935.

The pressures on a younger generation were different. To begin with, Russian graduates of Czech institutions were to some extent isolated from the local community. B.V. Novak, head of the Committee for the Provision of Education for Russian Students in Brno, recalled that housing the students in purpose-built barracks had its advantages as well as disadvantages. On the one hand, the fact that they lived together created an illusion of being at home, but on the other hand, they did not even try to learn Czech, to adjust to a different way of life or to get to know other nationalities. For this reason, more mature students were subsequently placed with Czech families. Another commentator, Dr Alfred Fuchs, noted that, although Russians had always been interested in foreign ideas and developments, they behaved with great self-confidence and did not seem to care what others thought of them. In this respect he compared them with the English. Although he thought that the Russians found it hard to assimilate into other societies, those in Czechoslovakia had adjusted both financially and spiritually. He stressed that he did not mean that this should be seen as either denationalisation or betrayal.[15]

Students who graduated during this period when Russian students lived together until their graduation had characteristic signs of dualism. For example, Fedor Nikolaevich Dosuzhkov can be regarded as a Russian poet but a Czech doctor. He was born in Baku in 1899 and before the Revolution he entered Rostov University. But the Civil War interrupted his studies, and he emigrated in 1920. At first he found himself in Constantinople, but in 1921 he moved to Prague to continue his studies. He graduated from the medical department of Charles University, and from 1927 worked as an assistant at the neurological clinic of the university. He was an active participant in the life of Russian Prague, and in the work of the Society of Russian Doctors in Czechoslovakia in particular. Although his most prominent medical works were written in Czech and he is considered one of the founders of psychoanalysis in Czechoslovakia, he wrote his poems, reminiscences and some of his more personal professional thoughts and ideas on psycho-neuroses in Russian, and had to publish these at his own expense. Having become part of the Czech professional community, he remained faithful to Prague, where he died in 1982. In general the Russian medical community showed a very broad spectrum of cultural interests; although, in order to practise, doctors were among the first to take on Czech nationality, in matters of culture they were always interested in Russian developments. Another doctor, N.A. Kelin (1896–1970), wrote poems and also gathered a valuable collection of Russian paintings.

Broadly speaking, those without wide cultural interests lost touch with Russian cultural life and became part of the Czech professional environment much quicker. This also applied to those who had to live and work outside the main centres of settlement where there were very few Russians. In such circumstances assimilation was inevitable. This of course is almost impossible to document from émigré sources as those who assimilated simply dropped out of view and left no records of this process.

Émigré Politics

The decline in government aid led to greater interest in politics among the emigration. During the heyday of Russian Action, the government had required all academic organisations to be apolitical. In fact, it had tolerated activity on the part of the moderate left while trying to prevent the expression of right-wing views and organisations. At the same time national and regional aspirations were suppressed. Once this pressure relaxed, political views could be more publicly expressed.

The first to emerge were monarchist leanings among the military. Openly monarchist and military émigré organisations could not be registered in republican Czechoslovakia, but their views were achieving wider currency. They were different from the groups of the pro-monarchist military in Paris or Yugoslavia where there were courses for retraining junior officers. The courses on higher military science in Paris also had a strong influence on the way in which people of this persuasion behaved.

In Prague, the extent of these views may be seen in various organisations. The first was the Circle for the Study of the World War of 1914–18, created under the auspices of the Russian People's University. The idea of examining Russian participation in the war was not new: it had been fairly widespread for some time. But it was only put into practice in the spring of 1927, when the Student Committee applied to organise a course. This was mentioned in the committee's report and it seems clear that prior to this, during Russian Action, the leaders of the émigré community realised that such a course would have been seen as a tactless irritant by the Czech authorities.

The course was extraordinarily successful. Seventy-six people applied to attend immediately, and before long the figure reached 220. This compares very favourably with the 18 people who joined the Circle of the Champions of the Russian Word, a figure that remained unchanged to the very end.[16] It is even more telling that study of the First World War did not simply concentrate on the obvious historical aspects. Discussions on current ideas of tactics and strategy were included in a special study group attached to the Circle for the Study of the World War.[17] This was beginning to look like the courses which various officers' organisations, including ROVS (Russkiy

Obshchevoinskiy Soyuz), the Russian veterans' organisation, had been trying to set up in order to keep military skills up to date within the emigration.

This type of organisation started appearing in Prague from 1927, but they never acquired a serious reputation. Some of them were 'anti-White', for example the Society of the Participants of the Volga Movement (1927). Its members were part of the predominantly Socialist Revolutionary movement, which with the help of the Czech legion had established itself in the Volga River region and later in Siberia, but was overthrown by Kolchak. The only influential military organisation, ROVS, existed initially, according to *Nedelia*, under the seemingly innocent title of 'The Russian Patriotic Union'. It was only on 23 May 1929 that this was changed to 'The Russian Military Union in Czechoslovakia'.[18] Subsequent to this, ROVS decided to create a separate branch in Czechoslovakia.[19]

The anniversary issue of the journal of the Brno branch of the Union of Russian Students in 1931 is a vivid example of the kinds of change which were occurring in Russian émigré society.[20] It opened with the customary greetings in Czech to the Czech people and to President Masaryk. But the issue was dedicated to Madame M. Lepařová, the chairwoman of the women's group, 'Slavs'. She was a philanthropist who shared Kramář's not Masaryk's views. This was followed by four portraits on separate pages, in the following order: the Grand Duke Nikolai Nikolaevich, President Masaryk, the Minister of Foreign Affairs Beneš, and K. Kramář. In the early 1920s it would have been impossible for this kind of publication to place the portrait of the Grand Duke first, because of the government's attitude to the Soviet Union. Moreover, the Communist and Social Democratic opposition in the 1920s frequently accused the government of spending the national budget on the forces of Russian counter-revolution. By 1931 almost all these restraints had disappeared. The Czechs had been unsuccessful in the role of international intermediary. The budget of Russian Action had been cut substantially and was no longer part of the opposition's arsenal against government policy. The anniversary volume was being published by the students with a view to raising money. Cutbacks in the government assistance available to them, combined with the international economic situation, meant that these students were in a very difficult situation financially.

With the changes in the nature of the emigration, its politics, too, had to change. The older generation had focused on the issues of the Russian Revolution and the Civil War. But this was increasingly being seen as irrelevant as those events receded into history. The nature of the emigration was changing and so was the Soviet Union. The predictions made by the generation that had been actively involved in the politics of late Imperial

Russia and the revolutionary period had not come about. The Bolshevik regime had not collapsed. An imminent return of military formations, backed by the forces of other European powers, was impossible. As the situation had evolved, so the emigration was rejecting the solutions propounded by the older generation. They looked for alternative ways of changing the Soviet regime.

This was made manifest in an unusual way. Prague, which had been the venue for the majority of academic, student, pedagogical and other non-political congresses for the Russian emigration, suddenly became the centre of party congresses. These congresses were quite different. It was no longer possible to invite participants from all over Europe. They were not held in large auditoriums or opened by politicians or leading members of the academic community. Czechoslovakia was no longer prepared to provide financial support for such undertakings. Nor was she so keen to issue entry visas for some of the delegates. But the main reason for the alteration in the nature of the congresses was that most of these organisations had an ever-decreasing number of committed and active supporters. Many of the groups had arisen in the conditions of emigration where arguments and dissension often turned erstwhile allies into opponents. However, they were unwilling to break away entirely from one another. Instead of forming new parties straight away, they tended to define themselves as factions or groups in the hope that eventually these would form the basis for a new organisation.

This was particularly true of the Socialist Revolutionary Party, which had a great many factions, fractions and subdivisions. One of the better known was Krest'yanskaya Rossiya (Peasant Russia) which had been formed by right-wing SRs and left-wing Kadets in Moscow in 1920.[21] It was referred to more often rather vaguely as a movement or tendency than as a party. It is difficult to ascribe many concrete actions to it within Russia although it claimed to have considerable influence there, 'perhaps on the majority of the intelligentsia'.[22]

Abroad it began its official émigré existence with the publication of S.S. Maslov's book, Rossiya posle 4-kh let revolyutsii (Russia after Four Years of Revolution). In 1922 in Prague a periodical, Krest'yanskaya Rossiya began to be published. It was edited by A.A. Argunov, A.L. Bem and S.S. Maslov and attracted attention owing to the standing of the contributors, who included Miliukov, Kizevetter and Sorokin. In 1925 it was replaced by Vestnik Krest'yanskoi Rossii (The Herald of Peasant Russia) published by the Central Bureau of the Foreign Groups of Peasant Russia. This new title and publication served to indicate that there had been a shift from theoretical to organisational and political work aimed at Russia. There were sections entitled 'News from Russia' and there were letters from Russia. The section 'In Russia' consisted of analyses by émigrés. Starting with issues 4–5 (June

1925) it was said that details of the organisation would be published, in addition to information about its achievements and decisions. *Vestnik Krest'yanskoi Rossii* alleged that it was in touch with five groups of sympathisers inside Russia. In issues 8–9, published in March 1926, it was said that the work in Russia was expanding and that there was now contact with eight groups of sympathisers. As such links expanded it became possible to send the publications to the Soviet Union. The editors argued that they should concentrate on the issues which were of immediate interest to those in Russia and that they needed to make the language of their articles more popular and accessible.[23]

In normal circumstances, eight groups of sympathisers could scarcely be considered sufficient to produce a political party of any significance. Nor would an interesting periodical which apparently influenced members of the intelligentsia be likely to do so. However, Krest'yanskaya Rossiya's leadership clearly drew parallels with Bolshevik experience. In 1912 the Sixth Conference of the Russian Social-Democratic Labour Party took place in Prague. Only 18 delegates attended and of these 16 were Bolshevik. A rival Menshevik conference organised by Trotsky was taking place in Vienna at the same time.[24] Most of the Russian population never even suspected that the former conference had taken place. Yet despite the splits within Russian Social Democracy and their apparent lack of support amongst the population as a whole, five years later the Bolsheviks seized power. Much later, Stalin was to explain that the conference had 'enormous impact on the history of our party'.[25]

Knowing how insignificant the Bolsheviks had appeared to be shortly before they took power inspired many émigré political activists, not only Krest'yanskaya Rossiya. They considered themselves to be in an analogous situation, with the potential to influence developments in Russia. Many émigré political groups began with a fairly vague idea which was gradually refined and made more appropriate to developments with the USSR. Activism in the Russian emigration took on a very specific connotation: it meant non-stop armed struggle with Soviet power. This could include the sending of terrorist or intelligence groups into Soviet territory, or negotiations with various governments over the possibility of armed intervention. Despite the fact that many émigrés had sympathy with this kind of activism, Prague was not a suitable place for it.

However, the emigration in Prague was also involved in a more peaceful kind of activism which rested on the power of language. Czech government policy towards the Soviet Union, with its emphasis on democracy, relied on the power of the written and the spoken word. In the early 1920s, the Socialist Revolutionary publication, *Revolutsionnaya Rossiya,* was printed on very thin cigarette paper with the aim of making it easier to smuggle into

Russia. In 1926, the March issue of *Krest'yanskaya Rossiya* which declared
the existence of growing groups of sympathisers in the Soviet Union, was
also published on this thin and light paper.

But the risks of infiltration into Soviet Russia were very high and the few
who managed to do so, or who read such émigré publications, frequently
paid for it with their lives. The character of the publications themselves and
the organisations which produced them were forced to change. It was no
longer possible to send in the traditional 'thick journals' containing a
detailed commentary which had fuelled dissent and public opinion in
Imperial Russia. Articles had to be short and to the point. All such work
took on an element of conspiracy, and this work – even in the emigration,
which seemed so cut off from Russia – began to seem more dangerous after
General Kutepov was kidnapped by Soviet agents in Paris in 1930. The need
to hide the identities of contributors, whether émigrés or from the Soviet
Union, increased the possibility of infiltration by Soviet agents. All of this
heightened the atmosphere of unhealthy suspicion within the emigration.
Political differences and debates evolved into accusations of criminal
activity. Denunciations to the police were not uncommon. People
wallowed in the mire of accusations and counter-accusations, passionate
defence and confessions in those cases where Soviet penetration could be
proved. However, the general need to become more conspiratorial meant
that, for the most part, suspicions could not be proved. Nonetheless, the
atmosphere remained unpleasant.

In 1928, Krest'yanskaya Rossiya organised a congress at which Trudovaya
krest'yanskaia partiia (the Peasant Labour Party) was founded. This
organisation stressed the extent of its links with Russia, which tended to
provoke the accusation that the scale of its activities in Russia was
exaggerated and it was alleged that letters supposedly written from Russia
were composed in the Prague editorial office. The political programme was
not particularly émigré in nature. In many ways this party resembled
agrarian parties in other democratic and capitalist states. It accepted the
socialist analysis that society was divided into classes while rejecting the idea
that class relationships had to be based on conflict. On the contrary, the
party considered that there were common interests between classes.
Members of Krest'yanskaya Rossiya argued that, although it was the party
of peasantry as a whole, it did not intend to pursue the interests of the
peasantry or any section of the peasantry at the expense of other social
classes. All forms of labour (*trud*), both manual and intellectual, were valued.
In many ways, Krest'yanskaya Rossiya's ideas were not particularly
innovative. Although the effect of the Russian Revolution was to turn them
into exiles, their ideas were part of the pre-revolutionary ideological
spectrum. Had they been in Russia during the period of NEP in the 1920s,

Krest'yanskaya Rossiya might have had a tangible impact. They claimed that during collectivisation Stalin resettled peasants in the border areas so that contacts across frontiers could not be maintained. But despite this hypothetical impact on the situation in their homeland, within the emigration itself Krest'yanskaya Rossiya was not particularly influential.

Eurasianism

By contrast, Eurasianism was conceived as a system of ideas which were to have universal application and would apply both to Russia and to the emigration. During the 1920s and 1930s this movement was influential in the major European centres. It has had a revival in Russia since the late 1980s and has received a great deal of attention there, although as G.S. Smith observes: 'As a body of doctrine, Eurasianism has been much more frequently summarised than critically examined.'[26] The texts have been republished and have given rise to a great deal of discussion. New archival material has come to light but much of the extensive correspondence between those who contributed to Eurasian publications and were influenced by Eurasian ideas has still to be studied. All this has stimulated interest in this particular group of émigré scholars and thinkers. Paradoxically, because of the renewed interest in these ideas and their application to the contemporary situation, the émigré context has often been obscured.

Eurasianism was inaugurated on 8 January 1921 when P.N. Savitsky published his review[27] of Prince N.S. Trubetskoy's work *Evropa i Chelovechestvo* (Europe and Mankind), although it is generally considered that the movement began its official existence in 1921 with the publication of *Iskhod k Vostoku* (Exodus to the East) in Sofia. Four little-known Russian intellectuals contributed to this volume of ten essays. They were Prince N.S. Trubetskoy, who was later to teach at the University of Vienna and would become a world famous authority on linguistics; P.N. Savitsky, a geographer and economist with a very wide range of intellectual interests, whom Struve considered one of his most brilliant pupils, and who spent most of his life in emigration in Prague; P.P. Suvchinsky, a music critic and many-sided intellectual, who left Sofia for Berlin; and G.V. Florovsky, a historian with enormous breadth of vision and a wide range of intellectual interests. Later he would become ordained as a priest and achieve renown as a theologian and proponent of ecumenism.

The essays dealt with a wide range of subjects and did not claim to follow a defined editorial line but they raised issues which were hotly debated. In the introduction it was stated that the authors were writing in a time of catastrophe and cataclysm and that they sensed the dying of the West and the rise of the East. That was accompanied by a redefinition of Russians and the peoples of the Russian world as neither European nor Asian but Eurasian.

The first essay by Savitsky discussed the turn to the East. This, he argued, was illustrated by the Russian Revolution which, for all its suffering and horror, showed that Russia was searching for truth. In other essays Savitsky was more down to earth. In one he discussed the correlation between centres of culture and the average temperature. In the civilisations of Mesopotamia and Egypt, cultures developed where the annual average temperature was 20°C. Since then, centres of culture had moved northwards. He argued that if this trend was to continue, then it seemed likely that the future centres of culture would be in Canada with adjacent districts in the United States, and parts of northern, central and eastern Russia and Siberia. The last essay by Savitsky, entitled ' "Continent-Ocean" (Russia and the World Market)', discussed the question of transport costs. Since transport by sea was so much cheaper than overland, the maritime nations had an important advantage. Savitsky examined various areas of Russia and suggested that Russia had to look at the problem in a different way. Her shoreline was largely frozen, or could be easily disrupted by hostile foreign powers, so Russia needed to develop a continental market independent of the world economy and the maritime powers. By producing and selling to neighbouring countries, Russia could create a diversified continental economy.

The essay by Suvchinsky, 'Strength to the Weak', addressed the old question of the split between the Russian intelligentsia and the people. Although many of the westernised intelligentsia had been forced into exile, the people had come under the domination of the most extreme representatives of that intelligentsia. Suvchinsky believed the time would soon come when the intelligentsia would repent, and at that point they would reunite with the Russian people under 'the one great all-resolving dome of the Russian Orthodox Church'. In a further essay, Suvchinsky expressed himself in near-apocalyptic terms: 'These are frightening times . . . terrifying epochs . . . times of great realisations of the Mystery, times frightening and blessed . . .'. To overcome the accompanying fear and disorientation, Suvchinsky called for a new culture and a new religious world view. Russian experience would lead in this new vision.

Florovsky attempted to analyse contemporary thought and culture. Both Slavophiles and Western Romantic thinkers had seen the fault of the West as being its rationalism. Such overvaluing of reason was seen as incorrect and it was considered that truth and vitality could only be found outside the West. In his essay 'Breaks and Connections', Florovsky addressed the fact that revolution had been a Russian ideal for a long period. It was clear that reality did not correspond to this vision. The only response and solution was total repentance. In another essay '"About non-Historical Peoples" (The Land of the Fathers and the Land of the Sons)' Florovsky discussed the question of historical creativity and how it was handed down the generations.

Trubetskoy discussed 'True and False Nationalism'. True nationalism was the product of self-awareness both for the individual and the nation. It had 'its origins in a unique national culture or was directed towards that culture'. Most false nationalisms, by contrast, focus on the idea of power. Trubetskoy considered that true nationalism had not existed in post-Petrine Russia and needed to be created in the future. He ended the article by saying: 'this will require the reversal in the consciousness of the Russian intelligentsia'. His next article was '"The Upper and Lower Storeys of Russian Culture" (The Ethnic Basis of Russian Culture)'. Here a long section is devoted to a linguistic examination of dialects in order to show the connections between various Slav groups and their connections with other foreign elements. The Slavs separated into three groups: the western Slavs whose lands adjoined the Romano–Germanic world, the southern Slavs who were within the Byzantine sphere of influence, and the eastern Slavs who chose the culture of Byzantium. Byzantine influence was beneficial for Russia whereas the West failed to inspire national creativity. Under Peter the Great this situation changed radically and Russians were supposed to be imbued with the Romano–Germanic spirit. But if Russia had been seen as a worthy successor to the cultural legacy of Byzantium, in terms of the West, Russian culture was at the tail end. This led to the creation of two gaping abysses, one between pre- and post-Petrine Russia and the other between the intelligentsia and the masses. However, the definition of Russian national life could not be limited simply to the distinction between the influence of Byzantine or of Romano–German culture. There also existed the Finno–Ugric and the Turkic peoples and their influence could be clearly seen in folk art and music, in ornamentation and literature. Any attempt to revive Russian culture had to take all these diverse elements into account and 'Russian culture . . . must rise up harmoniously from its foundations in Russian national life.'

The main themes of Eurasianism can be discerned in this volume. First, there was a need to define Russia's position in the world. If, as was stated, the Russians were part of neither Europe nor Asia but lived in Eurasia, this had to be analysed and explained. Such a definition involved the discussion of many subjects which had influenced the creation of Russian culture, including history and geography, economics, linguistics and ethnography. To some extent the discussion was a continuation of the nineteenth-century debates among the intelligentsia over Russia's situation and her relationship with Europe. The influence of Danilevsky's work, *Rossiya i Evropa* (Russia and Europe) published in 1869, is discernible. Trubetskoy's book, *Evropa i Chelovechestvo* (Europe and Mankind) appeared in Sofia in 1920 and its title seemed to echo these earlier concerns. But these essays must also be read in the light of the effects of revolution and civil war on émigré thinking and the pressing imperative of analysing the implications of the Russian Revolution. In Savitsky's words: 'The Russian Revolution is not an episode of European history only.'[28] He argued that Russia had become the ideological centre-point of the world. Much of this was associated with anti-Western feeling. This again harked back to Slavophile criticism of the West as being too rational and legalistic, and the imposition of Western forms of government had been blamed for deforming the Russian state and culture. The Bolsheviks could be seen as the most extreme example of Western culture. The Revolution was not so much a class struggle as the rising up of the Russian masses against the domination of a Europeanised governing class which had introduced a culture that was incomprehensible to them. All of this meant that Russia had to define herself correctly. This search for and refining of a definition was a major element in the programme of Eurasianism.

A second strand in their programme was more clearly political. In the context of the emigration this was hardly unexpected. As Trubetskoy argued in 1925,[29] Eurasianism began to formulate its ideas within the Russian emigration. As a result, it was ineluctably political. The emigration was a result of political events and, despite any desire on the part of émigrés to avoid politics, they could not do so as this would cause them to lose their identity as émigrés. Trubetskoy argued that since the main wish of the majority was to return to their homeland, they had to be constantly preoccupied with the conditions such as terror or famine which had made them leave. This meant that all ideas must first be examined from the point of view of their political content. Eurasianism was no different from other systems of thought in this respect. The introduction to *Iskhod k Vostoku* stated unequivocally that the Revolution had persuaded the authors that they had to oppose socialism. The question of what should supplant socialism was far less clear. Western forms of parliamentarianism were disliked. Parliamentary forms, it was argued, were too abstract, were not organic to society; it was too amorphous a form of individualism and left the individual too isolated. The Eurasians argued the need for an ideocratic state, which would be governed by an idea which incorporated the morality of the state. This idea would allow them to defeat Bolshevism. This theory led a number of opponents and critics to liken the Eurasians to their contemporary ideological opponents, both Bolshevik and Fascist. The Eurasians countered this by stating that Eurasianism was deeply anchored in a religious morality which was alien to both Communism and Fascism. However, the question of opposition to socialism was not undisputed. The literary critic Prince D. Sviatopolk-Mirsky,[30] an adherent of the movement, later became a Communist and returned to the Soviet Union where he died in the labour camps. The split in Eurasianism after 1928 was to a large extent over political questions.

This developed into the third part of the programme. The Revolution had a positive side: it brought about a search for deeper truth and meaning. The intelligentsia had to see the error of their ways and repent. This led to a religious world view as exemplified in Russian Orthodoxy. The difficulty for the Eurasians was how to reconcile these three diverse strands, and this was a task they never accomplished.

The publication of *Exodus to the East* was followed by a number of other volumes and periodicals in the 1920s and 1930s.[31] *Na Putyakh. Utverzdenie evraziitsev.* (On the way. The Affirmation of the Eurasians) and *Rossiya i Latinstvo* (Russia and the Latin West) were published in Berlin in 1922. *Evraziiskii vremennik* (The Eurasian Annals) appeared in Berlin in 1923 and 1925 and in Paris in 1927. A volume entitled *Tridsatye Gody* (The Thirties) appeared in 1931. Ten volumes of *Evraziiskaya khronika* (Eurasian Chronicle) were published between 1925 and 1928 in Paris, Prague and again in Paris. The programmes of the movement were published in Paris in 1926[32] and Prague in 1927.[33] A weekly publication appeared in Paris in 1928–29.[34] More authors joined the original four. A.V. Kartashev, a specialist on religion and the Church, and P.M. Bitsilli, a historian, contributed to *Na Putyakh* but did not participate in Eurasianism for very long. L.P. Karsavin, a religious thinker, and G.V. Vernadsky, who became the main Eurasian historian, along with D.S. Mirsky, contributed essays in 1925. The main authors engaged in vigorous polemic. Some of the original authors modified their views or even broke away. Florovsky criticised the movement in an article in 1928.[35] The Eurasian movement had received £10,000 from an English philanthropist, Henry Spalding, which meant that, unlike many other émigré enterprises in their early stages, financial problems did not dominate proceedings. Publications could be subsidised until 1928 when the money ran out. After 1928, the Eurasians split into the more left-wing section of the movement centred in Paris, and others, centred around Savitsky in Prague, who disagreed with the group in Paris. No doubt political splits were exacerbated by financial problems.

Eurasianism was a more all-embracing and more ambitious set of ideas than that of most political parties. It was an attempt to identify the processes in Russia which had led to the cataclysm of the Revolution, but it was more than that. It was also an attempt to define a new world view or *Welt-anschauung*. The ambitious scholarly programme interested many of the original theorists and adherents. A political aspect was integral to the Eurasianism, as well as a religious element, based on Eastern Orthodoxy. The tragedy of Eurasianism was that it was almost impossible to combine these three elements.

The basis of the Eurasian scholarly and academic programme is explained most fully in the introduction to N.S. Trubetskoy's essay: 'To the Problem of Russian Self-knowledge' and in Savitsky's article 'Eurasianism's Scholarly Tasks' published under the pseudonym of P. Logovikov in the volume *The Thirties. The Declaration of the Eurasianists (Tridsatye Gody. Utverzhdenie Evraziitsev*. no 7). Trubetskoy argued that the key concept in any complete understanding of world cultures is that of personality. This refers not just to the personal – that is, the individual reflection of a biological being – but can mean a composite personality, a reflection of many individuals; a symphonic personality. A symphonic personality would be, in the first instance, that of a people or nation and then a group of nations creating a particular culture. Every personality has different faces (*lik*) which are defined by particular circumstances. The individual, for example, might have a domestic face as a well as a public face for work. The nature of the individual alters with time. The composite personality simultaneously contains the faces of individual nations within a multinational personality. For Trubetskoy the important fact was that 'the personality does not coincide with any one of these faces or with any one of these individuals: the personality consists of the links between them and the totality of them all'.[36]

Having produced this complex definition of the personality, Trubetskoy suggested that there should be a scholarly discipline for the study of this subject, personology, which would be the key to a whole system of scholarship and would have to co-ordinate the efforts of many areas of knowledge: not simply those in the humanities and the social sciences, but also the natural sciences. The personality has its physical and physiological side as well and interacts actively with the surrounding environment. The first step towards achieving this grandiose plan would require wide-ranging descriptive work, but subsequently this would have to be analysed in many disciplines. From these analyses should arise 'the theory of the given personality' which would determine the inner links between the individual attributes of a particular personality and the specific characteristics which determine it. 'The theory of a particular personality, therefore, organically develops from the scholarly research and analyses and at the same time defines and determines the further direction of these studies.'[37]

The assessment of various nations and national characteristics was one of Prince Trubetskoy's fundamental concerns. In *Europe and Mankind* he put forward the case for a relativist assessment of differing cultures. He advocated the need for a complete revolution in thinking and a denial of egocentrism, according to which individuals saw themselves as the centre – or, in this case Europe, the product of Romano–Germanic civilisation, saw itself as the centre of development. Trubetskoy wanted to make it clear that no culture is central but that all peoples and cultures are equal and that one cannot refer to higher or lower civilisations.[38] He went on to emphasise that the important aspect of his book was that it was not anti-Western but against Eurocentrism. Further, it was not simply a product of his experience of the Revolution and emigration, which found Russians begging for favours and help from their European neighbours, but the product of ideas from ten years earlier. He had felt that earlier his ideas were so contrary to received opinion that no one was prepared to understand them, whereas now they received a slightly more sympathetic hearing.[39]

Thus, some of the ideas of the Eurasian movement arose before the Revolution. This applied not only to Trubetskoy but also to Vernadsky, who discussed the particular features of Russian colonialism before the Revolution in an article 'Protiv Solntsa' (Against the Sun) and Savitsky who was interested in geographical questions. This differentiated the Eurasian movement from other post-revolutionary émigré political movements, which were purely a reaction to the Revolution and Civil War and often were a complete reversal of previous assumptions. However, even if some of the Eurasian ideas had their genesis before 1917, it was the experience of the Revolution and Civil War that caused these ideas to be taken up by the Russian émigrés.

In his criticism of the ideas of Trubetskoy's book, Savitsky in his review began to develop some of the basic assumptions of Eurasianism. Trubetskoy's ideas were not dissimilar to other attempts to preserve national identity or other work directed against westernisation. Although overall Savitsky agreed with Trubetskoy, he thought that in some respects he was unrealistic. Cultures needed to be strong and powerful, and therefore unequal, in order to resist both military and cultural aggression. They could be considered equal in an ideological sense, which Savitsky understood as the main direction and aim of both a nation's and an individual's life: this could be achieved by technology and empirical knowledge. However, in order to resist cultural aggression, nations needed equality of methods, otherwise Romano–Germanic oppression would simply be replaced by some other kind of oppression. He considered that a call for cultural emancipation addressed to the whole of mankind would achieve some kind of mystical status but was not a practical programme that could be achieved in the near future.

Savitsky thought Trubetskoy mistaken in accusing the Romano–Germanic people of egocentrism and in his appeal that they shed the egocentrism which made them see their culture as perfect and superior. Savitsky argued that the appeal of any ideology was precisely that it appeared to be higher and more perfect. If one rejected the egocentrism in one's own ideology, then there was no reason to defend it. Conversely, egocentrism led nations to defend their position in relation to other nations.

Russia was considered strong enough to resist Romano–Germanic oppression, Savitsky continued. But she should not be seen in a traditional manner because her strength came from the fact that she was Eurasian. Thus Savitsky concludes that, in order to be rid of Trubetskoy's horror of universal Europeanisation, Eurocentrism must be counterbalanced by Eurasian egocentrism.

Here was one of the problems intrinsic to Eurasianism both in its older émigré variant and in more modern versions. What was its main aim? Was it intended to add to the number of national ideologies so that Eurasianism would be seen as the equal of existing ideas, or was it supposed to replace the existing dominant Romano–Germanic civilisation?

Although these arguments were largely theoretical and the questions discussed had been raised before the war, the experience of war, revolution and emigration had significant effects on the development of Eurasianism. In response to criticism that they were trying to create an ideology artificially, adherents replied that the spiritual core of Eurasian beliefs was a reflection of personal experience.[40]

In *Iskhod v Vostoku*, Savitsky pointed out that the French Revolution had occurred in a European country. Despite its new revolutionary message, the European states were able to restrain and occupy France. But, as a result of the Russian Revolution, the two faces of Russia were revealed. One was turned towards Europe and carried the 'new word' of proletarian revolution, while the other was turned away from Europe. This happened because Russia was East as well as West. From this position, the Eurasians argued that the significance of the Russian Revolution was much wider. Their efforts were largely directed towards trying to explain and analyse Russia's future evolution so that her particular nature could be seen positively in any development.

The Eurasians raised important questions in a way that found a ready audience among the emigration. Moreover, some of their attitudes and approaches mirrored wider European concerns. Some commentators have seen parallels not only between Eurasianism and the Russian debates among the intelligentsia in the nineteenth century, but also with European writers and thinkers such as Spengler and Toynbee who tried to chart the rise and fall of European civilisation and its values.

For the Russian émigrés in the early years, the burning question was not so much the causes of the Revolution as why the February Revolution, which had occurred without bloodshed, had turned into the three-year nightmare of cruelty and carnage of the Civil War, which was eventually won by the Bolsheviks. Almost everyone – and this included the leaders of the White movement such as Generals Kornilov and Denikin and Admiral Kolchak – had acknowledged the legitimacy of the February Revolution.

The pre-revolutionary democratic political parties appealed to Russia to follow a European path of development. But the Russian Revolution had not done so. It did not follow the plans of the Kadets, the Socialist Revolutionaries and Mensheviks, even though these groups held power for eight months in 1917 and attracted 75 per cent of votes during the elections to the Constituent Assembly which took place after the Bolshevik seizure of power. It seemed unlikely that either Miliukov's new tactics or the programmes of new political parties such as Krest'yanskaya Rossiya would help these groups to achieve their aims in the future. Political strategy was not the answer. The problem was much more serious and much deeper. Either Russia was still very backward and had not matured sufficiently either politically or socially to reach European standards or Russia had been betrayed by the traditional attitudes of 'Orthodoxy, Autocracy and Nationalism'. Many might have wished to believe that autocracy was entirely to blame, but it was hard to do so. They could still remember the powerlessness of tsarism when it came to dealing with many problems of the old regime. The period of Rasputin's influence had highlighted the weaknesses of the system, and immediately after the February Revolution all former monarchist sentiment seemed to have disappeared. Such examples clearly demonstrated that Imperial Russia had fallen far short of any ideal, but the difficulties of the present made nostalgia overwhelming. Attempts to lay the blame at the door of a Judaeo-German-Masonic conspiracy failed to convince most thoughtful individuals. *Smena Vekh* (Change of Landmarks), chronologically the first of the post-revolutionary émigré groups, called for repentance, declared the White movement mistaken historically, and announced the Bolsheviks to be the natural instruments of the national mission. This analysis and solution to the problem frightened the majority of the émigrés.

The Eurasians tried to deal with these questions more sympathetically. They acknowledged that Russia had a unique task and that the Bolsheviks had played a useful role in revealing this mission. They had rid Russia of historical trappings and shown that she was not simply a European country to be evaluated according to the standards of the most developed European states. But the Eurasians emphasised that the Communist experiments had ruined the Russian economy and it would take a very long time to rebuild it.

Prince Trubetskoy drew extreme conclusions from this analysis. He argued that Russia would become a Western colony in the near future. The

West would unite and create a super-coalition which would restore order in Russia. This would not happen at the behest of the emigration: it would occur at a moment when it seemed beneficial to the West. Russia would be left with the semblance of independence and the government would enjoy only the rights that other governments of colonial states enjoyed. The political complexion of such a government would be irrelevant. In Trubetskoy's opinion this would happen if the West provided economic support for Soviet Russia or even if the Bolsheviks brought about world revolution. Nothing could alter the situation. 'The well-being of European Communist states would be maintained by the blood and sweat of Russian workers and peasants.' Trubetskoy considered that, whereas in Europe people were thinking about their national identity, in Russia the position was worse as the Russian intelligentsia had been educated to European standards and thought they needed to learn from Europe. They would be prepared to submit to foreign oppressors and this could well be fatal for Russia.[41]

Trubetskoy went on to ask what the emigration could do in such circumstances. In his view, ways of restoring various aspects of the state in everyday life in Russia were impossible for émigrés. Instead they were left with a more intangible task. Members of the intelligentsia had to provide ways of resisting foreign dominance. He called on them to free themselves from Western blinkers and to reach for the treasures in Russian spiritual culture in order to create a new world outlook. This would be based on national culture, which would both develop from this outlook and strengthen it. He believed this task was far more important than all the political manoeuvring and argument which occupied the political élite.

In many ways this was a scholarly rather than a political programme. It was vast in scope, as Russia could not be properly understood by herself but had to be placed in the context of a world order. Savitsky stressed this by saying, 'Eurasianism contains the kernel of the search for universal truth.' [42] And it was this goal which attracted younger members of the Russian intelligentsia.

Many current commentators on Eurasianism argue that one of the problems of the movement was its inability simply to develop this academic research without becoming involved in politics. This led to infiltration of the movement by Soviet intelligence and eventually to its complete collapse. However, such criticism is based on a misunderstanding of the émigré situation. In the first place, as Trubetskoy had pointed out, the emigration was intrinsically political: to abandon politics would mean loss of identity. Secondly, no academic programme of research is likely to attract mass support. Moreover, it was difficult to introduce new ideas and new approaches into the academic world if, as Russian émigrés, they were not properly established within it. The history of Eurasianism shows that everything was more difficult in emigration. But, owing to the policy of Russian Action in Prague and the creation of a Russian academic community, some of the basic requirements needed to establish a new academic school were coming into existence. Scholars of Eurasianism emphasise that the enthusiasm for the idea in Prague was striking. This was sometimes connected to the charismatic personality of Savitsky and sometimes to the fact that Eurasians were involved in real scholarship. Some of the most talented scholars at the Russian Legal Faculty in Prague became involved in Eurasianism.

Savitsky and Florovsky had moved to Prague from Sofia. Immediately they found considerable support amongst younger scholars. Professor N.N. Alekseev, the political theorist and Vernadsky, the historian, began to contribute to Eurasian publications. S.G. Pushkarev, another historian, and M.V. Shakhmatov, another political theorist, joined them. Others such as M.A. Tsimmermann, a lawyer, sympathised with their ideas. The majority of these men were born between 1887 and 1895. Alekseev, the oldest, was born in 1879. Many of an older generation of scholars, such as Kizevetter, Struve and Spektorsky, all born between 1866 and 1875, opposed Eurasianism. For a short time this gave rise to an intense but fruitful intellectual environment. However, quite soon Florovsky left Prague and abandoned his Eurasian beliefs. Alekseev too left Prague, and moved to Berlin, where he could be contacted fairly easily, but Vernadsky left for Yale, where, especially during the first few years, he complained of the lack of intellectual contacts. As Russian students in Prague completed their studies, they also left and the intellectual life of the academic centre began to decline even before it was properly established. This signalled the end of most hopes for an independent role for the Russian emigration. As Izgoev put it: 'All hopes were directed over there [i.e. towards Russia].'[43]

Just as Krest'yanskaya Rossiya tried to turn its activities towards work within Soviet Russia, the Eurasians attempted to do the same. In 1926 Savitsky travelled to Russia illegally to attend an underground congress of Eurasians. He realised fairly quickly that he was being followed but thought he had managed to escape this surveillance. Perhaps he did do so at some point but he was not aware that the congress had in fact been organised by OGPU, the secret police. After this visit, the French section of Eurasianism, based in the Paris suburb of Clamart, was instructed to intensify contacts with visiting Soviet citizens. The newspaper *Evraziya* (Eurasia) was financed from the funds donated by Spalding, the British philanthropist. Even Prince Trubetskoy was seduced by these developments. In the first two issues of *Evraziya* he published an article 'Ideocracy and the Proletariat' which was very pro-Soviet. But this initiative did not work out as expected. Instead of attracting Communists the Clamart group 'themselves became attracted by Communism and Marxism'.[44]

Savitsky left the editorial board before the first issue of *Evraziya* was published. In issue 7, Trubetskoy declared that he had resigned. It led to the so-called 'Clamart split' within Eurasianism. This had a devastating effect. Not only did it mean that a number of Eurasians left, but the fact that Eurasianism had become so openly pro-Soviet and pro-Marxist scared away many sympathisers among the anti-Marxist émigré intelligentsia.

Nevertheless, Savitsky, Alekseev, Il'in and a few others tried to recreate Eurasianism in its academic form. They published the seventh volume of essays as *Utverzhdenii evraziitsev* (Declaration of Eurasians) and called it *Tridsatye Gody* (The Thirties). The difficulty of the enterprise may be judged by the fact that Savitsky had to write five out of 16 articles using the pseudonyms Logovikov and Lubensky. Alekseev and Il'in each wrote two articles. Ten authors contributed to the volume, which was more than in the first publications, even if the quality of the articles was lower.

Savitsky tried to explain the academic programme of Eurasianism fully and systematically in an article, 'Nauchnye zadachi evraziistva' (Scholarly Goals of Eurasianism) and showed how that programme had developed in the 1920s. But it was already too late. Political developments, the growing economic difficulties and the ageing of the core of the emigration showed that the original hope of a return home would not be realised.

In a letter to Savitsky in 1930 Trubetskoy pointed out that a change of direction was usually associated with mid-career difficulties. He identified the main problem of the article. 'Was it discussing Russian scholarship in general or the academic programme of Eurasianism?' Trubetskoy considered that there were only two serious scholars associated with Eurasianism at that moment – Savitsky and Vernadsky – adding in brackets that the rest did not count. Amongst Russian scholars in general, Eurasianism was just one of many theories and by no means widely accepted. This could be explained in part by the very different way in which Soviet scholarship was developing. Trubetskoy thought Savitsky's article illustrated one of the most salient features of Eurasianism: 'the disparity between the enormous scale of the work envisaged and the small amount of people involved'.[45] Even this short extract from a five page letter full of detailed argument demonstrates the poor timing of the whole programme.

For Trubetskoy there was only one possible solution: to free himself from Eurasianism, concentrate totally on his research in linguistics 'and . . . work for the all-European culture that claimed it would become universal'. Other Eurasians, while continuing with their research, tended to concentrate on political activities. As émigré politics seemed increasingly to be a side-show, it appeared that Eurasianism could only be fully developed in Russia, and they had to try to get there by any means available. All the problems associated with such underground activity affected the subsequent development of Eurasianism as well.

Although the cultural and academic achievements of the Russian emigration were considerable and often achieved at great personal cost, the political side of émigré life, with its plethora of leaders and insufficient followers, in addition to the difficulty and hopelessness of the causes espoused, could lead to both tragedy and, on occasions, farce. The first Eurasian congress was held on 1–5 September 1931. It attracted 18 delegates with V.N. Il'in arriving late. One exchange in the minutes illustrates the way in which trivia could attract far too much attention.

During a debate on work within the Soviet Union, N.N. Klepinina addressed K.A. Chkheidze as 'comrade Chkheidze'. Chkheidze drew the chairman's attention to the unusual mode of address, which he believed had been used in order to offend him. Then Klepinina addressed him as Mr (*gospodin*) Chkheidze, which did not improve matters as Chkheidze considered that the normal method of address was by name and patronymic. Klepinina, referring to Savitsky, stated that the word 'comrade' could not be considered insulting for a Eurasian. Chkheidze responded by saying that he had been familiar with the word 'comrade' since childhood but it was an odd way of copying the Soviet Union where it was more normal to address people as 'citizen'. Savitsky explained that this should not be seen as insulting. 'Comrade' was used in the USSR, as was the new orthography which they had also accepted. Klepinina then shook hands with Chkheidze – which was greeted with applause.[46]

Despite such seemingly ridiculous episodes, political activity was essential for the emigration. A good example was Trubetskoy's return to Eurasianism when he had argued convincingly and at length why he had to give it up.[47] Rising international tension in Europe and the rapid growth of German National Socialism had an impact on the younger generation of émigrés. Fascist sympathisers appeared even among Eurasians. When A.V. Meller-Zakomelsky, who ran the Circle for Russian Political and Cultural Studies in Berlin and regarded himself as a Eurasian, sent his programme to the Eurasian Central Committee it provoked a discussion on the subject of race at the meeting of the presidium of the committee with representatives of the Prague Eurasian group, on 9 July 1934. Savitsky opened the discussion by declaring 'there was some truth in the idea that spirituality was typical of a particular race, although there were no high or low races. Eurasianism meant the co-operation of races, their close unity in spiritual and creative work.' He suggested that Trubetskoy should write an essay on race to be published in the *Evraziiskya tetradi* simply for the benefit of members of the movement. This suggestion was accepted by the meeting.[48]

Trubetskoy's article 'On Racism' subsequently became widely known owing to Roman Jakobson's reprinting of it.[49] In the same year, 1935, Trubetskoy also published his article 'Of the Governing Idea of the Ideocratic State'. It was intended to illustrate that Eurasianism was different from Fascism. In the sequel to this, which appeared in the last edition of *Evraziiskya khronika,* Trubetskoy tried to show the difference between Eurasianism and the ideology of the Soviet Union, also an ideocratic state.[50]

Such articles by Trubetskoy and other Eurasians were important as, both directly and indirectly, they affected wide sections of the emigration and did so more effectively than the ever-decreasing membership of Eurasian organisations. But they needed a theory and borrowed it from Eurasianism. N. Arseniev, a member of the older generation, born in 1888, who was a philosopher and theologian, wrote an article for the Young Russian publication. He was a sympathiser of the Mladorossy (Young Russians) rather than a member and his article was a friendly critique of Eurasianism. The editors of the volume considered it necessary to add that Young Russians were 'close spiritual relatives of Eurasianism' and believed that they would co-operate both while in emigration and in Russia.[51] A. Izgoev, who saw himself as being separated from Eurasianism by 'an abyss', acknowledged that the young Russians revived Russian conservative and right-wing political thought. He considered that if any reasonable ideas emanated from the right, as opposed to pointless bloodthirsty gibberish, then that was a result of Eurasian writings. He identified the Mladorossy as a new political organisation which was achieving some success among émigré youth but thought they had no new ideas themselves. 'They simply picked up the scraps of Eurasian ideas and combined them with their leader, a legitimate autocratic emperor.'[52]

Young Russians

The Young Russians had far more members than the Eurasians. Their language was more accessible and did not require much intellectual effort on the part of their supporters. They attracted followers by means of their uniforms, banners, oaths, ceremonies and the like.[53] They were not supported by students but by the children of émigrés who had been unable to complete their studies and 'who had learned about work in factories and mines . . . and had experienced exploitation by the sweat of their brow'.[54]

The Young Russians originated in Munich where, in 1923, the Soiuz Molodoi Rossii (The Union of Young Russia) was formed. At that time they had almost no resonance in Prague; this occurred only after the winding up of Russian Action. It was in Prague that the Young Russians held their first congress, in 1932. The Young Russians themselves acknowledged their debt to Eurasianism. In 1928 their leader A. Kazem-Bek wrote that: 'The synthesis of Europe and Asia, our cradle and our school, will be carried out by Young Russia, which will bring about this Eurasian desire.' The other ideological leader, K. Elita-Velichkovsky, argued that their ideas were a revival of Russian thinking and were practical, not theoretical.

The Eurasians acknowledged the link with the Young Russians although they did so rather patronisingly. They saw them as accepting a monarchist idea while trying to accept Eurasianism as well. To the Eurasians they were a mixture of 'vulgarised Eurasianism and monarchist legitimacy' but since the Young Russians shared the political, social and religious ideas of Eurasianism, they were to be preferred to other émigré political parties.[55] This link may have played a role in the choice of Prague as the venue for the first conference of Young Russia.

As the international political situation in Europe altered, so did the dividing lines between the various émigré parties. Italian Fascism attracted youthful émigré supporters. However, as Iu. Arseniev, a supporter of Young Russia put it, it was not the ideology and in particular the religious and philosophical side which interested them, but Fascism's practical results and its approach to popular psychology.[56] In 1928, a wide spectrum of émigré politicians might have subscribed to this statement, including the Eurasians, the Change of Landmarks movement, and individuals such as Berdiaev or Struve, not to mention those Russian Fascists and pro-Fascist groups which arose in the mid–1920s. But the rise of German National Socialism changed the situation radically.

Race was the key to Nazism, and the Slavs were categorised as subhuman. It was no longer sufficient simply to see Fascism as a result of the crisis of democracy. With the rise of Hitler, it became increasingly clear to the emigration that Europe was facing a new war. Moreover, this war would be waged against the Slavs and in particular the Russians. Hitler's actions were variously interpreted. Some argued that he was being supported by the military-industrial complex while he suppressed the Communists. Others considered that the real political challenges he faced would make him abandon the ideas expressed in *Mein Kampf*. There was also a widely held belief that Hitler would start a war with the USSR, and with Stalin, rather than with Russia.

The possibility of a new war split the emigration again, cutting across previous political divides of right and left and the divisions produced by the Civil War. *Oboronchestvo* (defencism) united all those who felt that defence of Russia was paramount. It brought together people of widely divergent positions on both the right and left wing during the Revolution, Civil War and in emigration. On the other side, *porazhenchestvo* (defeatism) united those who felt that war was the only possibility of defeating Bolshevism and that it was legitimate to use any ally in this aim. On the whole, it was groupings on the right which occupied this position. But defencism and defeatism were dealing with one question only. Whom should they support when war broke out between Hitler's Germany and Stalin's Russia? The defencists were quite clear that Germany's aim was to enslave Russia and that they had to defend their compatriots against Nazism.

The Czech government realised the dangers inherent in National Socialism earlier than many others. Thus from the outset they supported émigré defencists and took various measures against defeatists who were looking for German support. As a result, for a short while between 1936 and 1938, Prague became a leading defencist centre, second only to Paris. The Eurasians with Savitsky were at their head. They were supported by Krest'yanskaya Rossiya led by Maslov and some of the left-wing Cossacks – representatives of those groups in Prague which still had some influence.

Some of the defencists in Paris, led by left-wing Eurasians, had organised the Union for the Return to the Motherland and more or less stopped criticising the Soviet regime. In Prague defencists abandoned Denikin's idea that they should try to influence the Red Army in order to turn it against the Bolsheviks. Instead they intensified their criticism of Soviet power. Eurasians noted that after 1935 Stalin turned away from internationalism to nationalism, which resulted in the massacre of old Bolsheviks. Subsequently, Stalin made overtures to the internationalists without abandoning his more nationalist policies. Although it was argued that it was unlikely that he had set out to create an ideological vacuum, he had done so through his various U-turns. The Eurasians came to the conclusion that their ideas should fill this vacuum.[57] This led to increased criticism of the Soviet regime. In addition to Trubetskoy's article 'The Decline in Creativity',[58] Savitsky published work illustrating the way in which the Soviet regime was destroying historical monuments.

The complex Eurasian position did not achieve widespread support. Most attitudes were polarised: either a complete acceptance of Soviet power or total rejection and willingness to see Hitler as an ally. The divisions on this question were particularly acute amongst the Young Russians. When Miliukov gave a defencist speech in Prague, one of the local leaders of the Young Russians, Colonel Chapchikov, criticised his position with the words: 'It is better to have a horrible end than endless horror.'[59] Nevertheless, the Paris leadership finally adopted a pro-Soviet position.

The National Labour Alliance

The émigré organisation which eventually, after various changes of name, became known as the NTS (Natsionalno'-Trudovoi Soiuz – National Labour Alliance) had its roots in the veterans' association, ROVS. One of its ideological leaders, Kyrill Vergun was based in Prague. The NTS began from a fairly pro-German position, and acquired the nickname *nats malchiki* (national boys). The prefix *nats* could also be understood as deriving from Nazi rather than national. In 1936, the secretary of the Belgrade section of the NTS, M.A. Georgievsky, travelled to Berlin to find out whether any common cause could be made with the Nazis. He was quickly disillusioned and realised that their racist perspective prevented them from understanding ideas which were anti-Communist and pro-Russian.[60]

Prague was never considered the political centre of the Russian emigration: that honour belonged to Berlin fairly briefly and then moved to Paris, the acknowledged political and cultural centre. The academic nature of émigré society in Prague played a role in the development and discussion of political ideas and the library collections made the publications of diverse political groups available. Eurasianism is the clearest example of this. Both established academics and students were fascinated by new ideas and approaches and Savitsky's presence in Prague undoubtedly stimulated this further. Government policy, which had always sought to attract moderate left-wing forces, also left its mark. In the early days of the émigré community these forces predominated, but by the late 1930s the nature of the community had changed. Many had left to create new lives elsewhere; others had assimilated into local society. Previous definitions of right and left had altered and blurred earlier political divisions but once again the moderate left dominated Russian political life in Prague.

New Links with the Local Community

Throughout the existence of the First Czechoslovak Republic, the position of the German minority was one which could not be ignored. Even if they were no longer in the position of dominance they had occupied under the Habsburgs, they still accounted for over 22 per cent of the population. In the early years of the Republic the German parties refused to join the government. The majority of émigrés expressed anti-German attitudes to begin with but these began to alter as a result of British and French behaviour at the Versailles conference and, more importantly, as a result of Allied policy towards the evacuated White forces from the Crimea. This led to the growth of pro-German feeling among the émigrés.

Anti-German feeling was seen by both Czechs and Russians as something unreal and temporary. German-speaking Czech circles included a high percentage of Jews, who were part of the Czech intellectual élite. Many Russian scholars had graduated from German universities and those who had published scholarly works abroad had largely done so in German. Paradoxically, Soviet citizens found it easier to align themselves with Germany, particularly once the Soviet government allied with Germany in the 1920s. This meant that they were not dependent on the Czech government or other social institutions, nor bound by any unwritten moral obligations. In Prague co-operation between the German and émigré communities usually involved the Germans who worked in the Department of Slavonic Studies in the German University in Prague. Nevertheless, despite support from Masaryk himself, this co-operation was never easy to achieve. Forces resisting attempts at Czech–German co-operation were strong on both sides of the divide. From time to time, tension between the communities would be expressed in street violence and fights between students at the two universities. Russian students were usually actively involved and always took the Czech side.

Roman Jakobson, who at the time was a representative of the Soviet authorities in Prague, was a crucial link between the émigrés and German scholars. He became the editor of the Russian section of the journal *Slavische Rundschau* (The Slav Review) of the German University in Prague founded in 1929. Immediately he invited Russian émigrés who were close to him both in age and ideological sympathies to contribute to the journal. Since at that time Jakobson was a Eurasian, Savitsky was invited to participate. He contributed an article: 'Deutsch-slavische Wissenschaft einst, jetzt und in Zukunft' (German–Slav Scholarship in the Past, Now and in the Future). The editor introduced it with the statement that it was of fundamental importance and that, although the conclusions were drawn from geography, it called for study in other areas of Russo–German scholarship.[61] The author argued that, in the area of geography, Russian and German scholarship had worked together very fruitfully and German scholarship had even been dominant. But political pressure had made the latter turn away from the study of the continental land mass to the ocean. Savitsky considered this regrettable, as the study of Russian geography in German had arisen as a result of the need to understand Europe's relationship with Russia. This had to be continued and Savitsky thought the study of the Slav and German worlds would illuminate the problem.

This approach signified an important new departure. Before 1935, most of the numerous academic publications by Russian scholars in Prague were aimed at an audience within Czechoslovakia and appeared in Russian. The foreign language most frequently used for summaries of articles was French.

After 1928, some articles appeared in Czech, but the first use of German came in 1934 with the appearance of *Notes of the Research Section of the Russian Free University*, which contained an article by S.I. Gessen, in German. Once the rise of Nazism began to strain German–Czech relations, French, English or Czech became preferable to German.

Nevertheless, the apparent ban on German restricted the possibilities open to the Russian intellectual élite. From the end of the 1920s, Russian scholars wrote for *Slavische Rundschau*, *Germanoslavica* and other publications of the Slavistischen Arbeitsgemeinschaft an der Deutschen Universität in Prag and for Czech and Slovak publications such as *Ruch filosofický*, or the Slovak *Sborník Matice slovenskej*. It became clear that the use of German allowed scholars to participate in the world academic community.

All of this indicated that the closed Russian academic world in Prague had to become a more open émigré community. The use of German and the possibility of entering German academic institutions created new opportunities. George Katkov, a fee-paying student, graduated from the German University in Prague.[62] Others such as Jakobson and Bem studied for their doctorates there. Jakobson, Savitsky and Chizhevsky, the Ukrainian philosopher, were even employed there.

The value of German was that it illustrated the extent to which the academic world in Slav countries was restricted by its use of Slav languages which were not widely known. The Prague Linguistic Circle, which was the most significant collaboration between young Czech and Russian scholars, published a large part of its work in foreign languages and republished Trubetskoy's fundamental work in German.[63]

Russian and Ukrainian members of the circle, particularly Jakobson and Chizhevsky, made valuable contributions to the development of Czech linguistics and literature. Moreover, Jakobson actively encouraged pro-Czech attitudes within the German University. In 1936 he reorganised the editorial board of *Slavische Rundschau* so that it was more sympathetic to the views of the Foreign Ministry. He initiated the debate over K. Bittner's work *Deutsche und Tschechen* (Germans and Czechs) which was very anti-Czech, and prevented Bittner from gaining promotion.[64]

Jakobson's interest in Czech culture continued after he fled Czechoslovakia following the Nazi occupation. In the USA he became involved in the work of the Institut de philologie et d'histoires orientales et slaves, which had been evacuated from Brussels. In 1942 he gave a course of lectures on Byzantium and the spirit of innovation in the Czech Middle Ages, and another course on early Czech poetry and ballads. In 1943, following an agreement between the exiled Czech government in London and L'École des Hautes Études, the professorship of Czechoslovak philology was re-established and Jakobson was appointed to the titular chair. He then began to organise a course on the subject of the Czech contribution to world culture[65] and invited George Vernadsky, formerly of Prague, as well as other Russians such as B. Mirkin-Getsevich and A. Koyré to contribute. Jakobson's connections with Czechoslovakia always remained close and he signed all the obituaries of Czech academics which appeared in the *Annuaire* of the Institute.

In the 1930s it became a little easier for Russian émigrés to interest Czech publishers and institutions in their publications and ideas. Savitsky's experience is a good example of this alteration. In 1933 his book, *The Sixth Part of the World. Russia as the Geographical and Historical Whole* was published in Czech in a series produced by the prestigious Czech publishing house, Melantrich[66] edited by V. Mathesius, founder of the Prague Linguistic Circle. He had probably met Savitsky at meetings of the circle and become interested in Eurasian ideas, the influence of which can be traced in some of the ideas of the circle.[67] Savitsky's book aroused interest in wider Czech circles and he was invited to join the editorial board of the Czech journal, *Social Problems* and also to write articles about the Soviet Union for the most prestigious Czech encyclopaedia *Ottův slovník naučný*. This meant that he was now writing for the full range of the Czech intelligentsia. Similar kinds of development affected other Russian émigrés. A.L. Bem's Dostoevsky Society united Russians, Czechs and Germans. After 1929, the Slavonic Institute in Prague became an important centre and published serious academic work in Czech,[68] which remained almost unknown in the West and in Russia, owing to language difficulties.

Overall, the older generation of Russian émigrés tended to remain marginalised despite their significant contribution not only to Russian and Soviet studies but also in the areas of technology, agronomy and natural science. This may be explained in part by the nature of Czech historical development. Scholars have only just begun to discuss this subject and much remains to be done.[69] The younger generation who were students in Czechoslovakia found it much easier to become assimilated into Czech society and institutions, as knowledge of the language eased their way. Nonetheless the rule formulated by D. Sugar, that 'every exile must work twice as well and for half the pay as a native if he wishes to reach the same level as the native-born',[70] was true for Russians in Czechoslovakia.

Hitler's rise to power caused an exodus of refugees from Germany to Czechoslovakia. The government did what it could to help them, but relations between these German refugees and the German minority within Czechoslovakia were never straightforward. In May 1935 the pro-Nazi party in the Sudeten area received 73 per cent of the vote, which signalled that three-quarters of the Germans in Czechoslovakia were opposed to the refugees. As a result Czechoslovakia became a country of transit for the anti-Nazi German refugees rather than a country of settlement.

This new influx of refugees had less effect on the Russian émigré community than the reorientation of Czechoslovak foreign and defence policy. In 1934 Prague entered into full diplomatic relations with the Kremlin. In 1935 a Czechoslovak–Soviet agreement was negotiated but any Soviet action on behalf of Czechoslovakia in the case of war with Germany was dependent on prior involvement by France. This *rapprochement* between Czechoslovakia and the USSR worsened the position of the Russian émigrés as the Soviet authorities urged the Czech government to stop any help to them. This, combined with the increasing danger posed by Nazism, forced many to move on and to become émigrés elsewhere.

The Munich agreement exacerbated the situation still further. When Czechs were thrown out of the Sudetenland after it was occupied by Germany, Czechoslovakia had to absorb all these new refugees. Meanwhile, separatist feelings were growing in Slovakia. The Germans invaded on 15 March 1939, a puppet Slovak state was formed, and Czechs were also expelled from Slovakia. Six months later all Czech higher educational institutions were closed.

Here, too, émigrés were prepared to take on jobs which nationals would not accept. Higher education in Slovakia experienced a shortage of specialists as a result of the expulsion of Czechs and some Russian scholars, led by N. Lossky and M. Novikov, were prepared to work there. This situation was forced on them and their response to it should not be interpreted as anti-Czech in any sense. According to the very limited sources available, the Czech community did not interpret these actions in that way.

Once the German forces began to be pushed back by the Red Army, some members of the emigration thought that it would be better to flee and to become refugees again rather than risk arrest by the Soviet authorities. Some were indeed arrested in 1945, while others left Czechoslovakia after the Communists came to power in 1948. Of those who remained in Czechoslovakia, a few managed to advance in their chosen field, although their émigré origins counted against them. Those who succeeded tended to prove the hypothesis that émigré communities are often more active than the indigenous inhabitants and that the very fact of emigrating is already a form of self-selection.

The Day of Russian Culture

The institution of a 'Day of Russian Culture' was a phenomenon of the Russian emigration.[71] It illustrated the need for Russian émigrés to assert the importance of their culture and link it to their identity.

The first Day of Russian Culture was held in Estonia in 1924. The form of this cultural festival was undoubtedly influenced by Estonian traditions dating back to the period of Estonian national revival when song festivals celebrated the indigenous nature of folk art at a time when the dominant culture was Russo–Germanic. This tradition left its mark on the Russian minority in Estonia. After the Revolution they tried to rid themselves of the stigma of being seen as former invaders or as a purely political counter-revolutionary phenomenon. Instead they tried to affirm the Russian culture which it was their duty to preserve.

In 1924 the Pedagogical Bureau in Prague held a meeting with a representative of the emigration from Estonia. This resulted in a decision to organise something similar across the Russian diaspora. In February 1925 A.L. Bem's proposal to make the Day of Russian Culture coincide with Pushkin's birthday was accepted and a committee chaired by Countess S.V. Panina was formed. Pushkin was chosen as a national symbol who would cut across all divides within the Russian emigration and who could even unite the émigrés with their Soviet compatriots. The idea of a Day of Russian Culture was also supported by such émigré umbrella organisations as the Union of Russian Teachers' Organisations, the student union, ORESO and the Union of Russian Academic Organisations Abroad, all of which were based in Prague. The purpose of the Day of Russian Culture was threefold: to unite the emigration, to strengthen its ties with Russian culture, which inevitably were becoming weaker, and to spread knowledge of Russian culture in the host societies.

The idea of émigré unity had existed from the first days of life as refugees. But the notion that ties with Russian culture needed strengthening was novel. Far-seeing leaders of the émigré community realised the danger of denationalisation, but the majority were convinced that at most they might have to spend two years abroad. Assimilation, it was thought, could not occur in such a short period. However, after four years abroad as emigrants and with the USSR now legally recognised by countries such as France, the possibility of denationalisation began to be a major concern. It is not coincidental that at the same time as the formation of the committee to organise the Day of Russian Culture, the Pedagogical Bureau organised a meeting to address the very subject of denationalisation.

It was essential for members of the emigration to be able to influence the governments of their host societies if they were to influence politics in the USSR. There was a clear paradox in this. In the first instance, the interest in the emigration lay in the fact that they were a source of political, military and economic information on the actual state of affairs in Russia. A considerable number of émigrés supported themselves by providing this kind of information and analysis. At the same time the émigrés tried to convince the authorities of their host societies of the disastrous nature of theSoviet regime and the danger it represented to those host societies. Their main mission was to persuade Russians everywhere of the rightness of their views and to attract the support of the government of their host society for their cause. The defence and maintenance of culture were hardly of prime importance. By 1925, all this was changing: now the emigration had to consider the problems arising from a long, and possibly lifelong, stay abroad.

The appeal of the Prague Committee on the subject of the Day of Russian Culture was immediately supported by representatives of the Russian emigration in 25 countries – a figure which eventually rose to 42. However, the nature and success of the Day of Russian Culture in the different countries varied considerably and did not achieve the avowed aim of unity.

The first Day of Russian Culture in Czechoslovakia took place on 8 June 1925 and its success encouraged its organisers both in Czechoslovakia and elsewhere. Many Czech cultural institutions participated. One of the biggest Czech publishing houses, J. Otto, published a series of three volumes entitled *The Cultural Heritage of the Russian People*. Czech radio focused on Russian culture for an entire week. The Prague National Theatre produced Tchaikovsky's opera *Eugene Onegin*. N.I. Astrov, a former mayor of Moscow, gave a lecture on Moscow at the Department of Philosophy of Charles University. As a result of all of this, along with the Russophile tradition in Czechoslovakia, the Russian emigration achieved much greater prominence than other émigré communities in Western Europe.

The climax of this kind of Russo–Czech endeavour came in 1928 when a parallel Czech committee was formed to help with the organisation. Various Czech organisations, including the Academy of Sciences were represented. Events were arranged both separately and jointly by the two committees and a government delegation led by the ministers M. Hodža and K. Krofta attended a gala performance of Rimsky Korsakov's opera *Sadko*.

But at the same time, the remaining Russian academic institutions in Prague were transferred to Czech jurisdiction. In that context, the Day of Russian Culture could be interpreted as an attempt to emphasise that the winding down of the policy of Russian Action did not mean that Czech society wanted to abandon its support either for Russian culture or the Russian émigré community. It signalled a different kind of relationship between Czech society and the emigration. However, by 1928 it was quite evident that this did not suit everyone and that the possibility of employment in Czechoslovakia for Russians was very limited.

The years 1928 to 1930 were the apogee of this kind of celebration. In 1930, Tchaikovsky's *Queen of Spades* was produced by the Prague National

Theatre but most of the other main events took place in Bratislava, including a production of Moussorgsky's *Boris Godunov* with Chaliapin, the world-famous Russian bass, in the title role. In 1930, the next volume in the series of *The Cultural Heritage of the Russian People* failed to appear and the world economic depression began to affect the organisation. This, it would seem, occasioned the attempt in 1934 by the Russian organisers to ask for support from the German community in Prague. The Vice-Chancellor of the German University in Prague, G. Gesemann, promised to give a lecture about Gogol before a performance of Gogol's *The Government Inspector* at the German Theatre in Prague, but neither of these events took place. Veber argues that the Czechs were offended by this.[72] Hitler had come to power in Germany and tension between Czechs and Germans was increasing. Countess Panina could merely express her gratitude for all the effort made.

But in the following year, 1935, the Czechs would no longer participate in the organisation. Although financial issues were the official excuse, this deceived no one. The real reason was that closer relations with the Soviet Union prevented the Czech government from openly supporting the Russian emigration. The Day of Russian Culture evolved into a series of lectures and church services. By 1938, the whole enterprise had been reduced to a church service, as the guest speaker A.V. Kartashev had not been granted a visa.

Throughout the ever-changing situation of the Russian emigration in Prague political events dominated both the emigration's relations with Czechoslovakia and Czech society and its attitudes to the West and the Soviet Union. Despite the demand by the Czech authorities that Russian émigrés be apolitical, this was never really possible as political questions were inextricably linked with questions of identity and survival. Although the attitude of the Soviet authorities towards the émigrés was in many respects very hostile, they realised that politics was ineluctably part of émigré life and their interrogation of those arrested in 1945 was based on this assumption. But if international politics dictated events over which Russian émigrés could have no influence, nevertheless the history of the Russian emigration in Prague, as in other places, demonstrates the great efforts that individuals made and the price they paid to remain true to their vision of Russian culture and Russia itself.

Chapter 5

The Russian Diaspora

To understand the nature of émigré society in Prague, some comparison with other cities of the Russian diaspora is necessary. This not only helps to highlight the specific character of Prague but also identifies features which were common to the whole of the Russian emigration. The émigrés existed in a peculiar form of limbo. They were cut off from the Russian nation but nevertheless justified all activities with reference to the needs of their compatriots. They saw themselves as forming a community, Russia Abroad, and shared many assumptions and ideas which they communicated as far as possible through the printed word. At the same time both political and economic factors served to isolate them in certain cities and areas so that each area of the Russian emigration acquired a particular character and reputation. This could have the effect of attracting more émigrés of a similar outlook. However, the situation was not static. Conditions altered and people moved on.

The majority of Russian refugees caught up in the Civil War had little choice in where they found themselves, but certain places were more welcoming or more desirable than others, and Russians with the means to do so began to choose their destinations. Johnston considers that

> Any of at least five reasons could be a factor in resolving where to settle. Financial resources were obviously one, availability of employment another, the willingness of governments to permit their entry, residence and work a notorious third. The existence of an already established Russian community and the political-cultural attractions of specific cities added their powerful inducements.[1]

To this list one might add that the attitude of the government and population of the host community to the Russians frequently determined the nature of émigré communities.

Some places, such as Paris or Berlin had historic ties with Russia. Others, including many of the new successor states in Eastern Europe, were seen as friendly brother Slavs. A few countries, like Britain, were the destination only of those with personal connections. Overall, however, most Russians wanted to stay in Europe since in broad terms they were familar with the culture and Russia did not appear to be too far away so that a return home still seemed to be possible.

Berlin

In the 1920s Berlin was an important staging post in the wanderings of the Russian emigration. In Karl Schlögel's words: 'No other place in the Russian diaspora between the two world wars had such intense contacts between Red and White Russia as there were in Berlin.'[2] This was reflected in both the political life and cultural developments within the emigration which changed more quickly in Germany than it did anywhere else. Refugees streamed into Germany until 1920; initially they largely happened to end up there, rather than making Germany the country of their choice. Disillusionment with the Allies and the Crimean disaster, which saw the end of the final struggle against the Bolsheviks, changed the situation and rather than being a temporary refuge, Germany became the destination of choice for very many. During the boom years of 1922–23 there were perhaps more than 300,000 Russians in Berlin and even Germans used to call the Kurfürstendamm 'Nevsky Prospekt'.

The First World War had severed traditional links between Germany and Russia but renewing them proved to be fairly easy. The incident of the sealed train in 1917 – when the German government allowed Lenin to travel through Germany in order to return to Russia to foment revolution – the Treaty of Brest-Litovsk and German support for an independent Ukraine all complicated Russo–German relations and virtually made them a taboo subject for some émigrés. But the Versailles peace conference removed these restraints for the majority of émigrés. Disappointment with the behaviour of the Allies was far more immediate than memories of the conflict of 1914–18 and of German support to the Bolsheviks in 1917 and 1918. Both Russia and Germany were victims of the Versailles system. This prompted Germany to seek *rapprochement* with Soviet Russia, and the émigrés to renew previous contacts.

The Rapallo Agreement which was signed on 16 April 1922, and which established normal diplomatic relations between Germany and Soviet Russia, opened the way to Germany for Soviet citizens. It also led to the introduction of the gold rouble to replace the currency introduced in 1917, which had become totally devalued in the period following the October Revolution. This made Berlin an inexpensive city not only for émigrés but for Soviet citizens as well.

At this juncture the Soviet authorities were relatively liberal in granting permission for Soviet citizens to travel abroad. This, combined with the policy of attacking the émigrés as well as the capitalist and imperialist West, meant that Berlin was flooded with Soviet agitators and secret service agents, but even more so with the carpetbaggers of the New Economic Policy dreaming of business deals on an international scale. There were also many members of the intelligentsia who had not yet made up their mind whether to choose life in Soviet Russia or to live in exile. Both seemed equally risky: in both cases they faced the danger of losing their identity. It was still a long way to the Stalinist terror. In Russia it seemed that life was returning to normal, that the New Economic Policy was being taken seriously and would provide stability for a long time to come. By contrast, life for the Russian émigrés was not easy. They were badly off and many projects never got off the ground for lack of finance. Audiences for writers or lecturers were small and a proper career required the mastery of a second language. This was difficult and seemed pointless to the émigrés, as it cut them off from those in Russia with whom they most wished to be linked. Freedom of speech had little value if they could not reach those with whom they most wanted to communicate. But Berlin was a gateway used not only by the Bolsheviks in their effort to penetrate the West and the émigré community, but also by the émigrés themselves in their hopes of influencing their compatriots in the Soviet Union. This, even more than the low cost of living, determined Berlin's extraordinary role in émigré life during the years of spiralling inflation.

In cultural terms Berlin was considered one of the most interesting places to be and represented an outpost of the Soviet Union in the heart of Europe. In the early 1920s Berlin was the only place where Russian intellectual life still existed, where exiles and Soviet writers, artists and literary scientists worked together. Berlin was a place for reflection and decisions. This was a place where those émigrés who contemplated a return to their homeland met. They included writers such as Alexei Tolstoy as well as Soviet citizens who had left their country legally and had not yet decided whether to return. In Berlin they could wait and think. But leaving Berlin, whether going East or West, involved making a decision. A whole range of writers including V. Shklovsky and I. Erenburg, V. Khodasevich, N. Berberova and R. Gul', came here to make up their minds. While they waited, Russian literary life blossomed. Publishing houses, such as Grzhebin, Vozrozhdenie, Epokha and Kniga also established bases both in Berlin and in Soviet Russia.[3] The frenzied atmosphere, associations of many different kinds, multitudes of Russian newspapers and magazines, and the existence of publishing houses all contributed to a genuine creative tension.

This did not last long. Bely's *Epopeya* (The Epic), Gorky's *Beseda*

(Discourse) and *Nakanune* (On the Eve), the newspaper of the Change of Landmarks movement, Yashchenko's *Russkaya kniga* (The Russian Book) and *Novaya russkaya kniga* (New Russian Book), which declared the need to promote unity between Soviet and Russian cultures abroad, all ceased to exist as early as 1923–24. Some contacts continued until 1930, when they stopped mainly due to the changing policies in the Soviet Union and the deteriorating political situation in Germany. The end of this period did not mean the end of the Russian emigration in Germany but it changed its direction and became more of a vehicle for the transmission of Russian culture and, paradoxically, for its re-emergence in the Soviet Union.[4] But the boom of 1922–23, when so many Russians were in Berlin, and which was immortalised in literature, correspondence and many memoirs, produced an illusion and a myth about the nature of the Russian emigration in Germany.

Politically, émigrés of very different views found support in Germany. The monarchists, as early as 1919, were the first to find Germany attractive. The first monarchist congress met in Reichenhall in 1921, with German help. The Imperial family, still bearing the name Romanov, had been of German blood since the time of Catherine the Great, and its numerous branches were closely linked with German ruling families. The same was true of the Petersburg court aristocracy. The Grand Duke Kirill Vladimirovich, and Prince Leuchtenberg (a member of a lesser branch of the Russian royal family), were representatives of these links between German dynasties and the Russian Imperial court.[5] Monarchist newspapers and periodicals were published in Germany: *Prizyv* (The Appeal), *Dvuglavyi orel* (The Double-headed Eagle) and *Gryadushchaya Rossiya* (Future Russia). The monarchist camp split into two factions almost immediately, with one supporting Kirill Vladimirovich and the other backing the Grand Duke Nikolai Nikolayevich. Kirill Vladimirovich was pro-German whereas Nikolai Nilolayevich's base was in France.

Furthermore, Germany had been united for just half a century when the Russian émigrés arrived, and after the collapse of the empire, particularist sentiment was strengthened. Developments in Bavaria were in many respects assuming a meaning of their own. In the Bavarian Soviet Republic a major role was played by Jews from Eastern Europe and Russia and this formed a focus for anti-Jewish sentiment among the right wing. The first to die in the beer hall putsch in the name of the Nazi ideal was Scheubner-Richter, a Baltic baron, one of the organisers of the Reichenhall Congress, who had secured funding for its organisation.

These 'Baltic barons' were descendants of the German conquerors of the Baltic region, who kept their titles and estates even after Peter I made the Baltic States part of the Russian empire. They held important positions at the court and were loyal to the Romanov family but the reforms of Alexander II and the Russification policy of Alexander III in the Baltic States, which undermined German influence in general and worsened the economic power of this group, contributed to the traditional anti-Russian sentiments in this part of Europe. This group played a significant role in right-wing German politics, and the Russian issue was a major part of their thinking. Alfred Rosenberg the ideologist of Nazism was familiar with these kinds of idea, and he was not an isolated case. Right-wing German circles relied on the expertise of these immigrants from the Russian empire, although most of them had not come from Bolshevik Russia itself but from the independent states of Latvia, Estonia and Lithuania. For a time Bavaria, and Munich in particular, became the unchallenged centre of the right wing of the Russian monarchists.

However, Berlin was dominated by more left-wing groups, not only among the Russian émigrés but in the Prussian government as well. Like the right, the left-wing émigré community in Berlin was not homogeneous. There was a whole range of groups from right-wing Kadets opposed to Miliukov's 'new tactics' to right-wing Socialist Revolutionaries and Mensheviks, as well as more pro-Soviet elements. The right-wing SRs led by Kerensky who had been the most numerous and influential in 1917 and who had to flee from the animosity of the Whites took a long time to organise the publication of their own newspaper. In the end they were able to publish *Dni* (Days) owing to a Czech subsidy. Shortly after the end of the period of massive inflation the newspaper transferred to Paris. This showed that Berlin, despite its economic and political instability, could compete with Paris as the émigré capital during the extraordinarily favourable conditions created by the combination of the low cost of living with very liberal possibilities of contacts with Soviet Russia.

The right-wing Kadet group which rallied around the newspaper *Rul'* (The Helm), was more fortunate. Even though this newspaper was more left-wing than a significant part of the emigration, it always defended the White cause and therefore was acceptable to the majority of émigrés. Moreover, it was produced by a commercial German publishing house and, no doubt under its influence, awarded less space to politics and more to reporting on the life of the Russian colony in Germany than *Dni*, with which it competed for readership. As a result, it survived until 1931 as a genuinely self-financing newspaper of the Russian colony in Germany, rather than as its political voice. Its end was connected with the economic crisis in Germany, which not only reduced the numbers in the Russian colony but also worsened the economic situation of those who stayed.

The Menshevik *Sotsialisticheskiy vestnik* (Socialist Herald), on the other hand, was not really connected with the émigré community, among whom it had very few readers. Ignoring the life of the émigrés, it survived in Berlin with the help of SPD (Sozialdemokratische Partei Deutschlands) which, even after it merged with USPD (Unabhängige Sozialdemokratische Partei Deutschlands), found it hard to maintain its position in the face of competition from the Nazis and the Communists.

These examples show that from 1924, when Germany achieved a temporary stability, Berlin was losing its importance as an émigré centre. The political position of Germany was too weak, its ties with the Soviet Union were too strong, and its economic situation offered little chance of good employment. Only those initiatives which could still play a role in the internal political struggle in Germany survived. The extreme right wing, however, was out of the game after the Munich putsch of 1923. With Hitler's imprisonment Nazism was pushed onto the extreme periphery of political life for five years. Furthermore, Hitler's writings exposed the aggressiveness of Nazism toward foreigners, especially the Slavs. In these conditions, nothing short of despair could move Russian exiles to attempt co-operation with the Nazis.

When Hitler assumed power in 1933, the semi-official representative of the dwindling Russian colony in Germany reacted by delivering greetings. Small groups of émigrés tried to conclude an agreement with or even make use of the Nazi regime in Germany in order to liberate Russia. But they, too, were to be disappointed. In the first place, once established, Hitler no longer needed the support of the Russian-Germans, let alone the support of pure Russians. Moreover, racial and national ideas were quickly gaining strength within Nazism. They had been present from the very beginning, but questions connected with the Versailles Treaty, the 'stab in the back', together with the struggle between the left and the right in the early 1920s, had pushed them into the background. Soon after Hitler's coming to power, the struggle against the alleged conspiracy of the Jews and Freemasons became central. However, contempt was also growing for all 'subhumans' (*Untermenschen*) who, in Hitler's schema, included Russians. Partly due to the significant role played by Russian Jews in the émigré community, anti-Semitic policies were extended to other Russian émigrés as well.

The attempts by pro-Nazi émigrés to establish good relations with the Nazi regime were lengthy and tortuous. They failed. As a result, Berlin in the mid–1930s did not attract even those few émigrés who were ready to support Hitler.[6] Not until the turning point in the course of the Second World War did the Nazi leadership start appreciating at least to some degree the potential of the Russian anti-Bolshevik forces. But the émigrés played a subsidiary role in General Vlasov's opposition movement which relied on Soviet citizens and prisoners of war. The Germans were no longer interested in the émigrés and considered that they no longer had a political role. Vlasov and his colleagues had careers in the Soviet Union and were products of the Soviet system. They had no common language with the older generation of émigrés.

Arguably, therefore, the Russian emigration ceased to exist in Germany by the middle of the 1930s. The conditions and attitudes which had made Germany, and Berlin in particular, a magnet for Russian refugees in the early 1920s no longer existed. Nazi attitudes meant that it was not safe to be a Slav in Germany and all those who were able to do so left. Those who remained acted not so much as an emigration but more as *zemlyachestva* (associations of people from the same region, province or locality) united by their common national origin and working to preserve their identity. They had little desire to become involved in politics.[7]

In terms of employment, like Czechoslovakia, Germany could not provide jobs for the émigrés. The Weimar Republic had to cope with massive unemployment within its borders throughout its existence and had no interest in or need for an immigrant labour force. Indeed, the mood at the beginning of the 1930s was marked by despair, and not only among the émigré community. The more economically advanced countries of North America and Europe had never experienced so many bankruptcies, and had never had such an immense army of the unemployed or such a high suicide rate. Proponents of the most extreme views had never been so well received. The crisis had an even heavier impact on the émigrés. Foreigners were the first to be made redundant; and xenophobia was on the increase. Furthermore the situation in the USSR was changing and émigrés were very sensitive to developments at home. From 1925, the Soviet authorities had been gradually abandoning the New Economic Policy. Social tension in the USSR was growing again and there were renewed hopes for an internal collapse of Soviet rule. Once again people began to dream of a new spring campaign against the Bolsheviks.

With the onset of collectivisation and industrialisation in the Soviet Union, a new mood could be sensed. Some émigrés were encouraged by the publication in *Pravda* on 2 March 1930 of Stalin's article entitled 'Giddy with Success'. The émigrés perceived this as the commander's call to his own people, those who had taken seriously the directives of the leader, and as marking a transfer of responsibility from the top power level to the executive. It was interpreted as an authoritative confirmation of the fact that the USSR was at the brink of anti-Communist revolution. People were fleeing the Soviet Union in increasing numbers, and the émigrés were well informed. Information was also supplied by foreign diplomats and by specialists, especially German ones, who had direct contacts with German farming colonies in the Volga river basin.

A new wave of appeals arose for reassessing relations with the Soviet

Union, exerting more pressure on it, and above all for a new military campaign, the success of which would be secured by a general peasant uprising. But at that very moment the capitalist-democratic world was becoming ever more deeply engrossed in a complicated tangle of its own controversies, and it not only stopped listening to the voice of the émigrés but started competing for a place in promising Soviet markets.

Therefore, instead of a united campaign against Communism, Russian émigré organisations were being closed and capitalist firms competed for Soviet contracts. Unexpectedly Stalin was proved right, the 'capitalists', though not attempting to 'catch up' with the Soviet Union, were trying to place their orders and make a profit. All this added to the increasing émigré disillusionment with Western democracy. In Germany too, that democracy not only seemed too weak to defend the émigrés but was also unable to defend itself. Russian émigrés had to find other places of refuge.

Paris

Paris was always seen as a most desirable destination and it came to be considered the capital of the emigration.[8] This was owing to an amalgam of historical and political ties as well as economic opportunities. Yet Russian culture was seen as inferior to French culture and although unskilled labour was welcomed in the 1920s, the professionally qualified were not. Paradoxically, the problem of maintaining Russian identity was especially acute in France, where freedom could also mean that the host society was indifferent to the position and views of the Russian refugees.

Paris had long exercised a fascination on Russian writers, artists and artistocratic visitors. In cultural terms, France set the standards and French literature was translated almost immediately into Russian throughout the nineteenth century. After 1870 Russian translations of Zola and other French writers were often published in Russia before the French originals. Napoleon's invasion of Russia and the periodic crises of the nineteenth century did little to dim the attraction. The humiliating defeat of Napoleon III in the Franco–Prussian War of 1870 and the rise of the Paris Commune led to a new stage in Franco–Russian relations when gradually it was recognised that Russia was a potential and extremely useful ally in the struggle against a united Germany. This led to the formation of the Entente and French investment in Russia.

Since the late nineteenth century Paris had been home to several short-lived Russian newspapers.[9] Russian exiles who arrived in Paris after the 1905 Revolution and who by 1907 numbered around 25,000 started worrying the Paris police, and French concierges found it impossible to count how many of those strange foreigners, speaking a totally incomprehensible language, actually lived in the rented apartments. But these people, 'mostly anarchists and Jews', kept to themselves, and though they could be seen on occasions in the cosmopolitan and bohemian foreign society of the French capital, they never established firm ties with the influential political and social circles in Paris.[10] And even though the newcomers among them who could be seen in Café Rotonde in Montparnasse 'sat down in the still warm seats vacated by the Bolsheviks',[11] this had no significant effect on Russian links with French society.

For Russians, French was still the language of diplomacy and the tendency to admire all things French in Russia was strengthened by her diplomatic alliances. During the First World War the Russian Expeditionary Force was sent to France in 1916 to help Russia's ally. Some Russian troops were already to be found in France and they acted as a magnet for other Russians. In 1920 Wrangel's army was evacuated from the Crimea under the protection of the French, although subsequently French policy towards the refugees was seen as betrayal.

The existence of an established Russian community tended to attract more Russians. France had greater employment possibilities than much of Eastern Europe and, in the 1920s in particular, France accepted most requests for political asylum. After the First World War labour was needed to rebuild the areas of northern France devastated in the conflict and farmers in south-west France actually seemed to try to settle the land.[12] The coal mines in the north of the country were operated almost entirely by immigrant labour and the fast-growing car industry attracted large numbers of immigrants in the 1920s. Thus in addition to the rather clichéd occupations for émigrés – working as taxi drivers, bouncers for night-clubs, or singing in Cossack choirs – there was a demand for unskilled Russian labour all over France. Small groups of Russians were dispersed throughout the country. Almost all were in types of employment for which they were not suited and which did not correspond with their educational level, and most in conditions which were worse than those of French workers in the same jobs. Only a small number of these Russians, mainly those working in agriculture, married Frenchwomen and became fully assimilated. After the period of hyperinflation in Germany and the ensuing slump, France became cheaper to live in than Germany. Professionally qualified people had a more difficult time as they were required to have French citizenship, pass French examinations and possess French diplomas. Following the depression in the 1930s, foreigners were the first to lose their jobs and might be subject to deportation if they did not possess valid permits.[13]

The story of émigré V.I. Yurkevich shows how difficult things could be. Yurkevich was well known in Russia as a shipbuilder but had to start as a

draughtsman in the Renault car factories in France before being able to
return to his profession and take a share of the credit for the fact that the
liner *Normandie* won the Blue Ribbon for the fastest sea journey between
New York and Southampton.[14] However for the émigrés as a group it was
of more importance that many unskilled labourers became skilled workers
and eventually foremen of their respective trades.

Although Paris became known as the political capital of the emigration
this was not equally true for the whole of the political spectrum. Many of
the left wing preferred the atmosphere in Berlin, although eventually the
Mensheviks left Germany via Paris for New York. Alexander Kerensky was
one of the first to seek exile in Paris. Kerensky had fled from Petrograd on
the eve of the Bolshevik seizure of power and gone to the Don, where it
must have rapidly become clear to him that the White movement, still in its
early stages, thought no better of him than did the Bolsheviks.[15] Kerensky
was not welcomed in Paris, either by the French or by the Russians. The
French were allied to the anti-Bolshevik forces fighting within Russia,
while the Russian ambassador in Paris, V.A. Maklakov, was the last envoy
of the Provisional Government and his sympathies lay closer to the Kadets.
He had been appointed to this post almost as a form of honourable exile
because of his close links to the Kornilov revolt in 1917. Subsequently,
representatives of all kinds of governments and would-be future administrations began to appear in France. These people spoke for movements and
conspiracies which they claimed offered almost a 100 per cent chance of
success. The result, according to Johnston, was that 'the cacophony of
voices claiming to speak for Russia's future did not manage to attract much
attention from the peacemakers of Versailles'.[16]

Arguably, this is too dismissive a judgement. Given the approaching Paris
Peace Conference, it was generally recognised that it was necessary to have
one body representing the forces of opposition to Bolshevism. For the only
time in its history, the Russian emigration managed to create a single body:
the Political Conference. This brought together those who at first sight had
little in common. It included former tsarist ministers, in particular Sazonov
who had been Foreign Minister between 1910 and 1916, and Savinkov who
as a terrorist had organised assassination attempts on those very ministers.
Savinkov had been termed 'a murderer' by Sazonov and was included
because a certain section of democratic Western society regarded him as a
hero. He became head of the conference press service.

The Political Conference was largely representative of the émigré
community, and if some leading personalities were missing, that was largely
the fault of the Allies. Thus Clemenceau and the French press were so
indignant about the expected arrival of Miliukov in Paris in December
1918, due to his alleged collaboration with the Germans in the Ukraine, that

Maklakov thought it better to send him to London instead. But it seems that even 'Kerensky ... had so irritated both the Allies and the Russian diplomats during 1918 that his participation in the Conference was never seriously considered'.[17] There were those who disapproved of the conference because they took offence at being left out, but most serious criticism of it was voiced after the end of the Paris Peace Conference. In the course of the Peace Conference the Political Conference worked in unexpected concord and presented a united front in relation not only to the Allies but also to the various rival anti-Bolshevik forces within Russia.

Yet the Russian anti-Bolshevik representation was never recognised as an official participant in the Paris Peace Conference. Czech observers were very close to the truth when they noted that Britain and France were not interested in a strong Russia and found it quite useful to be able to reject any of its representatives under the pretext of either Bolshevik betrayal or inadequate representation of various anti-Bolshevik forces. In Russia itself, the British and French had little difficulty in deciding whom they should or should not support; fatally for the anti-Bolshevik cause, they did not always support the same forces.

Right from the beginning, the Paris Peace Conference was a series of bitter disappointments for the Russians. K. Kramář, head of the Czechoslovak delegation, commented on the official opening of the conference in a letter to President Masaryk:

> It is a terrible future that is being set up here. The Poles, who have no government, have been invited to the conference, while the Russians have not. Neither Pich[on] nor Clem[enceau] said a word in their speeches about what Russia has done. Poincaré, too, failed to mention Russia in his address. . . . The unhappy Russians are dejected and say: 'If need be we shall ally with the Germans', and one can hardly blame them, because the way they are being treated by the Entente is a downright disgrace.[18]

The conference continued in this spirit, and it seems that all shades of Russian political opinion, both émigré and Bolshevik, regarded the outcome of the conference – the Versailles system – as shameful. The last blow dealt to whatever sympathies the Allies still enjoyed among the Russian refugees was the French attitude to Wrangel's evacuated army. After France announced that it felt free of any obligations towards the Russian army, and was administering aid only for humanitarian reasons, Wrangel approached the Russian representatives in Paris with a letter in which he wrote: 'I cannot believe that it is in the interest of France to let an organised friendly army, strong in spirit, turn into a herd of refugees, infuriated with the Allies, left to the mercy of fate.'[19] However, that was exactly what happened and it defined the sentiments of the Russian emigration towards the Allies. Disillusionment with the Allies accounted for the feeling amongst émigré politicians that Berlin provided a rather more sympathetic environment.

A German observer of current events was right to note, when commenting on the National Congress which was organised by Burtsev in Paris in June 1921 and which was dominated by right-wing Kadets, that the warm greetings extended to France were more a result of politeness than of politics and that there was no particularly pro-French feeling at the congress.[20] This applied to much of the Russian émigré press, particularly in Paris but also in Prague.

But despite the fact that various political groupings sought shelter in Paris, the political activities of the émigrés failed to find effective support in France. Burtsev's *Obshchee Delo* (The Common Cause) lacked funds, and closed altogether in 1922, even though Burtsev had been living in Paris since 1903 and had contacts in the French capital which dated from the time of his exile from Imperial Russia. *Poslednie Novosti* (Latest News), partly financed from Prague, became the only influential Russian political newspaper in Paris. At the same time in Berlin Russian dailies and periodicals of all political leanings were being published with the support of German money. Germany and Russia seemed to have very many links, sometimes of a most unexpected kind. France, seen as open-minded and loved by so many, seemed to show genuine interest in Russia's plight only when it came to the question of the destiny of the Russian government bonds which at one time flooded the French market. However, when the increasing cost of living in Berlin and growing political instability in the late 1920s and early 1930s made Germany more difficult for émigré political groups, with the exception of the extreme right, the traditional pre-revolutionary political élite once again turned to Paris.

Despite its pre-eminence in other areas, Paris was never the academic centre of the emigration. Part of the reason for this may lie in the structures of French universities.[21] But most developed countries suffered from too many rather than too few intellectuals and scholars. University departments everywhere reserved places for their own people, and French universities differed little in this from their English, German, Belgian, Austrian and Czech counterparts.

The reason why France became the target of reproach and criticism in the 1920s arose from the high expectations of the Russian élite. When clouds started gathering over the Russian academic world in Prague, five of its outstanding representatives departed for Paris. But people who had experienced Paris more or less in the role of eminent foreigners could not, despite their intelligence and awareness of the complexity of their position as exiles, reconcile themselves to the reception they got in the French capital in their new situation as refugees. Another stumbling block for Russian émigrés was that Paris virtually demanded that they abandon their mother tongue. The French were convinced that every cultured person must be proficient in French. The universality of French language and culture could not be challenged. Even at the Russian philological faculty of the Sorbonne, S. Eliseyev lectured on the Japanese novel and G.L. Lozinsky delivered a course on philology in French; only Professor A. V. Kartashev taught *Istoria khristianstva v Rossii* (History of Christianity in Russia) in Russian, on Saturdays.[22] In fact the Russian intelligentsia did fully agree that a person of culture was bound to speak and understand French. Moreover, the French could listen to lectures given in their own language and this could be very influential in opening a gateway to the inhospitable French academic world. But the idea of having Russian higher education institutions in France could not be justified, and they did not materialise. For the relatively few émigré graduates of French universities,[23] there were ways into the French academic community even if this was frequently in the colonies rather than in France itself.

The fact that the French government was not keen on expending large amounts to help the Russians meant that in the long term émigrés were better off financially in France than they were in Czechoslovakia or Yugoslavia, where a considerable percentage lived on grants and other handouts. In France they had to find occupations which could support them. Russian newspapers, magazines and books sold better in France than they did in other countries, although not well enough to make production cost-effective. A special role was played by the many Russian entrepreneurs who had managed to rescue part of their capital and had chosen Paris as a place of residence. Some of them supported the initiatives of the exile community: for example the oil magnate A.O. Gukasov funded the newspaper *Vozrozhdenie* (The Renaissance), which could not have existed without his support, although his frequent interventions were not to the benefit of the newspaper. Those members of the nobility who had not been reduced to poverty supported the Church and various charities. Assistance came from the YMCA, which after a short period of hesitation decided to support émigrés in Paris. Aid also came from Britain – Spalding supported the Eurasians and the Fellowship of St Alban and St Sergius indirectly supported the St Sergius Theological Institute and Seminary. Thus a number of émigré initiatives in Paris were funded from a variety of sources abroad. This in itself helped to make Paris a centre of activity.

Not only did this kind of funding concentrate in Paris but various organisations made it the base from which to continue their anti-Bolshevik campaigns. ROVS (Russkii Obshchevoinskii soyuz – the union of Russian veterans) was the leading organisation to do so. The veterans' union, with its large membership, could count on a steady income from subscriptions and donations. One must assume that a larger amount was raised by the Church but this would have been divided up into parishes or given to various charities and was thus less visible. The sums raised by ROVS were paid into Grand Duke Nikolai Nikolaevich's Special Treasury, and after his death into the Fund for the Salvation of the Fatherland. The changes of name had little significance, as the funds remained under ROVS's control. Although with the passage of time opportunities for action were curtailed and its membership declined, owing both to death and the further dispersion of its members, its income grew.[24] Many émigrés were becoming self-supporting and no longer relying on handouts. This could only happen from the outset because of what the mass of the emigration was able to earn. 'In Asnières for example, on the capital's grimy northern edge, an Orthodox priest arrived in 1931 to minister to Russians there. He had . . . seventy-five centimes in his pocket. Five years later he had a church and his budget exceeded 40,000 francs.'[25] By the beginning of 1926, the periodical *Russkaya shkola za rubezhom* (Russian School Abroad)[26] noted with satisfaction that 45–50 per cent of Russian cultural and educational activities in France were financed by the refugees themselves through the payment of school fees and voluntary contributions.

The gradual strengthening of contacts with French society played its role, too. There exists, for instance, a plentiful literature on French–Russian meetings on philosophical and socio-political issues, organised by Berdyaev. Much can be learned from the lives of other Russian scholars who distinguished themselves in French or American scholarship, for example Gurvitch, Kojève, Koyré, Yurkevich and Henri Troyat. However, the main factor which made it possible for a relatively large Russian cultural élite to exist in Paris, however reduced its circumstances, was that they were largely self-supporting. By being relatively independent of government support and of the vagaries of French politics, the Russian émigré community in France possessed exceptional stability. Paris became the capital of the Russian emigration because of its prestige and its indifference to the émigrés. This indifference resulted in a degree of freedom that did not exist in other centres of emigration.

Harbin

Harbin in north-east China was a fascinating example of an émigré community and displayed many of the characteristics of a border state in

Eastern Europe. There was the Russian life of pre-revolutionary Harbin, the immediate vicinity of the frontier with the USSR, which both attracted and repelled, and complicated relations with the local population which had been employed by the Russians on the railway but who also saw them as foreigners and imperialists. At the same time, Harbin had similarities with Prague. They were the only two cities of the Russian diaspora which created a proper Russian law faculty.

Pre-revolutionary Harbin was populated by Russians who worked on the railway as labourers and engineers and by merchants who used the opportunities available to trade in the Far East. Unlike Berlin and Paris, there were no Russian students and scholars, nor were there revolutionaries or members of the aristocracy. After the Revolution, émigré society in Harbin included people from the Russian provinces, as well as Cossacks and traders from Siberia, which was developing fast and becoming prosperous. The intelligentsia was essentially provincial, with lecturers from new rather than from historically prestigious universities. In the revolutionary years the ranks of this intelligentsia had been reinforced by leading scholars from the better-known universities as they were forced to leave Russia, via Siberia, for an eventual destination in Europe. Thus, temporarily, the nature of the Russian community in Harbin altered although many other refugees including prominent politicians and military representatives passed through without stopping.

Harbin was a railway city which grew up around the building of the Chinese Eastern Railway between 1897 and 1903.[27] It was also a colonial city intended to demonstrate the power of the Russian empire. Dubbed the 'Paris of the East', after the First World War and Russian Revolution it became separated from metropolitan Russia by the rapidly changing international situation as reflected in the politics of northern Manchuria. Following the Russian Civil War it became a veritable city on wheels as refugees lived in railway carriages and waited for a solution to their predicament.

There were similarities with Berlin despite the fact that the two cities belonged to different worlds. Relations between Russia and Harbin had been close prior to the Revolution. Afterwards the instability of the country allowed émigrés to become involved in its internal affairs. Harbin witnessed the coexistence of the Whites and the more pro-Soviet Russians. Whether someone had a Soviet passport or was an émigré did not provide an accurate guide to their attitudes. Many employees of the Chinese Eastern Railway applied for Soviet citizenship in order to keep their jobs while their political sympathies were with the Whites. Some of the émigrés were pro-Soviet and supported the Change of Landmarks movement. Extremists such as these and the Russian Fascists were mostly based in Harbin and Berlin.

The émigré community in Harbin was more democratic in terms of the social status of its members, considerably less intellectual and much more independent of the old order than other émigré centres. There were opportunities for adventurers and entrepreneurs from among the older generation as well as a clean slate for the activities of the younger émigrés who grew up on the only frontier where a real war was being waged. This represented the last and very significant difference. War was constant along the Russian–Chinese frontier: a petty and ugly war in which attempts to overthrow the Bolshevik regime in Siberia combined with the sorties of bandit groups composed of demoralised soldiers who, after many years spent fighting during the world war and civil war, could imagine no other way of life. The combination of the atmosphere of Berlin with a border state in Eastern Europe made Harbin both a destination which émigrés sought as well as an oasis of old Russia beyond the Soviet borders. Harbin was not only a transit point but also a natural regional centre of emigration, at least for the vast but sparsely populated and provincial Trans-Ural region of Russia.

Professor Raeff's assessment that 'the fact that the culturally active elements [in Harbin] were made up mainly of "provincials" (mostly from Siberia) was not as significant as the political frictions and economic hardships experienced by the Russian colony'[28] seems to downplay the fact that political bickering affected all émigrés and all émigré communities. The main difference lay in the fact that in some countries, such as Yugoslavia and Czechoslovakia, the authorities suppressed it directly and in others this was done indirectly by assessing and filtering those émigrés who were accepted. In conditions of instability such as prevailed in Germany and China in the early 1920s, such arguments come into the open. Equally misleading, at least as far as the first years of emigration are concerned, is the claim that compared with those in other places with a high concentration of émigrés, people in Harbin lived in poorer material conditions. The opposite was true: the 22,000 Russian employees of the Chinese Eastern Railway and hundreds, if not thousands, of Russians servicing this colony – as retail and wholesale traders, teachers, priests of the Orthodox Church, people with families who remained in employment – constituted a solid base for the development of émigré activities, probably comparable only with Riga, whose Russian population exceeded 30,000. Unlike those in Western Europe, the Russian émigrés in Harbin saw themselves as the bearers of progress with respect to the local population. Equipped with the achievements of European science, they undertook pioneering research in relation to the study of Manchuria, in the fields of geology, botany, agriculture and local crafts, or acted as intermediaries for their compatriots who lacked the necessary language skills in the area of Chinese law.

They also undertook a major study of Mongolian law. Bakich has calculated that this literature represents some 16 per cent of all Russian books published in Harbin between 1808 and 1960, and a high proportion of this was published in the 1918–31 period.[29] In Western Europe, including Czechoslovakia, such works in Russian about the host countries were practically non-existent. Russian authors writing about these issues published individual, largely popular articles in Russian, while books were published either in the local language or else in one of the world languages.

However, in Harbin Russian was regarded as a semi-global language, fully capable of competing with French and German,[30] but inferior to English. At the same time, assimilation into local society was very different from the accepted European norms and required linguistic competence, as the local language was not easy to master.[31] Nonetheless, by 1931 Usov's *Textbook of Colloquial Chinese* in four parts, which first appeared at the beginning of the 1920s, had gone through six editions.[32]

Moreover, in the 1920s, 19 Chinese students graduated from the Russian Law Faculty in Harbin, and they even started publishing a journal in Russian. This would have been unthinkable in Western Europe and it demonstrates the importance accorded to the language of the émigrés.

In the revolutionary period there are similarities between Harbin and Berlin. An attempt was made as early as December 1917 to organise Soviet power in the region of the Chinese Eastern Railway; it was suppressed by Chinese authorities with help from the interventionists. General Horvat was reinstated to the position of administrator which he had held under the Tsars. Three years later he was deposed by the Chinese because of his active involvement in the civil war in Siberia. In some ways this corresponded with the period of attempts to organise White forces on German territory and carry out joint Russo–German anti-Bolshevik operations in the Baltic region.

In January 1920, Harbin station offered an unusual spectacle:

> In all directions the tracks were congested with trains, inhabited by thousands of fugitives who had fled Siberia after the fall of Admiral Kolchak's government, setting up a township on wheels. This included all kinds of people, who had been blown by fate into the unknown wealthy region of a foreign state, where massive investment by the Russians in the Chinese Eastern Railway had created a tiny cultural oasis which provided shelter for the homeless Russian refugees. Their prospects were very grim: they did not and indeed could not have any future plans.[33]

The existence of a large and solvent Russian colony in Harbin nevertheless made it possible to organise courses on economics and law, which began on

1 March 1920 whilst at the same time, the territory of the Chinese Eastern
Railway served as a base for White troops that had withdrawn from Siberia,
enabling them to continue in their struggle.

During the Soviet period two agreements were signed with the Chinese
authorities: the first with the central but weak government, the second with
Marshal Zhang Zuolin. These transferred the pre-revolutionary Russian
rights to the Chinese Eastern Railway to the Soviet government in 1924.
The Soviet administration could have put an end to the existence of the Law
Faculty as an émigré initiative and driven it out of the Eastern Railway
building, forbidding the company's employees and their family members to
study there. Yet it did the opposite: it took the Law Faculty under its
protection and tripled its budget, while providing very acceptable
conditions for its operation – the head had to be a Soviet citizen, and the
professors had to refrain from political activities against Soviet power. On
this basis the faculty experienced a brief period of prosperity during
1925–28. The case of the Law Faculty was just one small part of the story of
Soviet cultural policy in Manchuria. The Soviet administration was more
tolerant towards the émigrés, striving to make use of the credit enjoyed by
Tsarist Russia in China for strengthening Soviet influence there. The
conjunction of a positive approach to the Whites and loyalty to the Soviet
administration, typical of some Harbin publications, was hard to find even
in work published in Berlin. This attitude contributed to relieving the
tension on the Soviet–Chinese border. Some of the Whites entered the
services of Zhang Zuolin, others, especially Cossacks, took up farming.[34]

From 1929 relations between China and the Soviet Union rapidly
deteriorated, as did relations between the émigrés and Soviet sympathisers
among the 60,000-strong Russian community in Harbin. In these
conditions the financial situation of the émigré part of the colony worsened
considerably. One aspect of Harbin became particularly clear: there was
nowhere to go. Harbin was on the direct route to Japan or the USA, but
this was hardly a practical option. Reaching Europe involved an expensive
journey around the world. Life in Shanghai, however pleasant it might have
been, also needed financial resources and did not offer an escape from the
Chinese chaos and the emerging Sino–Japanese conflict. Finally, the trap
snapped shut. In contrast to Berlin, the Russian colony in Harbin between
1929 and 1932 hardly changed in terms of numbers, but signs of decline and
a concurrent increase in extremism were observable in all areas. In 1931,
Russian Fascists began to become involved in major political issues.

During the Fascist period the nationalists in China never developed
programmes analogous to those of Nazism. The rise of Fascism came with
the occupation of Manchuria by the Japanese in March 1932 and the
installation of the Manchukuo government. Russian Fascists welcomed this

and, once again contrary to their counterparts in Berlin, found support among Japanese militarists. The Soviet government was forced to sell its rights to the Chinese Eastern Railway (in 1935) for a very low price, and its sympathisers had to leave Harbin. In the uneasy situation on the Soviet border, the Japanese were much more interested in winning the favour of the émigrés than Hitler was in Germany. The right-wing émigrés however lacked any real support; they often allied with various corrupt groups in the Japanese military, which was the only way the Russian Fascist movement was kept alive.

Much less is known about Harbin than about comparable Russian communities in Europe but a cursory overview allows one to see how far some features in all of the communities' understanding of their role and attitudes to Russian culture remained constant throughout the Russian diaspora. Other factors, like language and politics, were strongly influenced by local conditions. In Harbin these characteristics were magnified by its isolation.

Yugoslavia

Yugoslavia did a great deal for the Russian emigration. It had not been on the map of pre-war Europe and in the first months and years of Russian emigration even its name was confused. In 1929 the Kingdom of Serbia, Croatia and Slovenia was renamed Yugoslavia. The pre-war relationship of these areas to Russia had been complex. On the one hand they were brother Slavs, which argued that they had serious responsibilities for one another, particularly in the case of Serbia. On the other hand Russia could be too dominant and dangerous. The Kingdom of Serbia, Croatia and Slovenia had had a somewhat ambivalent position during the First World War, with troops fighting on both sides of the front. This ambiguity was echoed in its foreign policy towards the Entente, particularly France, and its participation in the Little Entente alliance, directed mainly against Hungary.

The Serb relationship with pre-revolutionary Russia had been close and Imperial Russia had provided Serbia with real help on many occasions, including the years of the world war. This played a decisive role in the attitude of the leadership of the Kingdom to the Russian émigrés. King Alexander I Karadjordjevic had attended the Corps des Pages, an élite military school in St Petersburg, and had close contacts with the Russian Imperial court and circles close to it. He also had close personal contacts with V.N. Schtrandman, who represented Russia in Serbia in 1914–18. In 1919 Schtrandman became the ambassador of Kolchak's government and a prominent official of the monarchist movement in exile, a target of constant attacks on the part of the exile democratic press. The king also maintained personal relations with V.A. Artamonov, Russian military attaché in Serbia between 1909 and 1917, and with S.N. Paleologue,[35] who was responsible for aid to Russian refugees. His work with his assistant P.V. Skarzhinsky, who later became the last representative of the Supreme Monarchist Council, was described as 'a comradeship for the exploitation of monarchist sentiments'.[36] Pašić, who became Prime Minister of the Kingdom of Serbia, Croatia and Slovenia in 1921, had co-operated with moderate Russian monarchists as leader of the Radical Party in the nineteenth century; subsequently he spent two years in St Petersburg as Serbian ambassador, and finally, from 1904 until 1918, as a more or less permanent Premier and Minister of Foreign Affairs for Serbia, he maintained constant and close relations with Imperial Russian diplomats.

Influential military circles in Serbia had contacts with Russian army officers of monarchist leanings. In addition to the 29,000 refugees registered in the census of April 1921, Yugoslavia received units of General Wrangel's army whom the census did not record.[37] Their number fluctuated, but at the end of 1921 it was no fewer than 10,000 men. They included graduates of military schools, staff officers and members of the rank-and-file. They had not given up the idea of returning home, nor had they left the armed forces. These people were devoted to the White cause. The high proportion of soldiers among the émigrés who had fled to Yugoslavia earlier on, mainly after the defeat of Denikin, meant that to a large extent the nature of the Russian émigré community in Yugoslavia was determined by professional members of the military.

The Council of United Officer Societies in the Kingdom of Serbs, Croats and Slovenes was active by 1921, and at the end of 1923 it included 16 organisations with a total of 3,580 members. Its proclaimed goal was to 'serve the cause of restoration of the Russian empire'. The council formed the Russian Officer Assembly; the individual societies organised courses, discussion meetings and competitions.[38] The creation of the All Russian Military Union (ROVS) was announced in Yugoslavia on 1 September 1924, and a ROVS centre remained in the country till 1927. This was a clear signal of the kind of émigrés the Yugoslav government supported, and all the republican Russian émigré press regularly published information on how émigrés of even moderate left-wing orientation were persecuted in Yugoslavia.

The officer societies possessed, in émigré terms, a sizeable income and wielded considerable influence thanks to their contacts both with the high ranks of the Russian émigré community in Yugoslavia and with Serb military circles. This meant that the officers, especially those of the engineer corps, technical units and topographers, who constituted nearly a third of all organised Russian officers, easily found jobs in the Yugoslav civil service. The military of monarchist sympathies set the tone in the Russian émigré community in Yugoslavia.

The prevalence of members of the military could not fail to have an impact on the cultural work of the émigrés. Data on publications in the Russian language serve as a good indicator. Thus out of the 897 non-periodical Russian émigré works published in Yugoslavia between 1920 and 1945, 179 can be defined as religious and 121 as military: together they constituted 33 per cent of the entire publishing output.[39] In comparison, of publishing ventures in Prague, no more than 3 per cent of output was of this kind, including works on the history of the First World War, which could be classified as historical as well as military.

The military were also a decisive factor in Russian education. There were three cadet corps, one cavalry training school and two institutes for the education of girls. Judging from émigré memoirs, this created an atmosphere very reminiscent of pre-revolutionary Russia.[40] In Yugoslavia, everyone was taught anti-Bolshevik views. This meant that they were deprived of familiarity with other ideas, and during Yugoslavia's occupation by Nazi Germany the graduates of these Russian educational institutions were guided by one simple belief: the enemy of our enemies is our ally. And the only enemy, under all conditions, was the Soviet Union. Thus, tragically, a great many were prepared to support Nazism in its struggle against Communism and did not seem to realise all the implications of this position.[41] The cultural climate of the émigré community was to a considerable extent shaped by its infrastructure, not only by the state and by émigré administration.

Serbia, too, was an Orthodox country, and a decisive role was played by the Serbian Orthodox Church. From 1930 this was headed by Patriarch Varnava, who had studied in Russia and was an 'implacable and active opponent of Soviet godlessness and atrocities, unheard of in the history of cultured nations, which culminated in the present usurpation of power in Russia'.[42] Religious issues played an important role in Yugoslavia. In almost all countries where Russian refugees settled, belonging to the Orthodox Church was regarded as an expression of loyalty to a person's native background. Orthodox parishes were a central focus for the émigré community and the meeting places for people of all callings and of varied social status. The main festivals saw even agnostics and atheists attending church. Despite this support, strife between the two main jurisdictions led to disintegration of the unity of the Orthodox Church in Yugoslavia. The main bone of contention between the Sobor and those who accepted the leadership of Metropolitan Evlogii was the question of the place that politics played in the life of the Church. The Russian Orthodox Church Abroad

(Russkaya Pravoslavnaya Tserkov Zagranitsei: RPTZ), led by Metropolitan Antonii, not only adopted a position of implacable rejection of Soviet power, which preached militant atheism, but went much further. It extricated itself from submission to the captive Patriarch Tikhon, elected by the All-Russian Regional Council which strove to place the Church outside politics, and rejected this principle altogether.

For example, with RPTZ's blessing, Orthodox brotherhoods started to emerge in Yugoslavia. These followed the model of those who had defended the Orthodox faith in the regions of the Ukraine that had been annexed by Poland in the sixteenth and seventeenth centuries, a time when there was severe pressure to convert to Catholicism or, at least, to unify the two Churches. But particularly in Orthodox Serbia, there was little reason to fear conversion to Catholicism, and the underlying motives for joining a brotherhood were of a different kind, for example 'to oppose Bolshevism and all those socialist and other parties which ran counter to the spirit of Christ's teaching; not to belong to the Masonry and its ramifications, to the Order of the Eastern Star'.[43] Anti-Semitism was rarely mentioned, because it was taken for granted that the Jews murdered Christ and the guilt of Christ's blood on their hands was passed from one generation to another. Jews were also represented as eternal revolutionaries.[44]

This form of the Church Militant was not acceptable in liberal countries, where even without this kind of activity the perception of émigrés was less favourable. Nor did this kind of attitude help in establishing contact with other faiths. As a result, in most of Europe, with the exception of Yugoslavia, Metropolitan Evlogii's views commanded support. The link with politics in the RPTZ was clearly manifested in the efforts of Nazi Germany to unify Russian Orthodox parishes under its leadership, but most parishioners continued to hold to their previous beliefs.

The nature of government policy had a strong effect on the views of those émigrés accepted into the country. In most of the Russian émigré press, Yugoslavia was seen as an epitome of reaction, with the exception of the monarchist press, which defined Yugoslavia as a 'haven for true patriots'. But the country was unable to provide the resources necessary to revive pre-revolutionary Russia. It needed specialists and people with university education. The help they extended to the refugees meant that by 1921 some 60 per cent of Russian students abroad continued their education in Yugoslavia and Czechoslovakia and in these two countries university establishments employed around 50 per cent of Russian academics working abroad. Initially Yugoslavia ranked first in terms of government spending on support for the émigrés, but was later overtaken by Czechoslovakia. There were similar numbers of Russian émigrés in both countries in the mid–1920s, oscillating between 25,000 and 42,000.

The linguistic barrier could be overcome relatively easily. The fact that Russian had considerable prestige enabled thousands of Russians to find skilled, specialist employment where their training was of use. In the conditions of émigré life this was a great advantage and meant that they could become involved in the life of the local community.For example, the Union of Russian Agronomists in Yugoslavia had 204 members, of whom 106 worked in the public sector and 84 for private employers.[45] As many as 93 per cent of people working in the field for which they had been trained was a figure of which émigrés in other countries could only dream.

However, as Russian émigrés began to be involved in local life, it was not always possible to remain loyal to their monarchist ideas and to the ruling family. There is a great deal of evidence that Russian émigrés in Croatia were perceived as champions of Serb centralist policies, and there were a number of apologists for Serbia and King Alexander in the émigré press. Perhaps even more telling is the fact that a Russian student group in Zagreb gave its address as Zagreb, Serbia. One must assume that students living in Zagreb realised that the city was the capital of Croatia, and the state in which they lived was called the Kingdom of Serbs, Croats and Slovenes. There is no doubt that centralised control over the émigré community as well as the religious affinity and difference of attitudes at the time of the world war, when the Serbs were allies of the Entente while the Croats fought on the side of the Central Powers, all played their role in placing most of the Russians on the side of the Serbs and the current government.

The émigré community contained a large number of specialists and professionals. Pio-Ulsky's obituary mentions that he had been head of the Union of Russian Engineers in Yugoslavia and that there was a complete absence of unemployment in the Union. The likelihood was that this had been relatively easy to achieve. 'In 1921, engineers, technicians, geodesists, educators, physicians and cultural workers did not have to exert any special effort to find employment,' wrote Kozlitin.[46] Moreover, in the first years of emigration the Union of Engineers even invited to Yugoslavia engineers who had found themselves in a difficult situation in other countries.[47]

Civil servants were the only professionials who had difficulty in finding appropriate employment. But since these were educated people, they were still able to find work. Since the majority of émigrés were better educated than the local population, even those without professional qualifications also found work. As I. Ilovaiskaya noted, since the knowledge of foreign languages was rare in Serbia, people who spoke them could earn a good living in the country once they had learned Serbo-Croat.[48]

Yugoslavia did not aspire to preserve the Russian intellectual élite but the new government, striving quickly to catch up with its competitors, welcomed Russian scholars who quickly found employment at local university establishments. A number of other problems emerged, however. Yugoslav libraries were poorly stocked, the equipment of old universities was inadequate, and a similar situation existed in the universities founded after the creation of the new state. There was a serious shortage of teaching materials and technical support personnel and financial resources were limited. All this made scientific and educational work extraordinarily difficult. The widespread mutual sympathies between the local population and the émigrés nonetheless helped to overcome many problems. Moreover, the teachers felt they were doing useful work when addressing their Yugoslav and Russian students. They knew that if their Russian students did not return to their homeland, they would come into their own in Yugoslavia

These vacillations can be clearly traced in the life of E.V. Spektorsky. One year before the war he was appointed as a professor in Warsaw University, so his peregrinations started with the wartime evacuation of the university. After the outbreak of the Civil War, Denikin appointed him Deputy Chief of Popular Education, but before Spektorskiy could start fulfilling his functions, he had to leave Odessa to escape the advancing Red Army troops. From Odessa he fled to Yugoslavia, where in 1920 he was immediately appointed to a professorship at Belgrade University, but in 1924 he moved to Prague, where he became Professor and Dean of the Russian Law Faculty. Soon afterwards, in 1927, he was forced to return to Belgrade. Back in the Serb capital, he took an active part in setting up the Russian Scientific Institute, subsequently becoming its first chairman, a position he held until 1930, when he moved to Ljubljana University in Slovenia.

The opening of the Russian Scientific Institute on 16 September 1928 coincided with the beginning of the Fourth Congress of Russian Academic Organisations Abroad, the first to be held not in Prague but in Belgrade. This was a signal to all Russians in the emigration that the Russian academic centre in Prague was in decline. Belgrade began to lead in the area,[49] but it was a completely different academic centre. There were no Russian university-level institutions in the city, and the conditions for scientific and educational work were totally different. At first the institute shared a building with the Serb Royal Academy of Sciences, from where it moved to the Russian House – which bore the name of Emperor Nicholas II – in 1933.

The biography of P.B. Struve vividly illustrates the nature of the academic world in Yugoslavia.[50] Interested in legal Marxism as a young man, his intellectual position evolved so that at the turn of the century he held views which were very close to Masaryk's; in the revolutionary period he turned to the right until he became Wrangel's Minister of Foreign Affairs, and in the Czechoslovak context was closer to Kramář than to

Masaryk. He started his émigré existence in Sofia, then moved to Prague, where he became actively involved in building up the academic centre; but, once it became clear that Russian academic life in Prague was unlikely to develop much further, he moved to Paris where he founded *Vozrozhdenie* (The Revival), the right-wing counterweight to Milyukov's left-liberal *Poslednie Novosti* (Latest News). He then chaired the Congress of the Russian Diaspora,[51] and moved to Yugoslavia after a dispute with Gukasov, the owner of *Vozrozhdenie*. In 1934 he refused to participate in the World Philosophical Congress in Prague which discussed, *inter alia*, the topic of a 'Crisis of Democracy', because 'the very spirit of the Prague community was alien and hateful to him', as S.L. Frank reminisced. 'I understood him well: I myself felt at the congress the oppressive predominance of banal democratic slogans stifling the free mind.'[52]

At first sight it might seem that Struve's conservatism was beyond doubt and that his more doubtful left-wing past could be ascribed to youthful rashness. For the Russian community in Belgrade he nevertheless remained a revolutionary, even though his conversion to right-wing beliefs was quite openly expressed by the time of the publication of *Vekhi* (Landmarks) in 1909. The right-wing leadership of the Russian Scientific Institute fully understood and appreciated this. Judging by the institute reports, he was one of its most active lecturers, and certainly also one of the most knowledgeable. Still, from various accounts we know that his lectures were poorly attended, and when he was invited to speak at Belgrade University, the students booed him off the rostrum and he had to cut short his lecture. Again according to Frank, this was a joint action of Serb Communists and Russian right-wingers. But even if it were not, all documents and Struve's biographers emphasise that Struve found Russian society in Belgrade stifling.

This kind of atmosphere hampered academic work. There were two ways out of it: one leading to the parochial, which did not provide access to international scholarship; the other to further emigration. Besides, although full employment in Yugoslavia secured for the émigrés conditions comparable with those of their local colleagues, by West European and North American standards their situation was at the level of general poverty. Gradually many Russian émigrés left the country which had given them such a cordial welcome.

Britain

Recent work on the Russian emigration in Britain shows that developments here were unlike those in other European countries.[53] England, and later

Britain, and Russia had a long history of dealing with each other's exiles. Edmund Ironside's children are supposed to have fled to their relatives in Kiev in the eleventh century. Much later, Britain became the first destination for the Russian political émigrés of the nineteenth century. This was where A.I. Herzen settled and where he published his *Polarnaya zvezda* (The Polar Star) and *Kolokol* (The Bell), the first Russian exile periodicals with a relatively wide circulation. This was where many Russian political figures came to pay him tribute, yet for most of these political activists it was usually a stay of relatively short duration and Britain never became a genuine émigré centre. In 1867, Herzen left London. The Russian centres of emigration were now to be found in Geneva, Germany, Paris and, after 1905, Italy, with émigrés visiting Britain only occasionally, as Lenin did, to work in the British Library. This may have been owing to the fact that in England the Russian exiles did not have financial support of the sort that Marx found in Engels, or to the operation of the latent mechanisms of 'splendid isolation' which made British culture less accessible to the Russians.

Contacts between the Russians and the British took a variety of forms in the nineteenth century. There were interesting attempts by Anglican and Russian Orthodox theologians to find a common language and seek a path to a single Christian Church. Business and scientific contacts occurred. The Anglophilia of the Russian nobility found expression in the establishment of the English Club and Anglomania spread amongst the highest ranks of the aristocracy in St Petersburg at the beginning of the twentieth century. But none of this resulted in the formation of a major Russian colony in Britian.

The relatively low number of direct contacts prevented widespread knowledge of the English language. Britain seemed too inaccessible and crossing the Channel made Russia seem even further away. Moreover, British Immigration Acts of 1905 and 1914 meant that very few Russians were able to come or were accepted.

The lack of contacts meant that Russian émigrés had no patrons and, with the exception of Sir Paul Vinogradoff, Professor of Jurisprudence at the University of Oxford from 1903 to 1925, no one to whom they could turn for help. The social make-up of the small Russian colony in Britain was quite specific compared with other émigré communities. The highest ranks of Russian pre-revolutionary society were represented and, according to P.P. Shilovsky, they 'strove to maintain, in their new and alien conditions, the structure of the old, pre-revolutionary Russia, complete and in every detail'.[54]

The social structure formed around the court of the Princess Xenia Alexandrovna and her family. There were representatives of the princely families of Golitsyn, Meshchersky and Trubetskoy, former ministers of the Imperial Government, high officials from the Duma, scholars, industrialists and financiers. They did not enjoy any special privileges but most of them had English friends, which greatly helped them to find work and housing and to obtain scholarships for their children. As a result, 'the material situation of the colony was much better than that of Russians in Paris or, say, the Belgrade Russian colony. Nor was there anything comparable to the tedious restrictions on employment that prevailed in France. . . . Nor was there any obligation to go to the police station or to pay dues.'[55]

The few who succeeded in obtaining permission to stay were thus spared the constant fear of losing employment or being subjected to police surveillance. Exiles in other countries believed that all Russians in Britain lived a life of ease, and they not only envied them but also requested financial aid from them. In actual fact, most Russians in Britain did not have enough resources of their own to provide substantial help to their compatriots in exile. But thanks to their contacts, they often managed to gain substantial subsidies from British organisations, assisted in the creation of organisations specially for this purpose, or received funding from private donors. For instance, the Anglo-Russian Committee chaired by Sir Paul Vinogradoff raised funds for the development of Russian academic work abroad. The Anglican Church financed the Fellowship of St Alban and St Sergius, and Prince Svyatopolk-Mirsky raised money for Eurasians, arranged the publication of Remizov's works in English translation and a soirée of Tsvetaeva's poetry in London. He supplied funding for the publication of the literary magazine *Versty* (Leagues), and was also able to ensure publication of Vernadsky's articles in the *Slavonic Review*. In the end he announced that he was tired of begging.[56] The importance of the Russian colony in Britain was consequently greater than its size and its resources. In the 1920s it was more than just a group of the better-off and played a significant role in the development of a whole series of émigré initiatives. Nevertheless, it remained a very small community of only a few thousand, with neglible political influence or impact on Britain itself.

Latvia and Estonia

The position of the Baltic States was very different. They had a long and tangled relationship with Russia and had been part of the empire. The population was familiar with Russian culture and Russian newspapers, periodicals and books were widely available. The Baltic States were an obvious destination for many émigrés. On the other hand, anti-Russian sentiment could be profound. Moreover, as in the rest of Eastern Europe, these countries were economically weak and became unstable politically as new states with new political élites were formed. They had a difficult course to steer between their own interests and those of their larger and ultimately more powerful neighbours, Soviet Russia and Germany. Russian refugees fled to the Baltic States and Eastern Europe.

Recent research has discovered a great deal of new material.[57] In particular analysis of the archives of the newspaper *Segodnya* (Today) has produced a fascinating picture not only of the changing situation of the fortunes of the Russian newspaper in Riga but also of its relations with other publications in the emigration as well as illuminating many aspects of the emigration.[58]

In Latvia, Russian was widely used and *Segodnya* was published from 17 August 1919 until 21 June 1940. A. Sedykh, visiting in the summer of 1929, commented:

> Russian can be heard everywhere in Riga. The first two or three days, a visitor from Paris looks back at the speakers, and then he gets accustomed to them. Much more difficult is getting used to the fact that everyone is holding the Russian newspaper *Segodnya* in their hands. It is the most widely read of morning papers, bought not only by Russians but by Germans and Latvians as well. In a train travelling from Vzmorye, a coastal resort, everybody in the carriage is holding *Segodnya*; by the end of the day, the evening edition of this newspaper literally covers the whole beach . . .'.[59]

This newspaper served not only the Russian émigrés, who had just arrived, but also Russians and those of Russian culture who had been in the area for a long time and of whom there were a great many. The paper paid particular attention to life in Latvia, Lithuania and Estonia, as well as reporting world events and the life of Russian émigrés in other centres.

The situation in Latvia was unusual. In the first 10 to 15 years after Latvia's declaration of independence in 1918, Russian could not only be heard everywhere, but could easily be used in routine everyday life, even though the number of Russian inhabitants of Riga was not more than 10 per cent of the total population. This was because the non-Russian population, including many Latvians and Germans, either used Russian as a colloquial language, or spoke it fluently. There was little obvious anti-Russian feeling. The Latvian, Russian and German languages coexisted peacefully in Riga. Some restrictions affected the Orthodox Church: the Alexei Monastery and the adjacent House of the Archierei were handed over to the Roman Catholic Church, and the memorial chapel on the main city square was subsequently pulled down. But other denominations also experienced difficulties and it is interesting that the German Lutheran church of St Yakov was given to the Catholic Church in 1921 under a concordat with the Vatican while the argument used for the demolition of the memorial chapel was that it obstructed traffic. The Russian press suspected that this was a pretext, but if so it was expressed in an ambiguous way, whereas the Orthodox cathedral in Warsaw and the garrison church in Grodno were pulled down as symbols of loathsome Russian occupation.

Russian émigrés constituted an insignificant minority. According to official data, by the end of 1921, 26,000 Russian refugees had entered Latvia; in 1935, émigrés without citizenship in Latvia numbered about 4,000, out of a total of 233,000 Russians living in the country. Despite the considerable outflow from Latvia to other centres of emigration, this provides evidence of the benevolent attitude of the authorities to naturalised émigrés and explains the attraction of Latvia. Of the Russians living in Latvia, 180,000 were peasants and small farmers in the southern regions of the country, semi-destitute people tending small plots of infertile land which could not provide them with a living. Therefore they had to rely on seasonal work. The adult population was semi-literate: only 66 per cent of Russian children of school age actually went to school.[60]

A policy offensive against minorities started at the beginning of the 1930s: in 1932, the 'Rules on state language' dramatically curtailed opportunities for the speaking of minority languages, banning their use during contact with the authorities and restraining them in other spheres as well. In 1934, after the *coup d'état* led by Karolis Ulmanis, an attack against minorities was launched on all fronts, including a ban on some Russian publications and the introduction of general censorship; non-Russian parents, including those of mixed marriages, were forbidden to send their children to Russian schools. As this policy, under the slogan 'Latvia for Latvians', began to show results, the Russian cause in Latvia started to languish.

But ideas in the Russian diaspora about Latvia, or more precisely, about the border states in general, changed in the opposite direction. Contrary to the initial widely held belief that in the 1930s the Russians of the border states were downtrodden, these states became attractive. At the end of the 1920s, Riga and Pechora became places of pilgrimage for émigrés from the main centres of Russian settlement, some of whom even moved there. The émigré hope for an early return to their homeland, where they would once again become immersed in the free flow of pure Russian, was fading and they started to value more and more those areas of uninterrupted occupation by Russian minorities where Russian had been preserved in its pure form, unspoilt by foreign influences. Moreover, these were places with Russian landscape, with Russian rural and urban architecture, with 'hearthstones of ancient piety', of uninterrupted tradition, some dating as far back as the fifteenth century, as in the case of the Pskovo-Pechersky Monastery on the Estonian border.

These regions attracted Russian journalists from abroad, such as A. Sedykh and Z. Shakhovskaya; as well as senior Russian professors and politicians, young post-revolutionary representatives, Eurasians and others who came to Riga and Tallinn to lecture. Many visited the Russian villages, especially those where the old believers still lived, the Pskovo-Pechersky Monastery and the border area, in order to look from accessible Russian soil across the river at the expanses of their inaccessible native country.

A research trip to the Pskovo-Pechersky Monastery was organised by N.E. Andreyev, for members of the Kondakov Institute in Prague to study the icons.[61] I.N. Okuneva, a student of art history at Charles University, immediately expressed the wish to join the expedition in order 'to see the wonders of Russian antiquity which still existed in the regions of Estonia bordering on Russia'. It 'appeared that a good many people travelled to Estonia from all countries, including Professor Elizaveta Eduardovna Maler from Basel, who came to record the folk songs of the Pskov region [and] Leonid Fedorovich Zurov, writer and amateur archaeologist' from France.[62]

Before the expedition reached the monastery, Andreyev visited a song festival in Narva in Estonia.

I was stunned by the intensity of Russian national feelings: the countryside was swept by a spirit of old times; wonderful costumes were stored in trunks, still waiting to be finished, ablaze with colour, with peculiar local ornaments, embroidery, elaborately decorated 'povoiniki' [veils worn by married Russian women, tied in bonnet-like fashion, to contain hair under a scarf] and 'kokoshniki' [headbands]. . . . The next morning there was a march of members of all the Russian organisations, who assembled on the village square in a grand rally, to the tune of Russian folk songs. . . . A ball was held in the evening in the city hall. . . . One hardly realised that this was Estonia. Everybody spoke Russian, Russian songs could be heard all over the place, all the numerous speeches of the Estonian Parliament officials – Russian deputies, representatives of other minorities, a certain minister – were delivered in Russian, too . . . .

This trip and the accounts of it are a perfect illustration of the fact that by the 1930s, when the materials and impressions imported from Russia had already been processed and were even starting to be re-processed, parts of the territory in the border states which had been Russian from time immemorial became the principal source of a revived interest in genuine Russian lifestyle and a living Russian language.

The local Russian minority and the Russian exiles in Estonia were in a less strong position. In the first place, there was no cosmopolitan environment in Estonia of the kind that existed in Riga. In Hanseatic times, Riga was already bigger than Revel (Tallinn), and in the nineteenth century it became one of the chief ports of Russia and a centre for trading firms, with a population in excess of half a million, while Revel, after it was linked with St Petersburg by a railway, grew as an industrial city in which industrialists from St Petersburg invested. The size of the population in pre-Soviet times never exceeded 160,000 and in Tallinn there was no Jewish colony of any significance to unite the Russian and the German minorities at least to some extent, as happened in Riga. The German colony in Revel tended to keep to themselves, and contacts between the two were not strong.

A substantial part of the émigré community were fugitives from St Petersburg, some of whom had dachas and relatives in the region: this was especially the case for high-ranking officials, writers, journalists and artists. In Tallinn cultural activities were conducted in a purely Russian spirit and were on the whole more lively and varied than in Riga, but due to the small base of support on which they relied, even the most successful undertakings were soon discontinued because of a shortage of funds. The peasant community, on the other hand, though not as poor as in Latvia, was considerably more nationally conscious, united in religious terms, and capable of organising such major events as the national song festival, undoubtedly under the influence of the surrounding Estonian population, for whom song festivals had become an important element in the movement of national revival in the nineteenth century. The level of the peasants' literacy was much higher too, especially among the younger generation.

Perhaps it was this more nationalistic orientation of the Russian colony in Estonia that gave rise to the more acute anti-Russian sentiment in Estonia in the first years of its independence, though it should be noted that anti-German feelings were quite strong, too, which justifies the assumption that the underlying reason consisted in the more developed national feelings of the Estonians themselves. Nevertheless, even some Russians admitted that they bore their share of blame for the difficulties of coexistence. In the spring of 1935, Bolshakova, a Russian émigré, wrote to her brother: 'according to Harbin papers, the situation of Russians there is not so bad as you wrote, and even if some have been brought low, it means that it had to be done – it would do no harm to upset this riffraff – the "Russians" – here as well. There is too much arrogance and self-complacency – why, some even lose sleep over the slogan "Russians United and Indivisible". Will they ever come to their senses!!!'[63]

The Place of Prague in the Diaspora

Emigration is a tragic phenomenon. People are torn away from their homes, families, country and culture. Many try to recreate these things in alien environments in the hope that they can be preserved for the long-awaited return home. The Russian refugees did not wish to become immigrants. They saw themselves as similar to the French émigrés after 1789 who had been able to return home within a generation. For this reason, the Russians did not draw parallels between themselves and the Polish emigration of 1832 which might have appeared a better comparison. Still less were they willing to draw upon the experience of the Huguenots or even the Jews. Nevertheless, just as with other émigré communities, the Russians stressed the special nature of their position. The Bolsheviks and the atrocities perpetrated in the name of Communism were seen as the epitome of evil. The suffering experienced by the refugees was represented in terms of the struggle between good and evil.

Although most held fast to their principles, they had to adapt to the circumstances in which they found themselves. Some thought that a return to Russia would take the form of a new military advance against Bolshevism. Others thought that the regime would evolve in such a way that a peaceful return would be possible and that those who had acquired new skills and expertise would be welcomed for the contribution they could make to Soviet Russian society. As these hopes faded, the emigration began to re-evaluate their position in relation not simply to Russia but also to the societies and countries in which they found themselves.

This can perhaps be most vividly illustrated in the area of education. Many young Russians had their education cut short by the Civil War when they enlisted in the White armies. Once they found themselves abroad, one of their earliest goals was to complete that education in readiness for future work in Russia. This was the main aim of Russian Action in Czechoslovakia. From the outset the government insisted that it did not wish to attract military refugees and did not want to emphasise any of the political polarities which had emerged as a result of the experience of the Civil War. Czech policy was based on a complex appreciation of the situation within Russia. Masaryk always considered that the monarchists did not have a particularly strong popular base and that it would be necessary to work within a left-wing coalition. It was also assumed that Bolshevism would have to evolve and develop more acceptable policies which would allow émigrés to return and to play a role in the rebuilding of the country and Russian society. Students were welcomed and supported, on the assumption that they would not be staying very long. The Law Faculty in Prague was developed because it was thought that an understanding of Russian law would be an essential tool for anyone returning to Russia to work in the adminstration. In Harbin a Russian Law Faculty was established with the same end in view. But this state of affairs could only last for a few years. As it became clear that the Soviet regime was more stable than anyone had expected and was evolving in unforeseen directions, the émigrés had to reconsider their position, and those who had completed their education in Czechoslovakia had to find employment elsewhere. Yugoslavia, by contrast, could provide employment for qualified people. It was more difficult to get accepted by French or German educational institutions, but those who managed to do so found they provided better openings and more employment possibilities.

For established scholars jobs in universities were greatly valued and people moved between the various centres of emigration.[64] But higher education in France, Britain and Germany was inhospitable to Russian émigré scholars. By contrast Yugoslav, Bulgarian, Estonian and Latvian universities opened their doors to Russian academics. Given their small population, Estonia and Latvia were particularly generous in this respect. In these countries, there was a shortage of highly qualified professionals. Moreover, the local intelligentsia were familiar with Russian culture and language and so it was easier for them to accept émigré Russians into such institutions. In Western Europe there was no such lack of qualified personnel. Few members of the Russian intelligentsia knew English or were familiar with British society. The older generation of university teachers were usually proficient in French and German but even this was of little help in gaining employment. Czechoslovakia came between these two extremes, initially supporting Russian scholars but in the long term being unable to provide them with employment in Czech institutions.

Undoubtedly age and family responsibilities had an important role to play. The overwhelming majority of those classified as students were unmarried. As a result of their wartime experience, they were older than was normal for most students, but they still were in a position to endure temporary difficulties when the long-term prospects seemed favourable. Thus those who found themselves in some of the Western European states considered that the benefits of being there would eventually outweigh the difficulties. Those who had to provide for a family – and this was more likely to apply to members of the academic staff – had to find ways of doing so immediately and were less likely to weigh up the question of future prospects. An invitation to teach at a university in Eastern Europe was a more attractive prospect for many than a lengthy and possibly fruitless struggle to be accepted by an institution in Western Europe.

The Russian intelligentsia is the section of the emigration that has always received the most attention and that has left the most distinct legacy.

However, the dominant group in the 1920s was the military. Many of them had no other skills, as they had been conscripted or had volunteered to serve in the armed forces before they had finished their education. Their period in the armed forces frequently deprived them of the habits of work and regular study. After the First World War, all over Europe erstwhile combatants had great difficulties in returning to civilian life. Most of those in Western Europe had spent less time in the trenches than the Russian forces. Moreover most of them had the support of their families, communities and governments when trying to re-integrate into their own societies. Things were much harder in this respect for Russians. Soviet literature of the 1920s vividly documents the situation in Soviet Russia. For the émigrés the situation was even worse. Their families and closest relatives had stayed in the Soviet Union. Europe was not very welcoming. The closest communities for many were their military units. Indeed, Wrangel's efforts to preserve the army were intended not only to maintain it as a fighting force but were also motivated by the feeling that the army was the last support for many and was seen as their family and 'homeland'.[65] Preserving unity was a psychological imperative for many, irrespective of their ideological differences. But in the end they failed to preserve the army or army organisation and eventually almost everyone, except for a select few in Yugoslavia and Harbin, had to transfer to a civilian way of life.

In the early years the political divisions of the Civil War predominated. The debate over intervention and the nature of the future forms of government in Russia was an extension of the debate over Russia's place in the world. Was she part of Western culture and development or did she have a special contribution because of her position as a bridge between East and West? This was all based on the assumption that it was inconceivable that Bolshevik barbarism would succeed. It was assumed that either the regime would collapse under the weight of its own inconsistencies or that the refugees would return seated on white chargers with flags unfurled to the rapturous cheers of their compatriots and that victory would inevitably be theirs.

Although phrased in altogether more measured and careful language, Czechoslovak policy was based on a similar expectation. Masaryk did not think that the Bolsheviks could continue their policies for long, so the Russians who had been educated in Prague would be able to return home. Their exposure to Western training and democratic practice would enable them to influence the Bolsheviks and would provide the specialists and administrators that the regime so obviously lacked. These people would be sympathetic to the views and needs of the Czechoslovak Republic, which would undoubtedly benefit from close ties with Russia.

However, it became clear that the Soviet regime was consolidating its position and was unlikely to evolve in the near future into something which would be broadly acceptable to the emigration. Émigré isolation was increasingly accentuated by the international situation, where foreign powers were prepared to recognise the Soviet Union. The USSR was recognised by the USA in 1933 and full diplomatic relations between Prague and the Kremlin were established in 1934. Hitler's rise to power was recognised by many as a sign not only that the political balance of Europe was changing but that war would be the outcome of Hitler's nationalistic and racist policies. All of this had an impact on émigré attitudes. In Czechoslovakia, the government had attempted, with partial success, to keep the emigration apolitical. Once Russian Action came to an end, political divisions re-emerged more clearly. Harbin became the birthplace of Russian Fascism. This was partly because the distance from Europe meant that the implications of Fascist ideology were not properly understood. But the rise of new groupings of this type was a response to the weakness of democracy, which seemed unable to protect itself and still less the interests of Russian refugees. The need to deal with the possibility of war between the Soviet Union and Nazi Germany meant that previous political divisions altered and émigrés had to decide which was their main enemy. The Bolsheviks had destroyed much that they held dear and deprived them of their homeland. The Nazis were prepared to fight the Bolsheviks but at the same time saw the Russians in racist terms. During the war the Russian émigrés met their Soviet counterparts. This was complicated as the values of the two groups were very different. Those who left the Soviet Union as a result of the Second World War are usually termed the second emigration or second wave. For the most part they left Europe for North America after the end of the war and inaugurated a new phase in the history of the Russian emigration.

The fact that an immediate return home was becoming increasingly unlikely was reflected in the changes in most areas of émigré life. The problem of maintaining Russian identity and Russian culture had to be reassessed. Although in the long term Russian culture had to be preserved for Russia itself, the needs and achievements of the emigration had to be given a higher priority, and not simply on the humanitarian level. The émigré press could only survive if it focused on the needs of the emigration. The Day of Russian Culture, celebrating Pushkin's birthday became a kind of émigré festival. Germany, which had been the magnet for Russian cultural life when it was seen as a meeting place for Soviet Russia and Europe, began to lose its attraction. Paris was more stable and drew the cultural élite towards it. Eastern Europe had provided an immediate haven after the Civil War since some countries had been part of the Russian empire and had a population familiar with Russian culture. Common Slav roots made the languages easier to learn and Russian culture could easily be seen as superior to indigenous ones. Yet, throughout the inter-war period these countries were seen as provincial, less desirable places to be. Paradoxically, it was in countries like France, which were not interested in the émigrés but which attracted large numbers of Russians, that the question of identity seemed to be particularly emphasised. The concentration of the political, social and cultural élite in Paris combined with the existence of large numbers of Russians, who were the audience or readership for émigré writers and artists of all kinds, allowed for a flowering of Russian culture abroad and its wider acceptance as part of world culture.

According to the Zemgor in 1924, 'the monthly expenditure by the Czechoslovak government on Russian Action . . . exceeded the sum total expended on Russian émigrés by all other European governments'.[66] This fact alone emphasises the unique role that Czechoslovakia played in Russian refugee life in the inter-war period. Other states were either not interested or not able to support the émigrés. Only Yugoslavia accepted comparable amounts of people but there the politics and atmosphere were very different. Czechoslovak policy towards the Russian refugees was extra-ordinarily generous. Humanitarian concerns meant that the initial assump-tions about the development of the Russian émigré community had to be modified. But in the heyday of the Russian academic centre in Prague, 20 per cent of the émigrés were students. In this respect, Prague was very influential in the emigration as a whole even if in absolute numbers Prague contained one of the smaller Russian communities.

The majority of Russians did not wish to stay in Czechoslovakia on a permanent basis. They were willing to stay temporarily, provided they could create a Russian micro-world of their own, a Russian academic world. Moreover, Czechoslovakia could not, and was not willing to, provide employment. Once the assumptions on which Russian Action was based were shown to be mistaken, subsidies to the emigration were cut and educational opportunities decreased. Only organisations which had links with the Czech academic world like the Prague Linguistic Circle could continue to operate in Prague. For those involved in the Russian academic world in Prague, this situation could not have been a surprise. From the outset, scholars had to face the question of how best to deal with the competing demands made on them. Focusing purely on Russian needs could be justified for a few years if Russia was going to benefit from this and if the scholars would return home. Once it was clear that this would not happen, Russian scholars had to find a place for themselves in the international scholarly community. It is noticeable how quickly scholars of international reputation, such as Sorokin, Vernadsky or even Jakobson, tended to leave Prague and move either to larger centres in Europe or to

America. These people were no less Russian after they left Prague: their work still encompassed Russian themes and bore the impress of their experience, but it was judged not simply in the narrow world of the emigration, but on a larger stage.

The End of the Emigration

Hitler's invasion of Czechoslovakia on 15 March 1939 ended the first independent Czechoslovak Republic. Ruthenia was annexed to Hungary, Slovakia was reorganised into an independent state with limited sovereignty and Bohemia and Moravia became a protectorate under, initially, the 'Reich Protector' Baron von Neurath. It also brought an end to the Russian émigré community.

Those who read the signs correctly had left before the outbreak of hostilities. Once Prague was occupied most émigré institutions were closed down or brought under the control of the German authorities. At that moment there were still 131 registered Russian émigré organisations. In his memoirs,[1] Nikolay Andreyev recalled the meeting at which Prince Dolgorukov, as a representative of the Committee of Russian organisations, had to transfer his responsibilities to General V.V. Biskupsky,[2] who had been appointed as head of the whole Russian emigration by the Nazis. K.A. Efremov, a taxi driver, was appointed head of the Prague centre of the Russian emigration. His job was not enviable, as he had to report to his superiors, the Gestapo. Remaining Russian émigrés tried to keep as low a profile as possible in order to survive.

There were still occasional lectures organised under the auspices of the Russian People's University. The Kondakov Institute was able to continue working as a result of having an independent source of income and provided help for a few individuals, including P.N. Savitsky who packed books after the German authorities dismissed him from his post as headmaster of the Russian secondary school. The Church continued to support and help its parishioners. But these were examples of individual effort rather than of activity by the emigration as a whole. The invasion of the USSR by the Third Reich on 22 June 1941 put added pressure on the remaining members of the emigration. Under Nazi jurisdiction they could not express sympathy for their compatriots, although many hoped that the war would force substantial changes in the USSR.

The end of the war saw the attempt to liberate Prague by the 1st KONR Division under the command of General Vlasov, the leader of the so-called

Russian Liberation Movement. On 6 May 1945 the KONR Division took part in the attack on German troops, including the SS division which had been sent to put down the Czech rising in Prague. However, the Americans had no intention of entering Prague: demarcation lines had already been agreed and Vlasov and his men had to retreat in the wake of the German troops. Three fronts of the Red Army met in Prague. Marshal Malinovsky's right wing had marched up from the Balkans, General Eremenko's troops who had previously been defenders of Stalingrad were in the centre, and were joined by Marshal Konev's men who had already fought in Germany near Berlin and Dresden. The occupation by the Soviet authorities was a severe shock to the remnants of the Russian emigration, most of whom had expected the Americans to occupy Prague.

SMERSH (the Soviet counter-intelligence organisation known by the contraction of Smert' Shpionam – Death to Spies) arrived in Prague in the wake of the Red Army. According to available information, 215 Russian émigrés were arrested by SMERSH, as well as by the NKVD and intelligence officers of military units.[3] Those arrested were mainly leading figures within the emigration but behaviour in the pre-war or the war years was not reflected in the arrests. Some Nazi collaborators were left in peace, yet others who had languished in German concentration camps were transferred to Soviet ones. Some, like S.P. Postnikov and P.N. Savitsky, survived years in the Gulag, were released in the amnesties following Stalin's death and were reunited with their families. Others were never heard of again. These arrests destroyed what was left of the emigration. Once the Communists took power in 1948, support for Russian émigrés and all their activities was forgotten even if their descendants still met in church and tended graves in the Olšansky cemetery. After 1948 many members of the Czech middle classes saw Communism as being typically Russian and their hatred of Communism led to a hatred of Russians. Russian émigrés became confused with Soviet Russians and this often had a deleterious effect on their lives, blighting careers and relationships. Many of the second generation of émigrés left for the West, but this meant abandoning the increasingly feeble hope that they would eventually be reunited with those who had been arrested and taken away to the Soviet Union.

For many of those who stayed, these reunions did take place. To the great surprise of their children, many of those who returned had become Soviet patriots. The late 1950s and early 1960s saw the beginnings of successful Soviet space travel and Yuri Gagarin became an international hero. The intellectual thaw in the USSR and the publication of Solzhenitsyn's *One Day in the Life of Ivan Denisovich* (1962) and Bulgakov's *The Master and Margarita* (1966–67), amongst others, allowed Russian first-generation émigrés to feel pride in their mother country in the same way as they had felt pride in the achievements of the Red Army in 1945. However, this sort of euphoria did not last very long.

When Czech Communism began to liberalise a little in the 1960s, some Czech specialists began to interest themselves again in the achievements of the Russians in Prague, especially the literary élite. But the Soviet invasion of Czechoslovakia in 1968 put a stop, once again, to this kind of activity. The younger generation of émigrés who had now grown up found it difficult to explain the difference between the Soviet Russia of their imagination and the way in which Czechoslovakia had been occupied by Soviet troops. For Czechs, it also blurred the distinction between émigrés and other Russians. Those Russians who still lived in Prague recall that it became impossible to speak Russian in public and the last traces of their identity had to be hidden.

The collapse of the Iron Curtain in 1989 opened a new phase, when previous taboos were dropped and interest in the Russian emigration in Prague and elsewhere could be expressed openly. The emigration was now a fashionable topic of study and new sources became available. Previously scholars had argued that it was not yet possible to write a history of the emigration,[4] and lamented the lack of sources both published and unpublished. Now the situation had changed radically and both types of source were made available.

Although the position of most Russian émigrés was very precarious in both financial and political terms, they had the freedom to discuss ideas which could not be developed inside Russia. Literature, theology and some political ideas, notably Eurasianism, developed within the emigration and are now of great interest to those who live inside the erstwhile borders of the Soviet Union. Marc Raeff has argued that not only did the émigré intelligentsia continue the creative ideas which emanated from the Silver Age and the early years of the Soviet Union but they also provided a conduit for Western ideas back to their Soviet compatriots.[5]

The experience of the Russian émigrés in Prague demonstrates how much their efforts were determined by their allegiance to Russia. International politics played a central role in influencing where they settled and what they were able to do. It also stresses how important it is to understand the various centres of the Russian emigration as being transient and in constant contact with one another, at least by means of the written word. This aspect is fundamental to an understanding of the dynamics of the Russian émigrés. Their experience as refugees elucidates our understanding of displacement in the twentieth century. On a world stage, the Russian emigration is yet another example of the way in which creative minorities can exist in exile and can have an impact on their surrounding societies.

Notes

INTRODUCTION

1. M. Tsvetaeva, 'Chekhiya ostalos' u menya v pamyati kak odin siniy den' i odna tumannaya noch'.', ed Z. Matgauser and V. Morkovin, *Pisma k Teskovoy*, Prague 1969, p. 126.
2. G. Vanecková, *Marina Tsvetaeva v Chekhii: putevoditel po mestam prebyvaniya v 1922–25 godakh* (Prague 1997) is a good guide to Tsvetaeva's life in Czechoslovakia.
3. The chaos of war and refugee existence means that no accurate statistics exist, so discussion of the extent of emigration continues. M. Alekhin and E. Belaya in 'Razmeshchenie emigratsii', *Bolshaya sovetskaya entsiklopediya*, vol. 64, cols 160–75 (Moscow, 1933) give the total number as 860,000 but omit a number of countries: Estonia, Latvia, Bulgaria, Turkey and Finland, where sizeable émigré communities were to be found. In the 3rd edition of the *Bolshaya sovetskaya entsiklopediya*, vol. 30, cols 163–4, (Moscow, 1978) the émigrés are said to number two million. L. K. Shkarenkov, in *Agoniya beloi emigratsii* (Moscow, 1981, p.18), considers that the maximum number was two million. Sir John Hope Simpson, *The Refugee Problem* (London, 1939) uses statistics provided by RZIA the Russian Historical Archive Abroad in Prague and discusses the various estimates (pp.80–3). In 1922, Dr Nansen, the first High Commissioner for Refugees, considered that there were one and a half million refugees in Europe. H.von Rimscha in *Der russische Bürgerkrieg und die russische Emigration, 1917–21* (Jena, 1924) pp. 50–1, gives the figure of 2.935 million on the basis of Red Cross statistics in *Volya Rossii* (28/12/1920) but that figure is rejected by others as too high. In 1926, the League of Nations statistics gave the figure of 1,160,000 as having left Russia. See M. Raeff, *Russia Abroad: A Cultural Study of the Russian Emigration, 1919–1939* (Oxford, 1990), pp. 23–4
4. RZIA statistics show that 107 émigré newspapers were published in 1934.
5. Claudena Skran, *Refugees in Inter-war Europe*, Oxford, 1995, p. 10.
6. Hope Simpson, *The Refugee Problem*, p. 3.
7. Louise W. Holborn, *Refugees: A Problem of our Time*, vol. 1, (Metuchen, NJ, 1975), p. 9.
8. Hans von Rimscha, *Der russische Bürgerkrieg* and *Russland jenseits der Grenzen 1921–1926* (Jena, 1927) are still of interest today. W. Chapin Huntington, *The Homesick Million* (Boston, 1933) was an attempt to produce a comprehensive picture of the Russian emigration but this lead was not followed in academic writing. A considerable amount was published in Soviet Russia, usually by those who had returned home and for the most part these were either political pamphlets or memoirs. V. Belov, *Beloe pokhmel'e.*

Russkaya emigratsiya na rasput'e. Opyt issledovaniya psikhologii, nastroeniya i bytovykh uslovii russkoi emigratsii v nashe vremya (Moscow and Petrograd, 1923) stands out from this genre.

9. D. Ivantsov 'Russkie bezhentsy v Yugoslavii v 1921g', *Russkiy ekonomicheskii sbornik*, 2, 1925, pp. 80–107.

10. S.S. Oldenburg in *Russkaya mysl'. Ezhemesyachnoe literaturno-politicheskoe izdanie pod redaktsiey Petra Struve*, vols 5–7, Sofia, 1921, pp. 234–7.

11. V.Kh., Davats and N.N. L'vov, *Russkaya armiya na chuzhbine*, Belgrade, 1923 (reprinted 1985). Davats never included this book in his academic bibliography.

12. P.N. Miliukov produced the most detailed account of this question, even though he has a clear bias in his book *Emigratsiya na pereput'e*, Paris, 1926. L.F. Magerovsky attempted to analyse the political divisions in Czechoslovakia in *Ročenka Československé republiky*, Prague, 1928.

13. See for example S.L. Voitsekhovskii, *Trest: vospominaniya i dokumenty*, London, Ontario, 1974; B. Prianishnikov, *Nezrimaia pautina*, Silver Spring, Illinois, private edn, 1979; G. Bailey, *The Conspirators*, New York, 1960, and P. Blackstock, *The Secret Road to World War Two*, Chicago, 1969.

14. L. Fleishman, Yu. Abyzov and B. Ravdin, *Russkaya pechat'v Rige: iz istorii gazety Segodnya 1930 godov*, vols 1–5, Stanford, 1997 (Stanford Slavic Studies, vol. 13–17) provides an excellent illustration of the way in which writers had to adjust to the demands of the authorities and of editors.

15. This process began earlier but was intensified by the depression. J. Baur, *Die russische Kolonie in München 1900–1945. Deutsch–russische Beziehungen im 20. Jahrhundert* Wiesbaden, 1998, p. 228 is overstating the case.

16. *Russkaya zarubezhnaya kniga. Trudy Komiteta russkoy knigi*, vols 1–2. Prague, 1924.

17. *Materialy dlya bibliografii russkikh nauchnykh trudov za rubezhom (1920–1930)*, vol. 1, Belgrade, 1931. The second volume was published in 1941 but almost the entire print run was destroyed by enemy bombing.

18. G.P. Struve, *Russkaya literatura v izgnanii*, New York, 1956, 2nd edn Paris, 1984. The fact that M. Slonim's, *Modern Russian Literature* (New York, 1953) devoted only 11 pages (396–406) to émigré writing provoked much criticism.

19. A guide to émigré debates can be found in the useful bibliographies in N.P. Poltaratskii (ed.), *Russkaia literatura v emigratsii–Sbornik statei*, Slavic series no.1 (Pittsburgh, 1972). See also Colloquium Proceedings, *Odna ili dve russkikh literatury?* Lausanne, 1981. E. Etkind, G. Nivat, I. Serman and V. Strada (eds), *Histoire de la littérature russe–Le XXe siècle: la révolution et les années vingt* (Paris, 1988) and *Le XXe siècle: Gels et dégels* (Paris, 1990) treat émigré literature as part of the entire corpus of twentieth-century Russian writing and provide a useful bibliography.

20. P.E. Kovalevsky, *Zarubezhnaya Rossiya: istoriya i kulturno-prosvititel'naya rabota russkogo zarubezhiya za pol veka (1920–1970)*, 2 vols, Paris, 1971, 1973.

21. Raeff, *Russia Abroad*.

22. Richard J. Kneeley and Edward Kasinec, 'The Prague RZIA Collection', *Slavic Review*, Spring 1992, pp. 122–30. T.F. Pavlova (ed.), *Fondy Russkogo Zagranichnogo Istoricheskogo Arkhiva v Prage*, Moscow, 1999.

23. D. Meisner, *Mirazhi i Deistvitelnost'* (Moscow, 1970) is an excellent example of this, making it necessary to treat such work even more carefully than most memoir material.

24. This resulted in perhaps only one work of lasting importance: Z. Matgauser and V. Morkovin (eds) Marina Tsvetaeva, *Pisma k A. Teskovoy*, Prague, 1969. The archival staff of the Museum of Czech Literature also catalogued much of the material in their collections and the Slavonic library staff saved the collections of RZIA in difficult times.

25. S.P. Postnikov (ed.) *Russkie v Prage 1918–1928g*, Prague, 1928; reprinted 1995.
26. For example V.V. Preobrazhenskiy (ed.), *Russkie v Latvii: sbornik 'Dnya Russkoy Kultury'*, 2 vols, Riga, 1933, 1934.
27. M.M. Novikov, *Ot Moskvy do Niu Iorka. Moya zhizn' v nauke i politike*, New York, 1952. N.E. Andreyev, 'O Russkoy Literaturnoy Prage', *Russkiy Almanakh*, Paris, 1981.
28. Von Rimscha, *Russlands jenseits der Grenzen*. 'Die Entwicklung der russländischen Emigranten nach den zweiten Weltkrieg', *Europa Arkhiv*, 7 (August/November/December 1952). H-E.Volkmann, *Die russische Emigration in Deutschland 1919–1929*, Würzburg, 1966. R.C. Williams, *Culture in Exile. Russian Émigrés in Germany 1871–1941*, Ithaca, NY, Cornell, 1972.
29. L.K. Shkarenkov, *Agoniya beloy emigratsii*, Moscow, revised 1986.
30. V. Kostikov, *Ne budem proklinat' izgnaniye . . . Puti i sud'by russkoy emigratsii*, 2nd edn, Moscow, 1994.
31. V.T. Pashuto, *Russkie istoriki emigranty v Evrope*, Moscow, 1992.
32. M. Dandová and M. Zahradníková, 'Rossica ve fondech literárního archívu Památníku národního písemnictví', *Sborník Literárního archívu*, 23, Prague, 1989.
33. The archives of Russian organisations under the Ministry of Foreign Affairs were separated and are now kept in the main government archive. See: *Russkya i ukrainskya emigratsiya v Chekhoslovatskoy respublike 1918–1938. Putevoditel' po arkhivnym fondam i sobraniyam v Cheshskoy Respublike*, Prague, 1995.
34. See for example: Z.Sládek, 'Russkaya i Ukrainskaya emigratsiya v Chekhoslovakii', *Sovetskoe Slavyanovedenie*, 1991. Z. Sládek, 'Prag: Das "russische Oxford"', in K. Schlögel (ed.), *Der grosse Exodus. Die russische Emigration und ihre Zentren 1917 bis 1941*, Munich, 1994. Z. Sládek 'České prostředí a ruská emigrace (1918–1938)', in *Duchovní proudy ruské a ukrajinské emigrace v Československé republice 1919–1939*, Prague, 1999.
35. *Slovanský přehled. Časopis pro dějiny střední, východní a jihovýchodní Evropy*, 1, 1993.
36. V. Veber, Z. Sládek and M. Bubeníková, *Ruská a ukrajinská emigrace v ČSR v letech 1918–1945*, Prague, 1996.
37. *Mezhdunarodnaya konferentsiya 'Russkaya, ukrainskaya i belorusskaya emigratsiya v Chekhoslovakii mezhdu dvumya mirovymi voinami. Rezul'taty i perespektivy issledovniy. Fondy Slavyanskoy biblioteki i prazhskikh arkhivov'*, Prague, 14–15 August 1995.
38. *Prace ruské, ukrajinské a běloruské emigrace vydané v Československu 1918–1945. (Bibliografie s biografickými údaji o autorech.)*, Bibliografii zpracovaly Z. Rachůnková a M. Řeháková. *Biografická hesla zpracoval*, J.Vacek za spolupráce a redakce Z. Rachůnkové a M. Řehákové, 3 vols, Prague, 1996.
39. Z. Sládek, L.Beloshevskaya et al. (eds), *Dokumenty k istorii russkoi i ukrainskoi emigratsii v Chekhoslovatskoi Respublike (1918–1939)*, Prague, 1998. L. Beloshevskya (ed.), *Dukhovnye techeniya russkoy i ukrainskoy emigratsii v Chekhoslovatskoy Respublike (1919–1939)*, Prague, 1999. *Khronika kulturnoy, nauchnoy i obshchestvennoy zhizni russkoy emigratsii v Chekhoslovatskoy Respublike. vol 1, 1919–1929*, Prague, 2000, vol.2, *1930–1939*, Prague, 2001.
40. For bibliography see *Rossica*, 2, 1997.
41. S. Tejchmanová, *Rusko v Československu. Bílá emigrace v ČSR (1917–1939)*, Jinočany, 1993.
42. M.C. Putna and Zadražilová, *Rusko mimo Rusko. Dějiny a kultura ruské emigrace 1917–1991*, vol. 1, Brno, 1993. Vol. 2, M.C. Putna and M. Zadražilová, Brno, 1994.
43. I. Savický, *Osudová setkání*, Prague, 1999. I. Savitsky, *Praga i Zarubezhnaya Rossiya*, Prague, 2002.
44. A. Kopřivova *Střediska ruského emigrantského života v Praze (1921–1952)*, Prague, 2001.
45. E. Chinyaeva, 'Ruská emigrace v Československu: vývoj ruské pomocné akce',

Slovanský přehled, 1, 1993. E. Chinyaeva, Russians outside Russia: The Émigré Community in Czechoslovakia, 1918–1938, Munich, 2001.

46. S. Tejchmanová, 'Ekonomický kabinet S.N. Prokopoviče v Praze', Slovanský přehled, 1, 1993, pp. 55–62. A.B. Ruchkin, 'Russkie uchenye-emigranty v 1920 gody. (Na primere Ekonomicheskogo kabineta S.N. Prokopovicha)', in Istoriya rossiiskogo zarubezhiya. Problemy adaptatsii migrantov v XIX–XX vekakh, Moscow, 1996, pp. 115–23.

47. E.P. Serapionova, Rossiiskaya emigratsiya v Chekhoslovatskoi respublike (20–30gody), Moscow, 1995.

48. Among the several hundred writers, scholars and intellectuals were such people as Nikolai Berdyaev, the philosopher, and Sergei Bulgakov, the theologian. See B. Lossky, 'K izgnaniyu lyudey mysli v 1922 godu', pp. 273–87 in M. Parkhomovsky and L. Yuniveg (eds), Evrei v kulture Russkogo Zarubezhiya. Sbornik statey, publikatsiy, memuarov i esse. 1. 1919–1939. Jerusalem, 1992.

49. Paul Tabori, Anatomy of Exile, London, 1972, p. 27.

50. F. Norwood, Strangers & Exiles, a History of Religious Refugees, Nashville, 1969, p. 475.

CHAPTER 1 – RELATIONS BETWEEN CZECHS AND RUSSIANS

1. J.V. Polišenský, History of Czechoslovakia in Outline (Prague, 1991) is an excellent short survey in English.

2. R.W. Seton-Watson, A History of the Czechs and Slovaks, London, 1943, p. 14.

3. See for example, ed. D.I.Čyževsky, Hegel bei dem Slaven, Reichenberg, 1934.

4. For example, most editions of English literature were first translated from German translations.

5. V.Černý, Vývoj a zločiny panslavismu, Prague,1995, p. 110.

6. T.G. Masaryk, Světová revoluce. Za války a ve válce 1914–1918. Vzpomíná a uva žuje . . . , Prague, Čin a Orbis, 1925, s.21. English version: The Making of a State. Memories and Observations 1914–1918, abridged and prepared with an introduction by H.W. Steed, London, 1927, p. 32.

7. Seton-Watson, A History of the Czechs and Slovaks, p. 285.

8. Masaryk, Světová revoluce, pp. 338–57; or in English trans., The Making of a State, with abbreviations, pp. 442–53.

9. Seton-Watson, A History of the Czechs and Slovaks, p. 286.

10. R. Seton-Watson, Masaryk in England, Cambridge, 1943, p. 21.

11. Masaryk, Světová revoluce, p. 111; English trans., The Making of a State, p. 103.

12. The Czechs and Slovaks are Slavs, but they were distinguished as a separate group, on a par with 'Slavs' in general. Thus, the Allied declaration can be interpreted as an undertaking to insist on the independence of Czechoslovakia, but not necessarily on the independence of, for example, Poland and Croatia. Was the liberation of Slavs from Slavs, Poles from Russians of equal importance? Did liberating Slavs assume the creation of an independent state, or the linking to an existing Slav state, for example joining the Croats to the Serbs, and so on? All this was unclear and contrasts sharply with the relative clarity of the statement about the Czechoslovaks.

13. Seton-Watson, A History of the Czechs and Slovaks, p. 292.

14. Z. Tobolka, Politické dějiny Československého národa od r.1848 až do dnešní doby, vol. 4, Prague, 1937, p. 220.

15. V.S. Mamatey and R. Luža (eds), A History of the Czechoslovak Republic, Princeton, 1973, p. 15.

16. Masaryk's and Beneš' memoirs (*Světová válka a naše revoluce,* vols 1–3, Prague, 1927–29) stand out from most memoir literature for their sincerity and factual accuracy, although it would be a mistake to take this as an absolute. The struggle between the Hrad group and those around Kramář was at its worst in 1925–28, reaching a climax in 1926, at the beginning of the decline of Russian Action. For that reason one cannot take too seriously statements of the kind, 'We had been acknowledged by the West, long ago (!) The Allies had announced our independence as one of the conditions of peace' (Masaryk *Světová revoluce,* p. 186. Eng. trans. p. 155). In this case Masaryk was thinking of President Wilson's reply to the Allies on 12 January 1917, but he understood perfectly well that this declaration did not guarantee the independence of Czechoslovakia. In his telegram of 5 July 1918, to the French Foreign Minister Pichon, in answer to Beneš's unpublished letter of 29 June 1918, he supported Czech claims and stated that the French government 'considère comme équitable et nécessaire de proclamer les droits de votre Nation à l'indépendance et de reconnaître publiquement et officiellement le Conseil National, comme l'organe suprême des intérêts généraux et la première assise du futur Gouvernement tchéco-slovaque.' In *Vznik Československa 1918. Dokumenty Československé zahraniční politiky,* Prague, 1994 (cited as *Vznik*) dok. 54, p. 142 Masaryk wrote: 'La France est ainsi la première à promettre son aide à notre nation et elle a tenu sa promesse à la conférence qui définit les buts de guerre dans la note au Président Wilson. De nouveau la France est la première à proclamer solennellement le droit de notre nation à l'independence' (ibid., dok 65, note 1, p. 159). The only realistic guarantee of Czech liberation and the creation of Czechoslovakia was the creation of a military force, the Czechoslovak army, and the basis for this could only be found in Russia.

17. By all accounts, Masaryk did not doubt the quality of the Czechoslovak troops. He was interested in the military side of things, but particularly paid attention to the morale of the rank and file, which he placed in a wider context than did the jingoists. Without doubt he knew the theories that 'the Prussian schoolmaster' won the Franco-Prussian War and considered that the Czechoslovak teacher had done no less. Furthermore, the Czechoslovak formations were volunteer units, which usually fight better than conscripts. The Czechoslovak corps in Russia justified all these hopes, to the surprise of the Western Allies.

18. It should be noted that Czechs and Slovaks can make themselves understood and understand Russians and Ukrainians without learning the language, although sometimes odd things occur as similar words in these languages can have very dissimilar meanings. Nevertheless, Masaryk in his note about the Czechoslovak formations, written in Russian on 3 March 1918 in Moscow, stated that 'commands in the Czechoslovak formations were given in Russian and Czech and that our soldiers had learnt Russian long ago' (*Vznik*, doc. 13, p. 56). In France or Italy, such a bilingual approach to the lower ranks and junior officers was unthinkable: in these countries the units were isolated and tended to become more nationalistic, whereas in Russia the units were faced with the possibility of 'dissolving' into the Russian upheavals, as the soldiers did not simply receive orders in Russian, but newspapers, leaflets and speeches at endless numbers of meetings were all accessible to them.

19. *Vznik,* doc. 8, p. 47.

20. Ibid., doc. 5, p. 41.

21. Masaryk provided a succinct summary of his views in a letter to Miliukov: TGM files, Box 299, Složka, 'Masaryk a Rusko', 22–7. I am grateful to Katya Kocourek for drawing my attention to this.

22. *Vznik,* doc. 22, pp. 81–3.

23. See J. Smele, *Civil War in Siberia*, Cambridge, 1996, pp. 26–7 and fn 36.

24. For example, the Soviet Central Executive Committee (*ispolkom*) in Siberia attempted to help the Czechs, but those involved in talks on both sides met with opposition from within their own ranks.

25. This recognition is dated 7 September 1918 (*Vznik*, doc. 108, p. 250). In this edition the SR Vladimir Kazimirovich Vol'sky is confused with the Menshevik Nikolay Vladislavovich (see index, p. 438). The SRs in Prague later used to like to emphasise the fact that this was the first instance of recognition of an independent Czechoslovakia (see *Volya Rossii*, 18, 1923, p. 73 et seq.). Legally that is correct, as the Allies expressed themselves more circumspectly without using the word state, but in the words of the USA on 2 September 1918, 'recognises the Czecho-Slovak National Council as a *de facto* belligerent Government, clothed with proper authority to direct the military and political affairs of the Czecho-Slovaks'. More to the point, perhaps, is that the Komuch was not recognised by anyone.

26. See Smele, *Civil War*, p. 45.

27. See A.F. Izyumov (ed.), 'Ufimskoe Gosudarstvennoe Soveshchanie', in *Russkiy istoricheskiy arkhiv*, vol. 1, a publication of Russkiy zagranichnyi istoricheskiy arkhiv v Prage, Prague, 1929, p. 253. Due to the notes which provide information about approximately 150 members of the Assembly, this publication is of particular interest. The biographical details make it easier to identify various protagonists of the Revolution where otherwise odd mistakes, confusion and typographical errors abound.

28. On 31 March 1918, J. Klecanda, secretary of the Russian section of the Czechoslovak National Committee, observed: 'From the conversation with the British representative [in Moscow] I got the impression that the main concern was that Russia should tie down more German troops. The restoration of Russia is of no great interest to Britain, and indeed the impoverishment of Russia in general may be more advantageous to England. . . . It is interesting to note that having taken the decision to support the Bolsheviks or rather Trotsky, the Allies have cut all links with Russian society. That is the unfortunate policy of our dear allies.' *Dokumenty a materialy k dějinám Československo-sovětských vztahů.* vol. 1, Prague, 1975 (cited as *DAM*), p. 65n. Masaryk considered Klecanda the most able of all his colleagues in Russia. But even after his sudden death, democratically inclined representatives of Czechoslovak organisations complained that the Allies ignored possibilities for the democratic development of Russia, and willingly bargained, if not with Bolsheviks, then with the extreme right.

29. At the last SR conference in Moscow, Chernov stated that the party had arrived at the conference like 'a collapsing building'. A section of the SRs at the conference did not sign the resolution setting up the All-Russian supreme power. This was the 'left' opposition. The more serious 'right' opposition was not even invited to the conference. The logic of the Revolution forced a considerable number of opponents to Bolshevism to move towards the right, so that they could be clearly distinguished from Bolshevism. Thus 'two Bolshevisms' were produced, which the democrats later described.

30. Richard H. Ullman, *Britain and the Russian Civil War. November 1918–February 1920*, Princeton, 1968, pp. 33–4.

31. *Dokumenty vneshney politiki SSSR*, vol. 1, Moscow, 1957, p. 69.

32. Masaryk, *The Making of a State*, New York, 1969, pp. 172–7.

33. V.A. Shishkin, *Chekhoslovatsko-Sovetskie Otnosheniya*, Moscow, 1962, p. 20.

34. I. Lukes, *Czechoslovakia between Stalin and Hitler*, Oxford, 1996, p. 7.

35. Lansing to Page, 29 May 1918, in *Papers Relating to the Foreign Relations of the United States, 1914–1946*. US Department of State, Washington, DC, 1922–7. Supplement 1 (2 vols, Washington, 1933), 1, pp. 808–9.

36. Mamatey and Luža (eds), *A History of the Czechoslovak Republic*, pp. 21–2.
37. Ibid., p. 26.
38. *Vznik*, doc. 113, p. 260.
39. V. Olivová, *Československo-sovětské vztahy v letech 1918–1922*, Prague, 1957, p. 66n.
40. Ibid., pp. 455–7. See the letter of Denikin's representative, staff captain Vyacheslav Mencel, to the Ministry of Defence on 8 April 1919.
41. Ibid., doc.16, pp. 462–3. Letter of Foreign Minister E.Beneš to an unnamed member of the cabinet [probably Rašín] on 16 February 1919.
42. Ibid., p. 464.
43. Ibid., doc. 14, p. 460. The report of the Ministry of Defence, of 27 June 1919.
44. Idem.
45. See C.M. Skran, *Refugees in Inter-War Europe*, Oxford, 1995, p. 66. Sir John Hope Simpson, *The Refugee Problem*, London, 1939, pp. 67–83. M. Marrus, *The Unwanted*, Oxford, 1985, p. 82.
46. Official policy was wholly in Czech hands and the Slovaks hardly influenced this aspect although Slovaks and the Slovak question had a significant role to play in the fate of the Russian emigration.
47. *DAM*, 1, No. 357. Report dated 2 March 1921.
48. Public organisations to help the refugees were being set up by 1920: The Committee for Russian Aid headed by the Mayor of Prague, Dr Baxa; Dr Kramář led the Committee for Help to the Crimea, and the Czechoslovak Red Cross was also working in this area. See Chinaeyeva, 'Ruská emigrace v Československu: vývoj ruské pomocné akce', *Slovanský přehled*, 1993, p. 17 and Z. Sládek 1996, 'České prostředi a ruská emigrace (1918–1938)', in *Duchovní proudy ruské a ukrajinské emigrace v československé republice 1919–1939*. Prague 1999, pp. 8–12.

CHAPTER 2 – POLITICS AND THE EMIGRATION

1. V.T. Rafal'sky was the head of the 'Russian mission'and the representative of Kolchak's government. It was officially recognised by the Czechoslovak government in the summer of 1919 and received financial support. See E.P. Serapionova, *Rossiiskaya Emigratsiya*, Moscow, 1995, p. 63.
2. The difference between Russia Reborn, New Russia and Future Russia can be confusing for the reader of the émigré press but gradually a consensus emerged. Russia Reborn meant a form of the state similar to that of the Russian empire before Nicholas II's abdication, New Russia meant the existing Soviet system, and Future Russia was the desired republican, democratic and in most instances, federal state. As the Civil War and subsequently émigré life developed, certain words such as 'patriots' or 'activism' acquired new emotional and political connotations. Other words such as *Sovdepia* (the state of soviets of workers' deputies) or *nepredreshentsy* (those who would not decide political questions before the convocation of a legitimate Constituent Assembly) were also coined.
3. *Russkoe Delo*, leading article, 4 November 1919.
4. *Slavyanskaya Zarya*, leading article, 12 November 1919.
5. *Russkoe Delo*, leading article 7 April 1920.
6. V. Olivová, 'Politika Československa v ruské krizi roku 1921 a 1922', in T.G. Masaryk and E. Beneš, *Otevřít Rusko Evropě*, Prague, 1992, p. 34.
7. E. Chinyaeva, *Russians outside Russia* (Munich, 2001, pp. 47–50) is a useful summary in English of the political structures in the First Republic.

8. M.V. Vishniak, *'Sovremennye Zapiski.' Vospominaniya redaktora*, Bloomington, 1957, p. 89. Cf. R.C. Williams, *Culture in Exile. Russian Emigrés in Germany, 1881–1941*, Ithaca, NY and London, 1972, pp. 233–6.

9. V. Veber, 'Strana eserů v moderních ruských dějinách a v Praze', V. Veber, Z. Sládek and M. Bubeníková, eds *Ruská a ukraiyská emigrace v ČSR v letech 1918–1945*. 1993, vol. 1, p. 26.

10. L.K. Shkarenkov, *Agoniya beloy emigratsii*, 2nd revised edn, Moscow, 1986, p. 39.

11. See for example Kondakov's diaries or Tsvetaeva's letters.

12. N. Berberova, *Kursiv Moy. Avtobiografiya*, vol. 1, 2nd edn, New York, 1983, pp. 241–2.

13. 'Чех - нежнее, чем овечка, в мире нет нежнее человечка.'

14. In his poem to Comrade Nette, the ship and the person, Mayakovsky addresses another Russian inhabitant of Prague, Roman Jakobson.

15. S.P. Postnikov (ed.), *Russkie v Prage 1918–1928*, Prague, 1928; reprinted 1995, p. 118.

16. According to *Obshchee Delo* (197, 28 January 1921): 'Censorship of the Russian press exists in the eating house. The Administration excludes all Russian publications with the exception of those produced by the SRs.'

17. See *Ocherk deyatel'nosti Ob'edineniya Rossiiskikh Zemskikh i Gorodoskikh Deyateley v Chekhoslovatskoy Respublike (Zemgor) 7 marta 1921–1 yanvarya 1925 g*, Prague, 1925, p. 8.

18. Serapionova, *Rossiyskaya emigratsiya*, pp. 57–8.

19. *Ocherk Zemgora*, pp. 49–50.

20. J.D. Smele, 'White Gold: The Imperial Russian Gold Reserve in the Anti-Bolshevik East 1918–? (An Unconcluded Chapter in the History of the Russian Civil War)', *Europe-Asia Studies*, 46 (8), 1994, pp. 1317–47. See also O.V. Budnitskii, 'Diplomaty i Den' gi', *Diaspora: Novye materialy*, 4, 2002, p. 81.

21. *Ocherk Zemgora*, pp. 21–2. Cf. V.V. Rudnev, *Russkoe Delo v Chekhoslovatskoy Respublike*, Paris. Rossiskii Zemsko-Gorodskoy Komitet pomoshchi rossiiskim grazhdanam zagranitsey, 1924, pp. 6–7.

22. *Russkoe Delo*, 24 April 1920, p. 3.

23. *Volya Rossii*, 22 April 1921, p. 5.

24. *Ogni*, 15 August 1921, p. 4; 22 August 1921, p. 4.

25. Sládek, 'České prostředi', p 12.

26. From documents in the Czechoslovak Foreign Office it is clear that grants were also paid to scholars and writers who did not live in Czechoslovakia. Some leading writers were more or less dependent on help from this source.

27. T.G. Masaryk, *Cesta demokracie*, vol. 2, Prague, 1934, p. 56.

28. Sládek, 'České prostředi', pp. 9–10; Sládek, 'Ruská emigrace v Československu' in *Slovanský přehled*, Prague 1993, p. 3.

29. See K. Schlögel (ed.), *Der Grosse Exodus*, Munich, 1994, p. 221.

30. *DAM*, 1, No. 403.

31. *Kazachiy Put'*, 12, 25 April 1924, p. 3.

32. Schlögel, *Der Grosse Exodus*, p. 240.

33. *Rossiiskaya emigratsiya v Turtsii, yugo-Vostochnoy i tsentral'noy Europe 20-kh godov . . . Uchebnoe Posobie*, Gottingen, 1994, p. 15.

34. D. Ivantsov 'Russkie bezhentsy v Yugoslavii v 1921g.', in *Russkiy Ekonomicheskiy Sbornik*, vol. 2, Prague, 1925, pp. 80–107. A study of 29,000 refugees in Yugoslavia in April 1921 showed that 23.7 per cent of men 'had worked in agriculture and had been involved in work in the fields'; however, some of them 'had been either amateur or temporary labour' and some 'had been forced into an accelerated labour programme by the revolutionary catastrophe' (pp. 90–91).

35. Postnikov, *Russkie v Prage*, p. 29, *Kazachiy Put'*, 7 Česká stránka,
36. *Kazachiy put'*, 7. Česká stránka.
37. *Khutor*, 10–11, 1 April 1923, pp. 33–4.
38. *Kazachiy Put'*, 9, p. 13.
39. *Khutor*, 28–9, 1 April 1923, p. 33.
40. *Khozyain*, 14, 9 April 1926, p. 8.
41. *Studencheskie Gody*, 2, 1922, p. 27.
42. *Slavyanskaya Zarya*, 3 January 1919, p. 5.
43. *Russkoe Delo*, 8 January 1920, p. 6.
44. O.S. Minor, 'Russkaya intelligentsia za granitsey', *Volya Rossii*, 28 September 1920, pp. 1–2.
45. There is no biography of A.V. Zhekulina, and details of her work are gathered bit by bit from a mass of sources. I am particularly grateful to Professor G.N. Zhekulin for valuable material on his grandmother. An obituary by Countess Panina was published in *Novy Zhurnal*, 24, New York, 1950.
46. Rudnev, *Russkoe Delo*, p. 32.
47. *Československá pomoc ruské a ukrajinské emigraci*, Prague, Ministerstvo zahraničí, 1924, pp. 47–8. Twenty-six per cent were the children of officers, 16 per cent the children of Cossacks; 16 per cent were children of landowners and government officials, 15 per cent children of professionals, 12 per cent children of merchants and artisans, 11 per cent children of agriculturalists.
48. Ibid., p. 52.
49. *Studencheskie Gody*, 2, 1922, pp. 27–8.
50. *Rossiiskaya emigratsiya*, p. 87.
51. He is not mentioned by Raeff at all and appears once in Schlögel's work as only one in a list of names. Serapionova mentions him only in connection with the Union of All-Russian Émigré Organisations which was formed in 1927, when his work on the creation of an academic Russian émigré centre was beginning to fade away. Perhaps the most vivid example of the way in which research on the emigration diverges from the reality is that in the valuable volumes edited by Veber, Sládek and Bubeníkova *(Ruská a ukrainská emigrace v ČSR v letech 1918–1945)*, Aleksei Stepanovich Lomshakov is misnamed as Alexander and the date of his arrival in Prague is wrongly given as 1922.
52. E.A. Vechorin, 'Inzhener-izobretatel, professor i drug molodezhi.' *St.Petersburgskiy Politekhnicheskiy Institut, Vol. 2.* Paris, 1958, pp. 172–7.
53. Postnikov, *Russkie v Prage*, p. 159.
54. *Bulleten'* (parizhskogo Zemgora), 7–8, 1921, p. 42.
55. *DAM*, pp. 22–3.
56. It is possible that Girsa decided to use the existing Russian Student Union as a way of carrying out Czech policies in the new conditions which had been created after the débâcle in the Crimea, and that it was he who initiated the re-election of the management and a new direction for the union's activities. But although it is logically feasible, there is no documentary evidence to support this hypothesis.
57. Serapionova, *Rossiiskaya emigratsiya*, p. 25.
58. At the height of Stalinism in 1953, a volume of documents was published – *Dokumenty o protilidové a protinárodní politice T.G. Masaryka* – in which there was one document about a conversation between A.S. Lomshakov and the President about help to the Russian emigration. In the footnotes Lomshakov is characterised as a dyed-in-the-wool 'White Guardist bandit'. In 1953, this kind of comment was usually a direct ticket to prison but Lomshakov was not arrested, perhaps in view of his age, or perhaps because

he still had protectors. In 1960, *Lidová demokracie* – a newspaper which supported the Christian national party – decided to note Lomshakov's 90th birthday. Although it was a much more liberal era, there was still a risk attached to this, and it was a vivid illustration of the effect of Lomshakov's personality, which made people willing to take risks.

59. SÚA, MZV-RPA, karton 39.
60. V.Kh. Davats and N.N. L'vov, *Russkaya armiya na chuzhbine*, Belgrade, 1923, p. 98.
61. *Russkoe Delo* (Sophia), 78, 12 February 1922.
62. Vechorin, 'Inzhener–izo bretatel', p. 176.
63. Postnikov (ed.), *Russkie v Prage*, 1928, p. 70.
64. *Volya Rossii*, 6, 1922, p. 24.
65. A.K., 'K istorii vozniknoveniya "Russkogo studencheskogo Soyuza" ', *Volya Rossii*, 15, 15 April 1922, pp. 22–4.
66. N.V. Bystrov, 'Russkoe studenchestvo v emigratsii', in *Krestyanskaya Rossiya*, vol. 4, Prague, 1923, pp. 158–61.
67. *Ročenka Československé Republiky*, 1923, p. 7.
68. *Volya Rossii*, 20, 27 May 1922, pp. 21–2.
69. *Volya Rossii*, 14, 8 April 1922, p. 24.
70. SÚA, MZV-RPA, karton 39, Zprávy o činnosti ruské a ukrajinské emigrace, 1925–32.
71. *Volya Rossii*, 17, 2 May 1922, p. 22.
72. Postnikov (ed.), *Russkie v Prage*, 1928 edn, pp. 113, 116.
73. Ibid., p. 112.
74. M.M. Novikov, *Ot Moskvy do N'yu-Yiorka. Moya zhizn' v nauke i politike*, New York, 1952, pp. 334–8.
75. A.A. Kizevetter, *Na rubezhe dvukh stoletii*, Prague, 1929, p. 489.
76. See the vivid account of this institution in ibid., pp. 470–95.
77. Petronik (pseudonym of P.N. Savitsky), *Recollections of Alexsei Stepanovich Lomshakov*, 1960. Typescript in the possession of I.P.Savický. Reproduced in *Transactions of the Association of Russian-American Scholars in the USA*, 31, 2001–2, pp. 562–7.

CHAPTER 3 – THE RUSSIAN ACADEMIC WORLD IN PRAGUE

1. Letter of N.N Alekseev to A.S.Yashchenko in November 1921 in L. Fleishman, R. Hughes and O. Raevsky-Hughes (eds), *Russkiy Berlin 1921–1923*, Paris, 1983, p. 257.
2. P. Boobbyer, *S.L.Frank*, Athens, Ohio, 1995, p. 122.
3. M.Yu. Dostal', 'V.A. Frantsev's correspondence', *Slavyanovedenie*, 4, 1994, p. 104.
4. J. Toman, *Letters, and Other Materials from the Moscow and Prague Linguistic Circles, 1912–1945*, Ann Arbor, 1994, pp. 27–8.
5. M.M. Novikov, 'Russkie emigranty v Prage', *Novyi Zhurnal*, 49, 1957, p. 251.
6. *N.S. Trubetskoy's Letters and Notes* prepared for publication by Roman Jakobson, Mouton, the Hague and Paris, 1975, pp. 470–71. The history of this article is interesting from a variety of points of view. In the first place, it deals with the attitudes of émigrés towards their host societies. Secondly, Trubetskoy expressed his ideas about the analogy between the Russian emigration and the Jewish diaspora,which had formed over a period of 2,000 years, to Petrovsky as early as August 1922 and judging from Trubetskoy's correspondence with others, e.g. Jakobson, he continued with this approach. It has been argued that Trubetskoy broke with Eurasianism in 1929–30 (e.g. O.A. Kaznina, 'N.S.Trubetskoy i krizis evraziistva', *Slavyanovedenie*, 4, 1995, pp. 89–95). It should be noted that Trubetskoy's article was written at the request of a meeting of

the Presidium of the Central Committee with members of the Prague Eurasian Group. On 9 July 1934, Savitsky raised the question of racial characteristics and Trubetskoy was asked to write an article on this subject. See *Evraziiskie tetradi*, 1934, 4.

7. S. Levitsky, 'Vospominaniya o Losskom', *Novyi Zhurnal*, 126, March 1977, pp. 174–5.

8. *Československá pomoc ruské a ukrajinské emigraci*, Prague 1924, p. 64.

9. S.P. Postnikov (ed.), *Russkie v Prage 1918–1928*, Prague, 1928; reprinted 1995.

10. *Práce ruské, ukrajinské a běloruské emigrace vydané v Československu 1918–1945*, 3 vols. Národní knihovna České republiky, Prague, 1996.

11. *Otchet . . . RYuF v Prage za 1926–1927 uchebny god s obshchim obzorom ego pyatiletney deyatel'nosti (1922–1927)*, Prague, 1927. It isn't clear when such courses ceased; probably at the opening of the Russian Law Faculty or the Russian People's University. Postnikov doesn't mention them.

12. This development from supplementary course to a quasi-fully fledged university is fairly characteristic of émigré efforts and can be seen clearly in the example of the Free Ukrainian University in Prague.

13. *Otchet . . . za 1926–27 . . . god.* pp. 8–9.

14. Ibid., p. 5.

15. *Russkii Narodnyi Universitet v Prage. Otchet o deyatelnosti za 1923–24 ucebnyi god.* Prague, 1924, p. 7.

16. *Obozrenie prepodavaniya v Russkom institute sel'sko-khozyaistvennoi kooperatsii v Prage*, Prague, 1929. *Československá pomoc*, pp. 62–4.

17. *Československá pomoc*, p. 64.

18. *Ocherk deyatelnosti Zemgora v Chekhoslovatskoi Respublike za 1921–1925*, p. 157.

19. See V.V. Zenkovsky, *Deti Emigratsii*, Prague, 1925.

20. E.P. Serapionova, *Rossiiskaya emigratsiya v Chekhoslovatskoi respublike*, Moscow, 1995, p. 122.

21. Postnikov (ed.), *Russkie v Prage*, pp. 100–8, Prague, 1925 *Ocherk Zemgora*, pp. 147–55, and *Zemgor v Prage 1921–1931*, pp. 110–12.

22. Amongst the more interesting scholarly articles are: R.J. Kneeley and E. Kasinec, 'The Slovanská knihovna in Prague and its RZIA Collection', *Slavic Review*, Spring 1992, pp. 122–30. T.F. Pavlova, 'Russkii Zagranichnii Istoricheskyi Arkhiv', *Voprosy Istorii*, 11, 1990, pp. 19–30. T.F. Pavlova (ed.), *Fondy Russkogo Zagranichnogo Istoricheskogo Arkhiva v Prage* (Moscow, 1999) is a most useful guide for researchers and indicates how much progress has been made in dealing with this subject.

23. J. Slavík (ed.), compiled by S.P. Postnikov, *Bibliografiya Russkoy Revolyutsii i Grazhdanskoy Voiny (1917–1921)*, Prague, 1938.

24. S. Varshavsky, 'Komitet Russkoi Knigi (Ocherk zadach i deyatel'nosti)', in *Russkaya Zarubezhnaya Kniga*, Part 1. Prague, Komitet Russkoi Knigi i Plamya, 1924, p. 5.

25. On 1 April 1924 a Russian Institute for the Study of Village Culture (Russkiy nauchnyi institut sel'skoy kul'tury) was created on the foundation of two parallel projects by S.S. Maslov and K.P. Kocharovskiy with the aid of A.N. Chelintsev. Lack of funds meant that they had to apply to the Zemgor to appoint three more people to the Council of the institute: V.M. Chernov, G.I. Shreyder and N.F. Novozhilov, who reorganised the work of the institute and gave it a new name and new constitution. See *Zapiski Instituta izucheniya Rossii*, vol. 1, Prague, 1925, pp. 259–64.

26. S. Tejchmanová, 'Ekonomický kabinet S.N. Prokopoviče v Praze', in *Slovanský přehled*, 1993, no. 1, pp. 55–62 provides an excellent account based on archival material of the institutional transformations of the Economic Bureau.

27. See Z. Skálová, 'Das Prager Seminarium Kondakovianum, später das Archäologische

Kondakov-Institut und sein Archiv (1925–1952)', *Slavica Gandesia*, 18, 1991, pp. 21–49. L. Hamilton Rhinelander, 'Exiled Russian Scholars in Prague: the Kondakov Seminar and Institute', *Canadian Slavonic Papers*, 16(3), Autumn 1974, pp. 331–52. N.E. Andreyev, *To, chto vspominaetsya*, Tallinn, 1996: vol. 1, pp. 289–303, vol. 2, pp. 72–80, 89–147 et seq.

28. *Sbornik statey posvyashchennykh pamyati N.P. Kondakova*, Seminarium Kondakovianum, Prague, 1926.

29. These figures are taken from the Committee to Guarantee the Education of Russian and Ukrainian Students, according to which, by 30 July 1928, 1,729 Russian students had graduated and 1,342 were still enrolled. But not all students came under the jurisdiction of this committee. The most accurate figures are provided by the Russian Law Faculty. By May 1925 when enrolment ceased, 439 students were studying and 14 per cent did not receive a government grant. These figures need to be added to the figures produced by the committee. The *Ročenky Československé republiky*, 10, 1931, p. 371 states that 1,591 students were still studying in Prague. Postnikov, *Russkie v Prage*, pp. 75–76, *Otchet.. za 1924–25 god*, p. 22.

30. This includes: 384 graduates from the Russian Law Faculty, 259 from the Institute for Agriculture and Co-operatives, 100 from the Pedagogical Institute, 41 from the Business School – 22 per cent of the total number of graduates.

31. G.V. Vernadsky, *Ocherk istorii prava Russkogo Gosudarstva XVIII–XIXvv. (Period imperii)*, Prague, Plamya, 1924, pp. 5–6.

32. M. Tsimmermann, *Istoriya mezhdunarodonogo prava s drevneishikh vremen do 1918g.* Prague, RYuF, 1924, pp. 7–8. The importance given to this idea by the author and by the Russian Academic Council is emphasised by the fact that these introductory remarks were republished in *Uchenye Zapiski, osnovannye Russkoy Uchebnoy Kollegiey v Prage*, 1 (3) pp. 257–85.

33. M.A. Wes, 'Michael Rostovtzeff, Historian in Exile', *Historia*, 65, (Stuttgart), 1990, pp. 59–74.

34. P. Sorokin, *Avtobiografiya*, Moscow, 1992, p. 147.

35. The most important scholarly books will be referred to regardless of whether or not they were published in Prague. It is extremely difficult to follow the physical movement of a number of people as they travelled in the early 1920s between various émigré communities. Their ideological evolution can in some cases be equally difficult to trace. P.M. Bitsilli lived and worked in Yugoslavia and Bulgaria. He had close links with Prague and was published there. S.I. Gessen worked in Prague between 1924 and 1934, yet his book was published in Berlin and the Introduction was written in Freiburg. P.B. Struve was published in the *Ekonomicheskiy Vestnik* in Berlin but he always signed his articles as written in Prague. L. Karsavin, *Filosofiya istorii*, Berlin, 1923. P.M. Bitsilli, *Ocherki teorii istoricheskoy nauki*, Prague, Plamya, 1925 (the Introduction includes a critical commentary on Karsavin). N.N. Alekseev, *Osnovy filosofii prava*, Prague, Plamya, 1924. S.I. Gessen, *Osnovy pedagogiki. Vvedenie v prikladnuyu filosofiyu*, Berlin, 1923.

36. D.D. Grimm, 'Osnovnye predpolozheniya i zadachi sotsial'nykh nayk' and P.B. Struve, 'Nekotorye osnovnye ponyatiya ekonomicheskoy nauki', in *Uchenye Zapiski*, 1(3), Prague, Plamya, 1924. E.V. Spektorskiy, *Nachala nauki o gosudarstve i obshchestve*, Belgrade, 1927.

37. P.B. Struve, 'Nauchnaya kartina ekonomicheskogo mira i ponyatiya ravnovesiya'; 'Khoz'aistvo, khozyastvovaniye, obshchestvo'; 'Pervichnost' i svoeobrazie obmena i problema ravnovesiya. Otvet A.D. Bilimovichu; and A. Bilimovich, 'Dva podkhoda k nauchnoy kartine ekonomicheskogo mira', in S.N. Prokopovich (ed.), *Ekonomicheskiy*

Vestnik, vols 1–3, Berlin, 1923–4.
38. V.V. Zenkovsky (ed.), *Pravoslavie i kultura. Sbornik religiozno-filosofskikh statey,* Berlin, 1923. E. Spektorskiy, *Khristianstvo i kul'tura,* Prague, Plamya, 1925.
39. The question of crisis has always achieved notoriety in general publications. Two examples will serve to illustrate the range of literature on this subject. S.N. Bulgakov, 'Tserkovnoe pravo i krizis pravosoznaniya', *Uchenye Zapiski,* 1(3), Prague, 1924, pp. 9–27, strove to prove the necessity of returning to church dogmatic discipline as the only way of justifying the rule of law, and blamed the ideas of natural law and the illusion of the legal state. V.F. Totomiants tried to discuss the crisis of European co-operation and tried to prove that that there was no crisis: 'Koopertatsiya i sel'skoe khozyaistvo', in *Kooperatsiya i sel'skoe khozyaistvo. Zapiski Russkogo instituta sel'sko-khozyaistvennoy kooperatsii v Prage,* Book 1, Prague, 1924.
40. E. Anitchkof, 'Qu'est-ce que l'art d'áprès les grand Maîtres de la scolastique', *Uchenye zapiski, osnovannye Russkoi uchebnoi kollegiey v Prage,* 1(2), Prague, 1924, pp. 9–43.

CHAPTER 4 – IDENTITY AND ATTITUDES

1. S.P. Postnikov (ed.), *Russkie v Prage, 1918–1928g,* Prague, 1928.
2. See *Pamiati Vladyki Sergiya Prazhskogo,* compiled by Olga Raevsky-Hughes, New York, 1987.
3. Metropolit Evlogii, *Put' Moey Zhizni. Memoirs,* transcribed by T. Manukhina, Paris, 1947, p. 286 et seq.
4. Ibid., p. 375.
5. See, for example, D.A. Olsufiev, *Mysli soborianina o nashey Tserkovnoi smute,* Paris, 1928.
6. Evlogii, *Put' Moey Zhizni,* p. 622.
7. S. Troitsky, *Razmezhevanie ili Raskol,* Paris, 1932.
8. Evlogii, *Put' Moey Zhizni,* p. 398.
9. I. Astrau in Raevsky-Hughes (ed.), *Pamyati Vladyki Sergiya Prazhskogo,* p. 35.
10. N.E. Andreyev, *To, chto vspominaetsya,* 2 vols, Tallinn, 1996, vol. 1, p. 307.
11. Postnikov (ed.), *Russkie v Prage,* pp. 234–8.
12. *Nedelia,* 24 May 1929, p. 1.
13. Ibid., 31 January 1930.
14. O. Kaznina, 'N.S. Trubetskoy i krizis evraziistva', *Slavyanovedenie,* 4, 1995, pp. 92–3.
15. *Yubileynyi Sbornik (Soyuza russkikh studentov v Brno). 1921 – Brno–1931,* Brno 1932, pp. 15,20.
16. *Otchet o deyatel'nosti (RNU) za 1923–24 g,* Prague, 1924, p. 11.
17. *Otchet o deyatel'nosti (RNU) za 1928–29 g,* Prague, 1929, pp. 10–13.
18. *Nedel'ia,* 31 May 1929.
19. L.K. Shkarenkov, *Agoniya beloy emigratsii,* Moscow, 1981; corrected and revised in 1986. p. 160.
20. *Yubileynyi Sbornik.*
21. For the history of the organisation see *Krest'yanskaya Rossiaya.Trudovaya Krest'yanskaya Partiya. Vvedenie.Ideologiya Programma.Taktika. Ustav,* Prague, 1928 and *Krest'yanskaya Rossiya. Sbornik statey,* 1, New York, 1953.
22. 'Ot redaktsii', *Krestyanskaia Rossiia,* vol. 1, Prague, 1922, pp. 3–5 and A. Argunov, 'Nasha positsiya', in *Krestyanskaia Rossiia,* vol. 7, Prague, 1924, pp. 78–94
23. *Vestnik Krest'yanskoi Rossii,* 8–9, March 1926, p. 170.
24. R. Service, *Lenin,* London, 2000, pp. 204–7.
25. J.V. Stalin, *Kratkiy kurs istorii VKP(b),* Moscow, 1938, p. 137.

26. G.S. Smith, *D.S.Mirsky. A Russian-English Life 1890–1939,* Oxford, 2000, p. 138.
27. P. Savitsky 'Evropa i Evraziya. (Po povodu broshury kn.N.S.Trubetskogo "Evropa i Chelovechestvo").' In P. Struve (ed.) *Russkaya mysl'.* *Ezhemesyachnoe literaturnoe-politicheskoe izdanie,* vols 1 and 2, Sofia, 1921, p. 138; reprinted in P. Savitsky, *Kontinent Evraziya,* (ed. A.G. Dugin), Moscow, 1997, pp. 141–60.
28. P. Savitsky, 'Povorot k Vostoku', in *Iskhod k Vostoku,* Sophia, 1921, p. 2.
29. N. Trubetskoy, 'My i drugie', *Evraziiskiy vremennik,* 4, 1925, reprinted in *Nasledie Chingiskhana,* Moscow, 1999, pp. 395–6.
30. An excellent biography is Smith, *D.S.Mirsky.*
31. Prior to the current revival within Russia, the most complete bibliography was published by O. Böss, *Die Lehre der Eurasier,* Wiesbaden,1961.
32. *Evraziistvo. Opyt sistematicheskogo izlozheniya,* Paris, 1926.
33. *Evraziistvo. Formulirovka 1927 goda,* Prague, 1927.
34. *Evraziya. Ezhenedel'nik po voprosam kul'tury i politiki* (Paris, vols 1–35, 24 November 1928–7 September 1929).
35. G.V. Florovsky, 'Evraziiskii soblazn', in *Sovremennye Zapiski,* Paris, 1928, vol. 34, pp. 312–46.
36. N.S. Trubetskoy, *K probleme russkogo samopoznaniya,* Paris, 1927, p. 94.
37. Ibid., p. 97.
38. R. Jakobson (ed.), *N.S. Trubetzkoy's Letters and Notes,* The Hague and Paris, 1975, p. 13.
39. N.S. Trubetskoy, *Evropa i Chelovechestvo,* Sofia, 1920, pp. iii–iv.
40. *Evraziiskiy vremennik,* vol. 3. Berlin, 1923, pp. 5–6. Unsigned introduction to the volume.
41. N.S. Trubetskoy, 'Russkaya Problema', in *Na Putyakh. Utverzhdenie Evraziitsev,* vol. 2, Moscow and Berlin, 1922, pp. 294–316.
42. P. Savitsky, 'Dva mira', ibid., p. 9.
43. A.S. Izgoev, *Rozhedennoe v revolutsionnoy smute, 1917–32,* Paris, 1933, p.16.
44. O. Kaznina, 'N.S. Trubetskoy i krizis evraziistva', *Slavyanovedenie,* 4, 1995, p. 90.
45. Kaznina, ibid., pp. 91–5. Letter dated 8–10 December 1930.
46. Perviy s'ezd evraziiskoy organizatsii. in *Protokol i materialy,* 1932, pp. 36–7.
47. See Kaznina, 'N.S. Trubetskoy'. Kaznina considers that Trubetskoy did not return to Eurasianism.
48. *Evraziiskiye tetradi. Chetvertoe, iyul'skoe 1934 soveshchanie,* Prague, 1934, p. 11.
49. Jakobson (ed.) *Trubetzkoy's Letters and Notes,* pp. 467–74.
50. *Evraziiskya khronika,* vol. 11, Berlin, pp. 29–37; vol. 12, Berlin, 1937, pp. 10–16.
51. *K molodoy Rossii . . . Sbornik mladorossov,* Paris, 1928, pp. 6, 9, 39, 45.
52. Izgoev, *Rozhedennoe,* pp. 11, 13.
53. M. Nazarov, *Missiya Russkoy emigratsii,* vol. 1, Stavropol', 1992, pp. 224–5.
54. V.S. Varshavsky, *Nezamechannoe pokolenie,* New York, 1956, p. 58.
55. 'Evraziiskaya rabota zagranitsei. Doklad N.A.Perfil'eva', *Pervyi s'ezd,* p. 77.
56. Iu.S. Arsen'iev, 'O fashizme', *K molodoy Rossii,* p. 141.
57. 'Rezolyutsiya 4–6.9.1936', *Evraziiskaya khronika,* 12, p. 5; cf. Savitsky's introduction.
58 N.S. Trubetskoy, 'Upadok tvorchestva'. *Evraziiskaya khronika,* vol. 9, Paris, 1935, pp. 29–87.
59. D. Meisner, *Mirazhi i deistvitel'nost',* Moscow, 1970, p. 231.
60. C. Andreyev, *Vlasov and the Russian Liberation Movement,* Cambridge, 1987, pp. 183–93.
61. *Slavische Rundschau,* 2, 1930, section 337.
62. G. Katkov, 'Masaryk's Guests', in M. Glenny and N. Stone (eds), *The Other Russia,* London, 1990, p. 254.

63. The Prague Linguistic Circle has been studied in depth in the works of L. Matejka., J. Toman, J. Vachek and others.

64. J. Toman (ed.), *Letters . . . from the Moscow and Prague Linguistic Circles 1912–1945*, Ann Arbor, 1994. Jakobson's letter to J. Hajek, head of the Third Section of the Czechoslovak Ministry of Foreign Affairs, 23 December 1936, pp. 166–7.

65. *Annuaire de l'Institut*, vol. 7, New York, 1944, pp. 480, 482, 484, 485, 489.

66. P. Savickij, *Šestina světa. (Rusko jako zeměpisný a historický celek.)* Prague, 1933.

67. N. Savický, 'O některých méně známých pramenech Tezí Pražského lingvistického kroužku', *Slovo a slovesnost*, 52, 1991, pp. 196–8.

68. For example, B. Jakovenko, *Dějiny ruské filosofie*, Prague, 1939, is an excellent study of the history of Russian philosophy and is almost unknown, in contrast to similar studies by Lossky and Zenkovsky published in the West.

69. J. Vacek, 'Interakce ruské a ukrajinské emigrace s českou a slovenskou vědou a kulturou v letech 1919–45', Veber et al. (eds) *Ruská*, vol. 2, pp. 1–40.

70. P. Tabori, *The Anatomy of Exile*, London, 1972, p. 165.

71. A considerable amount has been written about the Day of Russian Culture, which was organised in most countries of the Russian diaspora, but many authors seem to see it as a local phenomenon rather than acknowledging the links between the various émigré centres. Veber's article by contrast is based on archival material in Moscow. V. Veber, 'Dny ruské kultury', *Ruská ia ukrainská emigrace v ČSR v letech 1918–1945*, vol. 2, Prague, 1994, pp. 90–3.

72. V. Veber et al. (eds), *Ruská a ukrajinská emigrace v ČSR v letech 1918–1945*, vol. 2, p. 91.

CHAPTER 5 – THE RUSSIAN DIASPORA

1. R.H. Johnston, *'New Mecca, New Babylon': Paris and the Russian Exiles, 1920–1945*, Montreal, 1988, p. 20.

2. K. Schlögel (ed.), *Der Grosse Exodus*, Munich, 1994, p. 224.

3. R.C. Williams, *Culture in Exile*, Ithaca, NY, 1972, p. 276.

4. Ibid., p. 304.

5. N. Snesarev, *Kirill 1, Imperator . . . Koburgskiy*, n.p., 1925. Cf. Hans von Rimscha, *Russland jenseits der Grenzen 1921–1926*, Jena, 1927, p. 73ff.

6. I. Tsurganov, *Neudavshiisia revansh – Belaia emigratsiya vo vtoroi mirovoi voine*, Moscow, 2001, discusses émigré attitudes to the international situation and the Nazi regime.

7. I.V. Gessen, *Gody izgnaniya. Zhiznennyi otchet*, Paris, 1979; A.K. Nikitin, 'Etapy i metody unifikatsii russkoy pravoslavnoy obshchiny v Germanii v 1935–1939 godakh.' *Russkaya emigratsiya v Evrope 20e–30e gody XX veka*, Moscow, 1996, pp. 129–64.

8. The lowest and possibly the most accurate figure for Russians in France was recorded in the 1936 census: 91,577. However, this figure represents the number of those who arrived with Nansen passports and excludes those who arrived before these passports were in use or who had arrived illegally; see R. Gessain and M. Doré, 'Facteurs comparés d'assimilation chez les Russes et les Arméniens', *Population*, 1, 1946, p. 99. Moreover this was after the peak period for Russians in France simply because the age of the refugees meant that a larger proportion than usual had died of natural causes. Other estimates of the number of Russians in France doubled these figures.

   Schlögel, *Der Grosse Exodus*, p. 238 gives minimum figures for the number of refugees as 150,000 in 1930 and 100,000 in 1933. Estimates of the maximum number of Russian refugees in Germany reach 600,000 whereas clearly high estimates of the number of Russians in Bulgaria and Czechoslovakia are 35,000 and in Yugoslavia 60,000. M.

Jovanovič, *Doseljavanje Ruskikh izhbeglica u Kraljevinu SHS 1919–1924* (Belgrade, 1996, p. 274) gives a figure of 42,500.

9. T. Ossorguine-Bakounine, *L'émigration Russe en Europe. Catalog collectif des périodiques en langue russe 1855–1940*, Paris, 1976. J. Glad, *Russia Abroad,* Washington and Tenafly, NJ, 1999, p. 165.

10. M. Lesure (ed.), 'Les Réfugiés révolutionnaires à Paris', *Cahiers du monde russe et soviétique,* 6 (3), 1965, Paris, pp. 419–36.

11. Johnston, '*New Mecca, New Babylon*', p. 27.

12. A. Petrishchev, 'Russkoe zemledelie vo Frantsii', *Russkiy Ekonomicheskiy Sbornik,* vol. 12, Prague, 1928. L.L. Markov, *Kak russkie ustraivayutsya na frantsuzkoy zemle,* Paris, 1932.

13. M. Raeff, *Russia Abroad,* Oxford, 1990, pp. 37–8.

14. *Russkoe Zarubezh'e. Zolotaya kniga russkoy emigratsii. Pervaya tret' XX veka. Entsiklopedicheskiy biograficheskiy slovar',* Moscow, 1997, p. 736.

15. For example M. Astapenko, *Ataman Kaledin,* Rostov-on-the-Don, 1997, pp. 72, 78.

16. Johnston, '*New Mecca, New Babylon*', p. 33.

17. J.M. Thompson, *Russia, Bolshevism and the Versailles Peace,* Princeton, 1966, pp. 66–78.

18. *Dokumenty a materiály k dějinám československo-sovětských vztahů,* vol. 1, Prague, 1975, No. 174, p. 228. Letter of 23 January 1919.

19. V.Kh. Davats and N.N. L'vov, *Russkaya armiya na chuzhbine,* Belgrade, 1923, p. 31.

20. Von Rimscha, *Russland jenseits der Grenzen,* p. 90.

21. Raeff, *Russia Abroad,* p. 64.

22. *Russkoe Zarubezh'e. Khronika nauchnoy, kul'turnoy i obshchestvennoy zhizni. 1920–1940. Frantsiya,* vol. 1. Paris and Moscow, 1995, pp. 72–3.

23. A great deal of material was collected by the Society for the Preservation of Russian Culture (Obshchestvo okhraneniya russkikh kulturnykh tsennostey) under the chairmanship of D.P. Ryabushinsky. Unfortunately the inclusion and editing of this material by P.E. Kovalevsky in *Zarubezhnaya Rossiya. Istoriya i kul'turno prosvetitel'naya rabota russkogo zarubezh'ya za polveka, 1920–1970,* (2 vols, Paris, 1971, 1973) needs to be treated with care as he confused émigrés with *nevozvrashchentsy* (those who didn't return) as well as those from the first and second wave of émigrés.

24. Ivar Kreuger, the Swedish match king had 7 million francs on his ROVS account in 1932, when he went bankrupt. This was an immense amount for any émigré enterprise. See V. Kostikov, *Ne budem proklinat' izgnan'e ... Puti i sud'by russkoy emigratsii,* 2nd revised edn, Moscow, 1994, p. 420.

25. Johnston '*New Mecca, New Babylon*', p. 21.

26. *Russkaya shkola za rubezhom,* 23, 1926, p. 608.

27. The study of Harbin as a Russo-Chinese city has been complicated not only by distance but by the need to master Chinese, Russian and Japanese sources. In the last few years Russian sources and secondary literature have become more widely available, although Chinese sources are still largely closed to scholars. O. Bakich, 'Charbin "Russland jenseits der Grenzen" in Fernost', in Schlögel, *Der Grosse Exodus,* pp. 304–28 and J. Stephan, *The Russian Fascists. Tragedy and Farce in Exile 1925–1945* (New York, 1978) provide the basis for this section. R. Jones, 'Harbin as a Russo-Chinese City, 1917–1931' (M.Phil. thesis, Oxford, 2000) provides a useful overview of some of the historiography. A.A. Khisamutdinov, *Rossiiskaya emigratsiya v Aziatsko-Tikhookeanskom regione i Yuzhnoi Amerike* (Vladivostok, 2000) is an extensive bibliographical survey. D. Wolff, *To the Harbin Station – the Liberal Alternative in Russian Manchuria, 1898–1914* (Stanford, 1999) is useful for pre-revolutionary history of the city. M. Gamsa 'The Russian-Chinese

Encounter in Harbin, Manchuria, 1898–1932' (D.Phil. thesis, Oxford, 2003) has had access to new sources and contains useful criticism of existing literature.

28. Raeff, *Russia Abroad*, p. 23.
29. Bakich, 'Charbin "Russland jenseits der Grenzen" in Fernost', pp. 304–28.
30. Cf *Bibliograficheskiy Sbornik*, vol. 1 (IV) Obzor literatury po kitaevedeniyu, ed. N.V. Ustryalov (Harbin, 1932) which provides some idea of the literature available on China in various languages even though the emphasis is on Russian.
31. Gamsa, *The Russian–Chinese Encounter* discusses cultural relations and linguistic problems in detail.
32. *Izvestiya Yuridicheskogo Fakulteta*, vol. 9, Harbin, 1931, p. 356.
33. G.G., 'Yuridicheskiy Fakultet v Kharbine (1920–1930.) Ocherk', ibid., p. 308.
34. L.K. Shkarenkov, *Agoniya beloy emigratsii*, Moscow, 1981; corrected and revised edn 1986, pp. 163–9.
35. M. Jovanović, *Doseljavanje Ruskih izbeglica u kraljevinu SHS, 1919–1924*, Belgrade, 1996, pp. 66–8.
36. P.N. Miliukov, *Emigratsiya na pereput'e*, Paris, 1926, p. 35.
37. D. Ivantsov, 'Russkie bezhentsy v Yugoslavii v 1921 godu', *Russkiy ekonomicheskiy sbornik*, 2, 1925, p. 80.
38. V.O. Kozlitin, *Russkaya i ukrainskaya emigratsiya v Yugoslavii 1919–1945*, Kharkov, 1996.
39. J.N. Katchaki, *Bibliography of Russian Refugees in the Kingdom of the SCS (Yugoslavia) 1920–1945*, Arnhem, 1991, p. 27.
40. *Rossiiskaya . . . Uchebnoe posobie*, p 84.
41. V.I. Kosik, 'Russkaya Yugoslavia: Fragmenty istorii 1919–1941', *Slavyanovedenie*, 4, 1992, p. 25.
42. G.N. Pio-Ul'sky, *Russkaya emigratsiya i ee znachenie v zhizni drugikh narodov*, Belgrade, 1939, p. 40.
43. *Khutor*, 36, 1 March 1924.
44. Mitropolit Antoniy, *Khristos Spasitel' i evreyskaya revolytusiya*, Berlin, 1922.
45. *Khozyain*, 21–22, 1925, p. 5.
46. V.D. Kozlitin, 'Rossiiskaya emigratsiya v Korolevstve SHS (1919–1923)', *Slavyanovedenie*, 4, 1992, pp. 7–19.
47. T. Milenković, *Ruski inzhen'eri u Yugoslavii 1919–1941*, Belgrade, 1997.
48. Irina Ilovaiskaya-Alberti, 'Turning-Points' in M. Glenny and N. Stone (eds), *The Other Russia*, London, 1990, p. 231.
49. E.V. Spektorskiy, 'Desyatiletie Russkogo Nauchnogo Instituta v Belgrade', *Zapiski Russkogo Nauchnogo Instituta v Belgrade*, vol. 14, Belgrade, 1939, pp. 1–27.
50. R. Pipes, *Struve* (2 vols, Cambridge, Mass., 1970, 1980) is an excellent biography.
51. Ibid., pp. 381–6.
52. S.L. Frank, *Biografiya P.B.Struve*, New York, 1956, p. 164.
53. O. Kaznina, *Russkie v Anglii*, Moscow, 1997; E.B. Kudryakova, *Rossiiskaya emigratsiya v Velikobritanii v period mezhdu dvumya voinami*, Moscow, 1995; E.M. Multanen, 'British Policy towards Russian Refugees in the Aftermath of the Bolshevik Revolution', Ph.D. thesis, SSEES, London University, 2000; and the wonderfully lucid biography by G.S. Smith, *D.S.Mirsky*, Oxford, 2000. K. Schlögel in *Der Grosse Exodus* does not include a chapter on Britain.
54. P.P. Shilovsky, 'Here is Imperial Russia . . .', in Glenny and Stone (eds), *The Other Russia* p. 291.
55. Ibid., p. 293.
56. Smith, *D.S.Mirsky*, p. 156.

57. J.I. Abyzov, 'Riga: Der Lettische Zweig der russischen Emigration', in Schlögel (ed.), *Der Grosse Exodus*, pp. 112–40. The periodical publication *Baltiiskiy Arkhiv* also contains interesting material.

58. Y. Abyzov, *Russkoe pechatnoe slovo v Latvii 1917–1944gg. Bibliographicheskiy Spravochnik*, vols 1–4. Stanford, 1990–91. *Baltiiskiy Arkhiv*, 3 vols, Tallinn, 1995–97 and L. Fleishman, Y. Abyzov and B. Ravdin, *Russkaya Pechat' v Rige*, 4 vols, Stanford, 1997, are particularly valuable sources on the history of the emigration in these areas.

59. A. Sedykh, *Tam, gde byla Rossiya*, Paris, 1930, pp. 22–3.

60. D. Levitsky, 'V nezavisimoi Latvii', *Novyi Zhurnal*, 1980, p. 213.

61. N.E. Andreyev, *To, chto vspominaetsya*, Tallinn, 1996, vol. 2, p. 31.

62. Ibid., p. 29.

63. I. Belobrovtseva, 'Russkya emigratsiya: os' Tartu-Oxford-Harbin', *Baltiiskiy Arkhiv*, 1, 1995, p. 175.

64. *Materialy dlya bibliografii russkikh nauchnykh trudov za rubezhom* (Materials for Bibliography of Russian Scientific Works Produced Abroad) (1920–1930), Izdanie Russkogo Nauchnogo Instituta v Belgrade, Belgrade, 1931.

65. Paul Robinson, *The White Russian Army in Exile 1920–1941*, Oxford, 2002, p. 81.

66. *Ocherk deyatel'nosti Ob'edineniya . . . (Zemgor)*, 17 March 1921–1 January 1925, Prague, 1925, p. 24.

EPILOGUE: THE END OF THE EMIGRATION

1. N. Andreyev, *To, chto vspominaetsya*, 2 vols, Tallinn, 1996, vol. 2, p. 90.

2. After the Munich Agreement and the occupation there was a change of leadership in almost all the remaining Russian organisations. Countess Panina was replaced by someone with the same views but who was less well known. In other organisations this change was political. The head of the Russian Free University, the democrat M.M. Novikov, was replaced by V.S. Il'in, a prominent specialist in natural sciences whose views on the social sciences were dubious and who was also very vain. He was keen on collaboration with the invaders. A.S. Lomshakov was removed from his post as chairman of the Society of Russian Engineers and Technicians. The new leaders pursued a pro-German policy. The same can be said about the medical society and some other institutions. In émigré organisations created by the Nazi regime absolutely unknown people appeared, such as K.A. Efremov who was supposed to be responsible for émigrés in Prague. Kovalensky was nominated for the post of head of the united youth organisation; and N.V. Padalka became chairman of the Union of Russian Trade Unions.

3. A. Kopřivová-Vukolová 'Osudy ruské emigrace v ČSR po r.1945', in *Ruská a ukrajiská emigrace v ČSR,* 1993, pp. 80–94; V. Bystrov, 'Zrada dlouhá přes půl stolet, ibid., pp. 95–110, and E. Chinyaeva, *Russians outside Russia,* Munich, 2001, pp. 218–20.

4. G. Struve, *Russkaya literatura v izgnanii*, New York, 1956; 2nd edn Paris, 1984, p. 6. N. Andreyev, 'Ob osobennostyakh i osnovnykh etapakh razvitiya russkoy literatury za rubezhom', in N.P. Poltaratskii (ed.), *Russkaya literatura v emigratsii. Sbornik statei*, Pittsburg, 1972, p. 16.

5. M. Raeff, *Russia Abroad*, Oxford, 1990, p. 196.

Select Bibliography

Unpublished Material

ARCHIVES (WITH ABBREVIATIONS IN BOLD)

Archive of the Foreign Ministry, Prague (Archiv Ministerstva zahraničních věcí, – **AMZV**).

The T.G. Masaryk Institute, Prague (Ústav T.G. Masaryka – **TGM**).

The National Literary Archive, Prague (Literární archiv Památníku národního písemnictví).

State Central Archives, Prague (Státní ústřední archiv – **SÚA**).

The Kondakov Institute Archives, Prague (Ústav dějin umění AV ČR).

The Bakhmeteff Archive of Russian and East European History and Culture, Columbia University, New York.

State Archive of the Russian Federation, Moscow (Russkiy Zagranichnyi Istoricheskiy Arkhiv – fond **RZIA**).

Petronik (pseudonym of P.N. Savitsky) *Recollections of Alexsei Stepanovich Lomshakov*. 1960. Typescript, in the possession of I.P. Savicky. Reproduced in *Transactions of the Association of Russian–American Scholars in the USA*, 31, 2001–2, pp. 562–7.

Diary of Academician N.P. Kondakov. By kind permission of the late L.L. Kopecka.

DISSERTATIONS

Gamsa, M. 'The Russian–Chinese Encounter in Harbin, Manchuria, 1898–1932'. D. Phil. thesis, Oxford, 2003.

Jones, R. 'Harbin as a Russo-Chinese City, 1917–1931'. M. Phil. thesis, Oxford, 2000.

Multanen, E.M. 'British Policy towards Russian Refugees in the Aftermath of the Bolshevik Revolution'. Ph. D. thesis, SSEES, London University, 2000.

White, E. '*Svoimi Putyami*: Paths Back to Russia. An analysis of a Russian émigré journal'. M.St in Slavonic Studies, Oxford, 1995.

Periodicals

Evraziiskaya khronika, vols 1–4, Prague, 1925–26; vols 5–7, Paris, 1926.
Evraziiskiye tetradi, vols 1–6, Prague, 1934–36.
Evraziya. Ezhenedel'nik po voprosam kultury i politiki, 1–35, Paris, 1928–29.
Kazachiy Put', Prague, 1924–26.
Khozyain, Prague, 1924–38.
Khutor, Prague, 1922–24.
Nedelia, Prague, 1928–30.
Obshchee Delo, Petrograd, later Paris, 1917, 1918–22, 1928–33.
Ogni, Prague, 1921–22.
Russkaya shkola za rubezhom, vols 1–34, Prague, 1923–31.
Russkiy ekonomicheskiy sbornik, 12 vols, Prague, 1925–28.
Russkoe Delo, Prague, 1919–1920.
Russkoe Delo, Sofia, then Belgrade 1921–22.
Slavyanskaya Zarya, Prague, 1919–20.
Studencheskie Gody, Prague, 1922–25.
Uchenye Zapiski, osnovannye Russkoy Uchebnoy Kollegiey v Prag, 6 vols, Prague, 1924–26.
Vestnik Krest'yanskoi Rossii, Prague and Berlin, 1922–33.
Volya Rossii, Prague, 1922–32.
Zapiski Instituta izucheniya Rossii, vols 1–3, Prague, 1925–26.

Secondary Sources

Abyzov, Y. *Russkoe pechatnoe slovo v Latvii 1917–1944 gg. Bibliograficheskiy Spravochnik*, vols 1–4. Stanford, 1990–91.
Alekseev, N.N. *Osnovy filosofii prava*. Prague, 1924.
Andreyev, C. *Vlasov and the Russian Liberation Movement*. Cambridge, 1987.
Andreyev, N.E. 'O Russkoy Literaturnoy Prage', in *Russkiy Almanakh*. Paris, 1981.
——*To, chto vspominaetsya*, 2 vols. Tallinn, 1996.
Antoniy, Metropolit. *Khristos Spasitel' i evreyskaya revolyutsiya*. Berlin, 1922.
Astapenko, M. *Ataman Kaledin*. Rostov on the Don, 1997.
Bailey, G. *The Conspirators*. New York, 1960.
Baltiiskiy Arkhiv, 3 vols. Tallinn, 1995–97.
Baur, J. *Die russische Kolonie in München 1900–1945. Deutsch–russische Beziehungen im 20. Jahrhundert*. Wiesbaden, 1998.
Belobrovtseva, I. 'Russkaya emigratsiya: os' Tartu-Oxford-Harbin', *Baltiiskiy Arkhiv*, 1, 1995.
Beloshevskaya, L. (ed.) *Dukhovnye techeniya russkoy i ukrainskoy emigratsii v Chekhoslovatskoy Respublike (1919–1939)*. Prague, 1999.
——(ed.) *Khronika kulturnoy, naychnoy i obshchestvennoy zhizni russkoy emigratsii v Chekhoslovatskoy Respublike*, vol. 1, 1919–29. Prague, 2000; vol. 2, 1930–39. Prague, 2001.
Belov, V. *Beloe pokhmel'e. Russkaya emigratsiya na rasput'e. Opyt issledovaniya psikhologii, nastroeniy i bytovy usloviy russkoi emigratsii v nashe vremya*. Moscow and Petrograd, 1923.
Berberova, N. *The Italics Are Mine*. London and New York, 1969.
Bitsilli, P.M. *Ocherki teorii istoricheskoy nauki*. Prague, 1925.
Blackstock, P, *The Secret Road to World War Two*. Chicago, 1969.

Bobrinskoy, O. 'La Première République tchécoslovaque et l'émigration russe (1920–1938): la spécificité d'une politique d'asile', *Revue d'études comparatives Est–Ouest,* 1 (mars), 1995, pp.153–75.

Boobbyer, P. *S.L.Frank.* Athens, Ohio, 1995.

Böss, O. *Die Lehre der Eurasier.* Wiesbaden,1961.

Budnitskii, O.V. 'Diplomaty i Den'gi', *Diaspora,* vol. 4. Nov materialy, pp. 457–508, St Petersburg, 2002.

Bulgakov, S.N. 'Tserkovnoe pravo i krizis pravosoznaniya', in *Uchenye Zapiski,* vol. 1, Prague, 1924.

Černý, V. *Vývoj a zločiny panslavismu.* Prague, 1995.

Československá pomoc ruské a ukrajinské emigraci. Prague, Ministerstvo zahraničí, 1924.

Chinyaeva, E. 'Ruská emigrace v Československu: vývoj ruské pomocné akce', *Slovanský přehled,* 1, 1993.

——*Russians outside Russia.* Munich, 2001.

Čyževsky, D.I. (ed.) *Hegel bei dem Slaven.* Reichenberg, 1934.

Dandová, M. and Zahradniková, M. 'Rossica ve fondech literárního archívu Památníku národního písemnictví', *Sborník Literárního archívu,* 23, Prague, 1989.

Davats, V.Kh. and L'vov, N.N. *Russkaya armiya na chuzhbine.* Belgrade, 1923 (reprinted 1985).

Dokumenty a materiály k dějinám československo-sovětských vztahů, Díl 1. Prague, 1975.

Dokumenty o protilidové a protinárodní politice T.G.Masaryka. Prague, 1953.

Dokumenty vneshney politiki SSSR, vol. 1. Moscow, 1957.

Dostal', M.Yu. 'Perepiska V.A.Frantseva', *Slavyanovedenie,* 4, 1994, pp. 102–7.

Etkind, E. Nivat, G. Serman, I. and Strada,V. (eds) *Histoire de la littérature russe–Le XXe siècle: la révolution et les années vingt.* Paris, 1988 and *Le XXe siècle: Gels et dégels.* Paris, 1990.

Evlogii, Metropolit, *Put' Moey Zhizni. Memoirs,* transcribed by T. Manukhina. Paris, 1947.

'Evraziiskaya rabota zagranitsei. Doklad N.A. Perfil'eva.' *Pervyi s'ezd evraziiskoy organizatsii. Protokol i materialy,* 1923

Evraziistvo, Formulirovka 1927 goda. Prague, 1927.

Evraziistvo. Opyt sistimaticheskogo izlozheniya. Paris, 1926.

Fic,V.M. *Revolutionary War for Independence and the Russian Question: The Czechoslovak Army in Russia, 1914–1918.* New Delhi, 1977.

——*The Bolsheviks and the Czechoslovak Legion: The Origin of their Armed Conflict, March–May 1918.* New Delhi, 1978.

——*The Collapse of American Policy in Russia and Siberia, 1918: Wilson's Decision not to Intervene March–October 1918.* Boulder, Colorado, 1995.

——*The Rise of the Constitutional Alternative to Soviet Rule in 1918: Provisional Governments of Siberia and All Russia: Their Quest for Allied Intervention.* Boulder, Colorado and New York, 1998.

Fleishman, L., Abyzov, Yu. and Ravdin, B. *Russkaya pechat'v Rige: iz istorii gazety Segodnya 1930 godov,* vols 1–5. Stanford, 1997 (Stanford Slavic Studies, vol. 13–17).

Fleishman, L., Hughes, R. and Raevsky-Hughes, O. (eds) *Russkiy Berlin 1921–1923.* Paris, 1983.

Florovsky, G.V. 'Evraziiskii soblazn', in *Sovremennye Zapiski* (Paris 1928), vol. 34.

Frank, S.L. *Biografiya P.B.Struve.* New York, 1956.

Gessain, R. and Doré, M. 'Facteurs comparés d'assimilation chez des Russes et des Arméniens', *Population,* 1, 1946.

Gessen, S.I. *Osnovy pedagogiki. Vvedenie v prikladnuyu filosofiyu.* Berlin, 1923.

G.G. 'Yuridicheskiy Fakul'tet v Kharbine (1920–1930) Ocherk', *Izvestiya Yuridicheskovo Fakul'teta*, vol. 9, Harbin, 1931.

Glad, J. *Russia Abroad*. Washington DC and Tenafly, NJ, 1999.

Grimm, D.D. 'Osnovnye predpolozheniya i zadachi sotsialinykh nauk', *Uchenye Zapiski*, 1, Prague, 1924.

Halperin, C.J. 'Russia and the Steppe: George Vernadsky and Eurasianism', *Forschungen zur osteuropäischen Geschichte*, 36, 1985, pp. 55–194.

Hardeman, H. *Coming to Terms with the Soviet Regime: the Changing Signposts Movement among Russian Emigres in the early 1920s*. De Kalb, Illinois, 1994.

Holborn, L.W. *Refugees: A Problem of our Time*, vol. 1, Metuchen, NJ, 1975.

Huntington, W.C. *The Homesick Millions*. Boston, Mass., 1933.

Iskhod k vostoku. Predchuvstviya i Sversheniya. Utverzhdenie Evraziitsev. Sofia, 1921; repr. Moscow, 1997.

Ivantsov, D. 'Russkie bezhentsy v Yugoslavii v 1921g.' *Russkiy ekonomicheskiy sbornik*, 2, 1925.

Izgoev, A.S. *Rozhedennoe v revolutsionnoy smute, 1917–32*. Paris, 1933.

Izvestiya Yuridicheskogo Fakulteta, vol. 9. Harbin, 1931.

Izyumov, A.F. (ed.) 'Ufimskoe Gosudarstvennoe Soveshchanie', in *Russkiy istoricheskiy arkhiv*, vol. 1. Prague, 1929.

Jakobson, R. (ed.) *N.S. Trubetzkoy's Letters and Notes*. The Hague and Paris, 1975.

Jakovenko, B. *Dějiny ruské filosofie*. Prague, 1939.

Johnston, R.H. *'New Mecca, New Babylon': Paris and the Russian Exiles, 1920–1945.'* Montreal, 1988.

Jovanovič, M. *Doseljavanje Ruskikh izbeglica u Kraljevinu SMS 1919–1924*. Belgrade, 1996.

K desyatiletiyu prazhskogo Zemgora, Prague, 1931.

K molodoy Rossii . . . Sbornik mladorossov. Paris, 1928.

Kalvoda, J. *The Genesis of Czechoslovakia*, Boulder, Colorado, 1986.

Karsavin, L. *Filosofiya istorii*. Berlin, 1923.

Katchaki, J.N. *Bibliography of Russian Refugees in the Kingdom of the SCS (Yugoslavia) 1920–1945*. Arnhem, 1991.

Katkov, G. 'Masaryk's Guests', in M. Glenny and N. Stone (eds), *The Other Russia*, London, 1990.

Kaznina. O. 'N.S. Trubetskoy i krizis evraziistva', *Slavyanovedenie*, 4, 1995.

——*Russkie v Anglii*. Moscow, 1997.

Kelin, N.A. *Kazach'ya ispoved'*. Moscow, 1996.

Khisamutdinov, A.A. *Rossiiskaya emigratsiya v Aziatsko-Tikhookeanskom regione i Yuzhnoi Amerike*. Vladivostok, 2000.

'Khronika instituta', *Zapiski Instituta izucheniya Rossii*, vols 1 and 2. Prague, 1925.

Kiselev, A.F. (ed.) *Politicheskaya Istoriya Russkoi emigratsii 1920–1940 gg. Dokumenty i Materialy*. Moscow, 1999.

Kizevetter, A.A. *Na rubezhe dvukh stoletii*. Prague, 1929.

Kneeley, R.J. and Kasinec, E. 'The *Slovanská knihovna* in Prague and its RZIA Collection', *Slavic Review*, Spring 1992, pp. 122–30.

Kopřivová, A. *Rossiiskie emigranty vo Vshenorakh-Mokropsakh-Chernoshitsakh (Dvadtsatye gody 20-go veka)*. Prague, 2000.

——*Střediska ruského emigrantského života v Praze (1921–1952)*. Prague, 2001.

Kopřivová-Vukolová, A. 'Osudy ruské emigrace v ČSR po r.1945', in *Ruská a ukrajinská emigrace v ČSR, 1993*, pp. 80–94.

Kosik, V.I. 'Russkaya Yugoslavia: Fragmenty istorii 1919–1914', *Slavyanovedenie*, 4, 1992, p.25.

Kostikov, V. *Ne budem proklinat' izgnaniye . . . Puti i sud'by russkoy emigratsii*. 2nd edn. Moscow, 1994.

Kovalevsky, P.E. *Zarubezhnaya Rossiya: istoriya i kulturno-prosvititel'naya rabota russkogo zarubezhiya za pol veka (1920–1970)*, 2 vols. Paris, 1971, 1973.

Kozlitin, V.D. 'Rossiiskaya emigratsiya v Korolevstve Serbov, Khorvatov i Sloventsev (1919–1923)', *Slavyanovedenie*, 4, 1992, pp. 7–19.

——*Russkaya i ukrainskaya emigratsiya v Yugoslavii 1919–1945*. Kharkov, 1996.

Krest'yanskaya Rossiaya. Trudovaya Krest'yanskaya Partiya. Vvedenie. Ideologiya. Programma. Taktika. Ustav. Prague, 1928.

Krest'yanskaya Rossiya. Sbornik statey, vol. 1. New York, 1953.

Kudryakova, E.B. *Rossiiskaya emigratsiya v Velikobritanii v period mezhdu dvumya voinami*. Moscow, 1995.

Lesure, M. (ed.) 'Les Réfugiés révolutionnaires à Paris', *Cahiers du monde russe et soviétique*, 6(3), 1965, pp. 419–36.

Levitsky, S. 'Vospominaniya o Losskom', *Novyi Zhurnal*, March 1977, pp. 171–87.

Lossky, B., 'K izgnaniyu lyudey mysli v 1922 godu', in M. Parkhomovsky and L. Yuniveg (eds) *Evrei v kul'ture Russkogo Zarubezhiya. Sbornik statei, publikatsiy, memuarov i esse*. 1. 1919–1939. Jerusalem, 1992, pp. 273–87.

Lukes, I. *Czechoslovakia between Stalin and Hitler*. Oxford, 1996.

Mamatey, V.S. and Luža, R. (eds) *A History of the Czechoslovak Republic*. Princeton, 1973.

Markov, L.L. *Kak russkie ustraivayutsya na frantsuzkoy zemle*. Paris, 1932.

Marrus, M. *The Unwanted*. Oxford, 1985.

Masaryk, T.G. *Světová revoluce. Za války a ve válce 1914–1918. Vzpomíná a uvažuje . . .* Prague, 1925, English trans.: *The Making of a State. Memories and Observations 1914–1918*, abridged and prepared with an introduction by H.W. Steed. London, 1927.

——*Cesta demokracie*, vols 1–4. Prague, 1933–39.

——and Beneš, E. *Otevřít Rusko Evropě*. Prague, 1992.

Massip, M. *La Vérité est fille du temps. Alexandre Kasem-Beg et l'émigration russe en Occident 1902–1977*. Geneva, 1999.

Materialy dlya bibliografii russkikh nauchnykh trudov za rubezhom. 1920–1930. Izdanie Russkogo Nauchnogo Instituta v Belgrade, Belgrade, vol. 1, 1931; vol. 2, 1941.

Matgauser, Z. and Morkovin, V. (eds) Marina Tsvetaeva, *Pisma k A. Teskovoy*. Prague, 1969.

Meisner, D. *Mirazhi i Deistvitelnost'*. Moscow, 1970.

Mezhdunarodnaya konferentsiya 'Russkaya, ukrainskaya i belorusskaya emigratsiya v Chekhoslovakii mezhdu dvumya mirovymi voinami. Rezul'taty i perespektivy issledovniy. Fondy Slavyanskoy biblioteki i prazhskikh arkhivov'. Prague, 14–15 August 1995.

Milenkovič, T. *Ruski ingen'eri u Yugoslavii 1919–1941*. Belgrade, 1997.

Miliukov, P.M. *Emigratsiya na pereput'e*. Paris, 1926.

Na Putyakh. Utverzhdenie Evraziitsev, vol.2. Berlin, 1922.

Náš Majakovskij. *Sborník básní, statí, článků a vzpomínek k 20 výročí básnikovy smrti*. Prague, 1951.

Nazarov, M. *Missiya Russkoy emigratsii*. Stavropol', 1992.

Nikitin, A.K 'Etapy i metody unifikatsii russkoy pravoslavnoy obshchiny v Germanii v 1935–1939 godakh', in *Russkaya emigratsiya v Evrope 20–30e gody XX veka*. Moscow, 1996.

Norwood, F. *Strangers & Exiles, a History of Religious Refugees*. Nashville, 1969.

Novikov, M.M. *Ot Moskvy do Niu Iorka. Moya zhizn' v nauke i politike*. New York, 1952.

——'Russkie emigranty v Prage', *Novyi Zhurnal*, June 1957, pp. 243–56.

Obozrenie prepodavaniya v Russkom institute sel'sko-khozyaistvennoi kooperatsii v Prage. Prague, 1929.

Ocherk deyatel'nosti Ob'edineniya Rossiiskikh Zemskikh i Gorodoskikh Deyateley v Chekhoslovatskoy Respublike (Zemgor) 17 marta 1921 – 1 yanvarya 1925 g. Prague, 1925.

Odna ili dve russkikh literatury? Colloquium Proceedings, Lausanne, 1981.

Olivová, V. *československo-sovětské vztahy v letech 1918–1922.* Prague, 1957.

——'Politika Československa v ruské krizi roku 1921 a 1922', in T.G. Masaryk and E. Beneš, *Otevřít Rusko Evropě.* Prague, 1992.

Olsufiev, D.A. *Mysli Sobornianina o nashey Tserkovnoi smute.* Paris, 1928.

Ossorguine-Bakounine, T. *L'Émigration russe en Europe.Catalog collectif des périodiques en langue russe 1855–1940.* Paris, 1976.

Papers Relating to the Foreign Relations of the United States, 1914–1946. US Department of State, Washington, DC, 1922-7. Supplement 1. 2 vols, Washington, 1933.

Pashuto, V.T. *Russkie istoriki emigranty v Evrope.* Moscow, 1992.

Pavlova, T.F. 'Russkii Zagranichnii Istoricheskyi Arkhiv', *Voprosii Istorii,* 11, 1990, pp. 19–30.

——(ed.) *Fondy Russkogo Zagranichnogo Istoricheskogo Arkhiva v Prage.* Moscow, 1999.

Petrishchev, A. 'Russkoe zemledelie vo Frantsii', in *Russkiy Ekonomicheskiy Sbornik,* 12, Prague, 1928.

Pio-Ul'sky,G.N. *Russkaya emigratsiya i ee znachenie v zhizni drugikh narodov.* Belgrade, 1939.

Pipes, R. *Struve,* 2 vols. Cambridge, Mass., 1970, 1980.

Pivovar, E.I. *Rossiiskaya emigratsiya v Turtsii, Iugo-Vostochnoi i Tsentralnoi Evrope 20-kh godov. Uchebnoe posobie.* Göttingen, 1994.

Polishensky, J.V. *History of Czechoslovakia in Outline.* Prague, 1991.

Politicheskie partii Rossiii. Konets XX – pervaya tret' XX veka. Encyklopediya. Moscow, 1996.

Poltaratskii, N.P. (ed.) *Russkaya literatura v emigratsii. Sbornik statei.* Slavic series no.1. Pittsburgh, 1972.

Postnikov, S.P. (ed.) *Russkie v Prage 1918–1928g.* Prague, 1928, 1995.

Preobrazhenskiy, V.V. (ed.) *Russkie v Latvii: sbornik 'Dnya Russkoy Kultury',* 2 vols. Riga, 1933, 1934.

Prianishnikov, B. *Nezrimaia pautina.* Silver Spring, Maryland, 1979.

Protokoly zagranichnykh grupp konstitutsionno-demokraticheskoy partii, vol. 4, May 1920–June 1921; vol. 5, June–December 1921; vol. 6(i), 1922; vol. 6(ii), 1923–33. Moscow, 1996.

Putna, M.C. and Zadražilová, M. *Rusko mimo Rusko. Dějiny a kultura ruské emigrace 1917–1991,* 2 vols. Brno, 1993–94.

Rachůnková, Z. and Řeháková, M. (eds) *Práce ruské, ukrajinské a běloruské emigrace vydané v Československu 1918–1945. (Bibliografie s biografickými údaji o autorech.)* Bibliografii zpracovaly Rachůnková, Z. a Řeháková, M. Biografická hesla zpracoval Vacek, J. 3 vols. Prague, 1996.

Rachůnková, Z. and Řeháková, M. 'The Works of the First Wave of the Russian and Ukrainian Emigration [published in Czechoslovakia, later in the Czech Republic]. A Selected List in the years 1989–1996', *Rossica. Nauchnye issledovaniya po rusistike, ukrainistike, belorusistike,* 2, 1997, pp. 119–28.

Raeff, M. *Russia Abroad. A Cultural History of the Russian Emigration, 1919–1939.* Oxford, 1990.

Raevsky-Hughes, O. (ed.) *Pamiati Vladyki Sergia Prazhskogo.* New York, 1987.

Rhinelander, L.H. 'Exiled Russian Scholars in Prague: The Kondakov Seminar and Institute', *Canadian Slavonic Papers,* 16(3), Autumn 1974, pp. 331–52.

Riha,T. 'Russian Émigré Scholars in Prague after World War', *Slavic and East European Journal,* 16, 1958, pp. 22–6.

Rimscha, H. von. *Russlands jenseits der Grenzen 1921–1926.* Jena, 1922.

——*Der russische Bürgerkrieg und die russische Emigration, 1917–21*. Jena, 1924.

——'Die Entwicklung der russländischen Emigranten nach den zweiten Weltkrieg', *Europa Archiv*, 7 August/November/December 1952.

Ročenka Československé republiky, ed. A. Hajn, 12 vols. Prague, 1922–32.

Robinson, P. *The White Russian Army in Exile 1920–1941*. Oxford, 2002.

Rossiya v izgnanii. Sud'by rossiiskikh emigrantov za rubezhom. Moscow, 1999.

Ruchkin, A.B. 'Russkie uchenye-emigranty v 1920 gody. (Na primere Ekonomicheskogo kabineta S.N.Prokopovicha)' in *Istoriya rossiiskogo zarubezhiya. Problemy adaptatsii migrantov v XIX–XX vekakh*. Moscow, 1996, pp. 115–23.

Rudnev, V.V. *Russkoe Delo v Chekhoslovatskoy Respublike*. Rossiskii Zemsko-Gorodskoy Komitet pomoshchi rossiiskim grazhdanam zagranitsey. Paris, 1924.

Russkaya emigratsiya v Evrope 20e–30e gody XX veka. Moscow, 1996.

Russkaya molodezh' v vysshei shkole za granitsey. Deyatel'nost, Tsentral'nogo Komiteta po obespecheniyu vysshego obrazovaniya russkomu yunoshestvu za granitsei. Paris, 1933.

Russkaya zarubezhnaya kniga. Trudy Komiteta russkoy knigi, 2 vols. Prague, 1924.

Russkii narodnyi universitet v Prage. *Otchet o deyatel'nosti za 1923–24 [1927–1928] uchebny god*, 5 vols. Prague, 1924–28.

Russkii yuridicheskiy fakul'tet v Prage. *Otchet o sostoyanii i deyatel'nosti' 1923–24 [..1927–28] uchebnyi god,* 5 vols. Prague, 1925–28. *Otchet za 1926–28 uchebny god s obshchim obzorom ego pyatiletney deyatelnosti (1922–27)*.

Russkiy Parizh. Sostavlenie, predislovie i kommentarii T. Buslavskoi. Moscow, 1998.

Russkoe Zarubezh'e Khronika nauchnoy, kul'turnoy i obshchestvennoy zhizni. 1920–1940. Frantsiya, vol. 1. Paris and Moscow, 1995.

Russkoe Zarubezh'e. Zolotaya kniga russkoy emigratsii. Pervaya tret' XX veka. Entsiklopedicheskiy biograficheskiy slovar'. Moscow, 1997.

Russkaya i ukrainskaya emigratsiya v Chekhoslovatskoy respublike 1918–1938. Putevoditel' po arkhivnym fondam i sobraniyam v Cheshskoy Respublike. Prague, 1995.

Savickij, P. *Šestina světa. (Rusko jako zeměpisný a historický celek.)*. Prague, 1933.

Savický, I. *Osudová setkání. Češi v Rusku a Rosové v Čechách 1914–1938*. Prague, 1999.

——*Praga i zarubezhnaya Rossiya*. Prague, 2002.

Savický, N. 'O některých méně známých pramenech Tezí Pražského lingvistického kroužku', *Slovo a slovesnost*, 52, 1991, pp. 196–8.

Savitsky, P. 'Evropa i Evraziya. (Po povodu broshury kn.N.S.Trubetskogo 'Evropa i Chelovechestvo).' *Russkaya mysl'*. *Ezhemesyachnoe literaturno-politicheskoe izdanie* ed. P. Struve, vols 1 and 2. Sofia, 1921.

Savitsky, P, et al., *Iskhod k Vostoku*, Sophia, 1921; repr. Moscow, 1995.

——'Dva mira', in *Na Putyakh. Utverzhdenie Evraziitsev*, vol. 2. Berlin, 1922.

——'Povorot k Vostoku', in Savitsky et al., *Iskhod k Vostoku*, Sophia, 1921.

——*Kontinent Evraziya*, ed. A.G. Dugin. Moscow, 1997.

Sbornik statey posvyashchennykh pamyati N.P.Kondakova. Seminarium Kondakovianum, Prague, 1926.

Schlögel, K. (ed.) *Der Grosse Exodus. Die russische Emigration und ihre Zentren 1917 bis 1941*. Munich, 1994.

——(ed.) *Russische Emigranten in Deutschland 1918–1945. Leben im europäischen Bürgerkrieg*. Berlin, 1995.

——*Berlin, Ostbahnhof Europas. Russen und Deutsche in ihrem Jahrhundert*. Berlin, 1998.

Sedykh, A. *Tam, gde byla Rossiya*. Paris, 1930.

Serapionova, E.P. *Rossiiskaya emigratsiya v Chekhoslovatskoy respublike (20–30gody)*. Moscow, 1995.

Service, R. *Lenin*. London, 2000.

Seton-Watson, R.W. *A History of the Czechs and Slovaks*. London, 1943.

——*Masaryk in England*. Cambridge, 1943.

Shakhovskoy, Z. *Otrazheniya*. Paris, 1975.

Shishkin, V.A. *Chekhoslovatsko–Sovetskie Otnosheniya*. Moscow, 1962.

Shkarenkov, L.K. *Agoniya beloy emigratsii*. Moscow, 1981; 2nd revised edn 1986.

Simpson, Sir John Hope. *The Refugee Problem*. London, 1939.

Skálová, Z. 'Das Prager Seminarium Kondakovianum, später das Archäologische Kondakov-Institut und sein Archiv (1925–1952)', *Slavica Gandesia*, 18–1991, pp. 21–49.

Skran, C. *Refugees in Inter-war Europe*. Oxford, 1995.

Sládek, Z. 'Russkaya i ukrainskaya emigratsiya v Chekhoslovakii', in *Sovetskoe Slavyanovedenie*, b, 1991, pp. 24–36.

——'Ruská emigree v Československu' in *Slovanský přehled*, vol. 1, Prague 1993, pp. 1–13.

——'Prag: Das "russische Oxford"', in K.Schlögel (ed.) *Der Grosse Exodus. Die russische Emigration und ihre Zentren 1917 bis 1941*. Munich, 1994.

——'České prostředi a ruská emigrace (1918–1938)', in *Duchovní proudy ruské a ukrainské emigrace v Československé republice 1919–1939*. Prague, 1999.

——Beloshevskaya, L. et al. (eds) *Dokumenty k istorii russkoi i ukrainskoi emigratsii v Chekhoslovatskoi Respublike (1918–1939)*. Prague, 1998.

Slavik, J. (ed.) compiled by Postnikov, S.P. *Bibliografiya Russkoy Revolyutsii i Grazhdanskoy Voiny (1917–1921)*. Prague, 1938.

Slonim, M. *Modern Russian Literature*. New York, 1953.

Slonim, M.L. *Po zolotoy trope: chekhoslovatskie vpechatleniya*. Paris, 1928.

Smele, J.D. 'White Gold: The Imperial Russian Gold Reserve in the anti-Bolshevik East 1918–? (An Unconcluded Chapter in the History of the Russian Civil War)', *Europe–Asia Studies*, 46(8), 1994, pp. 1317–47.

——*Civil War in Siberia*. Cambridge, 1996.

Smith, G.S. *D.S.Mirsky. A Russian–English Life 1890–1939*. Oxford, 2000.

Snesarev, N. *Kirill 1, Imperator . . . Koburgskiy*. n.p., 1925.

Sorokin, P. *Avtobiografiya*. Moscow, 1992.

Spektorskiy, E.V. *Khristianstvo i kul'tura*. Prague, 1925.

——*Nachala nauki o gosudarstve i obshchestve*. Belgrade, 1927.

——'Desyatiletie Russkogo Nauchnogo Instituta v Belgrade', *Zapiski Russkogo Nauchnogo istituta v Belgrade*, vol. 14. Belgrade, 1939.

Stephan, J. *The Russian Fascists. Tragedy and Farce in Exile 1925–1945*. New York, 1978.

Struve, G.P. *Russkaya literatura v izgnanii*. New York, 1956; 2nd edn Paris, 1984.

Struve, P.B. 'Nauchnaya kartina ekonomicheskogo mira i ponyatiya ravnovesiya.' 'Khozyaistvo, khozyastvovaniye, obshchestvo'; 'Pervichnost' i svoeobrazie obmena i problema ravnovesiya. Otvet A.D.Bilimovichu; & A.Bilimovich 'Dva podkhoda k naychnoy kartine ekonomicheskogo mira', in S.N. Prokopovich (ed.) *Ekonomicheskiy Vestnik*, vols 1–3. Berlin, 1923–24.

——'Nekotorye osnovnye ponyatiya ekonomicheskoy nauki', in *Uchenye Zapiski*, 1, Prague, 1924.

Tabori, P. *The Anatomy of Exile*. London, 1972.

Taufer, J. *Majakovskij v Praze*. Prague, 1971.

Tejchmanová, S. 'Ekonomický kabinet S.N.Prokopoviče v Praze', *Slovanský přehled*, 1, 1993, pp. 55–62.

——*Rusko v Československu. Bílá emigrace v ČSR (1917–1939)*. Jinočany, 1993.

Thompson, J.M. *Russia, Bolshevism and the Versailles Peace*. Princeton, 1966.

Tobolka, Z. *Politické dějiny československého národa od r.1848 až do dnešní doby,* vol. 4. Prague, 1937.

Tolstoy, N. *Victims of Yalta,* revised edn. London, 1979.

Toman, J. (ed.) *Letters and Other Materials from the Moscow and Prague Linguistic Circles, 1912–1945.* Ann Arbor, 1994.

Totomiants, V.F. 'Kooperatsiya i sel'skoe khozyaistvo', in *Kooperatsiya i sel'skoe khozyaistvo. Zapiski Russkogo instituta sel'sko-khozyaistvennoi kooperatsii v Prage,* Prague, 1924.

Transactions of the Association of Russian–American Scholars in the USA, vol. 31, 2001–2.

Tridtsatye gody. Utverzhdenie Evraziitsev. Prague, 1931.

Troitsky, S. *Razmezhevanie ili Raskol.* Paris, 1932.

Trubetskoy, N.S. *Evropa i Chelovechestvo.* Sofia, 1920.

——'Russkaya Problema', in *Na Putyakh. Utverzhdenie Evraziitsev,* vol. 2. Moscow and Berlin, 1922.

——*K probleme russkogo samopoznaniya.* Paris, 1927.

——(ed.) A. Dugin, *Nasledie Chingiskhana.* Moscow, 1999.

Tsimmerman, M. *Istoriya mezhdunarodonogo prava s drevneishikh vremen do 1918g.* Prague, 1924.

Tsurganov, I. *Neudavshiysia revansh – Belaya emigratiya vo vtoroi mirovoi voine.* Moscow, 2001.

Ullman, R.H. *Britain and the Russian Civil War. November 1918 – February 1920.* Princeton, 1968.

Ustryalov, N.V (ed.) *Bibliograficheskiy Sbornik,* vol. 1 (IV) *Obzor literatury po kitaevedeniyu.* Harbin, 1932.

Vandalkovskya, M.G. *Istoricheskya Nauka Rossiiskoi Emigratsii.* Moscow, 1997.

Vaněčkova, G. *Marina Tsvetaeva v Chekhii: putevoditel' po mestam prebyvaniia v 1922–25 godakh.* Prague, 1997.

Varshavsky, S. 'Komitet Russkoi Knigi (Ocherk zadach i deyatel'nosti)', in *Russkaya Zarubezhnaya Kniga,* Part 1. Prague, Komitet Russkoi Knigi i Plamya, 1924.

Varshavsky, V.S. *Nezamechennoe pokolenie.* New York, 1956.

Veber,V., Z. Sládek, and M. Bukeníkova (eds) *Ruská a ukrainská emigrace v ČSR v letech 1918–1945.* Prague, 1993–5.

Vechorin, E.A. 'Inzhener-izobretatel', profuser in drug molodezhi, *St. Petersburgskiy Politekhnicheskiy Institut, Vol. 2.* Paris, 1958.

Vernadsky, G.V. *Ocherk istorii prava Russkogo Gosudarstva XVIII–XIXvv. (Period imperii).* Prague, 1924.

Vishniak, M.V. *'Sovremennye Zapiski.' Vospominaniya redaktora.* Bloomington, Indiana, 1957.

Voitsekhovskii, S.L. *Trest:vospominaniia i dokumenty.* London, Ontario, 1974.

Volkmann, H-E. *Die russische Emigration in Deutschland 1919–1929.* Würzburg, 1966.

Volkoff, A-M. *L'Émigration russe en Europe.Catalog collectif des périodiques en langue russe, 1940–1979.* Paris, 1981.

Vznik Československa 1918. Dokumenty československé zahraniční politiky. Prague, 1994.

Wells, H.G. *Rossiya vo mgle,* translated and with an introduction by N.S. Trubetskoy, Sofia, 1921.

Wes, M.A. 'Michael Rostovtzeff, Historian in Exile', *Historia,* 65 (Stuttgart), 1990.

Williams, R.C. *Culture in Exile. Russian Émigrés in Germany 1871–1941.* Ithaca, NY, 1972.

Yubileynyi Sbornik (Soyuza russkikh studentov v Brno). 1921–1931. Brno, 1932.

Zenkovsky, V.V. (ed.) *Pravoslavie i kultura. Sbornik religiozno-filosofskikh statey.* Berlin, 1923.

——*Deti Emigratsii.* Prague, 1925.

List of Names

Alekseev, Nikolai Nikolaevich (1879–1964) lawyer, philosopher, academic, publicist, leading Eurasian.

Aleksinskiy, Grigioriy Alekseevich (1879–1967) politician, member of Russian Social Democratic Party, publicist.

Amfiteatrov, Aleksandr Valentinovich (1862–1938) writer and journalist.

Andreyev, Nikolay Efremovich (1908–1982) historian, literary specialist, icon specialist.

Anichkov, Evgeniy Vasilievich (1866–1937) historian of literature.

Argunov, Andrei Alexandrovich (1866–1939) politician, SR, member of the Ufa Directorate and a leader of Krest'yanskaya Rossiya.

Arkhangelsky, Vasiliy Gavrilovich (1869–1948) politician, SR, publicist.

Arseniev, Nikolai Sergeevich (1888–1977) theologian, historian, writer.

Astrov, Nikolai Ivanovich (1868–1934) lawyer, Kadet, mayor of Moscow in 1917, involved in Paris Zemgor.

Bažant, Zdeněk (1879–1954) Czech engineer and Professor of the Czecho Polytechnical Institute, head of the administration of the Russian People's University.

Baxa, Karel (1862–1938) Czech lawyer, mayor of Prague; played an active part in helping émigré organisations in the early 1920s.

Bem, Alfred Ludvigovich (1886–1945?) literary specialist, critic, founder of the Dostoevsky Society, ran 'Skit', a literary circle for young writers and poets; lecturer at Charles University, leader of Krest'yanskaya Rossiya using the pseudonym 'Omelianov'.

Beneš, Edvard (1884–1948) Czech politician, Foreign Minister (1918–35) President 1935–39, head of government in exile (1939–45), President (1945–48).

Berberova, Nina Nikolaevna (1901–1993) writer.

Berdiaev, Nikolai Alexandrovich (1874–1948) philosopher and religious thinker.

Bilimovich, Alexandr Dimitrievich (1878–1863) economist and professor.

Bitsilli, Petr Mikhailovich (1879–1953) historian, literary critic, professor.

Bobrinskaya, Varvara Nikolaevna (1864/6?–19??) countess, active in public life and education.

Bogatyrev, Petr Grigorievich (1893–1971) Slavist, folklore expert, ethnographer, theatre critic, translator.

Breshko-Breshkovskaya, Ekaterina Konstantinovna (1844–1934) known as 'Grandmother of the Revolution'; one of the founders and leaders of the Socialist Revolutionary Party and a prominent political activist.

Brushvit, Ivan Mikhailovich (1879–1945?) engineer, member of Komuch, one of the leaders of the right-wing SRs in emigration, 1924–34 chairman of the Prague Zemgor.

Bulgakov, Sergei Nikolaevich (Father Sergei) (1871–1944) originally economist and philosopher; later theologian who became a priest and a professor at the Theological Academy in Paris.

Bystrov, Nikolai Vladimirovich (1899–1967) lawyer, public activist and representative of the 'second generation' of émigrés.

Chaliapin, Fedor Ivanovich (1873–1938) opera singer.

Chapchikov, Grigoriy Ivanovich (1897–?) army colonel, Cossack activist, member of the Mladorosy (Young Russians).

Chelintsev, Alexander Nikolaevich (1874–1962) economist and statistician.

Chernov, Victor Mikhailovich (1873–1952) leader of the SR Party.

Chirikov, Evgenii Nikolaevich (1864–1932) writer.

Chizhevsky, Dimitry Ivanovich (1894–1977) Russo-Ukrainian philosopher and historian of social thought.

Chkheidze, Konstantin Alexandrovich (1897–1974) Russo-Georgian writer, publicist and member of the Eurasians.

Chuprov, Alexander Alexandrovich (1874–1926) economist and statistician.

Crane, Charles (1858–1939) american industrialist, diplomat and philanthropist. Father of John, friend of Masaryk, supported the Kondakov Institute.

Crane, John (1899–1982) friend of Masaryk and his secretary in the 1920s.

Davats, Vladimir Khristianovich (1883–1944) mathematician, unofficial spokesman for Wrangel's army in emigration.

Denikin, Anton Ivanovich (1872–1947) general who in late 1918 was Commander-in-Chief of the Volunteer White Army. In the emigration he espoused moderate and even left-wing views.

Dolgorukov, Prince Peter Dimitrievich (1866–1945) right-wing Kadet and social activist.

Dosuzhkov, Fedor Nikolaevich (1899–1982) psychiatrist and psychoanalyst, poet; active in the Russian émigré colony in Czechoslovakia.

Durnovo, Nikolai Nikolaevich (1876–1936), philologist and Slavist.

Efron, Sergei Yakovlevich (1893–1941) editor, husband of Marina Tsvetaeva.

Elita-Velichkovsky, Kirill general secretary of the Mladorossy (Young Russians)

Evlogiy, (1868–1946) priest who became Metropolitan in 1923, accepted as leader of Russian Orthodox Church in Western Europe.

Fan-der-Flit, Alexander Petrovich (1870–1941) Russian engineer.

Florovsky, Georgii Vasilevich (1893–1979) theologian, priest, member of the World Council of Churches.

Frank, Semen Liudvigovich (1877–1950) philosopher.

Frantsev, Vladimir Andreevich (1867–1942) Slavist.

Gesemann, Gerhard (1888–1948) philologist and Slavist, Vice-Chancellor of the German University in Prague.

Gessen (Hessen), Sergei Iosifovich (1887–1950) philosopher and pedagogue.

Girsa, Václav (1875–1954) Czech doctor working in Kiev before the First World War, political spokesman for the Czech legion in Russia; subsequently head of Russian Action in the Minstry of Foreign Affairs in Czechoslovakia.

Goryanskiy, Valentin Ivanovich (real surname: Sulima-Grudzinskiy) (1887–1949) satirical poet and writer.

Grimm, David Davidovich (1864–1941) academic lawyer, 1910–11 Vice-Chancellor of the University of St Petersburg, member of the Central Committee of the Constitutional Democratic Party (Kadet).

Gurevich, Vissarion Yakovlevich (1876–1940) SR, 1921–22 chairman of the Prague Zemgor.

Gurvich, Georgy Davidovich (1894–1965) philosopher and sociologist.

Hajn, Antonin (1868–1949) Czech politician, close associate of Kramář.

Hajný, Josef employee of the Czechoslovak Ministry of Foreign Affairs, member of the administration of fund for help to Russian students.

Herzen, Alexander Ivanovich (1812–1870) thinker and writer, 'Father of Russian Socialism'; edited first influential Russian émigré journal.

Ikonnikov, Vladimir Stepanovich (1841–1923) historian and academician.

Il'in, Ivan Alexandrovich (1882–1954) philosopher and publicist.

Il'in, Vasiliy Sergeevich (1882–1957) botanist, rector (i.e. Vice-Chancellor) of the Russian People's University 1939–45.

Ivantsov, Dimitrii Nikolaevich (1886–1973) economist and statistician.

Izgoev, Alexander Solomonovich (1872–1935) social activist and publicist.

Jakobson, Roman Osipovich (1896–1982) philologist, linguist, literary critic, scholar.

Karsavin, Lev Platonovich (1885–1961) philosopher and historian.

Kartashev, Anton Vladimirovich (1885–1961) historian specialising in church history; active in religious and ecclesiastical questions, chairman of the Russian National Committee.

Katkov, Georgiy Mikhailovich (1903–1985) philosopher and historian.

Katkov, Kiril Mikhailovich (1905–1995) icon painter.

Kazem-Bek, Alexander Lvovich (1902–1977) President of Mladorossy (Young Russians).

Kelin, Nikolai Andreevich (1896–1970) doctor, poet, writer, art collector.

Kerensky, Alexander Feodorovich (1881–1970) socialist politician; in 1917 Minister of Justice in the first Provisional Government, War Minister in the Coalition, Prime Minister after the 'July crisis' and Supreme Commander-in-Chief after 1 September.

Kizevetter, Alexander Alexandrovich (1866–1933) historian.

Klimushkin, Prokopiy Diomidovich (1888–1960s) SR social activist and one of the founders of the Zemgor in Prague.

Kocharovsky, Karl-Avgust Romanovich (1870-after 1941) economist and publicist.

Kojeve, Alexander (1902–1968) philosopher.

Kolchak, Admiral Alexander Vasilievich (1873–1920) admiral, Supreme Ruler of Russia after *coup d'état* in Omsk 18 November 1918 to end 1919.

Kondakov, Nikodim Pavlovich (1844–1925) historian of art and Byzantinist, member of the Imperial Russian Academy of Sciences.

Kornilov, Lavr Georgievich (1870–1918) Commander-in-Chief of the army in 1917, one of the organisers of the Volunteer Army in 1918.

Kovalevsky, Peter Evgrafovich (1901–1978) historian of the emigration, and teacher.

Koyré, Alexandre (1892–1964) historian of science and philosophy.

Kramář, Karel (1860–1937) first Prime Minister of the Czechoslovak Republic.

Krofta, Kamil (1876–1945) Czech historian, diplomat and Foreign Minster of the Czechoslovak Republic 1936–38.

Kuskova, Ekaterina Dmitrievna (1869–1958) social and political activist and publicist.

Kutepov, Aleksey Pavlovich (1882–1930) general, became head of ROVS (the Russian veteran organisation) in 1928; kidnapped by Soviet agents in 1930.

Lapshin, Ivan Ivanovich (1870–1953) philosopher, historian of literature and music.

Levitsky, Sergei Aleksandrovich (1907–198?) philosopher.

Lomshakov, Aleksei Stepanovich (1870–1960) engineer, social activist, member of the Central Committee of the Kadet Party. Chairman of the Union of Russian Academic Organisations Abroad, founder of the Committee for the Provision of Education for Russian and Ukrainian students.

Lossky, Nikolai Onufrievich (1870–1965) philosopher.

Lyatskiy, Evgenii Alexandrovich (1868–1942) literary specialist.

Magerovsky, Lev Florianovich (1896–1986) social activist and archivist.

Maklakov, Vasiliy Alekseevich (1870–1957) jurist, member of Central Committee of the Kadet Party, Russian ambassador in France for Provisional Government of 1917, head of the Office des Refugiés Russes.

Makletsov, Alexander Vasilievich (1884–1948) jurist, specialist in criminal law and criminology.

Marakner, S.V. (?–1945?) head of the Agricultural, Co-operate Institute

Markov, Nikolai Evgenievich (1866–1945) known as Markov II, leading rightist Duma deputy before 1917, associated with the extreme right in émigré circles.

Masaryk, Tomáš Garrigue (1850–1937) philosopher, sociologist, politician and first President (1918–35) of the First Republic of Czechoslovakia.

Maslov, Sergei Semenovich (1887–1945?) Russian politician and publicist. Leader of Krest'yanskaya Rossiya.

Mathesius, Vilém (1882–1942) Czech philologist, one of the founders of the Prague Linguistic Circle.

Meisner, Dimitrii Ivanovich (1899–1980) journalist, publicist, social activist.

Miliukov, Pavel Nikolaevich (1859–1943) historian, politician and publicist, leader of the Kadet Party, editor of *Poslednie Novosti* in Paris.

Minor, Osip Solomonovich (1861–1934) SR politician and publicist.

Mirsky, D.S. (Prince Dimitry Petrovich Svyatopolk-Mirsky) (1890–1939) writer, critic, leading member of the left wing of the Eurasians, later member of Communist Party.

Mogiliansky, Nikolai Mikhailovich (1871–1934) anthropologist, geographer, ethnographer, professor.

Morkovin, Boris Vladimirovich (1882–1968) journalist and social activist.

Myakotin, Venedikt Alexandrovich (1867–1937) historian, publicist, professor.

Nabokov, Vladimir Dimitrievich (1869–1922) lawyer, publicist, newspaper editor and a leader of the Kadet Party; father of the writer V.V. Nabokov.

Nejedlý, Zdeněk (1878–1962) historian, musicologist, professor, Czech Communist, minister.

Nikolaevsky, Boris Ivanovich (1887–1966) historian, archivist, Menshevik politician.

Nikolai Nikolaevich, Grand Duke (1856–1929) Commander-in-Chief of the Imperial Russian forces 1914–15; in emigration the most popular member of the Romanov family; unofficial pretender to the Russian throne.

Novgorodtsev, Pavel Ivanovich (1866–1924) jurist, professor, member of the Central Committee of the Kadet Party, leading organiser of the Russian academic community in Prague.

Novikov, Mikhail Mikhailovich (1876–1960) zoologist, professor, Vice-Chancellor of Moscow University in 1917. Leading organiser of the Russian academic community in Prague. Director of the Russian People's University.

Novozhilov, Nikolai Fedorovich (1883–1963) teacher, social activist, SR.

Ogarev, Nikolai Platonovich (1813–1877) poet, publicist, revolutionary, émigré.

Ostrogorsky, Georgy Alexandrovich (1902–1976) historian and Byzantinist.

Ostrogorsky, Sergei Alekseevich (1866–1934) doctor, teacher, social activist.

Ostroukhov, Petr Alexandrovich (1885–1965) historian and economist.

Panina, Sofia Vladimirovna (1871–1957) social activist, member of the Central Committee of the Kadet party, founder of the 'Russian Hearth' in Prague; chair of the Committee for the Day of Russian Culture.

Pellé, Maurice (1863–1924) French general, commander of the Czech army in 1919; in command in Constantinople 1921–24.

Peshekhonov, Aleksei Vasilievich (1867–1933) statistician, political activist, publicist.

Postnikov, Sergei Porfir'evich (1883–1965) bibliographer and archivist, journalist, publicist and political activist.

Prokopovich, Sergei Nikolaevich (1871–1955) economist, statistician, publicist and political activist, minister in the Russian Provisional Government in 1917.

Pushkarev, Sergei Germanovich (1888–1984) historian.

Rafal'sky, Vladimir Trifil'evich (1886–1945?) Russian diplomat, Kolchak's representative in Czechoslovakia.

Rosenberg, Vladimir Alexandrovich (1860–1932) economist and publicist.

Rostovtsev, Mikhail Ivanovich (1870–1952) ancient historian and archaeologist.

Rudnev, Vadim Viktorovich (1879–1940) SR, social activist, journalist.

Savinkov, Boris Viktorovich (1879–1925) writer, revolutionary, SR, political activist.

Savinov, Sergei Yakovlevich (1897–?) writer, journalist, publicist.

Savitsky, Nikolai Petrovich (1867–1941) social activist, prior to 1917 a Marshal of the nobility, member of the Union of Russian Writers and Journalists.

Savitsky, Peter Nikolaevich (1895–1968) geographer, economist, historian; one of the founders of Eurasianism.

Shakhmatov, Mstislav Vyacheslavovich (1888–1943) historian of Russian law.

Shklovsky, Viktor Borisovich (1893–1984) writer and literary critic.

Shmurlo, Evgenii Frantsevich (1854–1934) historian and writer.

Slavík, Jan (1885–1978) Czech historian, social activist, director of the Russian Historical Archive Abroad.

Slonim, Mark L'vovich (1894–1976) SR and literary critic.

Sorokin, Pitirim Alexandrovich (1889–1968) sociologist.

Spektorskiy, Evgenii Vasilievich (1875–1951) jurist and sociologist, historian, Principal of the Russian Law Faculty in Prague.

Stakhevich, Mikhail Sergeevich (1893–1940?) social activist.

Struve, Peter Berngardovich (1870–1944) academician, economist, historian, politician, publicist.

Suvchinskiy, Peter Petrovich (1892–1985) musicologist, publicist, one of the founders of Eurasianism.

Timasheff, Nikolai Sergeevich (1886–1970) sociologist, jurist, philosopher of law, publicist.

Totomiants, Vakhan Fomich (1875–1964) economist, historian and theoretician of the co-operative movement, publicist.

Trubetskoy, Nikolai Sergeevich (1890–1938) linguist, philosopher; one of the founders of Eurasianism.

Tsegoev, Kirill Kirillovich (1894–1985) writer, journalist, publicist.

Tsimmerman (Zimmermann), Mikhail Arturovich (1887–1935) jurist and professor of international law.

Tsvetaeva, Marina Ivanovna(1892–1941) poet.

Ustryalov, Nikolai Vasilievich (1890–1937) jurist, philosopher, political activist, founder of the Smenovekh (Change of Landmarks) movement.

Varshavsky, Sergei Ivanovich (1879–1945?) lawyer. After the occupation of Czechoslovakia an active member of the Russian national movement.

Varshavsky, Vladimir Sergeevich (1906–1978) writer and literary critic.

Vasil'ev, Vasiliy Timofeevich (1885–1984) engineer and member of Prague Zemgor.

Vechorin, Evgenii Aleksandrovich (188?-after 1968?) engineer.

Vergun, Kirill Dmitrievich (1907–1944) engineer, President of National Union of the New Generation (later the National Labour Alliance) in Czechoslovakia.

Vernadsky, Georgii Vladimirovich (1887–1973) historian and leading Eurasian.

Vishniak, Mark Veniaminovich (1883–1977) journalist, secretary of Sovremmenye Zapiski, SR.

Yakovenko, Boris Valentinovich (1884–1949) philosopher.

Yashvil', Princess Nataliya Grigorievna (1861–1939) social activist and artist.

Yurkevich, V.I. (1885–1964) shipbuilder, designed the prize winning liner, *The Normandie*.

Zaitsev, Kirill Iosifovich (1887–1975) historian and theologian.

Zavadsky, Sergei Vladislavovich (1871–1935) jurist.

Zen'kovsky, Aleksandr Vasilievich (1878–?) economist.

Zhekulina, Adelaida Vladimirovna (1866–1950) teacher, social activist, chairman of the Association of Russian Teachers' Organisations Abroad deputy chairman of the Pedagogical Bureau, specialist and organiser of schools and pre-school education.

Zhiliaev, Uvar Dmitrievich (1886–?) economist, and director of the Russian Institute of Commercial Knowledge.

Index